Ruth Fiand

Care For You

English for Health and Social Care

3. Auflage

Bestellnummer 07524

Bildungsverlag EINS

Haben Sie Anregungen oder Kritikpunkte zu diesem Produkt?
Dann senden Sie eine E-Mail an 07524_003@bv-1.de
Autoren und Verlag freuen sich auf Ihre Rückmeldung.

www.bildungsverlag1.de

Bildungsverlag EINS GmbH
Hansestraße 115, 51149 Köln

ISBN 978-3-427-**07524**-0

Vorwort

Das Lehrwerk **Care For You** richtet sich an junge Erwachsene, die sich für eine Ausbildung im Bereich der Sozial- und Gesundheitspflege entschieden haben. Es eignet sich für die unterrichtliche Arbeit in Berufsschulklassen, Fachoberschulen sowie Fachschulen. Das Buch richtet sich an Lernende mit Vorkenntnissen und kann – auf Grund seiner Aufteilung in Lern-Module – in Klassen der Berufskollegs sowie in Vollzeit- und Teilzeitklassen eingesetzt werden, die die Lernenden bis zu einer Fachhochschulreife führen.

Care For You baut auf einen mittleren Bildungsabschluss auf und setzt einen Mindestwortschatz von etwa 1700 Wörtern sowie Grundkenntnisse der Grammatik und Kommunikationsfähigkeit voraus. In verschiedenen Lernniveaus angepassten Modulen können diese Grundkenntnisse aufgefrischt und je nach angestrebtem Abschluss vertieft und weiter ausgebaut werden.

In 10 Units werden Themenschwerpunkte aus Bereichen der Sozial- und Gesundheitspflege behandelt. Unit 1 (Modul 1–3) bis 3 (Modul 1) frischen Grundkenntnisse der Grammatik und des Textverständnisses sowie Basisvokabular auf.

Jede Unit umfasst drei Module, die verschiedenste Leistungsanforderungen repräsentieren. Modul 1 führt in das Thema allgemein ein und arbeitet sprachliche Grundkenntnisse auf. Über dieses Basismodul hinausgehend kann der Unterrichtende entscheiden, ob das Thema auf einem nächst höheren Leistungsniveau in den Modulen 2 und 3 vertieft oder ob auf einem höheren Niveau in das Thema „eingestiegen" werden soll. Insbesondere Modul 3 bietet weiterführende Texte und Aspekte des Themas der Unit sowie Sprachübungen und Comprehension-Aufgaben an, die ein mittleres Leistungsniveau übersteigen und die Erlangung der Fachhochschulreife vorbereiten.

Care For You ist auf Praxisnähe ausgerichtet. Realistische Situationen werden insbesondere in den Activity-Übungen angeboten, in denen handlungsorientierte Aufgaben dazu auffordern, in berufliche Handlungssituationen einzusteigen. Situationsgebundene Sprech- und Schreibanlässe sollen in diesen Aufgaben bewältigt werden.

Die Units bieten ein skills training an, das mit helpful phrases ergänzt wird. Hier findet der Lernende ein gezieltes Methodentraining und Fachvokabeln zu Themen wie introducing yourself, writing a curricullum vitae, description, comment, essay writing, discussing statements, summary, talking about statistics, explaining words, analysing posters and flyposters, cartoon analysis, mind mapping, presentation, giving advice, analysing case studies etc. Ebenso regelmäßig werden in den Units Translation-Übungen angeboten, die die sprachliche Sicherheit in der Zielsprache überprüfen.
Jede Unit wird durch Listening-Übungen ergänzt, die das Hörverständnis schulen und weitere Möglichkeiten der Diskussion sowie des freien Sprechens anbieten und die Inhalte der Unit somit noch einmal vertiefend einüben. Die Listening-Übungen sind zum Download zu finden unter **www.bildungsverlag1.de/audio-portal**.

Einige Unittexte sind Originaltexte, um die Lernenden an das Lesen authentischer Texte heranzuführen. Diese Texte sind mit der Überschrift „Authentic reading" gekennzeichnet.

Das nebenstehende Symbol weist auf unser Buchplusangebot hin. Unter **www.bildungsverlag1.de/buchplus/07524** werden ein Einstufungstest, Grammatikerläuterungen sowie ergänzende Übungen angeboten.

So take good 'care for you'!

Inhaltsverzeichnis

STARTER:
Getting to know each other

Why you need to introduce yourself to a group

It is difficult to work together and have productive conversations with people when you do not know who you are in a group with. For this reason you will have to introduce yourself and listen to what the others are doing and who they are. In a job it is interesting to get some information about what the other one is responsible for and what special skills she or he may bring into the team. One common way of introducing is to sit in a circle and everyone tells the group something about themselves. Generally it is good to know why someone joined the group and what she or he is trying to achieve. Some people feel nervous when they come into a new group and situation. Others are happy to meet new people because joining a new group can mean that you start something new and interesting. In any case an introduction can be useful. It may take away fear of the new situation and the 'strange face' sitting opposite to you. It can also motivate others when they hear about the positive feelings someone else brings into the group. Sometimes when a group of people comes together and the majority is not sure who everyone is, they may feel either cautious or intimidated. This often results in a quiet meeting where most people say nothing and only listen to the main speaker. But teamwork only works if everyone in the group feels 'safe' knowing who you are working with and what everyone can bring into the group. Do you remember your first day in a new team, for example a new class at school? What were your feelings when entering the class room for the first time and meeting your classmates who you did not know before?

Task 1

Can you remember typical situations of entering a new group?

a) What situations were these?
b) Say in a couple of sentences how you felt in these situations.

Introducing yourself to a new group

Here are some examples of students coming together in a new college doing studies on health and care. Their teacher asked them to sit in a circle and introduce themselves.

Anne: Hi, I'm Anne. I just want to pass my exam here and go to university. That's all, I think. I just don't know what future job I really want to do. Oh, I'm 17.

Kiasalam: Yes, okay, I'm next. My name is Kiasalam. My name already tells you that I have Indian roots. But I have never been in India. I live here in Britain since my birth. My father comes from India and he works for a British computer company. I'm 18 years old and I have two sisters, 14 and 9. Well, I want to do this class because I'm interested in care work. I already did a hospital placement and now I think of doing a care job, but before I start job training I want to do this class to achieve a university entrance qualification. Well, what else can I tell you? I like Indian food but also hamburgers and chips and I'm a member of a dance club.

Jean: Are you ready? Ah, yes. Okay then, I'm Jean and I also like hamburgers and chips. I also want to have my university entrance qualification. I'm 19 and I already started job training as businesswoman but did not like it. Now I'm sure I want to become a care worker but I first want to do a placement before doing the wrong job training again. Here I can achieve a qualification and work experience. This is why I'm here. Okay, you can go on.

Tim: I'm 16 and I live with my family. I have one brother of 13. I don't know what I want to do. My dad is a social worker and my mom a child care worker so I thought maybe a care job could be something for me, too. But I don't want to start a job training already. I think I'm too young. I like to be at school for some more time and pass my exams for a university entrance. What else? . . .Yes, I'm very sporty and do all kinds of sports, soccer of course but also skiing in winter and a lot more.

Comprehension

Task 2

Think about the following questions.

a) What basic information do the four students give you?
b) What do all four have in common?
c) Think of the class as a future working team. What information do the students give which is rather uninteresting?
d) What information is missing? If Anne, Kiasalam, Jean and Tim were your classmates what would you like to know?

Activity

Partner interview

- What is your name?
- Where do you live?
- …?
- …?
- Are you going to do a placement? What kind of?
- …?
- …?
- How do you like your placement/job training?
- Why do you want to become a care worker?
- …?

Task 3

Sit in pairs and look at the list above. These are some of the usual questions you are interested in when meeting a new classmate. What else could be interesting to know? Copy the list and add your questions.

Task 4

Do a partner interview.

a) Search for a new partner in class. Someone you do not know and use your list of questions to do a partner interview.
b) Introduce your interview partner to your class.

Task 5

Pick out one of the situations and imagine that you introduce yourself to the group. Prepare your introduction and present it to your classmates.

1. You are spending your holiday in a European summer camp. On the first evening all holiday participants come together at a getting-to-know-party.
2. You are doing a one-year placement at a British nursery school. On your first working day all your new colleagues come together in a staff meeting.
3. You are an exchange student at an American college. This is your first school day and you meet your new class.

4. You took over a holiday job on Mallorca. You are the hostess/host in a holiday centre park and you do all kinds of free-time activities with the holiday makers. This is the first day with a new group.

Have a look at the skills training and helpful phrases box for some help!

Skills Training

How to introduce yourself

Here are some basic rules how to introduce yourself:

1. If you have to introduce yourself to a large audience, make sure that your voice is loud enough for everyone to hear you. Speak clearly.
2. Do not stare down or at a point at the wall. The others might get the impression that you are uninterested in them or you feel very insecure. Move your gaze around the group and make eye contact with a few people without staring at them. If you feel very unsure to make eye contact and feel afraid of doing so, look at their forehead. The audience cannot tell the difference.
3. At a formal gathering say hello to the group and state your name first like 'Hello, my name is (first name) (second name)', but if you introduce yourself to your new class just tell your first name and maybe how you like to be called by your classmates. Maybe you have a nickname which you prefer.
4. Give some basic information about yourself. This information depends on the group you introduce yourself to. If you introduce yourself at a job meeting, say what exactly your job is, how long you have worked for your company, what special working skills and work experience you have etc.
   But if you introduce yourself to a new class, think of what your classmates are interested in, your age, where you come from, where you live, your family situation, your hobbies, maybe subjects you are good in or like most etc. If you do a placement, tell them what you do and how you like it. Maybe you already have some work experience which could be interesting to hear about.

5. Close the introduction. If you are going to work in a team for longer, you should tell the team what you like to achieve with the team in future and thank the group for their interest. You can also tell the group to ask questions if they like. If you introduce yourself to a school class, you can tell your classmates why you visit this school or class and what job you like to train in future.

Helpful phrases: Introducing yourself

Hello everyone, my name is … (but you can call me …).

Good morning / afternoon / evening, I'm ...

I live in ... with my family / partner ... I have got … sisters and brothers ...

I'm … years old.

I have (just) passed my exam at … school.

I'm a trained (nursery nurse).

I have … years of work experience as (a childminder)/in (minding children).

Right now I'm doing a placement at … /I already did a placement at (hospital).

I would like to become a (nurse). – In future I would like to work as a (nurse).

My future dream job is to (work with children)/is the job of a (nursery nurse)

I think I'm good at … My special skills are …

Here in this class I would like to achieve …

My hobbies are ... In my free time/leisure time I like to/prefer to …

I like ... / I dislike …

Thank you for listening.

Are there any questions? – What else do you like to know?

Activity

Icebreakers

Icebreakers can help you to get to know each other and they can be funny games to learn names and something about your classmates' personality. They can also support cooperation and understanding in the classroom. For example the partner interview which you already know is an icebreaker which helps you to get to know one of your classmates more closely and maybe the interview gives you the chance to make a first friend.

Task 6

Here are some more examples of icebreakers.
Look at the possibilities and choose one you like to do with your class!

Getting to know you bingo

This needs some preparation. You need a table with as many boxes as students in a class. The table should be drawn on a flip chart poster or blackboard. In a short introductory round every student writes down a short typical sentence, like for example 'I play soccer', 'I'm born in July', 'I speak two languages'. In a second round students should try to write the name of the student into the box with the description fitting to the student. Next lesson a copy of this table without names can be given to every student to do a bingo game as a repetition.

I play soccer. ***John***	I am born in July. ***Su***	I speak two languages. ***Ramon***
I have a lot of pets. ***Rany***	I have seven siblings. ***Harold***	I am born in another country. ***Lamaho***
I am in a theatre group. ***Julien***	I like spinach. ***Marian***	I am a real good skier. ***Tina***

Postcards

Students create their own postcard that reflects something typical of their life. They draw a picture and write a short text to the class beginning with 'Dear class'. If the class already knows each other and comes back to school after the summer break, students can also draw a summer happening. They write a short text but sign with a penname and the class has to guess who this postcard is from.

Name criss-cross

Students write down their first and second name to create a criss-cross. They add words to the letters of their name which tell something typical of them.

Personal Mandala

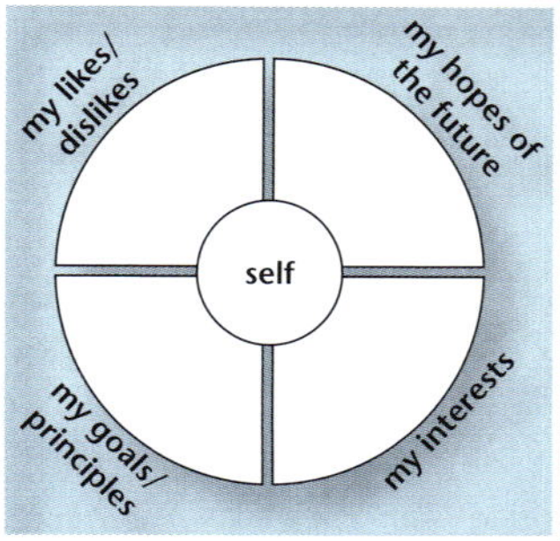

Students create their personal mandala to illustrate how they see themselves. A typical example is to subdivide the mandala circle into the following categories: my goals/principles, my likes/dislikes, my hopes for the future, my interests. These categories are only proposals. Students can also invent their own categories.

UNIT 1:

Care worker – a job with a difference

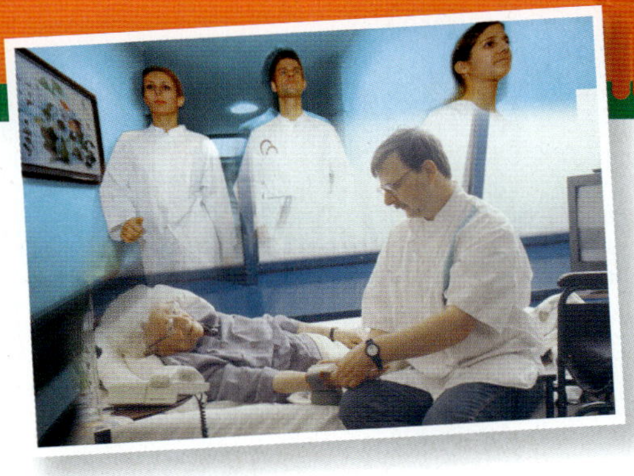

Module 1: The job of a care worker – can this job be good for me?

What is a care worker?

Sometimes people also speak of care assistants instead of care workers. But what is a care worker and what does she or he do?

Care workers help people in their daily life. They work with ill people, elderly people and those with special needs, or adults, teenagers and children who have some kind of social problem. Care workers can work as home care workers who assist at someone's home or they support young people or grown-ups in a residential setting. Their tasks include personal care, social care, basic medical care, first aid and domestic care. Most often a care worker keeps contact with relatives, nurses, doctors, social workers or other professionals who also look after the person who needs help.

Task 1

Sit in pairs and discuss the following tasks. The jobs listed below all work with people. But who is a care worker and who isn't?

a. Sort out the care workers. Give reasons for your decision.

event organiser · teacher · social worker · nurse · child care worker · educator · hairdresser · manager · medical assistant · nursery nurse · dietician · receptionist · occupational therapist · tour guide · psychologist · stewardess · correspondent · driving instructor · nanny · policeman · pharmacist · hostess / host

b. Do you know some more care workers?
c. Present your results in class.

Task 2

What job activities and working places belong to the different care workers? Make sentences. Sometimes there is more than one possibility to describe typical job activities.

Example:

A nurse works in a hospital and she changes dressings.

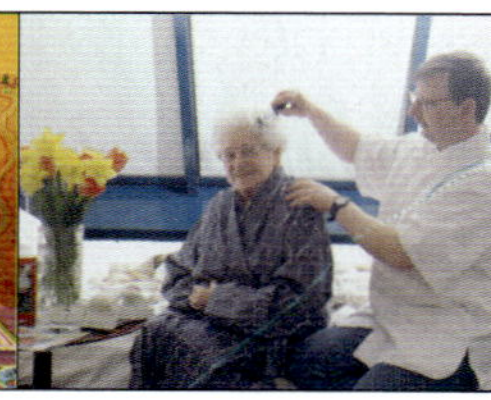

job	nurse nursery nurse home care worker street worker education worker child care worker old people's nurse
working place	child care home – hospital – drug scene of a city – the streets – school – old people's home – day care – nursery school
activity	change dressings – lift patients out of bed – plan activities – look after homeless people or drug addicts – counsel parents and children – sing – distribute medicine – prepare food – organise the household – teach and help children – supervise – read out children's books – do handcraft – help children with their homework – help with getting dressed

Task 3

What about you? Answer the following questions.

a. Are you doing a job, job training or placement at the moment? Describe your daily routines.
b. What do you like about your job, job training or placement?
c. Are there situations you dislike?

Task 4

Look at the list of verbs below. Make sure you understand their meaning. They all describe typical activities of care workers. Try to fill the gaps in the sentences. Again, there is sometimes more than one possibility.

supervise – look after – support – care for – watch – supply (with) – counsel

a. My mother is 82 years old. Last year her health condition became so bad that she had to go into an old people's home because she needs someone who can … her the whole day.
b. Mr Smith can't walk alone. Someone has to go beside him to hold his arm and … him.
c. Every morning nurses go around to change bandages, clean wounds and … the patients with the medicine they need.
d. Sometimes it's hard for nurses to be on the night shift because most often there is only one nurse to … all the patients of one ward.
e. As a social worker you need good communication skills because you must be able to speak with people and … them.
f. If you plan to go on an outing with your nursery school class you will need a second person to … the children.
g. As a nursery nurse you must always be very attentive and … what the children are doing.

Alice Morrison – a district nurse

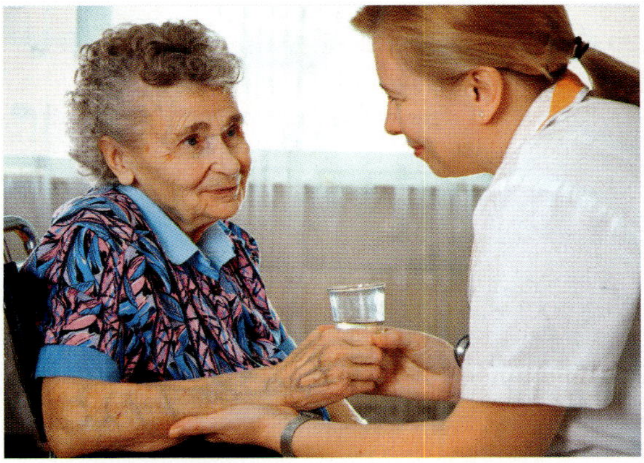

In Great Britain some nurses don't work in a hospital instead they are responsible for a whole district. They travel around and look after the sick and the elderly in a certain area. Alice Morrison is one of these district nurses.
Alice spent three years in a hospital training for her job and she had to take an extra exam showing that she can take responsibility for sick people without the help of a doctor.
Her exam results had to be excellent. She loves her work, although it can be very hard sometimes. There are days when she comes home late at night, but instead of relaxing she has to fill in the patients' files.
This is one of Alice's normal working days: It's four a.m. The telephone rings. It's John Baker and his voice sounds worried. 'The baby is arriving! Hurry up, please!' Alice dresses quickly, picks up her nurse's bag and within seconds she is on her way. Alice examines John Baker's wife, but she soon finds out that the baby is not ready to be born yet.
The Bakers are a very young couple and this is going to be their first baby. It's quite normal that every change in Mrs Baker's health worries them. You need routine and good medical knowledge to see that this was no emergency case. And this is exactly the responsibility every district nurse has to accept.
Then Alice goes home for breakfast. By eight she is in her car again and starts her routine rounds. Alice always takes a mobile phone with her so that emergency calls can reach her. She first visits Maureen Harper who had her baby only one day ago. She gives her a lesson in child care because it's Maureen's first baby and she has to learn what to do. Alice shows her how to bathe her baby carefully. Next Alice goes to see old Mr Johnson. His leg needs attention every day. She takes off his bandages and puts on a fresh dressing. But it's

not only the new dressing which Mr Johnson needs. He needs a good and warm chat because he lost his wife one year ago and feels very lonesome. Then Alice stops at the maternal clinic where she gives some courses to young women who are going to have a baby soon.
In case there is an emergency Alice can't deal with alone, she has to decide whether she calls a doctor, an ambulance or even a helicopter to bring her patient into hospital.
Alice sees many people every day. Even during the night she is called quite often. But although she works very hard, she is very contented with her job.
What does she like most? 'My responsibility and the freedom to organise my own working day! If you want to do this job, you must have a genuine interest in people. Sometimes the job is unpleasant and you must have a lot of energy to get through hard times. It helps to be a good listener, too'.

Comprehension

Task 5

Sit in pairs. Look through the job description again and fill in the table below. Present your results in class.

job requirements (What do you need to do the job of a district nurse?)	typical job activities (What does a district nurse do?)
– three years of hospital training	– visit sick people and young mothers
– excellent exam results	– examine sick people
…	…
…	…

Task 6

The ends of the following sentences are missing. Try to complete the sentences with what you learnt about Alice in the text.

a. Most often Alice's working day doesn't end in the evening because ...
b. Alice does not only care for young mothers at home but also ...
c. Old people not only need medical care but ...
d. Alice always carries a mobile phone with her because ...
e. Alice's job is a job with a high responsibility because ...

Writing

Task 7

Compare the job of a district nurse with the job of a hospital nurse. What are similarities and differences? Try to write about 100 words.

The words in the box may help you to work on this task.

Helpful phrases	
In contrast to ...	Im Gegensatz zu ...
Compared with/to ...	Verglichen mit ...
... has/have nothing in common ...	... hat/haben nichts gemeinsam ...
The job of ... differs from the job ... because ...	Der Beruf von ... unterscheidet sich von dem Beruf ... , weil ...
There are some differences ...	Es gibt einige Unterschiede ...
... is / are different from ...	... ist /sind verschieden von ...
... is /are similar to ...	... ist /sind ähnlich wie ...

Philip Soon – a child care worker

Philip Soon is a qualified child care worker. He manages a children's care home. If a child's family can't look after their children properly or if it's not safe for the child at home, the child may be sent into Vincent Children's Care Home, which Philip is in charge of. Together with his employees, Philip looks after children and young people who live there. Usually there are up to 15 children. If possible, each child has a bedroom and one care worker who looks particularly after this child. 'It's important to have one person who is mainly in charge of one child because the children need an atmosphere of trust,' Philip says.

'A child care worker is responsible for everything a parent would normally do – looking after a child's health, education and happiness. But we also keep constant contact with the child's family. We try to listen to both child and family to find out about their problems and wishes. We sort things out so that the family situation stabilises and the child can go home again.'

What qualification does a child care worker need? 'I had a high school diploma and I did some voluntary work in a nursery to find out if I can do this job. After five years of work experience in the job of a child care worker I applied for the job of a children's home manager. This is my personal story, but normally to enter the job training of a child care worker you don't need a lot of work experience with children. Most often a school or college degree is sufficient for the training. But I think it's better to do some voluntary work before you decide to do the job training. A voluntary year is a good chance to see if you can really do this job. There are some requirements for the job which you may easily fulfill, but there are personal qualifications which are also necessary to be a good care worker. It's a good help to be patient, for example. You must be flexible because every child's story is different and requires individual decisions. You will need good communication skills to talk to children and parents in such a way that they will understand what you want them to do. You must be able to listen to children and show them your understanding. You must be tolerant. And it's good to enjoy being together with people and doing activities such as dancing, painting, playing music or cooking so you can share them with children. You see, doing the job of a care worker is not a normal routine job. It's a job with a difference.'

Comprehension

Task 8

Sit in pairs. Look through the job description again and fill in the table below. Present your results in class.

job requirements (What do you need to do the job of a child care worker?)	typical job activities (What does a child care worker do?)
…	…
…	…

Task 9

The following statements are false. Please correct them.

a. Philip Soon is a qualified nursery nurse.
b. Two or three children share a bedroom.
c. There is one care worker who is mainly in charge of only five children to establish an atmosphere of trust.
d. The child care worker rarely keeps contact with the child's family.
e. Every child is treated in exactly the same manner.

Task 10

Say why

a. it is good to be flexible when you work as a child care worker.
b. it is advantageous when you enjoy sharing your hobbies with other people.
c. a care worker needs good communication skills.

Writing

Task 11

Choose one of the following questions and answer it. Don't write less than 100 words.

a. Can you imagine doing Alice's or Philip's job? Choose one and say why.
b. After reading the two job portraits and what Alice and Philip point out about their work, what characterises a good care worker?
c. Why is the job of a care worker, as Philip Soon says, 'a job with a difference'? Discuss.

Grammar

Web

Present Simple Tense

Bildung	Entspricht dem Infinitiv bei he, she, it + (e)s
Beispiele	*Child care workers (they) need to be patient.* *They don't spend a lot of time in their office.* *Philip (he) works in a child care home.* *He doesn't work in a hospital.*
Anwendung	Das Present Simple beschreibt häufig – Dauerzustände (wie Berufsbeschreibungen) – Gewohnheiten – regelmäßig wiederkehrende Vorgänge (hier z. B. bei Signalwörtern wie usually, normally, often, sometimes ...) – Fakten ('Water boils at 100 degrees.') – statische, gleich bleibende Zustände (→ mit dem Verb 'be' – 'He is very nice.')

If you want to do some more revision, use the internet link www. bildungsverlag1/ buchplus/07524 for detailed information and further exercises.

Task 12

This is one of Philip's normal working days. Fill in the correct Present Simple form of the verb in brackets.

a. Each morning Philip (check) his emails and (make) phone calls. This is something he (not forget). He (talk) to parents, teachers and social workers about what is going to happen with the children in the care home.

b. Most children in care (go) to school, but they also (have) an education worker who (help) them with their work.

c. Quite often Philip (have) a meeting with the education worker and one of the young people in the care home. They (talk) about the teenager's problems at school and how she or he (catch up) to improve school marks. In the care home they (not leave) the children alone with their school work.

d. Each early afternoon Philip (sit) together with his employees. This meeting (give) them the chance to talk about problems and to organise activities. Every care worker (report) about the child she or he (be) in charge of. Together they (make) decisions about how to help the child.

e. Philip (share) meals with the children and he (join) activities which (take place) regularly. He (not miss) the evening meal because it (be) a good chance to talk the day over and listen to the children's wishes. Usually Philip's working day (end) after the evening meal if there (not be) any need for him to stay for longer and talk with his employees or the children.

Word Order

Subject	Verb	Object	Place	Time
Philip	*speaks with*	*his staff*	*in their meeting room*	*every early afternoon.*
Time	**Subject**	**Verb**	**Object**	**Place**
Every early afternoon	*Philip*	*speaks with*	*his staff*	*in their meeting room.*

Task 13

Reconstruct the following sentences.

a. break – in – late – the – Philip – a – takes – afternoon.
b. he – plays – table – then – with – children – of – rooms – one – the – game – in – tennis – the
c. Philip – parents – every – meets – week – the – in – of – child – each – office – his – at – Care – Vincent – Children's – Home

Adverbs of Frequency

Adverbien der Häufigkeit: Satzstellung

- **am Satzende; z. B. bei weekly, daily, once etc.:**
  She visits him in hospital daily.
- **vor dem Vollverb oder nach dem ersten Hilfsverb:**
  She always supervises the children.
  She has always liked to be together with children.
- **hinter dem Verb, wenn das Verb 'to be' ist:**
  She is usually very polite to the children.

Adverbs of Frequency which take the Present Simple are:

never – seldom – sometimes – regularly – often – always ....

Task 14

Rewrite the sentences below with the Adverb of Frequency.

Example:

Philip misses the evening meal (never).
Philip never misses the evening meal.

a. All care workers keep close contact with the children's parents (regularly).
b. Children must be taken out of their family because their parents aren't able to take care of them (often).
c. Philip takes a break (once a day).
d. Alicia is a good child care worker, she has been fond of children (always).
e. It is hard to see that parents aren't able to care for their children (sometimes).

Writing

Task 15

Perhaps you started a job training or a placement. Describe a typical work day. Don't write less than 100 words.

Module 2: Applying for a job

At the job centre

Audio

Sandra Hopper passed her GCSE (General Certificate of Secondary Education) at the end of Secondary School. Now she is unsure about how to go on. For a higher education at a university she needs to pass an 'A-level' at an Upper Secondary School. Or should she register at a College of Further Education for a vocational training? For this reason Sandra talks to a careers adviser for young school-leavers.

Careers adviser: Have you already got some kind of idea of what you would like to do in the future?

Sandra: No, not really. I've just passed my GCSE and I'm still very indecisive. But I'm sure I would like to work with children or young people.

Careers adviser: Do you want to do job training or do you want to attend school for two more years for your A-levels and then register at university?

Sandra: I'm even indecisive about that. Right now I feel that I don't want to sit in school and learn, but perhaps in some months I will change my mind. But I'm quite sure I don't want to start school again that soon.

Careers adviser: You mentioned that you would like to work with children. Why?

Sandra: Well, I did some voluntary work in a nursery school for three weeks and I enjoyed that work. But I think I don't want to become a nursery nurse – perhaps there are other possibilities of working with children.

Careers adviser: A child care worker job training could be interesting for you. Child care workers can work in any institution which takes care of children. This does not have to be a nursery school, it could also be a children's home. Some care workers look after families and children at their home.

Sandra: What are the future prospects?

Careers adviser: There are about 60 000 children in care in the UK each year. There will always be a need for child care workers because the number of children under five will grow in future and more mothers are working. But I must tell you that care workers are not always well paid, so it's very important that you really enjoy your work and are sure you want to do this job.

Sandra: What do you suggest then?

Careers adviser: Well, perhaps you should do some voluntary work for more than three weeks. That's simply not enough to make a decision. Here, this is our monthly magazine 'Jobs & Placements'. There are always offers from children's homes which are going to provide placements.

Comprehension

Task 1

Answer the questions on the text.

a. Why does Sandra Hopper talk to a careers adviser?
b. How does Sandra feel about staying at school for some more time to pass A-levels?
c. Does Sandra have some kind of idea of what she would like to do in future?
d. How are her future prospects?
e. What does the careers adviser finally tell her to do and why?

Grammar

Web

Future

	'Will'-Futur (Future I)	'Going to'-Future
Bildung	**will + Infinitiv**	**is/are going to + Infinitiv**
Verneinung	**will not + Infinitiv =** **won't + Infinitiv**	**am not = I'm not going to + Infinitiv** **is not = isn't going to + Infinitiv** **are not = aren't going to + Infinitiv**
Beispiele	*Perhaps I will change my mind about attending school in future.* *I won't change my mind about high school.*	*On Monday I'm going to register at college.* *I'm not going to register on Friday this week.*
Anwendung	– bei zukünftigen Handlungen und Geschehen, die der Sprecher nicht beeinflussen kann. – bei einem Entschluss, der erst im Moment des Sprechens gefasst wurde.	– bei einem zukünftigen Geschehen, das bereits beschlossen oder geplant ist, bzw. für das bereits eine Absicht besteht (kein spontaner Entschluss).

Use the internet link www.bildungsverlag1/buchplus/07524 to work on more exercises.

Task 2

Transform the verb in brackets into the 'will'- or 'going-to'-future.

a. Looking through 'Jobs & Placements', I have just decided that I (draft) a letter of application to the Vincent Children's Care Home.
b. Exactly this time next week I (have) a job interview at St. Barbara Old People's Home.
c. This morning I have been informed about some trouble in the Johnson family. (you/visit) them tomorrow?
d. I (write) an application test tomorrow at nine in the morning. I got the invitation last week. I guess I (be) very nervous.
e. The new job (be) hard for him, but I know he is tough and I'm sure he (manage) everything.

Listening

Task 3

Look at the diagram and listen to Sandra Hopper talking about her education. After listening discuss with your partner and fill in the ages. Before you listen make sure you know what the word 'compulsory' means.

<table>
<tr><td>age ?</td><td colspan="2">Qualification:
High School Diploma
Higher Education University</td></tr>
<tr><td>age ?</td><td>Qualification
'A'-level
School
Upper Secondary general</td><td>Qualification
GNVQ: General National Vocational Qualification
Courses for students of 16 and over which teach them in subjects and skills needed for work. Possible courses: Catering, Health & Social Care, Information and Technology
C&G: City and Guilds Diploma
School
College of Further Education
(vocational, commercial, technical)</td></tr>
<tr><td>age ?</td><td colspan="2">Qualification:
GCSE: General Certificate of Secondary Education
Secondary School</td></tr>
<tr><td>age ?</td><td colspan="2">Primary School</td></tr>
<tr><td>age ?</td><td colspan="2">Infant School</td></tr>
<tr><td>age ?</td><td colspan="2">Nursery School</td></tr>
</table>

Task 4

The British school system is rather different from the German system but in some ways British schools correspond to German schools. Look at both lists of British and German schools and try to match.

British schools	German schools
Upper Secondary School ('A'-level)	Grundschule
Primary school	Gesamtschule
College of Further Education/Vocational School	Fachoberschule
University	Berufskolleg
Grammar School	Universität/Fachhochschule
Secondary School GCSE	Gymnasium

Curriculum vitae

Sandra decides to send a letter of application to Vincent Children's Care home. Part of a letter of application is the curriculum vitae (CV) or a résumé in which you write the course of your life in a short form.

Skills Training

Curriculum Vitae

Name	Sandra Hopper
Address	14, Oaktree Lane Stratford MG4 7GP Telephone No. 54 55 78 91 email: sandra.hopper@google.com
Date of Birth	July 20, 19..
Education	20.. – 20.. Stratford Primary School 20.. – 20.. Newton Secondary School
Qualifications	GCSE subjects: physics, biology, arts
Special Training	20.. – 20.. Guitar lessons 20.. Evening classes in home page design and Power Point
Work Experience	August 20.. three weeks voluntary work at a nursery school
References	Mrs Katherine Long Little Mice Nursery School 10 – 15 Chestnut Road Stratford MG4 7GP Telephone No. 74 78 99 11

Stratford, August 8, 20.. Sandra Hopper

Writing a curriculum vitae

Basics:

- A CV should be short, only one page. This means there are no full sentences.
- Make sure that you use correct language and do not use any abbreviations which can be confusing.
- Do not forget to update your CV with new qualifications or what you have achieved in your professional life.
- In contrast to German CVs, you do not include any hobbies or interests in a British CV, only extras connected with professional skills or qualifications. British people list references.

Structure:

1. Start with your personal details on top. Nowadays you do not have to include your date of birth, your nationality and your parents' names and professions. But you can add all or some of them if you like to or think it might be interesting for the job or placement you apply for. Sometimes students add some of them because otherwise their CVs would be too short.

2. Give basic information about your education and job career. This should not be more than two paragraphs of listing schools and workplaces with the full years.

3. Do not forget to add your qualifications, school and job qualifications; maybe you can add some information about special training courses you took, which could be of help for the job or placement you would like to do.

4. You can add references. But nowadays you do not have to include names and full addresses. Those people with a long work career normally add: "References available on request". This will do to keep the CV short.

5. End the CV with the current date and your signature.

Task 5

Now talk about Sandra's CV. The following phrases may help you.

Helpful phrases: Talking about CVs

From ... to ...	**she attended / went to**	**... school**	**in ...**
Then /After that ... **Only years later ...**	**she changed to**	**... school**	**in ...**
In addition to her school work	**she joined**	**... classes/courses**	**in ...**
She	**gained**	**some work experience**	**when ...** **in ...**
She	**finished / graduated from**	**... school**	**with ...**
She	**can produce**	**certificates**	**in ...**

Writing

Task 6

Write your own CV on a separate sheet of paper. Perhaps draft a CV first to see how much room you need. Then take down a neat final version.

Task 7

Sit together in pairs and tell your partner about your CV in English.

Letter of application

Skills Training

Writing a letter of application

A letter of application should always say ...

- how you learnt about the placement or job offered or where you saw the job advertised.
- what job you want to apply for.
- why you are interested in the job or placement.
- what kind of experiences or special skills you have.
- what exams you have passed and what qualifications you have got.
- what you enclosed in the letter (for example your CV and certificates).
- that you would like to be invited to an interview, so put in something like 'I'm looking forward to hearing from you' or 'Hoping to be invited to an interview'

Task 8

On the following page you will find Sandra's letter of application. Match the numbers from her letter with the following terms.

body of the letter – complimentary close – subject matter – salutation – inside address – date – enclosure – name and signature – letterhead

14, Oaktree Lane
① Stratford MG4 7GP

Telephone No. 54 55 78 91

Vincent Children's Care Home
Attn. Philip Soon ②
24-26 Cambridge Street
Oxford BT7 9LM

③ August 24, 20..

Dear Mr Soon, ④

Your advertisement in **Jobs & Placements** August 20.. ⑤

Referring to your advertisement in Jobs & Placements of August 20.., I would like to apply for a placement in your children's home.

I am very interested in working with children and young people and I would be pleased to work in your children's care home to gain some more work experience. ⑥

As you can see from my CV, I passed my GCSE in July 20.. and I did some voluntary work in a nursery school in August 20.. I have enclosed my school certificate and a reference from Mrs Katherine Long, head of the 'Little Mice Nursery School' in Stratford.
Because of the positive work experience I have been able to gather during my voluntary work, I would be pleased to work at your children's home.

I am hoping to be invited for an interview, I'm looking forward to hearing from you soon.

Yours sincerely, ⑦

Sandra Hopper
Sandra Hopper ⑧

Encl.: CV and school certificate ⑨

Skills Training

Writing letters – form and layout

1. Letterhead:	Your address (without your name) or company address, telephone, fax, e-mail address
2. Inside address:	Put FAO (= for the attention of), Attention or Attn., if you want to address a certain person.

3. Date:	5 August 20** → Great Britain June 2, 20** → USA Write the name of the month to avoid confusions!
4. Salutation:	*Dear Mrs Smith* *Dear Mr Smith* *Dear Sir or Dear Madam* if you don't know the person's name *Dear Sirs* (rather old fashioned) or *Dear Sir or Madam* if you don't know any person or name *Gentlemen:* → USA
5. Subject matter:	Say in a short sentence or keywords what the subject matter of the letter is.
6. Body of the letter:	Start the first word with a capital letter. All letters always have an introduction, main part and a close.
7. Complimentary close:	*Dear Sirs, Dear Sir, Dear Sir or Madam* → *Yours faithfully* *Dear Mr Smith* → *Yours sincerely* *Dear John* → *With kind regards, With best wishes, Kind regards, Best wishes* In the USA → *Yours truly, Yours very truly, Sincerely yours, Very truly yours*
8. Name and signature:	
9. Enclosure:	In short → Encl.

Writing

Task 9

Imagine you want to do a one-year-placement in America. You read the following advertisement in the magazine "Jobs & Placements" and you want to apply for the offered placement. Draft your letter of application.

Care workers/social tutors

Reference Number: DI 109 ■ Location: Great Rock Home for Deafblind Children, Great Rock, Philadelphia, 4500 Summer Ave, PA 18769 US, Ph: 215-966-2983 ■ Staff Manager: John Burton

About the job:
We are looking for care workers or social tutors. We want to attract dynamic and energetic people who want to support deafblind children. We provide good work conditions, training and development opportunities. Our working hours are flexible. Even if you can only spare 8 hours/month or if you are searching for a placement we can probably offer you a place to work in our home.

Some knowledge of disability or work experience is advantageous. For us reliability, patience and flexibility are vital qualities.

The job interview

Case study

Great Rock Home for Deafblind Children takes part in an international exchange programme offering placements for a social gap year in America. This exchange programme is organised by a London agency which set up an assessment centre for the allocation of placements. Tim Roberts, aged 18, applied for a placement at Great Rock Home. Right now Tim is going to a vocational college class, focusing on health and care. He already did a hospital placement but did not really like it. He loves to work with people but is quite sure that a medical job is nothing for him. During the last months he became fed up with school and he now thinks a gap year might help him to make a decision whether he really wants to do job training or school. Tim is invited to the London assessment centre. This is his first job interview after writing about 20 applications of all kinds. For the hospital placement he did not have to do an interview because his mother who works in the hospital as a nurse arranged everything for him. On the morning of the job interview Tim gets up as usual. He has to go by train. Tim was expected for the interview at 9 a.m. but he arrives at 9:30 a.m. He caught his train in time but had some problems to find the assessment centre. 'Half an hour won't be a problem', Tim thinks. He wears his casual clothes, jeans, T-shirt and his old but comfortable sneakers because he does not want to convey the impression that he changed his style for the interview and believes his casual clothes make him look 'cool' and 'relaxed'. He also believes his outward appearance does not play a role because he applied for a care job placement and he is sure that clothes do not play a role in this job compared to business jobs. The assessment board consists of three people. Tim is taken by surprise when he enters the room seeing the board because he thought there would only be the personnel manager. He is confused and sits down not saying a word. He does not want anybody to notice that he feels uncomfortable with the situation and crosses his arms waiting for the board to begin asking questions. There is a long, awkward silence. Then one of the interviewers asks him to tell something about his life and qualifications. Tim starts talking about his hobbies. When being asked about his qualifications again, especially his qualifications for the placement at Great Rock Home, he gets stuck because he did not have a look at his CV once again and he forgot about what he wrote in this application letter. 'Why did I not do any research?', comes into his mind. Now Tim becomes very nervous, feels hot and is sure that his face must be red all over. He cannot sit still, starts stuttering and biting his lips. He has also the impression that one of the interviewers does not like him, 'Is he smiling or laughing at me?' Feeling unpleasant he purposely avoids looking at him. In his CV Tim wrote that he can offer references. But now when being asked for them he cannot present any because he did not take his school certificates or references with him. After 20 minutes the job interview comes to an end. Tim is glad to leave the room and he is sure that this interview was a total failure.

Comprehension

Task 10

'The first impression counts'. Take up this statement and try to say what impression you get from Tim during his job interview. Do a brainstorming once around your class completing one of the following sentences:

a. In his job interview Tim gives the impression that ...
b. I have the impression that ...
c. I cannot help thinking that Tim ...
d. I think Tim is out to make the impression that ... but fails because ...

Task 11

Now sit in small groups and discuss Tim's job interview and work on the following tasks:

a. Make a list of Tim's faults and
b. Say what Tim can do better for and during his next job interview.

Take down your results on a flip chart poster to present them in class.

Body Language

Task 12

'Body language speaks loud words'. This statement expresses that body language always plays an important role in our daily interaction, as Tim's example shows in a job interview. From your body language everyone can see what you feel. Facial expressions and postures give you a lot of information about your communication partner. They are part of the non-verbal communication.

Here is a list of typical body signals and what they can express. Match the signals with the explanations and compare your results in class.

a. touch communication partner	1. It is a posture to build up a barrier and show that you feel uncomfortable, defensive or uninterested, but sure not willing to do something. Sometimes people use objects to build up barriers too, like holding a folder in front of them.
b. foot tapping, drumming with a pen, being restless on your chair	2. It is a positive signal to show that you are open towards your communication partner and willing to communicate. It is like a welcome. People tend to look longer and more often at those they like and trust or avoid eye contact with those they dislike or mistrust.

c. playing with your hair, fidgeting, turning red	3. This means that you feel attracted by your partner, showing that you like to talk. People lean away from people they do not like.
d. wringing hands	4. It is a signal that you really like your partner, but be aware, touching is a "don't" at your workplace.
e. crossed arms	5. This shows that the one who does that is really concerned about something
f. lean towards your partner	6. These are all signals showing that someone is nervous or even worried about something.
g. smile combined with eye contact	7. This can show that someone is impatient or bored of something.

Task 13

a. Look at Tim's job interview again and say what body language he shows and what it reveals about his feelings.
b. Now look at the pictures below and discuss with your partner what the postures reveal about the people's feelings. Talk about your results in class.

Task 14

In a typical job interview you are going to be asked some of the questions below. Sit together in small groups and imagine that you are doing the job interview at the assessment centre. Think of further questions and present your role-play in class.

Questions you may face in a job interview include the following:

- Can you briefly tell us something about yourself and your qualifications?
- Were you a good student at school?
- What were your favourite subjects?
- Have you got some work experience?
- What do you know about Great Rock Home for Deafblind Children?
- Why do you want to work for us?
- What could you offer us if we decided to give you the placement?
- Do you have any references?

Task 15

Look at the body language and say what signals you saw during the role play performance.

Module 3: At work – first working day

Making a tour of the house

After a job interview Sandra was offered the chance for a one-year-placement at Vincent Children's Care Home. Sandra accepted right away. Now she is sitting in the entrance waiting for Philip Soon.

Philip Soon: Good morning, Sandra, how are you?

Sandra: Fine, thank you. And how are you?

Philip Soon: Quite okay. Well, I think before we sit down in my office to talk about your tasks, I would like to take you on a tour of the house. And if possible I would like to introduce you to your colleagues at our daily staff meeting.

Sandra: All right

Philip Soon: Our home has three floors. Here on the first floor there are some offices, the canteen kitchen and some common rooms. On the second and third floor there are the children's bedrooms, mainly. Oh, this is Mr Malcom, our care taker. Good morning, Mr Malcom, may I introduce you to Sandra Hopper. She is going to do a period of practical training in our house.

Mr Malcom: How do you do?

Sandra: How do you do?

Philip Soon: Well, let's start. We are standing right in front of our large dining room. Here all children and staff members meet for daily meals. We have a second and third small kitchen on the bedroom floors, so that children can have something to drink whenever they like and have something to eat, if they miss a meal. Down here we have a canteen kitchen. We'd better not enter the kitchen, they are preparing our dinner and there is a great hurry. Next to the kitchen there is our meeting room. Our meeting room is equipped with an overhead projector, a beamer, a flip chart, white board just everything we need for training and lectures. Opposite the meeting room there are three offices. The office next to the caretaker's is mine. Well, let's turn around and go down the hall. The last room on the right is our game room. There are two table tennis tables and one pool billiard table. Right now no one is playing because most of our children are in class, but in the afternoon the room is full of children. On the

left there is the education worker's office, Mrs Taylor. Children come to her for extra lessons. For this reason she has a blackboard and a large table with some chairs in her office. Let's have a look, perhaps she is sitting at her desk.
(Philip Soon knocks at the door)

Mrs Taylor: Come in.
Philip Soon: What are you doing? I hope we may interrupt you?
Mrs Taylor: No problem. Oh, this must be our new volunteer.
Philip Soon: Yes, this is Sandra Hopper.
Mrs Taylor: Nice to meet you.
Sandra: Nice to meet you, too.

Vincent Children's Care Home – plan of the house

Task 1

Read through the dialogue again and find out what kind of rooms 1, 2, 3 and 4 on the first floor are.

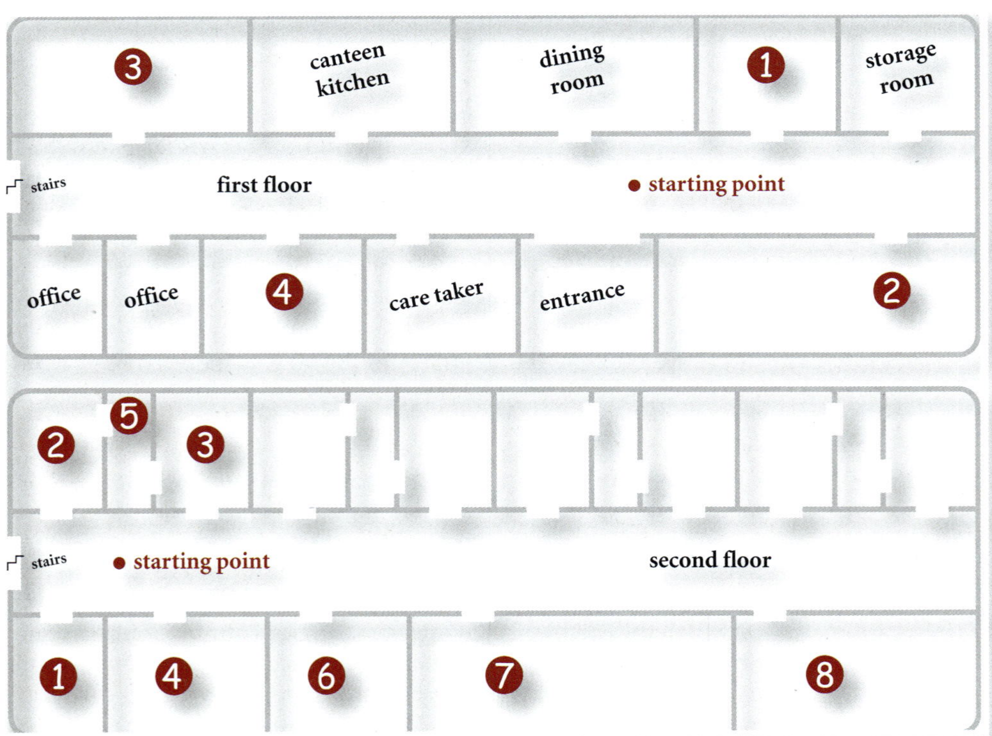

The third floor is identical to the second floor. Here the teenagers have their bedrooms.

Listening

Task 2

a. After having a short chat with Mrs Taylor, Philip Soon and Sandra reach the second floor. Listen to them and match the room numbers of the second floor with the rooms listed below. You can find some vocabulary help in the vocabulary appendix on page 243. Discuss your results with your partner.

living room – staff room – Harry's bedroom – first aid room – Michael's bedroom – Harry's and Michael's bathroom – kitchen – TV room

b. If necessary, listen to the recording a second time and answer the following questions.

1. Who of the staff do they meet?
2. What kind of problem does this staff member tell Philip about?
3. What are Harry and Michael doing when they enter Harry's bedroom?

Activity

Task 3

Choose one of the following tasks.

a. Describe your workplace. First draw a map of your workplace or the place where you're doing a placement (maybe on a transparency) and talk about it in class.
b. Imagine a new trainee or volunteer has her or his first day at your workplace. Take this person around and introduce her or him to some of your colleagues. Make sure you know how to introduce someone new and design a possible dialogue.

   Are you working with children, teenagers, sick people, old people or people with special needs? In the box below you find some words which may help you. Also look at the skills training boxes.

child sized bath facilities – child sized kitchen sink – shelves – cupboards – play carpet – cloakroom – quiet corner – pillows and blankets – mattresses – boxes with toys, blocks and children's books – bookcase – child sized tables and chairs – children's cutlery and dishes – notice board – board with drawing – wall bars – climbing frames – sick bed – invalid chair – invalid toilet seat – wheelchair – medical files – sick room – hospital room – ward – doctor's room – nurses' room – treatment room – stretcher – operating theatre – ward – day room – smokers' corner

Skills Training

Workplace description

1. **First tell your classmates about where you work.**
   I work at St. Katherine's old people's home in London.
   I am doing my hospital placement at our town hospital and I work at the ward for …
2. **Next you could say how many rooms your workplace consists of.**
   Our nursery school consists of … rooms.
   There are 10 patients' rooms and … rooms in my ward.
   There is one large group room and some smaller rooms like …
3. **Give a short overview of where the most important rooms are.**
   When you enter my ward there are six patients' rooms at the left and …
   Next to/right of/left of the kitchen there is a group room.
4. **Say what the rooms are used for.**
   We have one large room which we use as a small gym to do some exercises with the children.
   Most of the rooms are patients' rooms.
   There is also a kitchen where we prepare snacks and tea or coffee for the old people.
5. **Say something about the equipment.**
   In our group rooms we have child-sized tables and chairs and …
   All patients' rooms are equipped with …

Introducing people

Philip Soon introduces Sandra to her new colleagues and he uses different ways for doing this. To introduce someone it is very common to use:

– May I introduce you to ... ?
– Have you met ... ?
– This is ...

People who have been introduced greet each other with:

'How do you do?'	→ when people meet for the very first time. The answer to this question is **'How do you do?'**
'How are you?'	→ when you want to 'break the ice'. The person asked most often answers with **'Fine, thank you (thanks)'** and may add **'And you?'** or **'And how are you?'**
'Nice to meet you.'	→ it is also an icebreaker, which is answered with **'Nice to meet you, too'**.

Web

Grammar

Present Tense Continuous

Bildungsweise	am/is/are + ing-Form des Verbs am not/isn't/aren't + ing-Form des Verbs
Beispiele	On their tour of the house Philip Soon says: *We are standing right in front of our large dining room.* *We'd better not enter the kitchen, they are preparing our dinner.* *Let's have a look, perhaps Mrs Taylor is sitting at her desk.*
Anwendung	– bei momentanen Handlungen – bei Handlungen, die sich in einem bestimmten Zeitraum der Gegenwart wiederholt abspielen: At the moment I'm searching for a placement. – bei zukünftigen, bereits vereinbarten Handlungen: The training is taking place August 1st till 5th.

Task 4

Fill in the correct Present Continuous form of the verb.

When Sandra comes into the meeting room with Philip Soon, she encounters the following situation: Eight people **1 (sit)** around the conference table. They **2 (wait)** for the meeting to begin. There is another male person who **3 (stand)** at a small high desk. Obviously he **4 (try)** to install a beamer. A second person **5 (roll)** out a screen. Sandra recognises Mrs Taylor. She **6 (take)** some cups from a serving table and she **7 (distribute)** them among her colleagues. When she sees Philip, she holds in and asks him, 'Hi, Philip, we **8 (still/wait)** for Maren, Henry and Peter. **9 (they not come)** to our meeting? Do you know what they **10 (do)** at the moment?'

Task 5

Now decide whether the verb in brackets must be transformed into the Present Simple or Present Continuous form.

a. Look! Philip Soon (**already sit**) in his office and (**he telephone**) with Harry's parents. Usually he (**start**) his work at 9 o'clock.
b. There (**be**) always some trouble with the teenagers. They (**know**) that it is forbidden to smoke. But right now they (**hide**) in one bedroom and they (**smoke**).
c. The smaller children (**go**) on an outing next Saturday morning till late afternoon.
d. Some of the children (**not eat**) spinach, but the kitchen staff (**prepare**) some for this dinner.
e. Listen! What a terrible noise (**come**) down from the second floor? (**you know**) what the children (**do**)? Yes, right now they (**watch**) a football match and they (**shout**) because their favourite team (**play**).

Questions in the Present and Future

„Satzbauschema" – Informationsfragen

Fragewort	Hilfsverb	Subjekt	Verb	Satzergänzung	
Where Where Where	**do** **does** **do**	you Sandra her friends	do do do	your placement? her placement? their placement?	**Present Tense Simple**
Where Where Where	**are** **is** **are**	you Sandra her friends	going going going	to college? to college? to college?	**Present Tense Continuous**
Where Where Where	**will** **will** **will**	you Sandra her friends	start start start	your placement? her placement? their placement?	**Future I**

Who (=Wer) Who Who	does is starting will start	a placement a placement a placement	in Vincent Children's Care Home? in Vincent Children's Care Home? in Vincent Children's Care Home?

Fragewörter			
Where? Who? Who? What? Which?	Wo? Wer? Wen? Was? Welche(n)?	How? How much? How many? Why? When?	Wie? Wie viel? Wie viele? Warum? Wann?

Task 6

Ask for the part of the sentence printed in bold.

Example:

John works ***in the Vincent Children's Care Home.***
Where does John work?

a. **In six weeks** Joanne is going to start her job training as an old people's nurse.
b. This job training will be **hard.**
c. Peter is doing some voluntary work **at Little Mice Nursery School.**
d. John always welcomes **new employees.**
e. John always welcomes new people, **because he is the manager of the care home.**
f. **Sandra** wants to train as a child care worker.
g. At the moment she is doing **some voluntary work.**
h. Sandra supervises **eight** children when she stays for a night shift.
i. **This work experience** will help her to find a job later.

UNIT 2: Working world

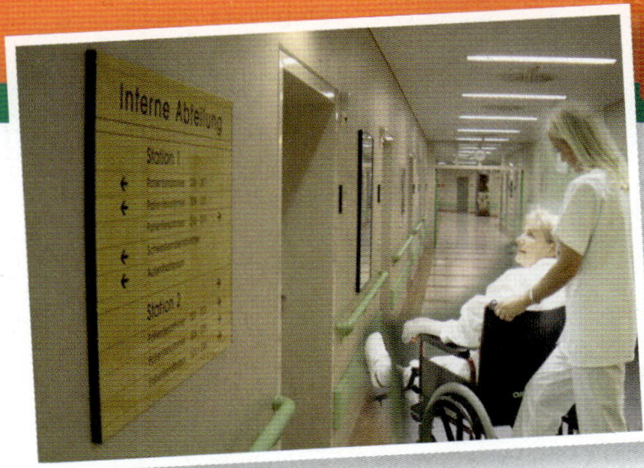

Module 1: Problems at work

Atiye, 29:

I love my job, I always wanted to be a nurse and I'm really glad not to be unemployed. I had my children and went back to work when they were three and five years old. Now I work on night shift mainly.

During the day I look after my children and in the evening and night I am responsible for the patients of one ward all alone. Sometimes the situation is very difficult when there are patients who just have had surgery or who are very ill. Sure, I can call a doctor, but only if there is a real emergency. Besides, I miss having someone to talk to, a colleague who I can ask for help or some advice. It's hard to be alone during the night.

All this is making me very nervous. I hardly get any sleep when I come home and during work I'm always worried about making a mistake. I don't want to lose my job. This would be a serious problem for us, because we bought a house and we have to pay off our bank loan.

Task 1

Answer the following questions.

a. Why does Atiye work at night shift?
b. How does she feel during night shift?
c. Why can't Atiye give up her job and stay at home with her children?
d. Doing the job of a nurse, can you imagine situations at work which are unpleasant or difficult?

Unemployment in Europe

Unemployment (percent)

Task 2

Linda is afraid of becoming unemployed. Look at Europe's unemployment rates and compare them.

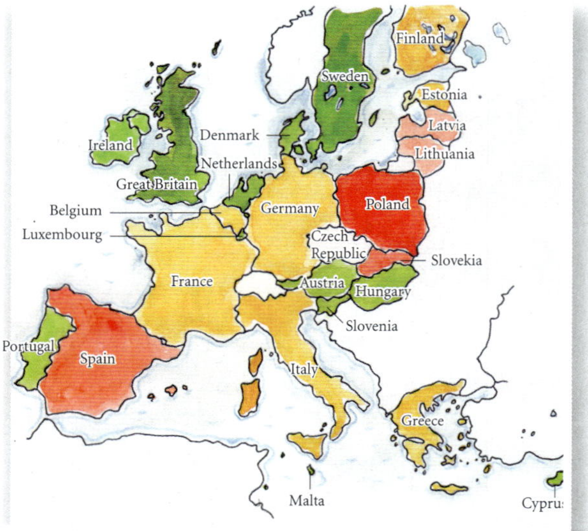

Source: UNECE Statistical Division/United Nations: Statistical Database – Unemployment, August 2012, http://w3.unece.org/pxweb [01.10.2012]

Austria	5,2
Belgium	7,4
Czech Republic	6,6
Denmark	7,6
Estonia	10,8
Finland	7,6
France	10,2
Germany	5,4
Great Britain	8,1
Greece	22,6
Hungary	10,7
Ireland	14,9
Italy	10,2
Latvia	15,2
Lithuania	13,8
Luxembourg	5,2
Malta	5,7
Netherlands	5,2
Norway	3,0
Poland	9,9
Portugal	15,2
Slovakia	13,7
Slovenia	8,7
Spain	24,6
Sweden	7,3
Switzerland	3,1

Helpful phrases

Sentences with comparisons		
The rate of unemployment in... is	as high as as low as almost the same as much the same as not as high as not as low as	(the rate of unemployment) in...
	less high than higher than lower than	
... is the country with	the highest the lowest	rate of unemployment in Europe
The	highest lowest	rate can be found in...

Task 3

Do your own research and find out about the unemployment rate in the town or area you live in. Compare your results with your country's unemployment rate and the rates of the other European countries.

Why nurses can't be angels

Audio

Beth is a nurse in St Margret's Hospital in Leeds. She is annoyed about certain kinds of TV series.

Beth: I'm angry about all kinds of hospital series which show constantly smiling nurses. Their white coats always look clean and freshly ironed. Of course these nurses have lots of time for each patient although their ward is full of fatally ill people. And what a surprise! After a dramatic surgery and the best care of the nurse, the patients jump out of their sick beds more energetic and fitter than ever before. These nurses are no human beings. They are white angels who smile every illness away.

All these series give no or perhaps just very little insight into what being a modern-day nurse is about. Nurses are no angels. In reality the job isn't as romantic as some series make people believe. Shortage of hospital staff is a problem today. This means an immense strain for us. To give the best care to everyone has become much harder.

I love my job and I'm inspired to work because of all the people I meet. The gratitude some patients show you when you can really help them keeps me working. I would like to give best care to everyone at any time, but after 12 days in hospital without a day off I feel almost crazy with tiredness. To keep on smiling at my patients and do my job with vigour is very hard at times like these. You feel just too exhausted to show the enthusiasm which you should have in this job.

This year I was caring for an old lady who was very sick. Right from the beginning of her stay in hospital it was clear that she was going to die. She didn't have any relatives who cared for her. I had some intense conversations with her. She spoke to me about her coming death and was not frightened at all. On the day she died there were three patients who had just had surgery. They needed special care. On my rounds I dropped into the old lady's room again and again. And when I took her blood pressure it was very low. I kept the door open to be at her side when she needed me, but another patient was very short of breath. I gave this patient some oxygen, called the doctor and stayed with him for treatment. When I finally went back to the old lady she was already dead. I felt deeply sad that no one had sat at her bedside and held her hand. During our training we are told that to accompany someone dying is one of the most privileged things a nurse can do. But what can we do if time is always short? Even if someone dies in the presence of their family we can only give some consoling words. But then the room is prepared for the next patient as soon as possible. Today hospitals must work efficiently. Beds must be occupied, but there is no money for more staff. That is a real problem! I'm glad I still love my job!

Comprehension

Task 4

Are these statements true or false? Correct the false statements and point out text passages which show that some statements are true.

a. Beth enjoys to watch hospital series on TV.
b. She believes that there are some series which show a quite realistic picture of the work in a hospital.
c. To be efficient some hospitals reduce their staff.
d. Sometimes Beth is too exhausted to stay friendly and keep on smiling at patients.
e. When the old lady died there was a great hurry on the ward because some of the patients needed special care.
f. Beth had a lot of work on that day, but she was still able to look after the old lady and be at her side when she died.
g. Beth has totally lost enthusiasm and the love for her job.

Task 5

Match the sentence beginnings with suitable endings.

1. Hospital series are totally unrealistic …	a. … when there is a constant strain at work.
2. It's hard to keep on smiling and being patient …	b. … when one of her patients dies.
3. Sometimes Beth feels very exhausted …	c. … because hospital beds must be occupied and many patients must be cared for.
4. Beth feels deeply sad …	d. … because they show fatally ill people who suddenly become healthy again.
5. There is not much time to speak to and console relatives of someone who died …	e. … but Beth knows about this work and still loves her job.
6. Doing the job of a nurse means a lot of work which is sometimes very hard …	f. … because she has to keep on working without a break.

Task 6

Find words in the text which mean

a. a bed in a hospital
b. a creature that is no human being
c. reducing staff
d. being tired
e. everything you do with a patient

Task 7

Answer the following questions.

a. Why are nurses no angels? You may give some examples from the text.
b. Why does Beth believe that the shortage of hospital staff is a problem today? Again, try to give some examples from the text.
c. What could be the reasons why Beth still loves to do her job?

Discussion

Ramon Sanchez: I think people make a real fuss about hospital jobs; as soon as someone wears a white coat people glorify their work. My God, it's just a job like any other.

Cindy White: You're wrong. I think working in a hospital is a job with a lot of stress, both physical and emotional. I respect anybody who does these jobs which I could never do.

Job centres do regular information days at school. These are two statements of a student's class being informed about all kinds of hospital jobs. There is a discussion about the image these jobs have. Look at the statements and divide your class into groups, one taking the role of Ramon Sanchez and the other that of Cindy White.

Task 8

a. First collect arguments which speak for the opinion you have to support.
b. Choose a speaker of your group and do the discussion in a role-play.

Listening

Task 9

Audio

Stress at hospital is a problem for nurses. But there may be more kinds of problems at work. Listen to the people and fill the gaps with their names and the problems they have.

Have a look at the vocabulary appendix, which gives you some help with the words.

Andrew	**unemployment**
Monica	**boring and repetitive job**
Surat	**racial discrimination**
Karen	**sexual harassment**

a. ... is very unhappy because he thinks he does a ...
b. ... sometimes hates to get up and go into her office because she suffers from ...
c. ... is irritated and sad about the way his colleagues speak to him. He is afraid of ...
d. ... is very nervous because there is a constant fear of ...

Grammar

Comparison of Adjectives – Die Steigerung der Adjektive

Regelmäßige Steigerung mit *„-er"*, *„-est"*	
einsilbige Adjektive	high – higher – highest low – lower – lowest
zweisilbige Adjektive auf *„-er"*, *„-le"*, *„-ow"*, *„-y"*	clever – cleverer – cleverest narrow – narrower – narrowest heavy – heavier – heaviest

Regelmäßige Steigerung mit *„more"* – *„most"*	
zweisilbige Adjektive, die nicht auf *„-er"*, *„-le"*, *„-ow"*, *„-y"* enden	careful – more careful – most careful nervous – more nervous – most nervous
drei- und mehrsilbige Adjektive	interesting – more interesting – most interesting astonishing – more astonishing – most astonishing

Unregelmäßige Steigerung		
good	better	best
bad	worse	worst
ill	worse	worst
little (klein)	small	smaller
little (wenig)	less	least
much	more	most
many	more	most

Task 10

Write down the comparatives and superlatives of the following adjectives.
If you need some more information on adjectives and their comparisons, use the internet link www.bildungsverlag1.de/buchplus/07524. Here you can find some more irregular comparison forms.

a. sensitive
b. efficient
c. sporty
d. nervous
e. energetic
f. disappointed
g. miserable
h. difficult
i. simple
j. healthy
k. polite
l. enthusiastic

Task 11

Transform the adjectives in brackets into the comparative or superlative, when necessary.

Example:

Beth believes that her job is much (hard) than an office job. The (hard) thing in her job is to see someone die.

Beth believes that her job is much harder than an office job. The hardest thing in her job is to see someone die.

Beth points out that TV hospital series are very **1 (unrealistic)**. The image they try to show has nothing in common with the **2 (real)** work of a nurse. Compared to these series hospital work is **3 (exhausting)** and **4 (hard)**. TV nurses never feel **5 (bad)** or are **6 (angry)** about their work. But in reality the situation of nurses has become **7 (bad)**. Because of shortages there is **8 (little)** staff than in earlier times but the work is still as **9 (much)** as it was ten years ago. For this reason the work of a nurse has become **10 (much)**. The situation is even **11 (difficult)** at weekends because there is **12 (little)** staff than during the week. One of the **13 (bad)** situations Beth went through was when one of her patients died and she was too **14 (busy)** to stay with this patient.

Translation

Task 12

Sit in pairs and translate the following sentences into English. Take care of irregular comparisons.

a. Am schwierigsten ist die Situation am Wochenende.
b. Alles könnte leichter sein, wenn mehr Personal auf einer Station arbeiten würde.
c. Die Situation ist schlechter als vor zehn Jahren.
d. Jeder Patient sollte die beste Pflege erhalten.
e. Oft bleibt zu wenig Zeit, um mit Patienten zu reden.

Module 2: Working mothers

Working mothers – two full-time jobs

In former times men went out to work and women stayed at home doing the household and caring for the children. Luckily this is an outdated understanding of the male and female role. The rise of our living standards is not the only explanation for the increasing number of working women who have to contribute to the family's income. Today women take their full part in the world of work. But some pay a high price because to be a mother and work means a lot of stress. Very often working mothers with small children feel exhausted and emotionally drained because there is rarely time to relax. The number of men who take a year off for bringing up their child or who take an equal share at home with the children and household is limited but rising gradually. A lot of working mothers still have two full-time jobs at work and at home and feel overwhelmed and guilty about everything: the time they spend for work, the lack of time they have for their children and the amount of time their children have to spend in childcare.

Task 1

Emily is 28 years old and a working mother. She does a full-time job with two small children Sally (4 years) and Samuel (aged 18 months). Her husband also works full-time. He is very career-oriented and therefore does a lot of hours overtime.

Do a brainstorming with your partner or in a small group and think of problem situations Emily may be confronted with or have to organise as a working mother at home with her family or at work.

at home	at work
➢…	➢…
➢…	➢…
➢…	➢…

Here is an example of a working mother, Kate Morrison, who would give up her job if she could afford to live without her wages. Kate is a mother of two children, aged 6 and 22 months, respectively. She misses both her children when she is at work.

Kate: It's really a financial thing. We just can't live on my husband's salary alone. I do feel that if I didn't work, I would have a lot more time to teach my children things and support them. Since I'm working I can't do things like taking my children to the museum, to the park or horse riding. When I'm at home I have so many things to do in the house that I don't have much time to spend with them. I did not plan to return to work after the birth of my youngest daughter, but I had to. Now we pay a childminder and we spend the rest of the money I earn on food and clothes. With the childminder it's not the same as with me. She is there and supervises the children. She plays with them and sometimes watches TV with our eldest daughter. But it's very different. When I'm with my eldest daughter even if we watch TV we learn together. I explain things to her and it's interactive rather than just sitting in front of TV and keeping silent until I come home.

I used to think that people who leave their children to a childminder are irresponsible. Today I do the same. When one of my children is ill the situation almost tears me apart. Most often I stay at home then. My employers are very child-friendly, but I feel my repeated days off are a problem for my colleagues. And if I stay at home too often, I'm sure I will lose my job. Last year the childminder was ill and I had to stay at home. Shortly afterwards my youngest daughter got ill as well. I was too afraid to ask for some more time off at work then and I left the childminder alone with her having a bad fever. It was terrible, but I had to do it.

Comprehension

Task 2

Answer the following questions on the text.

a. Why does Kate Morrison go to work?
b. How does Kate manage her daily life?
c. Do you believe Kate would prefer to stay at home or not? Give reasons from the text.
d. How do her employer and her colleagues react to Kate as a working mother?

Giving up your job means giving up your personality

Ronda Miller has a different point of view.

Ronda: I would never think of giving up my job. I have two children, 12 and 16, and it's sometimes really hard to organise our daily life. But I believe that if you give up your job you give up your own personality. Having no job makes you vulnerable and weak. You constantly rely on your husband's income. I don't know, but I would feel pretty bad if I had to ask my husband for money. But I must say that since the birth of my children my attitude changed. Work doesn't rule my life that much any more. Before I met my husband and we decided to have children, I sometimes was in the office from 7am until midnight. I didn't have a social life. Work was my life and I rewarded myself with expensive clothes or exotic holidays. Now I don't need these things any more, because my family life has become more important to me. But it's good to have your own money. I can buy anything I want to have without asking my husband. Staying at home and giving up work would never come into my mind because this would mean giving up a very important part of my life. I would regret not leaving the house for some time. Going to work also means meeting people you can talk to, who respect you as the woman you are and don't only look at you as a mother. Sometimes it's good to have a break from the children. It's also important to show your children that you are an independent woman, who can do more than just do the cooking, cleaning and washing. Today there is the possibility to send your child into a day care nursery school. You can also pay a childminder. Children don't want to be together with their parents all day long. They sometimes need a break, too.

Comprehension

Task 3

This is a short summary of Kate's and Ronda's attitude towards going to work. Fill in the missing words from the box.

childminder – respect – financial – home – independent – support – personality

Kate Morrison feels that her family would do better if she stayed at **(1)** with the children. She is sure that she could **(2)** her children a lot more then. Leaving the children alone with a **(3)** who only supervises the children is a bad compromise in her eyes. But because of **(4)** reasons there is no chance for her to stay with the children.
Ronda decided to keep her job because it's most important for her to stay **(5)**. She also wants her children to **(6)** her as a working woman. For her doing a job is a very important part of her **(7)** .

Task 4

Answer the following questions about Ronda.

a. What does Ronda do with the money she earns?
b. Why does staying at home never come into her mind? Think about what doing a job means to Ronda.
c. Ronda says that having no job makes you 'vulnerable and weak'. What kind of situations may she have in mind when she says that?

Discussion/Writing

Task 5

"All men should take a year off for the upbringing of their children."

Discuss this statement. Don't write much less than 100 words.

Activity

Task 6

Are you a working mother or do you stay at home?
How many children have you got? How old are your children?
Do you plan to go back to work?
How do you manage your working day?
Why did you decide to go back to work? What are your reasons for staying at home?

Carry out your own survey on the situation of working mothers. The questions above could be part of your questionnaire. Ask working mothers and those who prefer to stay at home with their children. Design your questionnaire first and then carry out your survey. Collect your results in class and discuss them

Task 7

Lisa Summer (aged 28) and her husband Tom (aged 27) are parents of 15 months old twins. Lisa stopped working because of the twins but now she thinks of going back to work. She discusses her future plans with her husband. Sit in pairs and design a dialogue between Lisa and Tom. Read out your dialogue in class.

Task 8

Imagine the topic 'working mothers' is discussed on the radio. Kate and Ronda take part in this discussion. What would they say? What could be their arguments? Sit in pairs or small groups and develop a dialogue between Kate and Ronda. Read out your dialogue in class.

The phrases in the box below may give you some help to develop your dialogues.

Helpful phrases:

When I leave my children in the morning I feel ...
There is no reason to feel this way because ...
The best thing you can do is to ...
It's much / not much better to ... because ...
It's wrong to say that ...
I believe it's bad/even worse/much better for children to ...
It's always a problem to ...
But what if ...
The situation is even worse when...
Why not...
What's the problem with...

Grammar

Formation of Adverbs – Die Bildung des Adverbs

Adverbien werden durch Anhängen von „-ly" an das Adjektiv gebildet.	nice (Adjektiv) → nicely (Adverb) correct → correctly nervous → nervously
l → lly le → ly y → ily	careful → carefully terrible → terribly happy → happily
Adjektiv und Adverb haben manchmal die gleiche Form und die gleiche Bedeutung.	daily, hourly, weekly, monthly, early, likely, fast, long, far, straight, low
weitere Ausnahmen	good (adj.) → well (better, best) little → little (less, least) bad/ill → badly (worse, worst) hard → hard fast → fast near → near soon → soon

Use of the Adjective and Adverb – Gebrauch des Adjektivs und Adverbs

Adjektiv	Adverb
Bezieht sich immer auf Nomen (z. B. Personen und Gegenstände) *Working mothers must be patient.* *Working mothers do a hard job.*	**Kann sich beziehen auf** • **ein Verb** *Ronda manages her household and job very well.* • **auf ein Adjektiv** *Some working mothers are totally exhausted.* • **auf ein anderes Adverb** *Ronda manages her family life and job particularly well.* • **auf einen ganzen Satz** *Fortunately, she has a husband who helps her a lot.*

- **kein** Adverb nach Verben, die einen Zustand beschreiben → to be, to become, to get, to grow, to turn (werden), to remain, to stay, to keep (bleiben), to seem (scheinen)
- kein Adverb bei Verben der Sinneswahrnehmung → to look, to feel, to smell, to sound, to taste

Task 9

Transform the adjective of the first sentence into an adverb to fill the gap of the second sentence.

Example:

It's very sensible to pay a childminder who can stay with the children when you are away. But before you decide everything must sensibly be discussed.

a. Working mothers need to be powerful to find the energy to work and manage their family's household. Sometimes they have to speak to their family … to make clear to everyone what her or his task is.
b. Some working women are nervous because they have to leave their children at home with a childminder. But being at work and reacting … can be a problem, too.
c. It's quite difficult to find a good childminder. Not everyone knows how to supervise and care for the children … .
d. Our new childminder is a very polite person. She always … draws my attention to problems with my children at home or at nursery school.
e. Children need to have a regular day. Sometimes it's quite helpful to sit together with them … and talk about the coming week.

Task 10

Fill in the adjective or adverb.

1. Being a working mother isn't always **(easy)**. 2. Sometimes it's **(extreme) (difficult)** to organise your **(daily)** life. 3. To fulfil the **(clear)** wishes and **(constant)** demands of your family, employers and colleagues can be **(particular) (hard)**. 4. Everything must be **(good)** organised. 5. **(Various)** problems arise when a child **(sudden)** becomes **(ill)**.

6. Then the working mother has to make a **(quick)** decision. 7. A **(good)** solution must be found. 8. How can a **(normal)** working day be organised in a **(complete) (different)** way? 9. Some mothers stay at home with their **(ill)** child but feel **(bad)** about their decision. 10. Not every employer or colleague reacts **(friendly)**. 11. This is a **(great)** problem. 12. **(Quite)** often colleagues are not **(real)** willing to take over some **(additional)** work because of their **(absent)** colleague. 13. And if these days off happen **(repeated)**, the risk of losing the job becomes very **(high)**.

Module 3: How to find out about job preferences

Getting to know your strength and weakness – a voluntary social year

Audio

Are you 16 or slightly over 16? Have you just left school and don't have a clue what to do in future? This is a typical situation many young people have to face. More and more youngsters take a gap year before they decide to do job training or go to university. Some students plan to travel the world.
Mike Hilton, a career adviser for young school leavers and university graduates says, 'taking a gap year is becoming more and more popular. And no matter whether you take the year before or after university it can be extremely valuable. If this year off is well planned, students can learn and develop skills which will be of good help to them in their future'. To travel the world can be expensive and some students take the chance to do a voluntary social year in a foreign country. Those youngsters who decide for a voluntary social year work in any kind of institution which takes care of people. For one year you take part in the daily work of an old people's home, a nursing home, a child care home, or a hospital. And it's not just any kind of work, the volunteer takes an active part. Those who want to do a social year must be willing to lend a hand and be able to cope with difficult situations.
Janet Turner, who did a voluntary social year in a nursing home for children with special needs, says, 'you should think it over again and again. Do you really want to do it? It sometimes is hard work and you really must want to do it. You are not just standing there watching. The work I do in the nursing home is demanding. After a period of introduction you are independent and do the full job. This is hard work and a great challenge. During the first weeks I was constantly exhausted. One or two times I cried because it was very difficult for me to decide who to care for first and what to do next. I wanted to do my best, but sometimes you have to ask for help. And there is always somebody there for you who you can ask anything you need to know. Day after day you feel better and more secure. Today I know that I am strong enough to care for children with special needs. A voluntary year shows you your weaknesses, but now I know that I have a lot of strength.'
Eric Batts applied for a voluntary social year in France because he wants to work in a foreign country. He was offered a placement in an old people's home in Bayeux. Eric says, 'this is a very special experience. On the one hand there are the old people who I have to care for. On the other hand I have to learn to manage all this in a foreign language. I'm really proud that I can cope with the situation and I'm sure this work experience will be a good thing to mention in my application documents.'

Comprehension

Task 1

Explain in your own words what the following figures and words mean.

a. gap year
b. voluntary social year
c. period of introduction
d. take an active part

Task 2

Who are these people? Explain who they are and what they do.

a. Mike Hilton
b. Janet Turner
c. Eric Batts

Task 3

Find a word in the text which means

a. learning a job.
b. someone who helps you to find a job.
c. something you can do or learn to do.
d. a country which is not your home country.
e. someone who does something without getting paid for it.

Task 4

Some students have wrong ideas about a voluntary social year. Look at their statements and explain to them why they are wrong.

Sally: I'm 18 years old. I already started job training which I didn't finish. Now I'm too old to do a voluntary social year because they only take fresh school leavers at the age of 16.

Brian: My grandmother is German and I speak German fluently. I would be interested in doing a voluntary social year in Germany. But you can only do a social year in your own home country. This would be Great Britain in my case.

Ruby: It would be interesting to do some voluntary work in a nursing home to get to know all about working with disabled people. But they only let you do some cleaning jobs. Or just boring jobs which anyone can do.

Mike: Only during the last two or three months you are allowed to do more demanding jobs. During the first seven or eight months you only stand beside the care workers and watch them.

Writing

Task 5

Imagine you are Eric Batts and before you decide to do a voluntary social year; you want to be sure about the positive and possible negative aspects of taking a gap year. Eric started to take down a list of pros and cons. Look at the list and try to complete it. Compare your entries with your classmates.

Pros	Cons
A gap year in France will help me to improve my French. … …	I will have to leave my family and friends for one year. … …

Activity

Task 6

Imagine that after his voluntary social year in a French old people's home Eric comes back to his former school to speak to the final class of school leavers and tries to convince them to do the same. Take the notes from your list as a help to prepare Eric's speech. Decide who is going to speak in class and do your speech.

Grammar

Web

The use of some and any

some	any
im bejahten Satz	**im verneinten Satz**
There are some students who want to take a gap year.	*Nowadays there aren't any students who don't see advantages in a social year.*
in Fragesätzen, die positiv beantwortet werden bzw. auf die eine positive Antwort erwartet wird	**im Fragesatz**
Did you gain some work experience during your voluntary social year?	*Did you find any placements you want to apply for?*
Die gleichen Regeln gelten für:	
something – etwas **somebody – jemand** **someone – jemand** **somewhere – irgendwo**	**anything – irgendetwas** **anybody – irgendjemand** **anyone – irgendjemand** **anywhere – irgendwo**

Task 7

Look at this dialogue. Susan and Henry are talking about what they want to do after school. Fill in 'some', 'any', 'someone', 'anyone', 'something' or 'anything'.

Susan: Have you got **1** … clue what you want to do in future?

Henry: I'm not really sure. Perhaps I'll do **2** … kind of job training with children. I did **3** … voluntary work in a nursery school and I liked it.

Susan: I don't know about what kind of job training I would like to do. But I'm quite sure that I want to do **4** … kind of work with people. I can't imagine sitting in an office working with papers. I don't like **5** … kind of office work, I want to work with human beings.

Henry: Do you know **6** … who can give you **7** … good advice?

Susan: Well, I spoke to a career adviser and he told me about different kinds of care worker jobs. He gave me **8** … brochures I can read through. And Eric Batts, who did a voluntary social year at a French old people's home, visited our class and told us **9** … about his time in France.

Henry: I don't know **10** … about caring for old people. But I think it must be hard work.

Susan: I'm not interested in working with old people but I'm interested in doing a voluntary social year here in Great Britain and I applied at **11** … child care homes.

Henry: That seems to be a good idea. If I had known **12** … about a voluntary social year, I would have tried to apply for it, too. It surely helps you to gain **13** … work experience.

Uncountable Nouns

- **Nomen wie – advice, information, knowledge, news, progress, strength, work and homework haben keine „normale" Pluralform wie book – books oder school – schools.**
- **Zum Beispiel:** *'His advice was very good', 'The information he gave me was of great help'.*
- **Um diese Nomen zählbar zu machen, sagt man zum Beispiel** *'He gave me two good pieces of advice'* **oder** *'This bit of news is very interesting'.*
- **Nomen wie people, police stehen im Plural.**
- **Um diese Nomen in den Singular zu setzen, sagt man zum Beispiel:** *One person, one police officer.*

Translation

Task 8

Translate the following sentences and compare your translation with your partner before you present them in class.

a. Ich arbeite gerne mit Menschen.
b. Einige seiner Informationen über das freiwillige soziale Jahr sind sehr interessant.
c. Ein soziales Jahr zu machen war ein wirklich guter Ratschlag.
d. Bei einem freiwilligen sozialen Jahr lernt man seine Stärken kennen.

UNIT 3:
Living in a family

Module 1: What does a family mean to you?

How would you like your future to be?

It's astonishing to see that although birth and marriage rates are decreasing, a lot of youngsters think of their future in a very traditional way. Mostly they take their own family and parents as a role model and wish to have the same living standard and family. Here is what Fiona (15) wishes for her future.

Fiona: My wishes are very simple. First I would like to finish school, get my driving licence and find a job. I would like to be a correspondent for French because I'm quite good at French and perhaps I can learn Spanish as well. My Mum worked as a correspondent for French and German. But I'm not very interested in learning German. When I'm about 24 I would like to marry and raise a family. I don't think I want to have only one child, perhaps two children. We're two children in our family as well. Me and my elder sister Rosalind. Maybe we'll have enough money to build a house. I would like to live in my parents' neighbourhood. At the moment I can't imagine living without my family. One of my friends lost her mother because of cancer. I would be desperate without Mum. And of course Dad and my elder sister. You need someone who cares for you. If there's a problem at school, with friends or anything else, I can always talk to Mum or Rosalind. They often give me some good advice.

Task 1

a. Fiona's future wishes are very traditional. Find examples from the text which show that this statement is true.
b. Why is family important to Fiona?
c. What do your future plans look like? Give a short talk in class.

What does a family mean to you?

Janet Young interviews people on the street for her daily radio programme 'Street Voices' – the picture shows her in her studio. Here are some of the answers she got to the question: What does living in a family mean to you?

Tim (20): Living in a family means a lot. It's the place where you grow up. It teaches you about the world and it gives you a lot of warmth. I love Mum and Dad.

Janet Young: Are you still living at home?

Tim: Yes, I have been talking about moving away from home and into my own flat for some time but I never actually do something about it. It's not that I haven't got the money to rent my own place and sometimes I think it would be better because I can sleep late and be untidy without Mum nagging at me. But when it comes to moving out I back off. I am very fond of my parents.

Miriam (64): I'm a grandma and all of my children left the family long ago. On the one hand this is a sad experience because you have to let them go. On the other hand it made me proud to see that they can manage their life alone. It's some kind of success as a parent.

Janet Young: Do you keep close contact to your children?

Miriam: Well, yes and no. I know they have their own families and not much time left over. But when my husband died five years ago our contact grew closer again. My family helped me through a very sad time. You're not alone. My grandchildren keep me active. I'm glad that there is still someone who needs me.

Simon (17): Everyone needs a family to grow up. A family supplies you with everything you need. That's not only clothes or food. I mean, a family introduces you into society. You need someone who knows 'the rules' and tells you what is right or wrong. Everyone needs education and your family can offer it to you. The family is the first to teach you, then of course nursery school, primary school and so on.

Janet Young: Are you still living with your family?
Simon: Yes, at the moment I'm still living at home but I'm going to move out soon. I want to go to college. When you're grown up, time has come to break free. I'm glad to leave my family and live alone. It's time to go. I love all of them, but now I am going to share a flat with some of my friends.

Comprehension

Task 2

This is a summary of the different opinions presented in the text. Read through the text again and fill the gaps with words from the text only. Don't repeat any word. Sometimes you have to change the grammatical form of a verb.

Tim, aged 20, believes that a family is most important because it's where you (1) and it also (2) you everything you have to know. It offers you love and (3), too. This may be the reason why Tim is still living at home. He earns enough money to (4) his own flat, but he (5) of his parents.

Miriam is 64 and her children already have their own families. She feels (6) and (7) at the same time. All her children left home, but she thinks it's a (8) to see that they can lead their own life. After her husband's death the (9) to her children became (10) again.

Simon thinks that the main thing a family supplies you with is (11) because this is what you need to become a member of (12). Simon is 17 now and feels that his time has come to (13). First he wants to (14) a flat with some of his friends.

Discussion/Writing

Task 3

Write a short comment on one of the following questions. "Skills Training" and the "Helpful phrases" - box may help you.

a. What does living in a family mean to you?
b. Why should young grown-ups leave their family and live alone?
c. Or should they live at home as long as they want to?

Skills Training

Writing a comment

In a comment you write or talk about a problem or questions from your personal point of view. It is your personal statement. You do not have to discuss a problem from different points of view or think of the pros and cons. A comment only concentrates on your personal opinion. It is written in the simple present.

Your personal comment should have the following points:

1. **An introduction:** Say what you want to talk about, e.g. *I like to talk about the question what family means to me.* Or just start with the question, e.g. *What does family mean to me? I think living in a family means that …* You can also use a formal introduction like *My/This comment deals with the questions … (Mein/Dieser Kommentar handelt von …)*
2. **Your personal opinion: State your opinion but do not forget to give reasons!** One strategy is to start with a 'weak' argument and leave the strongest one for the end of your comment to lay emphasis on it.
3. **Examples:** You can also support your point of view with giving one or more examples.
4. **Closing sentence:** Give a short summary of your point of view in a last sentence, e.g. *Finally there is no doubt that living in a family means …*, (Schließlich besteht kein Zweifel daran, dass..), *So all in all I believe …* (Alles in allem glaube ich, dass…)

There are more useful phrases in the box below!

Helpful phrases: Writing a comment

I think that ...	Ich denke, dass ...
I believe that ...	Ich glaube, dass ...
In my opinion it's better to ...	Meiner Meinung nach ist es besser ...
My point of view is that ...	Meine Meinung ist, dass ...
In his/her place I would prefer to ...	An seiner/ihrer Stelle würde ich es bevorzugen ...
As I see it …/From my point of view …	So wie ich das sehe …
I can imagine that …	Ich kann mir vorstellen, dass ...
That is why I think …	Darum denke ich …
I'm sure/certain/convinced …	Ich bin mir sicher/überzeugt …
The fact is that …	Fakt ist, dass …
It is clear/obvious that …	Es ist klar/offensichtlich, dass …
Take for example (the case of) …	Nehmen wir zum Beispiel (den Fall von…) …
Let me give an example.	Ich möchte ein Beispiel anführen.
I would never like to ...	Ich möchte auf gar keinen Fall ...
I reject this attitude because ...	Ich lehne diese Haltung ab, weil ...
I support people who ...	Ich unterstütze Leute, die ...
I think it's understandable that ...	Ich denke, es ist verständlich, dass ...
At last one can say …	Zum Schluss kann man sagen …
All this proves that …	All das beweist, dass …
The (main) point is …	Der (wichtigste) Punkt ist …

Language

Task 4

Find the noun forms of these verbs in the text.

a. to live b. to advise c. to experience
d. to succeed e. to warm up f. to educate

Linking words used to express cause and effect

Linking words that can be used to express cause and effect:

because – as – since – due to – therefore

Task 5

Look at the examples and try to link the phrases in the columns A and B. Sometimes it's possible to form more than one sentence by using different linking words. If possible, try to form more than one sentence.

because – weil (Nebensatz)
as – da, weil (Satzanfang)
since – da, weil (Satzanfang)
due to – auf Grund
therefore – deshalb

Examples:

Many young grown-ups don't want to leave their family.	A family offers many advantages.

Many young grown-ups don't want to leave their family, ***because*** *a family offers many advantages.*
Since/As *a family offers a lot of advantages, many young people don't want to leave their families.*
A family offers a lot of advantages, ***therefore*** *many young people don't want to leave their family.*
Due to *the fact that a family offers a lot of advantages, many young grown-ups don't want to leave their family.*

A	B
a. Tim still lives at home	he is fond of his parents
b. a family teaches children everything they need to know	children need a family
c. a family can support you when there is a problem or some trouble	it's good to have a family in bad times
d. high teenage unemployment	some young people are glad to have a family
e. a family can help old people to keep active	grandchildren need their grandparents
f. the help received by grandparents	both husband and wife can have a job and leave the children at home

Family types

Not every family has the same structure, e.g. there are large and small families. Mainly, families are divided into four family types: the extended family, the nuclear family, the patchwork family and the single-parent family.

The extended family

A typical extended family consists of father and mother most often with more than two children and the family's household also includes grandparents who live with the family or sometimes aunts and uncles and their children. Compared to former times extended families are rare nowadays.

The nuclear family

This is the most common type of family. It's mother and father with one or more children. Statistics today say that in most European families there live '1.5 children on average', which means that most families consist of mum, dad and one or two children. To have three or more children seems to be an exception these days.

The patchwork family

Since there are a lot more divorces today than in former times, patchwork families are becoming more widespread. In a patchwork family parents who are divorced or lost a partner come together to start a new family. One or both partners may have children stemming from their former partnership. This means that in a patchwork family you have a natural mother or father, a stepmother or stepfather with natural children and stepchildren.

The single-parent family

Statistics show that families with only one parent, are increasing. It's not only because of divorce or the loss of one partner. Today a lot of women choose to bring up a child without a partner.

Comprehension

Task 6

What do you think about the following statements? Please correct those sentences that contain wrong information.

a. Most European families consist of parents and two children.
b. In former times households were much smaller, because people were poorer than today.
c. Today extended families are increasing again.
d. In industrialised countries like those of Europe it's normal to have three and more children in one household.
e. Since it is difficult to bring up a child without a partner, single parent families are rare.

Discussion

Task 7

With your partner choose one of these questions. Discuss the question and take down keywords to present your point of view in class.

a. Can you think of reasons why extended families have become rare today?
b. Statistics show that families are becoming smaller nowadays. What could be the reasons?
c. Why is there an increase in single-parent families?

Task 8

Read through these different family examples first.

Ronda is her parents' only child.She is eight years old. Her father works full-time, her mother part-time.	Robin is four and he has got an elder sister, Liz, six years old, their mother works as a teacher and their father stays at home. Sometimes he works at home for his former company.	Thomas is five. He visits a day nursery school because his mother works fulltime. They live in a single-parent household.	Maggie is seven. She has got three sisters, two smaller ones and one older sister. There are also two older brothers and baby Ralph. Their mother stays at home and their father works fulltime. Quite often he works overtime.

Now imagine all these families have to master typical family situations like the following

- a child's birthday party
- buying new winter clothes for the whole family
- a child is ill
- father or mother is ill
- a child has problems at school, in nursery school or with a best friend
- father or mother becomes unemployed
- the family wants to go on a holiday
- the family searches for a new flat or house

Do these situations mean a special problem to some of these family types? Can a certain family type master one of these situations more easily?
Sit together in small groups and pick out two situations for discussion. Present your results in class.

Audio

Atina Forester – an independent business woman talks about her family

Atina: I come from a Greek family. My mother came over to America with her parents to find work here. They worked hard and as one of our early family photos shows they first lived in a poor working-class area. But later they ran a Greek restaurant with the whole family. My grandma, granddad, my mother and all of my aunts and uncles used to work in this restaurant. Later my parents had their own restaurant with my grandparents' support and everyone, my sisters and brothers and me, worked in this restaurant. That's typical of Greek people, everything is a family business.
One thing was always clear to my mother even when she emigrated to America: She would marry a Greek and bring up a typical large Greek family. Greek people meet Greek people no matter in which country they are living. Together they celebrate family parties which are not only large but huge. At one of these parties my mother met my father Paco. Some time later they got married. These family parties were a kind of 'marriage market' in my parents' teenage time. In my great-grandparents' time women were promised to their husband without really asking them and they accepted what their fathers – the heads of their family – decided for them.
I always had the impression that my mother was satisfied with her life and happy. I think she loved to care for her 'big Greek' family. Greek people are proud to bring up lots of children and have large families. They believe that only lots of children make you rich and for this reason I have four sisters and three brothers.
I married an American and I was always sure I didn't want to lead on our family tradition with lots of children and me staying at home looking after the household or our restaurant. Now I live alone with my daughter Nina and son José as a single parent. Our marriage broke up and we got divorced ten years ago. First I felt ashamed that I wasn't able to keep up the marriage. Perhaps this was my Greek soul. It needed some time, but I learnt to become independent. I built up my own business. Today I run my own travel agency and I can afford a good life for all of us.
It's strange, but when I look at my sisters and brothers I believe that we all decided for another family type than we grew up in. Only one sister – Donna – has got six children and lives a very traditional family life as a housewife who looks after the house and the children and keeps all trouble away from her working husband. Gracia and Bernardo have got two children like me, Esmeralda is married but decided not to have children. Isabela has got a little son, but she didn't want to marry her boy's father. Manolo and Placido are still singles and have changing relationships. Manolo says he won't ever get married and have a family because he got so fed up with having no privacy in a large family. But typically Greek, we all stick together. Everyone knows what the other one is doing and if someone needs help he or she will get it from the family.
That was different in my former husband's family. John has only his sister Betty and during our ten years of marriage he only met her four of five times. He never knew what she was doing. Thank God, that's different in a large Greek family!

Comprehension

Task 9

Answer the following questions on the text.

a. How were marriages 'arranged' in Atina's parents' and great-grandparents' time?
b. What was Atina's mother always sure about?
c. What does Atina think of how her mother feels about her family and family life?
d. Atina talks about her sisters' and brothers' family lives. What types of families do they have?
e. What does Atina like about her family compared to her former husband's family life?

Listening

Task 10

Audio

There is a story behind this family photo. Listen to the story of its owner and try to answer the following questions.

a. When was the photo taken?
b. Who took the photo?
c. What happened on that day?

Before you present your answers in class exchange your results with your partner.

Task 11

Look through your family photos or ask your grandparents for a family photo which was taken on a special occasion. What is the 'story behind the photo'? Present this photo in class and tell the story.

Grammar

Web

Simple Past Tense

Anwendung	beschreibt eine Handlung, die in der Vergangenheit stattfand und abgeschlossen wurde.
Beispiel	*Last year Mary married John.* *Atina built up her own business ten years ago.*
Bildung	Regelmäßige Verben → Infinitiv (Grundform) + „ed" Unregelmäßige Verben → 2. Verbform Verneinung des Vollverbs → didn't + Verb im Infinitiv (Grundform)
Beispiel	*John didn't arrive in time for the wedding.* *I didn't see you at Mary's wedding.*
Bildung	Fragen im Past Tense werden (bei Vollverben) mit „did" gebildet.
Beispiele	*Did you meet your cousin on this family party?* *Where did the family party take place?*

Task 12

When Atina talks about her family history, she uses a lot of past tense, because she talks about what happened a long time ago. Now Atina tells the story of her wedding day. This report must be put into the past tense because her wedding took place ten years ago.

My 'Greek' Wedding – Atina talks about her wedding ten years ago

When I **1** (**marry**) John ten years ago we **2** (**be**) sure we **3** (**want**) a little romantic wedding in a small chapel with only a few best friends and my and John's close family. But when I **4** (**tell**) my parents about our plans they **5** (**not understand**). My parents **6** (**think**) of a huge family party with all our relatives and friends. Instead of marrying in a small chapel with only best friends we **7** (**celebrate**) with hundreds of guests and the wedding **8** (**take place**) in our large town church. On my wedding day I **9** (**meet**) relatives I had never seen before and family friends who **10** (**come**) to join our wedding party I **11** (**not know**) about.

This is what Greek weddings are like. Besides I **12** (**not be**) able to choose my own wedding dress. I **13** (**fall**) in love with an off-the-shoulder silk dress in a light grey and instead of a veil I wanted to wear some flowers in my hair. But this time my mother **14** (**break**) into tears and I **15** (**promise**) her I would wear a 'modest' wedding dress and of course the wedding veil she and my grandmother already **16** (**wear**) at their weddings. I **17** (**keep**) up our family tradition and my mother **18** (**stop**) crying.

Task 13

Atina's daughter Nina wants to know more about her mother's wedding and about the time before her parents' marriage. Here are Atina's answers. Can you think of her questions? Use one of the question words in the box below.

who – where – when – how – why – how many

a. 'I remember this very well. I met your Dad at my best friend's party. He was one of her husband's friends'.
b. 'We married almost one year after we first met on the 1st of May.'
c. 'Oh, I think I fell in love with him, because he looked very handsome and he was very different from all the boys I met before'.
d. 'I don't know exactly. But I'm sure there were more than 300 people at our wedding.'
e. 'Of course, daddy, your grandfather was my witness at our marriage ceremony.'
f. 'We both felt very exhausted after our wedding day and I was really glad to go on a three weeks holiday'.

Language

Task 14

Family Tree

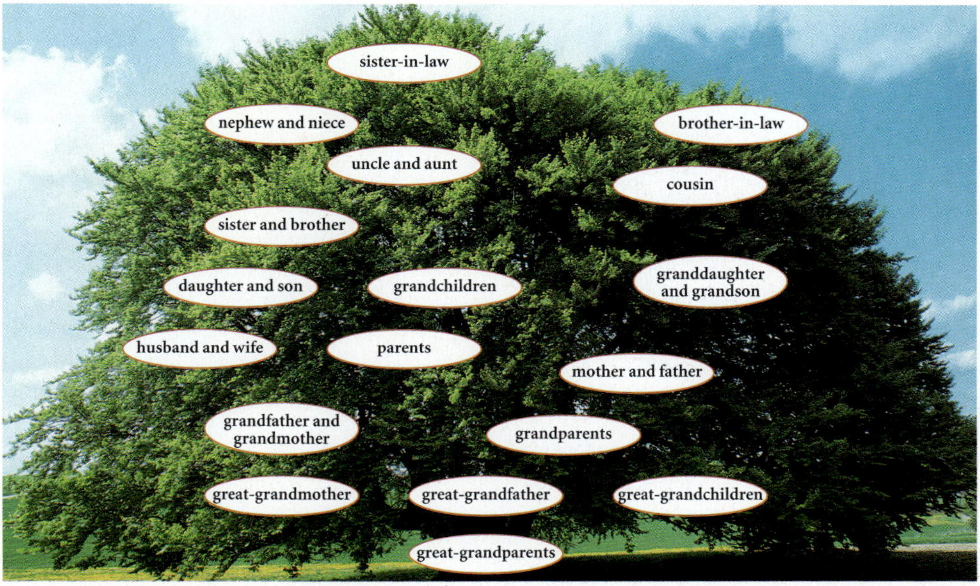

Do you remember all the family names? If you need help, look at the family tree with all the different relatives. Then try to fill in the gaps of the following text about Atina's family.

a. Atina's mother came over to America with her parents, Atina's (**1**).
b. The family built up their own Greek restaurant and Atina's mother worked in this restaurant with her sisters and brothers, Atina's (**2**) and (**3**).
c. After her marriage Atina's mother ran her own restaurant with her (**4**) Paco and her parents' support. As a teenager Atina worked in this restaurant together with her four (**5**) and three (**6**).
d. Now everyone is grown up and with the exception of Manolo and Placido they have got children. Donna has got six children. Three girls and three boys who are Atina's (**7**) and (**8**).
e. But they are not the only (**9**) Atina's (**10**) Nina and her (**11**) José have. Gracia, Esmeralda and Isabela have got children, too.
f. Whereas Atina's family is a large one, her former husband's family is small. He has only got one sister Betty, Atina's former (**12**).

Module 2: Does a child need brothers or sisters?

Talking about statistics

Types of households in the United Kingdom in per cent of all households

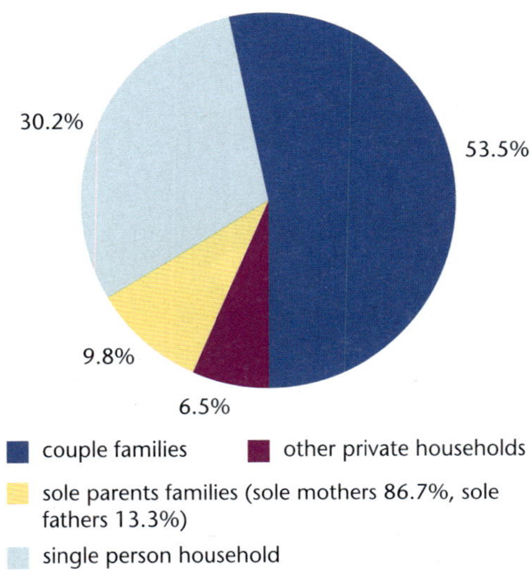

Households by number of children in the United Kingdom in per cent of all households

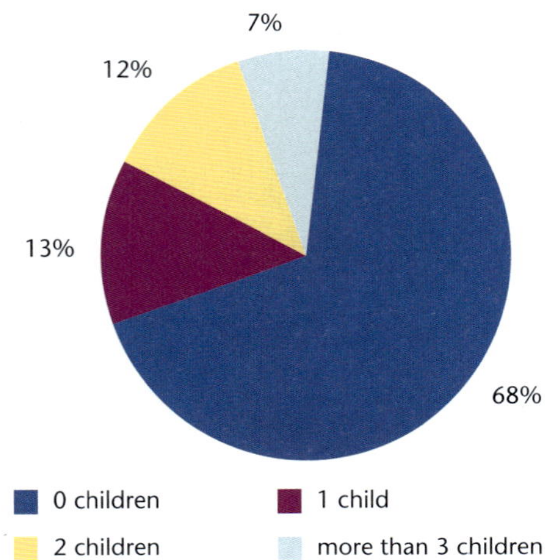

Adapted from OECD: Family database – The structure of families (SF), August 2012, www.oecd.org/social/family/database [01.10.2012]

Task 1

What do the pie charts tell you about Britain's family structures? Prepare a talk in class making use of the skills training and helpful phrases boxes given in the next page.

Activity

Task 2

Do you believe these pie charts are only typical of Britain or are there similar trends in your country?

a. Sit in groups and search the Web to gather some information. Then write a short report to inform your class.
b. Choose one more country to compare your results with, e.g. the United States, Japan, China and the Russian Federation. Tell your class about your results.

Skills Training

Talking about statistics: Analysing charts

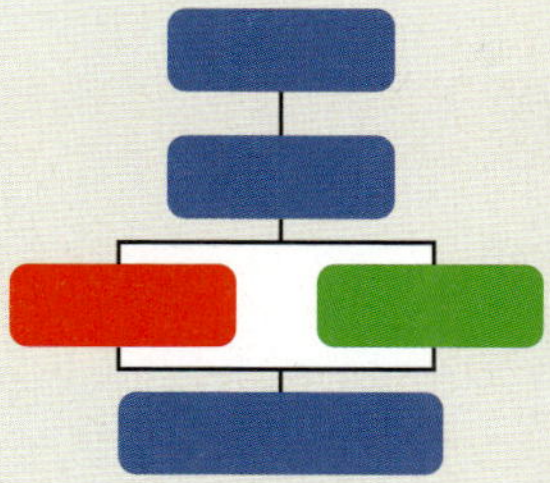

flow chart or diagram

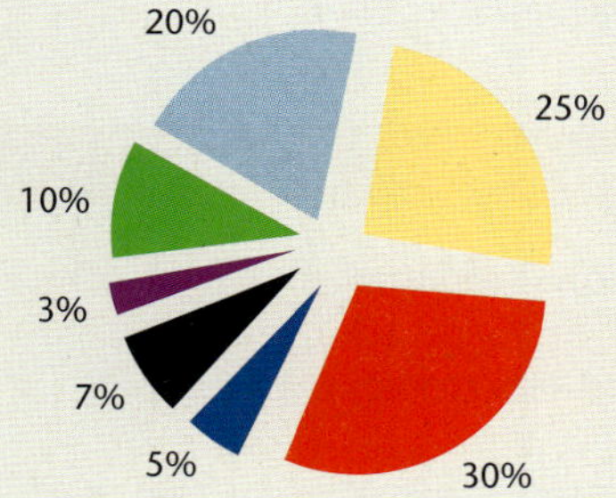

pie chart

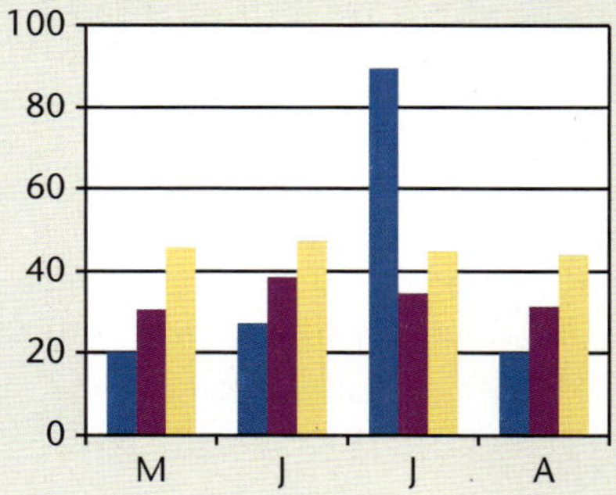

bar chart

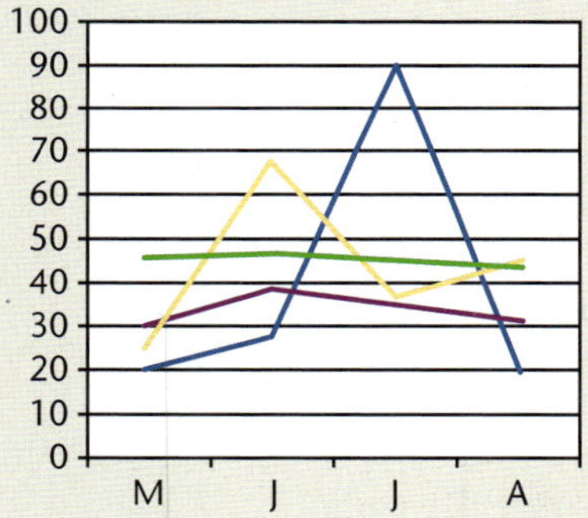

line chart

month / year	M	J	J	A
1965	12.1	10.9	9.2	9.8
1970	13.5	14.1	12.1	12.1
1975	13.9	12.1	11.5	12.2
1980	14.1	14.2	19.3	14.0
1985	12.9	14.9	21.8	13.1
1990	12.5	14.9	22.8	12.9
...	...	...	...	...

table chart

There are flow, pie, bar, line and table charts. A flow chart or diagram shows a progress of something or arrangements like, e.g. the organisation of an institution. Who is the overall manager? What are the different departments and who are their heads? Who is in charge of what? etc. Or a process like how to install a computer programme. What do you do first? Then next? etc. Line charts really show a line. They are good to look at changes over a long period of time, like the development of unemployment in a country. Pie charts are good to look at the percentage something takes from a whole. Bar charts are good to compare rates. With the different bars you can directly make out low and high rates. And table charts are a good way to show lots of data in a small space, countries are often compared in tables. But for any chart there are some basic rules how to build up their analysis:

1. Start with saying what the chart depicts **(= topic)** and the period of time and the country it refers to **(= circumstances)**.
   For example *This table chart lists the changes in unemployment in European countries over the past ten years.*
2. Take down **basic trends** like *There is a general increase in unemployment.*

3. Prove your results with giving **figures**, The unemployment rate rose from 5.8% up to 10.8% in only three years.
4. Speak about striking **changes**, like a dramatic fall or rise.
5. **Compare** the different data, e.g. *The unemployment rate in (country) is much higher than the unemployment rate in (country).*

Helpful phrases: Analysing pie charts

This graph shows (topic) of (country) in the year …	Dieser Graph zeigt (Thema) in (Land) in den Jahren …
The table chart lists (topic) over the past … years.	Die Tabelle listet (Thema) der letzten … Jahre auf.
The pie chart represents the changes in/of (topic) in (country) since (year).	Das Kuchendiagramm repräsentiert die Veränderungen in (Thema) in (Land) seit (Jahr).
The number of … increased/rose/grew/stepped up/went up from … to … per cent.	Die Zahl der… nahm zu/stieg an/wuchs/steigerte sich/ging hoch von … zu … Prozent.
The number of … decreased/fell/reduced/dropped/went down from … to …	Die Zahl der … nahm ab/fiel/reduzierte sich/sank ab/ging herunter von … zu …
The number(s) of … reach(es) a peak of … per cent.	Die Zahl(en) des/der … erreicht(en) einen Höchststand von … Prozent.
(the) increase, rise, growth, step-up	Zunahme, Anstieg, Anwachsen, Steigerung
The number of … collapsed/plunged dramatically.	The Zahl der … brach ein (kollabierte)/stürzte dramatisch.
(the) decrease/the fall/the drop/the downswing/the collapse	Abnahme/Fall/Absinken/Abschwung/Einbruch (Kollaps)
… kept/remained stable.	… blieb(en) stabil.
The number(s) of … is/are steady.	Die Zahl(en) … ist/sind gleichbleibend.
The number(s) of … remained constant.	Die Zahl(en) … blieb(en) konstant.
The number(s) of … seems to be stabilized.	Die Zahl(en) … scheint/scheinen sich zu stabilisieren.
… is/are at … per cent	… ist/sind (liegen) bei … Prozent.
Compared to … with … per cent, XY hold(s)/take(s) the highest/lowest share with … per cent.	Verglichen mit … mit .. Prozent, hält/nimmt XY den höchsten/niedrigsten Anteil mit .. Prozent ein.
The share XY take(s) is much higher/lower than …	Der Anteil, den XY einnimmt/einnehmen ist sehr viel höher/niedriger als …
Half of/a third of/a quarter of …	Die Hälfte/ein Drittel/ein Viertel der (von) …
All in all these figures show the general trend …	Insgesamt zeigen die Zahlen den allgemeinen Trend …

Does a child need brothers or sisters?

Today most couples decide consciously whether they want to have children or not and how many children they want to have. Looking at research results there is a clear trend in European countries: More and more parents choose to have a single child. But are single children better off than those who live in larger families? Agatha Henderson and Frances Turner talk about their experience and opinion on having children.

Agatha Henderson: I'm the mother of one daughter and this is exactly how I want it to be. It never came into my mind to have more than one child. Children need love, attention, time and money. If there were more children, I would have a problem providing every child with all he or she needs. I myself grew up in a large family. I had three sisters and two brothers and I remember very well that sharing and showing consideration for the family was a large part of my childhood. People say that's the great advantage of large families, because children become more independent and learn to share. But they don't see that children are suffering because they are missing a lot: their parents' attention, time spent together with them and enough money. I wanted just one child because I knew this was my only chance to give my child the necessary attention and the best education possible. It's also a money problem. I decided to stay at home for my daughter and we have to live on my husband's salary. Actually, we can't afford to have more than one child. There are of course fewer financial worries with one child and as soon as Lisa is old enough it's easier to take up a job again.

Frances Turner: After some time of deep thought I finally decided to have one child. I was 34 by that time and I loved my job. I was in a conflict. As a career woman I didn't want to lose my work. It meant and still means a lot to me. At the same time I didn't want to live without having a child. For this reason having one child was the only way to have both career and a family. It's easier with one child. There is more flexibility and freedom to organise a working day.

I keep up contact to my firm via Internet and work at home if possible or part-time in the office. For me it's important to show Tom that he has a working mum who participates in the working world and can earn her own living.

But I was worried about spoiling my child and bringing up a self-centered person. Today I'm sure everything lies in the hands of the parents. I read the book 'The single child' and other studies, but there is no real proof that single children are lonely or will later turn out to be difficult and egoistic people. Single children and those with siblings are just the same. Of course our family life is different from those with more than one child and perhaps we can offer Tom more possibilities. But we're always worried about pampering him and are sometimes stricter than other parents. Tom doesn't suffer from loneliness. He has many friends and he meets his 'best friend' almost every day. He doesn't miss brothers or sisters.

Comprehension

Task 3

Answer the questions on the text.

a. 'Love', 'attention', 'time' and 'money' seem to be reasons for Agatha Henderson's decision to have just one child. Explain why. What does she have in mind when she uses these keywords?
b. Describe the experiences she herself had in the family she came from.

c. Why didn't and doesn't Frances Turner want to give up her job?
d. What might she think of when she talks about having more 'flexibility' and 'freedom' to organise a working day with only one child?
e. How does she organise her working day?
f. What was she worried about at first?
g. Why is she sure she won't bring up a self-centered and lonely child?

Task 4

Janet Young interviewed Agatha Henderson and Frances Young for her radio programme. Here are some statements taken out of this interview. Try to say who could have said what and why.

Example:

I think statement a is Agatha Henderson's statement, because in the text she says in line 6 to 9 that she comes from a large family and that...

a. I myself suffered in my own family. My mother was always in a hurry and totally exhausted because of the large household and there were days when I didn't see my father at all, because he was always working over-time.
b. Only one child means that I can be much more flexible.
c. I believe my child is proud seeing me sit in front of my laptop and managing my working life.
d. My child has never asked for a brother or sister, there are lots of friends and one best friend.
e. Sure with more than one child we wouldn't have the chance to go on a holiday once or sometimes twice a year. There is only one of us who earns money.
f. I read a lot of books because I was unsure, but now I know that single children are not much different from other children.
g. No, we don't bring up egoistic little monsters. Compared to other parents we're much stricter.

Discussion/Writing

Task 5

There are some prejudices against single children. Choose one of the following statements and discuss why you think the statement isn't true or only partly true. Try not to write less than 100 words.

a. Most single children are lazy and stay at home until they marry. They depend on their parents and like to be pampered in 'Mum's hotel'.
b. Single children don't learn to share, because they are used to having everything.
c. Parents who don't want to have more than one child are egoistic.

The words in the word box below may help you to write your rejection.

Helpful phrases

reject	ablehnen
The first/second ... statement represents a common prejudice against ...	Die erste/zweite ... Behauptung repräsentiert (stellt dar) ein gängiges Vorurteil gegen ...
I (totally) disagree with ...	Ich bin (völlig) gegen ...
I can't understand this point of view ...	Ich kann diesen Standpunkt nicht verstehen ...
I only partly agree with this statement ...	Ich stimme dieser Aussage nur teilweise zu ...
The impression this statement wants to convey is wrong ...	Der Eindruck, den diese Aussage vermitteln möchte, ist falsch ...
on the one hand ... on the other hand ...	einerseits ... andererseits ...
I would never support this opinion ...	Ich würde diese Meinung nie unterstützen ...
I prefer to ...	Ich bevorzuge es zu ...

Don't forget to say why you don't consent to the statement!

Activity

Task 6

All single children are spoilt.

Take this statement as a starting point for a radio discussion between Ronda (aged 17), a single child, Mary (aged 16), who has one more younger sister, Andrew (aged 18), who stems from a family with four more children, and Charly (aged 15), who is a single child like Ronda but lives alone with his mother. Sit in groups and work out a role-play.

Radio reporter: Welcome everyone to our today's discussion with the somewhat provocative topic 'All single children are spoilt'. Ronda, you are a single child, are you spoilt?

Go on!

Module 3: XL – extra-large families

American celebrities love big families. To have four and more children seems to be trendy, for example Angelina Jolie and Brad Pitt jet off to everywhere around the world with an extra-large family as a result of having natural children and adoption. To adopt children has become very popular among American celebrities. But there is not a general upspring of extra-large families. Most American families stick to a two-kid norm. Only

certain groups of people in America seem to prefer having more than three or four children. There are religious groups who prefer having big families. Extra-large families with poorer women with less education are another group and mothers who stem from a big family. But astonishingly, a government survey shows that professional and wealthy mothers are having bigger families.
Wealthier couples seem to like the idea of having four and more children.
TV programmes showing extra-large families in their daily life have become popular and the text below is part of a radio documentary about the Dunhams, a family with 17 children.

Discussion

Task 1

Before you go on reading the case study, look at the following statements and discuss them.

a. Think of the statements first and exchange your thoughts with your partner.

1. It is irresponsible to have more than four children because no one can provide enough love and attention for all of them.
2. It is irresponsible to have an extra-large family only because it is trendy and you can show how wealthy you are.
3. Poor couples should not have extra-large families.
4. Wealthier couples should have more than four children because they have enough money to supply every child with everything.

b. Tell your class why you agree or disagree with the statements.

Case study

Here is an example of an extra-large family living in Minnesota (USA)

Hi, my name is Paula Duncan and I'm the mother of a mega-family. With our 16 children we are seen as extraordinary people. Most families around here are small families. Only one of my boys has a friend from a family with five children. Our family is a combination of birth and adoption. We have ten natural children and adopted six Filipino siblings who were living in children's homes. I love my mega-family and maybe we will adopt more children in future.
Already our mornings look different. Very early in the morning I get up and brew my first coffee. Maybe this is the only peaceful moment of only a quarter of an hour which I have all for myself during the day. Soon, I will have to make a wake-up call for my kids. Running a family of this size feels very much like a military operation. And much the same as a general I make a wake-up call for the four smallest girls first, give them their breakfast and while they get ready in the bathroom I wake up the five older girls, and then finally the seven boys. When you have that many children you have to be well-organised, otherwise you just sink. Each day we follow a strict organisational plan which we stick to. A big family of this size only works with discipline and good organisational skills which we adopted and perfected with every new child. For example, although we have two bathrooms our mornings

only work with a plan for their occupation and strict time limits. And, every child has to take over chores that range from clearing the dishes, to mowing the lawn, to cleaning the bathrooms.

We don't have a normal car. Our family car is a van which is still not large enough for all of us. When we head to the supermarket, we pick up many pounds of meat, six to eight loaves of bread, countless bags of chips, at least 15 milk cartons, and endless bottles of ketchup. At least two to three of my children have to accompany me because all the food I have to buy does not fit into one supermarket trolley. We need three of them. And all this food is just enough for two to three days. Our family meals are big enough to feed an army.

Back home from these shopping tours I have to stuff all the food and directly start making sandwiches for the seven youngest. The others can help themselves but this kitchen work very often feels like being in a frontline with all the children around you having their demands. I constantly check our chore list. Very often I have to take over the role of "general mum" remembering the children to do their chores, because I wouldn't survive without the help of every family member.

And the laundry, compared to other households we have four loads of dirty clothes for the washing machine each day. And very often I feel that we have more than hundreds of socks each day as well.

Sure, this mega-family keeps you busy all the time. My days are full of small wounds, hugs, kisses, runny noses, and work, work, work. But I love my family and would never want to have a different life. There is also a big advantage for the children. They always have a playmate and someone they can talk to if they are in need for help. And, we laugh a lot, each day funny things happen. All this keeps me alive. I love the evenings, I feel deeply satisfied when the day is over and I'm not too tired to tell bedtime stories. It still feels joyful to give every child a good-night-kiss at the end of a lovely mega-family day.

Comprehension

Task 2

Answer the following questions.

a. Explain why Paula Duncan calls her family a mega-family.
b. How did her family come together?
c. Can you say, why Paula thinks people believe them to be "extraordinary people"?

Task 3

Look at the Duncan's daily life. How does their mega-family 'work'? Here are some questions which help you to gather some information. Discuss your results with your partner and present them in class.

a. How do they organise their family day? Look at the special organisational skills they developed.

b. How do they differ from a normal-sized family? For example, look at their mornings, supermarket story, the laundry etc.
c. Why does Paula call herself "general mum"? What role does she have in her family?

Task 4

Are there questions about the Duncan's family life which are left open? Think of what you would like to know about them.

a. Make a list of questions.
b. Read out your list in class and say why you would like to ask them.

Language

Task 5

Paula compares her family life to a military operation.

a. First search for more words which belong to military language and compare your word list with your partner.
b. Explain what Paula tries to express using military language.

Are big families good for children?

Task 6

Before you go on reading the text, look at this cartoon first and work on the following tasks:

a. Describe what you see. (The animals you see on the picture are a frog with its brood which are called tadpoles.)
b. Can this situation be compared with typical situations in an extra-large family? With your partner, think of example situations and present them in class.
c. Say what problem of an extra-large family this cartoon wants to point at.

Source: www.CartoonStock.com

'A big advantage of an extra-large family is that children learn much from each other at a very early age.' 'Children learn responsibility, sharing, and caring for each other in a big family'. These are the usual answers you get from big-family mums and that is the general cliché we have of children who grow up in large families. And there are studies which support the idea that brothers and sisters teach each other social skills. Children with brothers and sisters are said to be better in making friends, better at helping other children, and they respond to other children's feelings sooner and more intensively than single children. But all these social skills can already be supported in a family with just one more sibling. Studies show that it does not need lots of brothers and sisters. With regard to social skills children with lots of siblings do not have an advantage over those who have just one.

Roberta Jennings, who does the yearly school entrance examinations at primary school, tells from her experience that children from large families seem to be less intelligent than those children who stem from the classical family type, mother and father with one or two children. She argues that as a family grows parents have less time and money to support each child in their education and intellectual development.

Mothers of extra-large families have to be good managers because caring for a family with more than five siblings is very much the same as managing a company. Carmen Stallon, a mother of six children, says, 'One of the biggest challenges for me is that my children's interests and needs aren't the same but I have to give every child the attention they need. My 4-year-old daughter's interests are just very different from my oldest daughter's interests who is now 16 and deep in her puberty. This is the hardest thing for me, managing the household is of minor importance. But very often I go to bed mentally exhausted after trying to deal with a teenager's first love and the spelling problems of a primary school child.'

Parents of large families very often have to face lots of prejudices and meet with disapproval. Helen Brown, who has seven children, says, 'There are lots of unwelcome comments. Even my sister asked me: 'Don't you know how to take precautions?'

John Down, a sociologist, believes that children of large families not only have to suffer from a lack of money and time but also from these prejudices. He is sure that children from large families are looked down upon by their classmates and can't make friends easily because most of the children do not want to associate with them because they are looked at as being disadvantaged because of their family situation. He also thinks that big-family children are raised to believe that they are part of a group and that their individuality means nothing and therefore very often suffer from a feeling of inferiority.

Joanne Romney who works at a family advice centre and knows lots of big-family mums says, 'The large majority of all big-family mums have one thing in common. They love their kids and want lots of them. They just enjoy their kids and think that two are not enough. Big-family kids don't lack anything. Their mums give up their life for the kids. They don't want their job as mum of school-age kids to end so quickly.'

Comprehension

Task 7

Fill in the missing words taken from the text.

A lot of people think that children who grow up in an **1.** ... family will learn **2.** ..., **3.** ... and **4.** ... a lot sooner than children of small families. But studies show that this is only a **5.** ... because it only needs one more **6.** ... to take up **7.** ... faster than single children might do. This shows that children from extra-large families do not have an **8.** ... over those with just one brother or sister. But living in extra-large families is one of the biggest **9.** ... for every mother because they have to be good **10.** ... to organise the family life. For example Carmen Stallon believes that the different **11.** ... and **12.** ... of her six children are very exhausting. She has to give full **13.** ... to every child's problem which can be very different because of their age difference. Compared to this problem she believes managing the household is just of **14.** ... importance.

Writing

Task 8

The text presents some very controversial opinions. Have a closer look at them.

a. The sentences below take up the different points of view. Complete the sentences by giving reasons. Try not to copy the text and use your own words mainly.

1. From her experience with school entrance examinations Roberta Jennings draws the conclusion that children from bigger families are less intelligent because …
2. John Down points out that not only the lack of money and time are a problem in an extra-large family but also the prejudices the children of those families have to meet with because …
3. He also thinks that children in extra-large families cannot develop their individuality because …
4. Joanne Romney believes that compared to normal-sized families children from extra-large families do not lack anything because …

b. Pick out one of these points of view and write your own personal comment of about 100 words.

Language

Task 9

Here are some words and expressions from the text. What do they mean? Some of these expressions are not easy to explain. Try to give your explanation mainly in your own words. Use the skills training and helpful phrases boxes for help.

a. l. 6 cliché
b. l. 25–26 mentally exhausted
c. l. 8 social skills
d. l. 29 unwelcome comments
e. l. 18 intellectual development
f. l. 37–38 suffer from a feeling of inferiority

Skills Training

Explaining words and expressions

Find a word with a similar meaning	Search for a more general term which the word may relate to
'Grandmother' is another word for 'granny'. A word with a similar meaning is called … 'Granny' is the same as …	A wheelchair is a kind of chair with … An old people's home is a home where …
Find a word with opposite meaning	**Give an example**
'Sour' is just the opposite of 'sweet'.	For example brother and sister, father and mother, uncle and aunt are all relatives.

Say what a person mainly does or what a thing is mainly used for	Describe some details
A nurse is a person who cares for people in a hospital ... A wheelchair is something disabled people use to ...	An extended family is a family type which consists of ... A wheelchair is a chair with two wheels. Disabled people use it to ... With a wheelchair they can ...

Helpful phrases: Explaining words and expressions

similar meaning	gleiche Bedeutung
opposite meaning	entgegengesetzte Bedeutung
different meaning	andere Bedeutung
The word ... is the same as ...	Das Wort ... ist das Gleiche wie ...
The word ... is the opposite of ...	Das Wort ... ist das Entgegengesetzte von ...
This word ... describes something you use for ...	Das Wort ... beschreibt etwas, das man nutzt für ...
The is a person who ...	Dies ist eine Person, die ...
This is a thing which ...	Dies ist ein Gegenstand, der/den ...
A/An .. consists of ...	Ein/Eine .. besteht aus ...
A/An is part of ...	Ein/Eine ist Teil von ...
The word ... stands for ...	Das Wort ... steht für ...
The word ... describes a situation/feeling like ...	Das Wort ... beschreibt eine Situation/ein Gefühl wie ...
The word ... is used for a situation like for example .../for a person who ...	Das Wort ... wird für eine Situation wie zum Beispiel ... genutzt/für eine Person, die ...
When you call s.o./s.th ... you want to say/express/convey the impression that ...	Wenn man jemanden/etwas ... nennt, möchte man sagen/ausdrücken / den Eindruck vermitteln, dass ...
When you use the expression ... you want to point out/emphasize that ...	Wenn man den Ausdruck ... nutzt, dann möchte man hervorheben/betonen, dass ...

money problems/child labour – income based on family business, e.g. farm work – family as a health insurance and provision for old age – no contraception – influence of church/religion – children as a status symbol – high mortality/ second marriages – patchwork families

Task 10

Discuss why extra-large families were the norm in former times. Have a look at the keywords in the word box above which may give you a clue.

UNIT 4:
Growing up

Module 1: Puberty – a hard time for teenagers and parents

You perfectly understand what I mean.

Not in some minutes or later, do it now!

I absolutely don't want to hear that again!

I need nerves like steel to stand your moods.

Why can't I, all of my friends are allowed to do so!

That's a must, not a maybe!

Not with them, they're teek, you know.

Stop arguing, just do what I told you!

Turn off that thing! At once.

My stiff ones. They make me feel owned.

He's so hissy, doesn't want me to chill out with my chick. But she's a proper fit and he's a wasteman.

Absolutely no way with this outfit!

Task 1

Look at the statements.

a. Translate them. If you need help, look at the word box.
b. Who is talking, parent or teenage child?
c. Can you think of typical situations someone uses these statements?

Teenage slang/ "teenglish"
hissy – angry or losing temper
chill out – relax
chick – girlfriend
proper – good, good-looking
fit – (good/fitting) partner
wasteman – fool, idiot
teek – antique, old-fashioned
stiff ones – parents
owned – to feel humiliated or embarrassed

Activity

Task 2

Now sit together in pairs and imagine a typical 'teenage – parent situation'. Write down your dialogue and present it to the class.

Task 3

When children come into puberty both parents and children pass a time of trouble and change. Here are some keywords which can be used to describe typical experiences people make during puberty.

rebellion – arising sexuality – personality – appearance – ups and downs – bad temper – lack of understanding – withdrawal – arguments – spots

First make sure you understand the meaning of these keywords and then fill them into the gaps of the following text.

Amanda, a 15-year-old teenager, says, 'One day I am on top of the world, next day I feel down and don't want to talk to anybody'. Amanda's statement shows how young people feel during puberty. Puberty is a time of rapid changes and **(1)**. Some parents think it is a period in which their child shows **(2)** and hope it will soon be over. 'Puberty is a time of **(3)** on the face of the teenager and wrinkles on the face of the parent'. This sentence does not only hint at the hormone changes in the teenage body but also at the conflicts between parents and their teenage child during puberty. Teenagers don't want to accept their parents' orders and opinions any more. Puberty is a time of **(4)** against parents. There are lots of **(5)** between parent and child. The teenage boys and girls develop their own **(6)**. They want to make their own decisions about what they do and who they meet. And of course, teenagers want to decide about their **(7)** without their parents. They like to experiment with their clothes and outfits. For example most often parents are shocked to see their daughter or son all dressed in black or with a tattoo or piercing. In situations like these teenagers complain about their parents' **(8)**. They can't see that their parents are worried about them. Often teenagers react with **(9)** from the family. They prefer to stay alone in their room or to stay together with their friends instead of sitting around the table with their parents, sisters and brothers. This often worries their parents even more, because puberty is also a time of **(10)**. At this time youngsters make their first experiences with a partner and a lot of parents fear the possibility of unwanted pregnancy. It's difficult for parents to accept that their son or daughter has a relationship which involves more than only holding hands. This is a very natural development but it's not easy for parents to talk with their children about 'safer sex' and suitable methods of contraception such as taking the pill or using a condom.

A mother-daughter conflict

Audio

My daughter's older boyfriend must get out of her life

Betty: Samantha has become some kind of a problem since she started seeing an older guy, 25, half a year ago. She's crazy about him and she does everything he says. She meets him secretly because we don't allow her to see him. When we had a talk about her boyfriend one month ago she couldn't understand our point of view. We don't want her to be together with this person. No way! He's not good for her and Samantha's behaviour has been worse for the last three months. This must be the boy's or let's say guy's bad influence.
His outfit is just unbelievable, he dyed his hair green and blue and he wears six earrings. He works as a DJ in a popular teenage disco nearby. Last week we managed to have a serious talk with Samantha once again. We told her the guy was too old and weird for her to go out with. Her only answer was that she is madly in love with him and won't give him up. We strongly forbade him to come to our house, but the other day I saw his car in our neighbourhood and we are pretty sure that Samantha still meets him and I don't want to think about what they are doing together. We're worried about her. We don't want anybody to hurt her feelings. She acts like we don't exist any more and this really, really upsets me.

Betty Miller from Staffordshire, aged 43

I will never leave my boyfriend

Samantha: That's typical of Mum. She's making a fuss about everything! Perhaps Mike, that's my boyfriend's name, is a bit different, but he's a very nice person. But Mum can't see that. My parents just see his outfit and are sure that he is some kind of a criminal or a bad guy. I don't know what they think about him. But as long as they refuse to talk to Mike or meet him for some time in peace they won't find out about him. I'm not a little girl any more. I'm almost grown up and I can decide for myself. But that's what Mum can't accept. We didn't

Betty's daughter Samantha, aged 16 and a half

really talk about my boyfriend. She didn't even try to listen to me. She only bombarded me with reproaches and didn't listen to any of my words. She just forbade me to see Mike again without telling me why. Only because of his outfit? That's unfair. Mike does not fit into her image of a nice boy, you know, the old-fashioned boy with a short hair cut and so called good manners. Someone who brings her flowers and asks her if he may take her little girl out. Just take her out, no sex of course. But we don't live in the Middle Ages. I can handle everything. I know perfectly well what I'm doing and I take care.
What Mum can't see is that I'm really, really sad, because all this makes me think that she wasn't and still isn't interested in my feelings and thoughts. I'm madly in love with Mike and I don't want to give him up.

Comprehension

Task 4

True or false? Correct the false statements.

a. Samantha has fallen in love with a boy the same age who is just a bit weird.
b. Her mother doesn't like her boyfriend's outfit.
c. Samantha and her parents had a good and long talk about the new relationship.
d. Her mother thinks Samantha's behaviour has changed because she's together with Mike.
e. Samantha thinks she is mature enough to keep up this relationship.
f. Samantha believes that her parents think about Mike in a wrong way because they only see his outer appearance.

Discussion

Task 5

Look at Mrs Miller's and Samantha's points of view and discuss the questions below. Present your results in class.

a. Can you imagine why Mrs Miller is worried about her daughter's new relationship?
b. What does Samantha criticise about her mother? Can you understand her point of view?
c. What could Samantha do to give their mother-daughter-relationship a new chance?

Activity

Task 6

Imagine Mrs Miller and her daughter Samantha talk once again to settle their conflict. Since they both really want to find a solution they ask a friend to act as a go-between. Now work out a more peaceful dialogue. Sit together in groups of three so everyone can take over one part. Present your dialogue in class.

Translation

Task 7

Translate the following sentences and discuss your results with your partner before reading out in class.

a. In der Pubertät akzeptieren Jugendliche die Meinung ihrer Eltern nicht mehr.
b. Jetzt wollen sie ihre eigenen Entscheidungen treffen.
c. Jugendliche beklagen sich oft über das mangelnde Verständnis ihrer Eltern.
d. Eltern machen sich um ihre Kinder Sorgen.
e. Für die Eltern ist es nicht einfach, mit ihren Kindern über Verhütung zu reden.

Language

Task 8

Look at the examples and try to link the following sentences by filling in one of them.

'But, although, despite/in spite of' are linking words used to express a contrast.

although – obwohl, obgleich (im täglichen Umgang kann auch „though" genutzt werden)
but – aber
not x but y – nicht x sondern y
despite/in spite of – trotz

Examples:

She met her boyfriend, ***although*** *she knew that her parents didn't want her to see him again.*
She met her boyfriend ***despite/in spite of*** *her parents' worries.*
She knew her parents wanted her to break up the relationship with her boyfriend, ***but*** *she didn't do so.*
She doesn't want to leave her boyfriend, ***but*** *keeps up the relationship.*

a. Samantha meets her boyfriend, (…?) she knows her parents wouldn't allow her to see him.
b. Maybe they'll find a way to settle their conflict. (…?) as long as both don't listen to each other, they won't have a chance to live in peace.
c. Samantha doesn't want to give up Mike (…?) her parents' wish her to leave him.
d. Samantha's grandparents try to keep out of the conflict, (…?) they are also worried about their granddaughter.
e. Samantha loves Mike (…?) the fact that he is much older than her.
f. (…?) Mrs Miller knows that her constant arguments with her daughter will destroy their relationship, she can't stop warning her daughter.

Listening

Audio

Task 9

Listen to the following father-son dialogue and find out what kind of conflict both have. Before you start listening make sure you know what the word 'play truant' means. Then listen to the dialogue and try to answer the following questions.

a. What did the father find out about his son?
b. Why does Jerome think it's not that serious?
c. What consequences does his father speak about?
d. How do both settle their conflict?

Grammar

Simple Past and Present Perfect

Task 10

Mrs Miller says: 'Samantha **has become** some kind of a problem, since she **started** seeing an older guy half a year ago.'

Mr Miller uses Present Perfect and Past Tense. Do you remember why?

Simple Past beschreibt immer Handlungen, die in der Vergangenheit abgeschlosssen wurden → Last week the weather was nice.
Present Perfect beschreibt dagegen Handlungen, die in der Vergangenheit begonnen haben und bis in die Gegenwart andauern oder deren Folgen bis in die Gegenwart reichen → The weather has been bad since the beginning of this week.

Transform the verb in brackets into its present perfect or past tense form.

Jerome's conflict with his father

a. Jerome's father is angry with his son, because on Monday morning last week he (**see**) him sitting in the new fast food restaurant with a girl.
b. This wouldn't be something to be angry about, but Jerome (**be**) playing truant on that day.
c. Up till now Jerome (**never/have**) a serious conflict with his father, but since Monday the situation (**change**).
d. Jerome's father (**lose**) trust in his son, because he (**lie**) to him.
e. Recently Jerome's school marks (**become**) bad and most of the school term (**already/ go**).
f. (**he/start**) to revise for his final exams yet?
g. Jerome feels that his father (**react**) too hard towards him on that Monday, because he can't believe that he (**not do**) something like that in his own teenage years.

for =	**seit → Zeitspanne (wie lange?)**	Sandra writes in her letter: *'For more than one year we have been talking on the Net'.*
since =	**seit → Zeitpunkt (seit wann?)**	*'Since last May we have been talking on the Net'.*
→ Since und for stehen mit dem Present Perfect, wenn der Zeitraum bis zur Gegenwart reicht.		

Task 11

Fill in since or for.

a. She hasn't met her boyfriend... more than two weeks.
b. I have tried to contact him via e-mail... some hours now. But I can't get through again. ...last Monday there has been something wrong.

c. ...as long as I can remember my parents have always told me not to hesitate to ask them for help if I need to.
d. ...Donna met her new boyfriend her life has totally changed.
e. He has always loved to stay at the sea... his childhood.

UK agony aunts

www.CartoonStock.com

Agony aunts are very British. In every daily newspaper it still is a tradition to have a so called 'problem page' with an agony aunt answering letters of readers. Agony aunts are females with names like Barbara, Deidra, Jackie, Kathy, and Claire. Males also give advice but most likely as Dr. Whatshisname mainly giving medical or psychological expert counselling. Marjorie Proops was a legendary agony aunt of the *Daily Mirror*, who started the boom of agony aunts in all newspapers in the late 1950s and beginning 1960s, the golden age of problem pages. Writing to the agony aunt became so popular in that time that editors had to hire lots of writers answering letters under the name of the newspaper's agony aunt. But, there were restrictions. The agony aunts of this age had to avoid being political or referring to anything combined with sex. Modern agony aunthood beginning with the 1970s is much different. From now on agony aunts are off limits. They speak out in favour of contraception, gay rights and comprehensive sex education for children and work with counselling services and helplines. Talking about sex is not a taboo any more. Today people criticise that these pages have more and more become pages full of extreme stories of human tragedies and sexual fantasies, attracting readers but not suitable for young people. Teenagers still use the agony aunt advice corner to talk about problems which they do not want to talk about with their parents. Now they use the Internet and don't take a pen in their hand to write a letter, but lovesickness and first sexual experience are still the favourite topics like in the early 1970s.
Here are two typical letters of teenagers asking for advice.

Teenagers who have some kind of love problem which they do not want to talk about with their parents sometimes write to an advice corner of their teenage magazine hoping to receive help.

Here are the letters of two teenagers who are asking for advice.

Dear agony aunt ...

I am deeply in love with a boy of 20. I am almost 17 and I think I am mature enough to keep up this relationship. It's a secret because it would drive my parents crazy if they knew about it.
My parents always believe that I'm with my best friend Anne when in reality I'm with him. So I always have to lie to them because my parents would never accept this relationship. Now my boyfriend asked me to have sex with him and I have refused because I am afraid of getting pregnant. I am confused because I love him very much and I don't want to lose him. What should I do?

Confused girl from Manchester

I thought I was talking to an 18-year-old boy on the Internet, but now it turned out he is already 30 years old and, even worse, he is married and has got a child. I feel so sad and betrayed because I trusted him and told him about my love for him.

I am 15 years old and for more than one year we have been talking on the Net. Then suddenly two weeks ago he told me he wanted to break up our relationship. I was desperate and asked him why, but he didn't want to answer my questions any more. Then I phoned his old number and a lady answered the phone. When I told her my name she burst out laughing because she knew about everything we talked about on the Net. She told me she was his wife. It's a great shock. I'm so upset because I loved him so much and I'm deeply shocked and embarrassed because I told him all my intimate thoughts and they must have been laughing about me all the time.

Sandra (15) from Newport

Comprehension

Task 12

Here are short summaries of the letters. Read them and fill the gaps with words from the letters only.

a. The girl from Manchester wants to keep up her relationship with a boy of 20 because she believes she is (1) enough, although she is only 17. But she has to keep the relationship a secret because she is sure that her parents would never (2) it. Another problem has come up for her because her boyfriend asked her to have sex with him. Now she is (3) and doesn't know what to do. Up till now she has (4) to have sex with her boyfriend because she is worried about (5), but she doesn't want to (6) him.

b. Sandra from Newport feels (1) by someone she was talking to on the (2) who she believed to be a boy of 18. She fell in love with him but now this boy (3) to be a married father of 30. Since Sandra (4) her Internet friend she told him about her (5) thoughts not knowing he and his wife were playing a mean trick on her. For this reason Sandra suffers from a deep shock and feels (6).

Writing

Task 13

Choose one of the letters and draft an answer.
You can find some phrases which may help you to write your answer in the "Helpful phrases" – box below.

Helpful phrases: giving advice

I am sorry for you because your situation seems to be ...	Du tust mir leid, deine Situation scheint ... zu sein.
It's quite clear/obvious that ...	Es ist klar/offensichtlich, dass ...
But it's never as bad as you believe it to be because ...	Aber es ist nie so schlecht, wie du glaubst, weil ...
Don't give up, there is always a solution ...	Gib nicht auf, es gibt immer eine Lösung ...
You will feel much better if ...	Du wirst dich viel besser fühlen, wenn ...
Talk to ... He/she knows the situation and can give you good advice.	Spreche mit ... Er/Sie kennt die Situation und kann dir einen guten Rat geben.
In your situation you should .../ It would be better if you ... (→ Verb des Satzes im Past Tense)	In deiner Situation solltest du .../Es wäre besser, wenn du ...
Think everything over again and make your own decision about ...	Denke noch einmal über alles nach und treffe deine eigene Entscheidung über ...
Don't hesitate to talk to ...	Zögere nicht mit ... zu sprechen ...
Don't rush things, first you should ...	Übereile nichts, zuerst solltest du ...
Don't keep silent, try to talk to ...	Bleibe nicht stumm, versuche mit ... zu sprechen.
Discuss your feelings and doubts with ...	Diskutiere deine Gefühle und Zweifel mit ...
Speak everything over with ...	Besprich alles mit ...
You may also contact our helpline with the number/our counselling service with the web address ...	Du könntest auch unseren telefonischen Hilfsservice mit der Nummer .../unseren Beratungsservice mit der Webadresse ... kontaktieren ...
You should take counselling because ...	Du solltest eine Beratung warnehmen, weil ...
Chin up, don't be desperate!	Kopf hoch, sei nicht verzweifelt!

Module 2: Unwanted pregnancies

Task 1

Have a look at the cartoon.

a. First describe what the cartoon shows.
b. Discuss its message with your partner and tell your class about your results. Do not forget to give reasons.

Source: www.CartoonStock.com

Task 2

Sit in groups and prepare a talk in class on the topic 'young parents'. Do a mind map first to collect the various aspects you want to talk about.

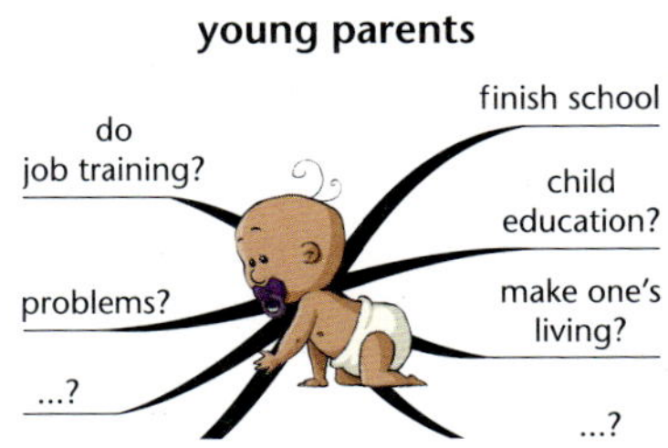

Britain's teenage mothers

Every morning Mary gets up at seven to make breakfast for her three-year-old son Henry. She dresses and feeds him and then escorts him to nursery school. For the few hours he's there she runs her household, does the shopping, pays bills. After she picks him up, they spend the evening together, playing, watching television, making dinner. This is the sort of day-to-day routine many single mothers will be accustomed to. But Mary is a young mother who fell pregnant when she was a teenage girl of 16. 'I have no regrets, but it's been hard,' says the now 19-year-old Mary on a BBC Internet page for single mothers. 'Sometimes I wish I could just go out to a club but I know I'll have to pay too much for it. We need the money and I'll really feel ill in the morning. All the responsibility lies on me. There is plenty of time for that.'

Mary's story is one of many. In 2003, the year Mary's son was born, Britain's constantly rising teenage pregnancy rate reached a climax of 13 000 girls 16 and under who became pregnant. UK still has one of the highest teenage pregnancy rates in Europe, although new statistics show that there is a downward trend in the under-16 pregnancies.

Britain's government reacted to the teenage pregnancy rates with a 'Teenage Pregnancy Strategy', a campaign which addresses youngsters and provides them with sexual health advice. Comprehensive sex and relationship education, a large offer of young people services and a more open attitude to sex are the integral parts of this campaign. One aspect is that every schoolchild of 10 should have some lessons of sex education in school. But unlike in Germany, parents have the right to withdraw their child from these lessons and some do.

The stated goal of the 'Teenage Pregnancy Strategy' is to 'halve the under-18 conception rate in future'. With the under-16 rate it's easy to see the reasoning. Compulsory schooling runs until 16.

Adapted from OECD: Family database- the structure of families (SF 2.4), August 2012, www.oecd.org/els/socialpoliciesanddata/oecdfamilydatabase.htm[01.10.2012]

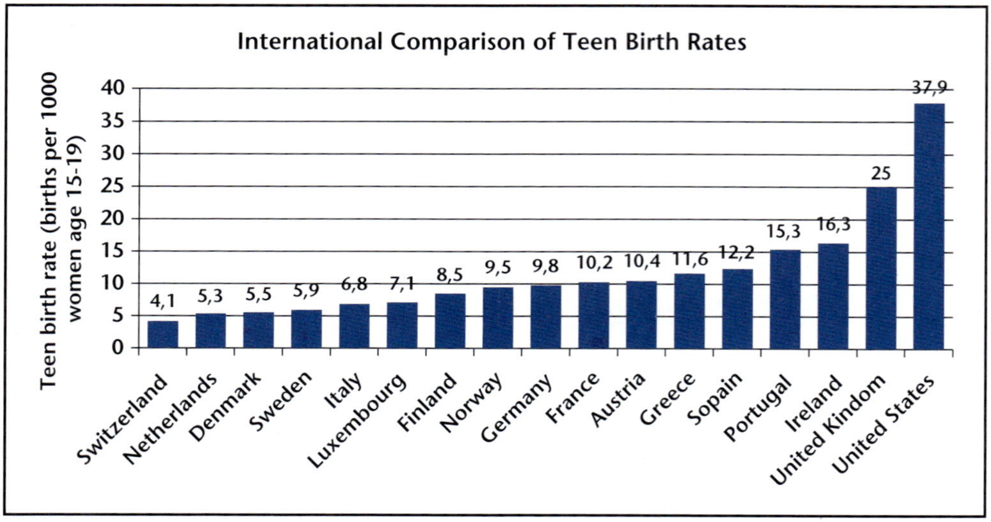

Comprehension

Task 3

Answer the following questions.

a. Mary leads the typical single mother's life, but can you think of the reasons why her life may even be harder or more difficult?
b. Explain how the government wants to reduce the high teenage pregnancy rates.
c. Can you think of the reasons why the government takes special care to firm the downward trend in the under-16 rate?
d. Why do so many young girls fall pregnant? Think of possible reasons.

Language

Task 4

Find words in the text which mean …

a. expecting a baby (adjective)
b. expecting a baby (noun)
c. young mothers of 16 and under
d. everyday routine
e. feel bad about something you did
f. something the government does to inform the people
g. teaching children about sexuality.

Writing

Task 5

With your partner first discuss statistical trends and figures based on the text and the bar chart. Then write an analysis.

Activity

Task 6

Role-play

Imagine Linda Franklin, who is just 15, finds out that she is pregnant by her new boyfriend Dennis, who is 17. Linda has just started a two-year-course in child care at Birmingham College of Further Education. Besides school she is on a nursery school placement once a week. It is Sunday morning and Linda decided to tell her parents – Shirly Franklin 45 and Ted Franklin 47 – about her situation and maybe find a solution to her problem. Split in groups and take over the role of Linda, Shirly or Ted. How do you want them to react? What is their point of view? Act out your role-play in class.

Case Study 1 – A young mother talks about her experience

Donna Downman gave birth to her daughters Rachel and Rebecca when she was only 14. This made her Britain's youngest-ever mother of twins. In an interview she gave to the 'Sun Woman' she talks about her life and experiences as a teenage mother.

During the interview she says that she experienced the first signs of puberty already at seven and fell pregnant at 13. At this age she entered a sexual relationship. Since the birth of her children Donna has muddled through, bringing up her girls with her mother's help. Here is an extract of this interview.

Authentic reading

Donna Dowman – a girl who had her twins at 13

'I definitely felt a certain pressure to have sex. All my friends were talking about it and a few had slept with their boyfriends. I guess I didn't want to be left behind.'

'I looked and felt older than my years, too. Going through puberty so young meant that by the time I reached 12 my figure had already blossomed.'

'I could easily have passed for a 16-year-old.'

'I lost my virginity to a boy I'd only been seeing for three weeks. It was horrible and I regretted it immediately.'

'Looking back I was neither emotionally or physically ready for such a big step.'

'I told Mum straight away and although I know she was disappointed we had a long chat about the responsibilities of a sexual relationship.'

(Shortly after her first sexual experience Donna met her twins' 16-year-old father and very soon she became pregnant.)

'Mum knew I was pregnant even before I did.

I suffered morning sickness and felt tired all the time.'

'She was with me when I took the test and when the blue line appeared we both burst into tears. I was just a child myself.'

'I haven't had much of a childhood,' she reflects.'

'As for falling pregnant, Mum gave me all the talks and all the warnings, yet I still wasn't as careful as I should have been.'

'I've only myself to blame for that. But looking at my two beautiful girls it's very hard to say that they were a mistake. I love them so much.'

'When the twins grow up I'm going to make sure they don't make the same mistake that I did.'

'I'll sit them down and tell them all about the facts of life. Hopefully, unlike me, this time they'll listen to their mum.'

Source: Interview with Donna Dowman, in: Sun Woman (UK), 21.06.2000

Comprehension

Task 7

There is a wrong word in each sentence. Look at Donna's life story and replace the wrong word with a correct one.

a. Donna refused a sexual relationship at 13.
b. It's unusual that a girl of only seven experiences first signs of childhood.
c. Donna felt a certain freedom to choose her time to have her first sex.
d. Donna was pleased to go through her first sexual experience.
e. When Donna found out about her pregnancy she burst into laughter.
f. Donna was only 13 when she fell pregnant, so she was just a grown-up.

Task 8

Try to analyse Donna's case and answer the following questions.

a. Why do you think Donna had already had sex at 13?
b. What kind of relationship does Donna have towards her mother? Describe the mother-daughter-relationship.
c. How does Donna feel about her life as a young mother?
d. What does she want to do to prevent her twin daughters from having a baby as early as their mother? What does she mean when she talks about telling them 'the facts of life' (l. 43)?

Language

Task 9

Find words or phrases in the text which mean the same as the phrases in bold letters.

a. Donna felt **some kind of stress** to have her first sexual experience.
b. She thinks at 12 her figure **was looking like the one of a woman.**

c. **Right after** her first sexual experience she regretted everything.
d. She **directly** told everything to her mother.
e. She knew she was **expecting a baby**.

Case Study 2 – A young mother's son talks about his experience

Thomas Vipond knows how children of teenage mothers feel. He is only 17 years younger than his mother. Here is an interview he gave to the Guardian.

Authentic reading

'People are constantly judging us'

People tend to look at me strangely when I am introduced as my mother's son. Sometimes they find it impossible to hide their disbelief and say 'No' several times with increasing degrees of astonishment. This is usually followed by: 'But he's so big.' They then look at my mum up and down as if to say: 'How did this 6ft 2in chubby monster come out of you?'

My mother is 33 and I am 16. She was my age when she gave birth to me and going through everything I am now – GCSEs and wondering what she wanted to do in life – but she had a baby to look after too. I can't imagine how difficult that was.

The only blessing was that she had a very supportive family who helped her every step along the way. It wasn't always easy: financially, things have always been pretty tight. When my mum went to university, we didn't have much money at all. I was there from the age of two to six and I spent most of my young days in the university creche. (I feel as if I've already been to university).

One of the worst things about having a young mother is that sometimes people assume, because I'm big and she's young, that I am her boyfriend – a bit of a toyboy.

Once, on a visit to Ireland a couple of years ago, we stopped at a tourist information centre in Boyle and had a chat with the lady working there. At first it was fine – she told us about the local history and tourist attractions, places to stay, and I found it interesting and informative. But then she suddenly veered off into dangerous territory, telling us about a lovely little place called Lovers Island. I sensed what was coming and looked at the door. It wasn't far and I thought I could make it. I sprang like a puma, but before I could reach the salvation of outside, she said, with a grin and a wink: 'It's very romantic.' This was too embarrassing. I ran to the nearest body of cool water and threw myself in, hoping to wash away my mortification. My mum thought it was all very funny. Needless to say, I didn't, and for the rest of the journey I maintained a certain distance from her.

That was one of my worst experiences of having a young mother. It has been difficult, but nowadays I think it's great. I think I have a really good relationship with my mum: it's a very open one and I can talk to her about most things. She – dare I say it – is kind of cool. She knows what's happening out there – well, sort of.

But even though things are great now, and in general people have become accustomed to our situation, there was a time when my mum only encountered negativity about our situation. Once a teacher in my mum's school summed her up with the words: 'Well, she's made her bed... ' Attitudes like that really annoy me. Highly judgmental, they only conform to the stereotypical image of young mothers. My mother only experienced a little bit of this treatment; fortunately for her, it made her determined to succeed.

Source: Vipond, Thomas: 'People are constantly judging us', in: The Guardian, 07.07.2003

Comprehension

Task 10

How does the child of a teenage mother feel? Try to find out by answering the following questions.

a. Describe how people react when they are introduced to Thomas Vipond and his mother.
b. Thomas talks about a special holiday situation he had to experience.
   Explain in your own words what happened to him.
c. Can you think of why he talks about the incident as a 'mortification'?
d. Are there any other negative aspects he talks about?
e. What advantages of being a young mother's son does he mention?
f. What kind of negative stereotypical image of young mothers was Thomas' mother confronted with? Explain.

Discussion

Baby-flaps- a good idea for mothers in distress?

All over Europe the rate of babies abandoned by mostly young mothers is rising. In Britain it has tripled in the last ten years. In 2007 Britain discussed the 'baby-flap' which Germany first introduced. Hospitals and private organisations offer this flap. The baby can be placed on a platform, setting off an alarm which alerts a nurse or volunteer to the baby's arrival. The mother picks up a letter from the box informing her about where she can find help and that there is a time of eight weeks during which the mother can make up her mind and pick up the baby again without any legal consequences.
If the mother does not turn up again, police will be informed and efforts are made to place the baby with a family. The German example meets critical voices in Britain. A lot of people argue that 'baby-flaps' actively encourage mothers to 'dump' their children and thus lead to an even higher rate of abandoned babies. Supporters say it will save the lives of many foundlings who would otherwise die.

Writing

Task 11

What is your attitude towards baby-flaps? Write a comment of about 150 words.

Activity

Task 12

Imagine you're working in a young mothers' home and your organisation decided to install a baby-flap. You think of designing posters and fly posters to inform young pregnant girls.
Sit in small groups and design a poster or fly poster. Present your results in class. Don't forget to tell your classmates why you decided to design a poster or fly-poster.

Skills Training

Creating posters and fly-posters

Posters and fly-posters work with the same layout principles:

- If you decide to create a fly poster, stick to a small size ('pocket-size').
- Take down only the most important facts.
- Use keywords or (very) short sentences.
- Use headlines so that the most important pieces of information can be seen at first glance.
- Use colours, different print layouts (fat and small) or some other kind of eye-catcher (e.g. photos, cartoons and clip arts) to arouse people's interest and underline the most important facts.
- Try to address the person you design your poster for. For example use a language the addressee can understand or address the person directly: 'Listen to me! This is your decision! I want you!'
- Advertising posters always work with a slogan, e.g. 'Always Coca Cola!'
- Do not forget to put a contact address, e-mail or phone number at the end of your poster or fly-poster. Very often posters and fly-posters present a contact person with the name and photo to build up a personal relationship and an atmosphere of trust.

Helpful phrases: Analysing posters and fly-posters

In the foreground/background/upper part/lower part you can see …	Im Vordergrund/Hintergrund/oberen/unteren Teil kann man … sehen …
In the right/left/central part of the poster a/an … is presented …	Im rechten/linken/mittleren Teil des Posters wird ein/eine … präsentiert.
The poster works with light/dark colours to convey the impression that …	Das Poster arbeitet mit hellen/dunklen Farben, um den Eindruck zu vermitteln, dass …
Bold type headlines directly give/transfer the most important information that …	Fettdruck-Überschriften übermitteln direkt die wichtigste Information, dass…
A detailed text about … informs the reader about the most important facts.	Ein detaillierter Text über … informiert den Leser über die wichtigsten Fakten.
All contact information is given like …	Alle Kontaktinformationen werden gegeben wie …
The poster presents a picture/some pictures showing …	Das Poster präsentiert ein Bild/einige Bilder, die … zeigen.
In the picture you can see …	Auf dem Bild sieht man …
The picture shows a person/scene/place...	Das Bild zeigt eine Person/eine Szene/einen Ort …
… gives the impression that …	… vermittelt den Eindruck, dass …
The viewer's interest/attention will be aroused with … as an eye-catcher.	Das Interesse/die Aufmerksamkeit des Betrachters wird mit … als ein Blickfang geweckt.
… works as an eye-catcher.	… dient als ein Blickfang.
The picture is eye-catching.	Das Bild ist auffallend.
The viewer's attention is focused on …	Die Aufmerksamkeit des Betrachters wird auf … gelenkt.
The viewer finds it difficult to withdraw his eyes from the poster because …	Der Betrachtet kann sich dem Poster nicht entziehen, weil …
The eye-catcher inspires the viewer to think about …	Der Blickfang inspiriert den Betrachteter, über … nachzudenken.

Audio

Module 3: Sex education

Discussing sex education

New research results show that children today grow up quicker, which also means that young girls are already entering puberty between the age of eight to ten. This was very different one generation ago, then it was just one girl out of 100 who was sexually fully developed by that age. One shocking fact may be that girls are physically able to get pregnant while they are still attending primary school and are far away from being mature enough to have a child. Boys are also growing quicker. This development does not only mean that parents have to cope with typical teenage behaviour much earlier. It also means that parents have to take into consideration that their children may have sexual experiences as early as the age of ten. Children may have sex long before parents think of talking about it with their child.

Here are different points of view on the topic:

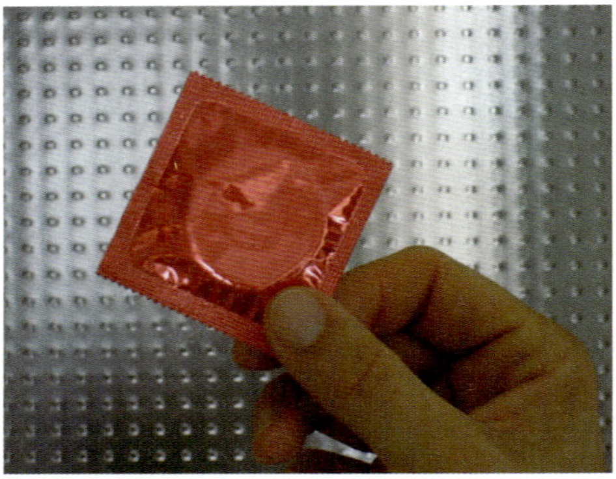

Dr Russel Winner (child health expert): First of all, parents have to accept that puberty comes much earlier today and of course they have to act on it. Parents need to be more aware about sex education to protect their kids from unwanted pregnancy and they have to be more honest with them. They often leave sex education until their children are 14 or 16. But this won't work, they need to speak to their children about sex much earlier. If the children are not actually asking, parents should raise the subject just to make sure about their child's interest and sexual experiences.
Parents should never give their children the impression that sexuality is something they don't want to talk about, or even worse, something the child should not talk about. What if in puberty there really is some kind of problem and your son or daughter won't find the courage to ask you for help?

Helen Reilly (nursery nurse): We try to be frank with the children. Quite often they ask us about where babies come from and we try to give them an honest and simple answer. No details, but they should understand the main thing.
At nursery school age they ask simple questions and as soon as you've said as much as they need they switch off. We want to have a climate of openness in our nursery school and this is exactly what we suggest to the parents. Be open and accept every question from your child and try to answer it. There are lots of picture books which give you help if you can't find the right words.

Claire Winters (agony aunt of a daily newspaper): Sometimes I'm astonished when a girl of 13 or even 12 writes to me asking me about having sex. These cases become more and more frequent and they should be a warning for parents. But on the other hand there are still letters from 17- or 18-year-old girls asking me if they can become pregnant by a French kiss. These examples show that sex education is important. Children and especially teenagers must be well-informed about sex. Parents have to recognise the right moment when they should give their child the necessary information. Good, well-informed sex education within a caring family encourages children to wait before they experiment with sex themselves.

Robert Downsend (primary school teacher): Sex education in primary school means that children are mainly taught to realise that there are different sexes; they learn about the different sex organs and that babies aren't found under the gooseberry bush. Only when pupils reach the age of 15 and 16 sex education plays a role again. Now the sex act is talked about but on a very scientific basis. But looking at the new study results we have to change our concept. It's too late then to talk about arising sexuality when most pupils start their puberty at age eight. We should talk about the consequences it may have and be 'more practical'. For example, we have to talk about why it's important to use a condom and how to use it. Most youngsters don't use a condom or any other kind of contraception during their first night.

Writing

Task 1

Here are some of the main statements. Can you say why the speaker comes to her or his conclusion? Add the missing reasons.

Example:

Dr Russel Winter: Parents should be aware of sex education.
Dr Russel Winter thinks parents should be aware of sex education because this will protect their kids from unwanted pregnancy.

Dr Russel Winter

a. Parents can't leave sex education until 14 and 16 years of age.
b. Parents should never refuse or hesitate to answer their children's questions on sex.

Helen Reilly

c. At nursery school age parents shouldn't be afraid of their child's questions.

Helpful phrases

Remember to vary the usage of connectors such as

- because – weil
- since/for (Satzanfang) – weil
- therefore – deshalb
- for this reason – aus diesem Grund

and verbs

- think – denken, meinen
- believe – glauben, meinen
- be of the opinion that... – der Meinung sein, dass...
- suggest to... – vorschlagen zu ...
- conclude/come to the conclusion – schließen, zusammenfassen/zu dem Entschluss kommen

Claire Winter

d. Teenagers must be well-informed and feel that a family cares about them.

Robert Downsend

e. Sex education at school should be 'more practical'.

Activity

Task 2

Imagine that you are working in a family advice centre. Parents come to you asking for some counselling about how to talk about sex with their children and teenagers. Here are some questions asked by worried parents. On the basis of what you learnt about sex education in this module, give some advice to the parents.

a. Mary Smith: My daughter is 12 years old now and she looks much older, but she is very naive and I think in many ways she is still a child. She sure has no sexual interest. Can't I wait to talk about sex with her until she is 16 and really interested in boys?

b. John Henderson: I feel awkward talking about sex with my boy of 11. Most often I try to avoid talking about 'it'. I don't raise the subject and I told my boy to ask his teacher about everything. Perhaps it's better to leave sex education to school. They're better at explaining difficult things to children. I know, I'm not. Or shouldn't I?

c. Martha Robertson: My daughter of 5 asked me about my neighbour who is pregnant. She is very interested to know what is going on in 'Mrs Miller's tummy'. Can I talk about it with her? And how? Is there any help I can make use of?

d. Timothy Duck: I don't worry at all. Why should I? Today there are those teenage magazines which tell them about everything. I'm convinced that there is no question left over for my 14-year-old son. I don't believe that I have to talk about sex with him or should I?

Task 3

Britain still discusses whether sex education should be introduced at nursery school and how successful the old concept is? Sex education starts at primary school age with teaching the sex organs and provides some more lessons for teenagers aged 15 to 16, teaching them about the act of procreation. Here is one cartoon.

Work on the cartoon.

a. Describe what you see.
b. Discuss the message of the cartoon. What does the cartoon want to say about sex education?

The consequences of failing to properly educate our children.

Discussion

Task 4

Here are two voices on the government plans to introduce sex education in nursery school.

Don't destroy our children's innocence

What causes the furore was not that our children were being given sex education at school, nor that it was being given to them by the age of 10. No. The fear came from the government's experts who suggested sex should be taught to four-year-olds.

Why? Four-year-olds have no interest in sex. They have no interest in knowing the correct names for body parts or how they fit together. Government has to accept that some parents do not want to have 'that conversation' with their children. A child's innocence is a precious thing. It should not be stolen by sex education in nursery school.

Andrew Herberd, Manchester

I suspect that sex education will never work as long as classes of 'giggling 14-year-olds' exist and so long as parents in this country remain embarrassed when it comes to talking about sex. My mother is Dutch, my father English and our household has always had a more liberal attitude than those of my very 'British' friends; my mother presented me with a condom when I was six or seven. This may seem irresponsible, but it is largely the norm in the Netherlands. And, the age of first sexual experience is far lower than in Britain. This is mainly because Dutch parents normalise it by informing children about respectful, loving sex from a young age. Perhaps the policy of 'protecting children's innocence' is just an excuse to protect parents from the dreaded 'sex talk'.

Janneke Earl, Lincoln

Source: Voices from the Internet page 'The big issue', Observer.co.uk, Saturday July 27, 2008

Work on the statements.

a. Try to sum up the main ideas of both statements in a couple of sentences.
b. What does Andrew Herberd want to express when he talks about 'innocence' as a 'precious thing' that 'should not be stolen'?
c. How does Janneke Earl feel about British parents?
d. Take up the issue and write your own comment.

Europe against AIDS

Since the late 1980s the HIV/AIDS epidemic has been a major health problem for the EU. For this reason the campaign 'Europe against AIDS' was launched by various European governments to inform young people about AIDS to prevent new infections. There was a decrease in infections in the late 1990s but in 2012 the European Conference on AIDS announced that the number of newly diagnosed HIV infections has increased again in many EU Member States which led to a reinforcement of the measures and actions already taken like poster campaigns all over Europe. The cartoons below are typical examples of this campaign.

AIDS – acquired immunodeficiency syndrome

– Is a disease you get when HIV destroys your body's immune system. HIV – human immunodeficiency virus – is a virus that kills your body's CD4 cells. These cells help your body fight off infections and disease.

- AIDS is mainly a sexually transmitted disease. Most people are infected by having sexual intercourse with an infected person.
- The virus can be passed from an infected person to another in semen and vaginal fluid. So you can get AIDS/HIV by having unprotected sex – sex without a condom – with someone who has HIV.
- There is also the risk for those people who inject drugs to be infected, e.g. by sharing needles. Some people were infected from blood transfusions before 1985. Today it is unlikely you could get infected that way because all blood has been tested since 1985.
- Babies who are born to mothers with AIDS/HIV infections have a high risk to carry the virus.
- You cannot get HIV/AIDS by working with or being around someone who has HIV. From sweat, spit, tears, clothes, phones, toilet seats, drinking fountains or through everyday things like sharing a meal or drink. From insect bites or stings. From donating blood. From French kissing (there is a small chance if there is a possible blood contact with the infected person).

Task 5

Look at the cartoons with your partner and try to understand the situation they depict.

Task 6

Working with the cartoons.

a. Describe the different situations in the cartoons.
b. The campaign cartoons want to inform about the dealing with AIDS. What can we learn from them? Think of the message every poster wants to bring forward to us.
c. What do you think about the dealing with AIDS in a rather funny way?
d. Which cartoon do you like best? Why?

Task 7

One of the most recognized HIV/AIDS posters ever produced is the image of a child with outstretched arms saying, "I have AIDS. Please hug me. I can't make you sick." It has become a worldwide icon in the fight against HIV/AIDS discrimination. The poster was inspired by the experience of Ryan White, a 13-year-old haemophiliac with AIDS who was barred from school. It became a symbol of the intolerance that is inflicted on AIDS victims.

a. Surf the Web and search for posters dealing with HIV/AIDS.
b. Choose one you like best and present it in class telling your classmates why you picked out this poster.
c. Compare your posters in class. What message do they want to bring forward and how do they work?

Activity

Task 8

a. Advertising posters must always be simple in design so that their message can be understood quickly. Most consist of a catchy and easily remembered slogan with an eye-catcher, sometimes a small advertising text is added.
Now try to design your own HIV/AIDS poster and present it to your class.
b. Which of your posters do you like best? Give reasons.

Task 9

Imagine you are working in a nursery school. Jane, 5 years old, suffers from AIDS. More and more parents get to know about her and are worried. After talking to Jane's parents you decided to inform the parents of the situation in a circular. What information do you want to give to the parents? Sit in pairs or small groups and design the circular. Present it to your class.

UNIT 5:
When families break apart

Module 1: Trouble kids – how should parents handle them?

The thing about children is that if you are lucky they misbehave only sometimes. Misbehaving is a very normal thing, but there are also kids who often show temper tantrums and won't take No for an answer. Those kids who won't do as they are told and who constantly say rude things or fight with their siblings are called 'trouble kids'. With these kids the most patient parent can end up losing patience and yelling. Trouble kids can drive their parents insane and disturb the family life. Parents will feel tired and stressed and even start arguing with their partner over how to manage this kid.

Comprehension

Task 1

Look at the cartoon first.

a. What situation does it show? Describe the situation.
b. Do you think the picture shows a typical situation and a typical reaction of both parent and child? Could there be another way of handling the problem? Dicuss with your partner.

Task 2

Now look at the text.

a. Explain what a 'trouble kid' is.
b. Why can families break apart because of a trouble kid? Discuss reasons with your partner.

Parenting programmes – a solution to the problem?

Audio

Some yelling at a misbehaving child is normal, but when yelling becomes a daily routine something is wrong. Always yelling at a child will have a negative impact on both parents and children.

A parenting programme can be a solution to the problem. With the help of a trained and experienced 'troubleshooter', families can find out the reasons why a child constantly misbehaves. They can find new ways of communicating and learn how to settle an argument peacefully. These new ways of treating each other may change a trouble kid into a well-behaved child and a troubled family into a happy family.

Here are two examples of families who found a new basis for their family life after they took part in a parenting programme.

Simon: When our youngest daughter Emma was born we were soon pushed to our limits. Mary, our oldest daughter, was very good at provoking us until both of us started yelling at her.

Katherine: Yes, she was very impulsive and she threw herself onto the floor each time I forbade her to do something. Then she started damaging things wilfully. I didn't know what to do and yelled at her again.

Simon: With the parenting course I learnt not to just yell at my child listen to them. Now I know each differently. Mary needed positiv 'don'ts'. She felt pushed aside.

Katherine: Today our family life is much more harmonious and it was good to see that other parents have the same problems.

Doris: We're both working full-time and I think because I'm a working mum I developed some kind of bad conscience. I wanted to have a perfect family. So I put a lot of pressure on Frederick. He should be a well-behaved son and a good pupil.

schlecht benehmen
Wutanfall
unhöflich
streiten
schreien
in den Wahnsinn treiben
stören
Auswirkung
Streit lösen
Grenze
reizen, provozieren
bis
forbid - forbade - forbidden - verbieten
mutwillig
to set a rule Regel aufstellen
to handle - behandeln
Lob
schlechtes Gewissen
Druck
verweigern
Befehl
[illegible]

Joshua and Doris Jennings with Frederick, aged eight

But he reacted with tantrums. Each time he came home from school and I told him to sit down to do his homework he shouted at me. He refused to listen to what I was telling him. And he treated me like his personal slave. Now I know that I put Frederick under pressure because I expected too much of him. I found a better way of communicating with him than giving him orders all the time. Now when he comes home from school I leave it to him when he does his homework. But I tell him clearly that his homework must be done before supper. It works!

Comprehension

Task 3

Say whether the statements are true or false. Correct the false ones and give examples from the text which show that the true statements are true.

a. A parenting programme teaches parents how to stay firm and strict towards their children's demands.
b. Mary Burns started to be a trouble kid after her brother Michael was born.
c. Mary didn't accept her parents' orders and even reacted destructively.
d. With the help of the parenting programme Simon Burns was able to see that Mary was afraid of losing her parents' love after Emma's birth.
e. Frederick tried to rebel against his mother's constant orders with tantrums and the refusal to do what his mother told him to do.
f. Having participated in the parental programme Doris doesn't set Frederick rules anymore.

Language

Task 4

Find words and expressions in the first texts of this module which fit these definitions. You can follow the order of the texts to find them.

a. Children who often show bad behaviour.
b. To show bad behaviour.
c. To bring a conflict to a positive end.
d. Strong fits of bad behaviour.
e. How people talk to each other.
f. Another word for destroy.
g. Expert who looks at a family situation to find out about the reasons for conflicts.
h. Courses for parents in which they can learn how to handle family conflicts.
i. Telling someone that he is doing well (2 words possible).

Task 5

This is a short summary of the text. Fill the gaps with some of the words and expressions you matched to the definitions in task 4.

The text 'Parenting programmes – a solution to the problem' deals with ways of how to change a trouble kid into a well-behaved child. The text points out that parents can take part in a **1** ... which shows them how to develop new **2** ... and handling family conflicts. A so called **3** ... helps them to find out about the reasons for their child's bad behaviour. Two examples of families with trouble kids clearly show that if families change their communication they can **4** ... peacefully and solve their conflicts. Both examples underline that children need clear rules but also a **5** ... and some freedom to make their own decisions.

Grammar

Web

Frederick Jennings' grandfather believes that his grandson has a lot more freedom than he had when he was a young boy. Here he talks about his childhood.

He makes use of can, may, might, and must which are modal auxiliaries. They can (with the exception of can) only form the present tense. To form other tenses you must use another verb (Ersatzverb).

Look at the grammar box which gives you some help on modal auxiliaries and try to work on the different tasks.

Modal Auxiliaries – Unvollständige Hilfsverben

Hilfsverb	Bedeutung	Ersatzverb
I can	Ich kann/habe die Fähigkeit etwas zu tun	I am able to (Past Tense: I was able to...)
I could	Ich könnte/ich habe die Möglichkeit, etwas zu tun	I was able to
I may	Ich kann (vielleicht)/ich darf	I am allowed to (Past Tense: I was allowed to...)
I might I must	Ich könnte vielleicht Ich muss	I am allowed to I have to
I mustn't	Ich darf nicht (= strenges Gebot und Verbot)	(Past Tense: I had to)
I should/I ought to	Ich sollte etwas tun/einen Ratschlag befolgen	Kein Ersatzverb
I need not + Infinitiv ohne to	Ich brauche nicht zu	Steht nur im Simple Present und nur in Sätzen mit negativem Sinn
I need	Ich brauche	kein Ersatzverb notwendig

Task 6

Things were different when I was young. Form sentences.

Example:

children/can swim in the river
Children could/were able to swim in the river.

a. We were farmers and I/must go onto the fields with my father.
b. I/may not sleep long on weekends.
c. My father/cannot spend a lot of time with the family he/must work till late and at weekends.
d. I/must do what my parents told me.
e. But I/can play outside without any dangers from traffic.

Task 7

Fill in the appropriate verb.

a. You have got plenty of time. Your parents told you to be back at eleven and you ... hurry.
b. My parents are very strict and they told me that I always ... work hard for school.
c. Parents of trouble kids ... to have good nerves.
d. Children ... some clear rules but also love and affection.
e. I ... tell Tom to do his homework, he does it of his own accord.
f. You ... always give in when Tom has some of his tantrums. This will only spoil him.

Translation

Task 8

Translate the following sentences. Be careful which auxiliaries you make use of. Sometimes in German people make use of the word 'müssen' in a totally different meaning from the English word 'must'.

a. Marc muss seine Hausaufgaben immer direkt nach der Schule machen.
b. Du musst Frederick nicht immer sagen, was er tun sollte. Er ist alt genug, seinen eigenen Weg zu finden.
c. Kinder brauchen klare Regeln.
d. Du darfst Fiona nicht unter Druck setzen. Sie kann unter Druck nicht arbeiten.

Parenting styles

The following texts inform you about four different parenting styles educators speak of.

Task 9

Work through the four definitions first and then turn to task 10 and 11.

Authoritative or democratic parents

These are loving parents who accept their child as the person she or he is. Although they watch their children closely they do not interfere with the children's personal development. They are always at their children's side when they need help and a positive feedback. They support them in their personal development but they also set firm rules.

Authoritarian parents

In former times this was the common parenting style. Authoritarian parents expect their children to do what they are told without asking why. They give no explanation to their children and demand best performances at school and at home. There is constant control and children can't develop their own private interests. Educational methods such as threatening and punishing are the usual way to keep discipline.

Indulgent parents

They are loving parents who listen to their children attentively. To fulfil their children's wishes is very important to these parents. They let their children do whatever they want to. They believe children can only develop their own personality without setting rules. For this reason they seldom or never punish their children for misbehaving.

Uninvolved parents

These parents do not set rules because they don't care for their children. Most often children are left alone. At worst their way of treating their children is some kind of neglect.

Comprehension

Task 10

Read the four statements and decide which parenting style they may stand for. Explain your decision.

A: 'Laissez faire'. That's my philosophy of life. My children can gain their own experience and do what they want to. No boundaries! If they do something wrong, it's their own problem. I totally condemn any kind of punishment.

B: Our neighbour Mrs Smith complained about Mike. He kicked his football into her car. I told her it's none of my business. I don't know where he is and what he is doing. I can't be bothered!

C: As long as you live in my house you must do as I tell you to do. That's how things were in my parents' house and that's how things are here at home.

D: I'm glad to see that Toby has his own interests. He is a real good tennis player. I'm not very sporty, but I'm proud to see Toby and tell him so. Everyone in our family supports him. We accompany him to every match. During the week he spends many hours on his tennis training, but he knows that he must work for school as well. We spoke about it and we decided that he has to finish school first.

Task 11

Today experts are sure that the 'authoritative' parenting style is the best basis for a happy family life. Can you think of reasons why?

Supernannies – educational heroes?

Jo Frost made lots of parents acquainted with educational methods which are said to have become the educational repertoire of the 2000-parents-generation. She is the star of a British television reality show called Supernanny. In Britain people regard her as a child expert. In addition to her show she wrote some books on child education explaining and speaking for her methods and all her books have become bestsellers. Lots of parents also make use of her chat room asking for help. In her television show Jo visits some desperate parents who are not able to manage their children any more. She works with the parents to find some methods to transform their children's wild ways. In the end the viewer will see a well-behaved daughter or son who seems to have changed into 'mum's and dad's darling'.

Some people call Jo Frost's methods down to earth. Jo is not a child psychologist or behavioural scientist. After college she worked as a nanny for over 15 years and calls herself 'someone who is well-experienced in real-life child-rearing situations'.

Each episode shows the parents with their child in their day-to-day conflict situations. Jo watches them for some time and shows them a new way of how to handle their child to transform the unwanted behaviour into good behaviour.

After demonstrating her methods parents are left alone to try to implement the suggested methods with their child. Then Jo visits them a second time to see how everything works and to give some more advice if necessary.

The methods she uses are quite simple. She tells parents to set rules and to explain them to their children. In her eyes a child should clearly know what the rules are and why they are needed. Parents have to make an effort to explain the rules. In particular they should tell their children that breaking the rules is going to have negative consequences. Therefore parents should make sure that children understand what these rules mean.

One standard punishment in Jo's parenting programme is a short time-out period on the 'naughty step' or, for older children, in the 'naughty room' – a room without any toys, TV or other distractions.

Jo is convinced that children are soon tired of the timeouts and conform to better behaviour. She does not want parents to turn into extremely strict people but she points out to them where they need to be more decisive or simply more flexible. She tells parents that their children need discipline but also a lot of affection, 'a loving firmness' in setting rules, as she calls it.

Language

Task 12

Read through the text and find a word with the same meaning.

a. cope with
b. change
c. very practical
d. bringing-up of a child
e. carry out/put into effect
f. amusement
g. follow the rules

Task 13

Now find opposites in the text.

a. happy
b. misbehaved
c. complicated
d. exception
e. indecisive
f. inflexible

Comprehension

Task 14

Guided summary
Answer the following questions in short sentences to form a summary.

a. What is *Supernanny* and who is Jo Frost?
b. Why does she visit parents in their homes?
c. What does Jo Frost do at first when she visits parents with their children?
d. What happens after Jo's visit?
e. What kind of methods does Jo Frost use and recommend?
f. What are the consequences of misbehaving?

Task 15

Now combine the answers and write the summary of the text. Make use of the skills training and helpful phrases boxes below. Also look into the vocabulary at the end of your book. Here you will find a word box with useful connectors you can work with.

Skills Training

Writing a summary

To summarise a text means to take down important aspects in your own words mainly. You may take important aspects and facts from the text as keywords but do not copy the text in detail. Here are some tips how to avoid copying the text.

- Read the text once again and mark important words and text passages with a coloured pen.
- Take down important aspects in keywords.
- Some people subdivide the text into paragraphs and take down headlines or short sentences for each paragraph.
- Start with an introductory sentence which should at least mention the title and the topic of the text.

- Summarise the content of the text, but make sure that you only pick out the most important information on the topic.
- Use connectors to link the sentences.
- Use the Simple Present.

Helpful phrases: Writing and structuring a summary

The text (title) is taken from (source) and it was published (date).	Der Text (Titel) wurde aus (Quelle) entnommen und (Datum) veröffentlicht.
The text chooses ... as its topic.	Der Text wählt … zum Thema.
In (title), (author) discusses (topic).	In (Titel) diskutiert (Autor/in) (Thema).
In (title), (author) explains the principles of (topic).	In (Titel) erklärt (Autor/in) die Prinzipien von (Thema).
(Title) offers a detailed information on/introduction to (topic).	(Titel) bietet eine detaillierte Information über/eine Einführung in (Thema).
The text is a detailed account of (topic).	Der Text ist ein detaillierter Bericht über (Thema).
(Author) reports about …/gives an account of…/gives information on …	(Autor/in) berichtet über…/gibt einen Bericht über …/gibt Informationen über…
The text (title) deals with (topic).	Der Text (Titel) handelt von (Thema).
The text (title) gives a survey of …	Der Text (Titel) gibt einen Überblick über …
(Author) provides the reader with details about/ information on …	(Autor/in) versorgt den Leser mit Details über/Informationen von …
(Author)/(title) begins with explaining how …/why…	(Autor)/(Titel) beginnt damit, zu erklären, wie… /warum …
Then (author) explains that …	Dann erklärt (Autor/in), dass …
(Author) begins by explaining how/why …	(Autor/in) beginnt mit der Erklärung, wie…/ warum …
The next paragraph focuses on …	Der nächste Paragraph beschäftigt sich mit …
Finally (author) comes to the conclusion …	Schließlich kommt (Autor/in) zu dem Schluss, dass …
One of the last/most important aspects (author) mentions is that …	Einer der letzten/ wichtigsten Aspekte, die (Autor/in) erwähnt, ist, dass …
At last (author) emphasises that …	Zum Schluss betont (Autor/in), dass …
The author presents some statistical data to support his point of view that …	Der Autor/in präsentiert einige statistische Daten, um seinen/ihren Standpunkt zu unterstützen, dass …
The text ends with …	Der Text endet mit …
One of the most important aspects of the text is that …	Einer der wichtigsten Aspekte ist, dass …

Task 16

Discuss the following questions with your partner and talk about them in class.

a. Jo Frost advises parents to show a 'loving firmness'. What does she mean? Explain.
b. What do you think of her educational methods like the 'naughty step' and the 'naughty room'?

Discussion/Writing

Task 17

After the British TV channel ABC started the reality show *Supernanny*, European TV channels copied the show's concept with their own supernannies. All over Europe viewing figures were soon rising. Although reality shows seem to be very popular, there are critical voices. Some say it's good for parents because they can take some good advice from the different family situations it depicts. Others say the show flaunts a family at a time and in a situation in which they are extremely vulnerable.

What do you think of these programmes? Write a comment of about 150 words.

Activity

Case study

Edgar and Miriam Waters have got two children, Benjamin, two years and two months old, and Eve, four and a half years old.
Eve is allowed to sit with her parents on a normal chair at the table. Benjamin has to sit in his high chair because this prevents him from grabbing food from the table. Each time he sat next to his sister Eve, Benjamin started fooling around. Once he tore down the table cloth and everything on the table.
Besides Benjamin still needs help with eating and those times he sat on a normal chair, he didn't sit firm enough. He still seems to be too small to sit without some kind of hold. Before Miriam realised that it's still better for Benjamin to sit in his high chair, Benjamin was allowed to sit on a normal chair for some time. Now each time that Miriam or Edgar try to place him into his high chair, Benjamin starts yelling and kicking his feet. When he sits in his high chair he doesn't stop crying vehemently. Sometimes Miriam or Edgar give in, because Benjamin's temper tantrums become worse. More often he reacts aggressively towards his sister Eve. Last time he was placed in his high chair, he reached for Eve's hair and pulled some out.

Task 18

Can you think of reasons why Benjamin doesn't want to sit in his high chair and misbehaves?

Task 19

What should Miriam and Edgar do to handle Benjamin's temper tantrums? Do a role play taking over Jo Frost's role giving advice to Miriam and Edgar.

Listening

Task 20

There are three people who talk about some kind of disturbed family situation. Listen to their account and find out whether these statements are true or false. Discuss with your partner and correct the false statements.

a. The 53-year-old widow works full-time.
b. She does not want to be her grandson's babysitter that often.
c. Her grandson is a very well-behaved child.
d. Joshua is the eldest son of the family.
e. He canot accept that his brothers can do some things better.
f. Each time one of his brothers talks about some kind of success, he withdraws and becomes very silent.
g. The 22-year-old boyfriend feels too young to have children.
h. His girlfriend does not want to wait much longer.
i. He loves to be together with his sister's children.

Task 21

Work on the following questions.

a. With the help of a bilingual dictionary work through the following newspaper article on your own and take down a brief survey of its main aspects in German.
b. Write a short summary of the text.
c. Read out your summaries in class and compare them. Which one did succeed in summarising the main aspects in a short text?

Authentic reading

'Supernannies' to tackle antisocial children

A team of "supernannies" is to be sent to some of Britain's most deprived areas to help parents control antisocial children, the Prime Minister revealed today.

The parenting experts will be sent to 77 areas with high levels of unruly behaviour, teenage pregnancies and truancy from school.

The £4m scheme will also force the parents of disruptive children to attend parenting courses.

Writing in the Sun newspaper, the Prime Minister claimed the initiative would tackle the root causes of crime and disorder.

He said the experts would "be able to step in – either through one-to-one support or in group sessions – to offer a helping hand to parents who are beginning to struggle with their children before the problems get out of hand".

The Prime Minister denied the scheme would involve "interfering with normal family life", adding: "Life isn't normal if you've got 12-year-olds out every night, drinking and creating nuisance on the street with their parents not knowing or even caring."

The plans coincide with a government study revealing that 85% of people think bad parenting is responsible for bad behaviour.

Commenting on the findings, the Prime Minister said: "This should be no surprise given the huge popularity of television programmes in which experts help parents with their problem kids."

More details of the "supernanny scheme" will be revealed by the home secretary, John Reid, later today.

Mr Cavadino (an expert on juvenile crime) said blaming parents was "unproductive". "Many parents are at their wits' end to know how to control their children's behaviour", he said. Mr Cavadino said parents should not be forced to attend courses.

"However, a voluntary approach is usually more likely to engage parents than compulsion, which can run the risk of breeding resentment."

He pointed out that youth courts were already able to order parents to attend parenting courses when their children were convicted of criminal offences.

The government's coordinator, Louise Casey, insisted evidence showed compulsory courses were "equally effective as voluntary".

"Almost nine times out of 10, those parents do not have to be forced to do it – they are actually taking help when they get the right wake-up call," she told the BBC Radio 4 Today programme.

"I am very comfortable – as is every member of the public, the government study shows – that if you need to force people on to parenting courses to get help, then you should."

Source: Weaver, Matt: 'Supernannies' to tackle antisocial children, in: guardian.co.uk, 21.11.2006, www.guardian.co.uk/society/2006/nov/21/childrensservices.pupilbehaviour?INTCMP=SSRC [01.10.2012]

Module 2: Divorce

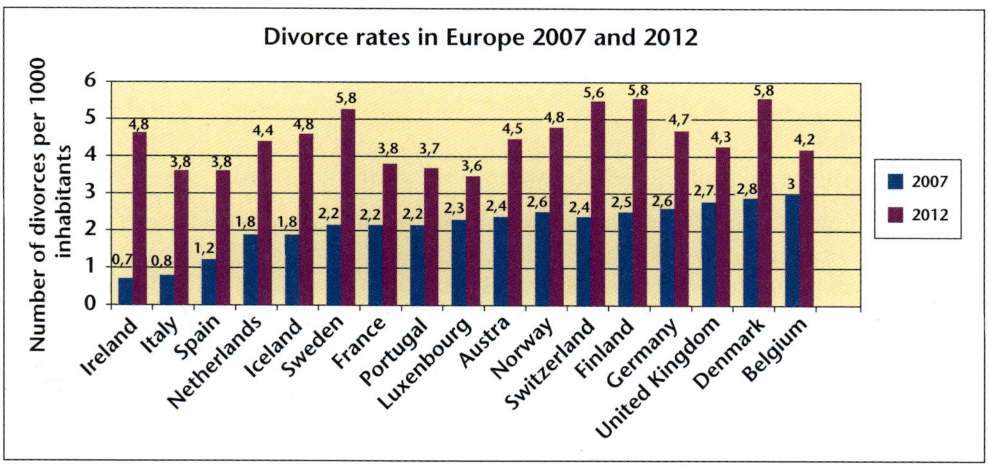

Adapted from OECD: Family database – The structure of families (SF 3.1), August 2012, www.oecd.org/els/socialpoliciesanddata/oecdfamilydatabase.htm

Task 1

Look at the information given in the chart and talk about the changes in the divorce rates in Europe. Here are some questions which might help you.

a. Is there a general trend? Are there interesting exceptions?
b. Which European country has the highest rate? Which one has the lowest rate? Are there countries which have almost the same rates?

c. What role does the church play? What kind of status does marriage have in different European countries?

Present your result in class.

Why is there an increase in divorce?

During the last twenty years divorce rates have gone up in almost every European country. In Britain the divorce rate has increased by more than 200 %. But what caused this increase? What are the factors to persuade unhappy couples to get divorced?
In former times the sentence 'till death do us part' was an irrevocable principle. Religious belief forbade divorces. Besides, divorce wasn't socially accepted. After a divorce women became social outsiders and most often a divorce meant financial ruin. In those days women were financially dependent on their husbands. Today this situation has totally changed. Because of changes in the divorce law it's much easier to get divorced nowadays. Women can earn their own money and don't depend on their husbands. And above all, today there is less social stigma and blame attached to divorce. Divorce has become something normal. Nevertheless divorce means a time of stress and distress. This hasn't changed over the years. There is no such thing as a 'victimless divorce'. Children involved in divorce tend to suffer from depressions. In the first years after divorce many children are likely to show aggressive behaviour and a lot of them have problems at school. Studies have shown that most children want their parents to stay together.

Comprehension

Task 2

Explain with the help of the text but mainly in your own words:

a. Why in former times divorce meant social and financial ruin, especially to women.
b. How the situation of women has changed today.
c. Why there is no such thing as a 'victimless divorce'.

Working in a family advice centre

Audio

Sabrina Wagner, 42 years old, studied behavioural science and concentrated on educational problems in families and the family law. She is now working in a family advice centre. Parents who have some kind of problem with a child come to her. She also advises families before or after divorce. This is an interview she gave to the magazine 'Happy Family'.

Reporter: Mrs Wagner, how would you describe your work?

Wagner: Well, I think the main thing is giving advice to troubled families. Most often I accompany them through a hard time, for example after a divorce. I give them intensive counselling to find ways to keep up the family or to find ways to handle the situation after divorce. It's my aim to bring back some kind of harmonic cooperation after a family separates. All family members have to see that it is better to work with each other than against each other.

Reporter: How do families get to know about your advice centre?

Wagner: Most often the youth welfare department contacts us because they believe a family needs counselling. Or families contact us directly because they feel that something is going wrong and they can't solve their problem alone.

Reporter: What are the main problems?

Wagner: There are lots of different problems. You can't just point out typical problems. Usually divorce is a first step to end a long period of arguing and psychic strain which of course has a negative impact on a child's development. Children suffer from divorce and this will sure leave its mark on the child's behaviour.

Reporter: What do you advise parents who want to divorce?

Wagner: It's difficult to give some general advice. You always have to look at the individual situation. But there are some important things parents should take into consideration. Both partners should tell their children about divorce and explain in clear and simple words why they came to this decision. If only one partner speaks to the children, they will believe that the other partner has to take the blame for it. It's also important to clearly tell the child that if mom and dad stopped loving each other this does not mean they also stopped loving the child. Some children believe they will lose their parents' love after divorce. And it's very important to give the child the chance to keep contact with both parents and meet them regularly. There should be clear arrangements about visiting days.

Reporter: What do you suggest?

Wagner: Children need both, mom and dad. So it's quite sensible to let them see the parent they don't live with every second weekend. And parents should make it possible for the children to spend holidays with each parent.

Comprehension

Task 3

These statements are false. Exchange just one word to transform the sentence into a true statement.

a. Sabrina Wagner studied psychology and did some studies in educational problems and family law.
b. She works in a drug advice centre.
c. Most often Sabrina gives families short counselling to find ways out of their family crisis.
d. Normally divorce sets off a long period of arguing.
e. It's not easy to give some individual advice to parents who want to divorce.
f. Children are afraid they will gain the love of a parent after divorce.

Task 4

Find phrases in the text which mean the same as these. Sometimes the expression you will find in the text is shorter.

a. Sabrina talks to the families a lot to give them some good advice.
b. Together they find ways of how to cope with the time after divorce.
c. She wants to achieve a good atmosphere among the family members.
d. Some families can't find a way out of a problem alone.
e. Divorce also means a lot of pressure on every family member's psyche.
f. Divorce always has a long-lasting negative influence on the child's behaviour.
g. A child should clearly know when he/she can meet a parent and for how long.

Task 5

Answer the questions on the text.

a. What kind of job does Sabrina do in the familiy advice centre? Briefly summarise her main tasks.
b. Sabrina says that every family member has to see that 'it is better to work with each other than against each other' (l. 15–16). What does she want to express with this sentence?
c. What should parents who want to divorce do with regard to their children?

Activity

Case Study

Wendy Barnes, a mother of three children, visits Sabrina Wagner after her son got noticed in school because of his aggressive behaviour. Here is what she told Sabrina about her divorce.

Wendy: At the beginning of the year my marriage broke up. I was granted custody of my children Tom, 11, Janet, 9 and Peter, 5 years old. My husband is paying maintenance. Now he asks to see the children more frequently. At the moment I don't want my children to visit him too often. I think they need to calm down again because we all went through a hard time. I was quarrelling all the time with my husband and during the last weeks before my husband went to live with another woman we even shouted at each other in front of the children. I told my children that I wanted a divorce because their Dad loved someone else and this deeply hurt them. We need some more time to overcome all this.

Peter cries very often and he doesn't want me to go out. He clings to me. Janet is doing poorly in school. Yesterday Tom's teacher phoned me and asked me to fetch him from school because he started a fist fight with one of his classmates. What if they are torn between the two of us again? Should I really allow my husband to see them more frequently? And how often?

Task 6

Take over Sabrina's role and give Wendy some advice on how to solve her family problem. Take the following questions into consideration.

a. Explain to Wendy how her children are suffering from divorce and which negative impact the family situation already had on her children.
b. Show her what she did and is doing wrong at the moment. Tell her why.
c. Give Wendy some advice on the question of how often her husband should be allowed to meet his children.

Task 7

Imagine Sabrina suggested to have a conversation together with Wendy's husband to make clear arrangements about visiting times. Sit together in pairs or small groups and design a dialogue between Sabrina, Wendy and her husband. Present your results in class.

Module 3: Inappropriate Parenting

Task 1

Look at the following cartoon and describe it. Here are some questions which may be of help.

a. Who are the people shown in the different pictures?
b. What is happening in each picture?
c. How does the child react? Has the way of reacting changed?

Task 2

The cartoon has no subtitle. Can you think of one? Say why you think your title fits to the cartoon.

Child abuse

The term 'child abuse' refers to any kind of violence a child or an adolescent may experience while she or he is in the care of someone they trust in or depend on. There are four main forms of child abuse.

- **Physical abuse:** It may happen once or repeatedly and it always is inflicted on the child deliberately. Those who impel physical abuse use physical power against the child and even take the risk to injure. Physical abuse includes beating, shaking, pushing, choking, burning, kicking or even attacking a child with a weapon.
- **Sexual abuse:** This involves using the child for sexual purposes in any way such as fondling, inviting a child to touch or be touched sexually, intercourse, rape or prostituting a child.
- **Neglect:** It involves any kind of failing to provide a child with basic needs which are important for his or her physical, psychological and emotional development. Examples include not providing a child with food, clothes or shelter, medical care and parental love.
- **Emotional abuse:** It includes any kind of verbal threats and intimidation, but also ignoring the child.

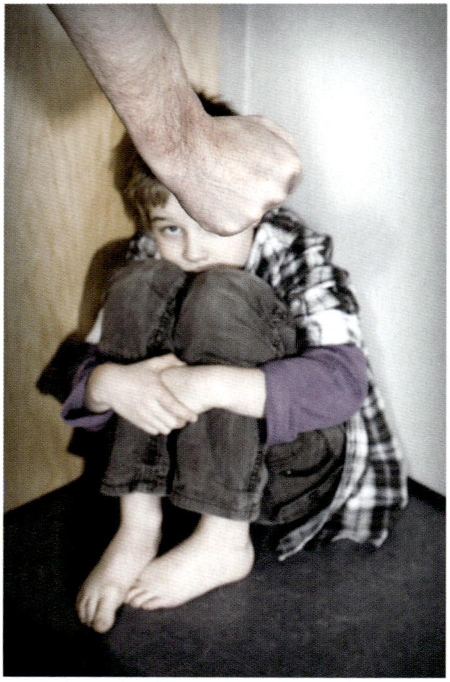

Writing

Task 3

Look at the charts below, all dealing with child abuse in America.

a. First discuss your first impression in class. Is there anything striking? Shocking? Anything you did not expect?
b. Choose one of the charts and write an analysis. Remember that there is a skills training box on analysing charts on pages 67–68 which you may use.

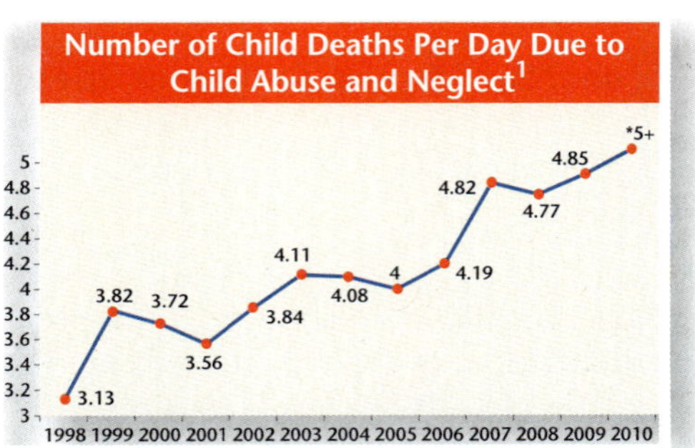

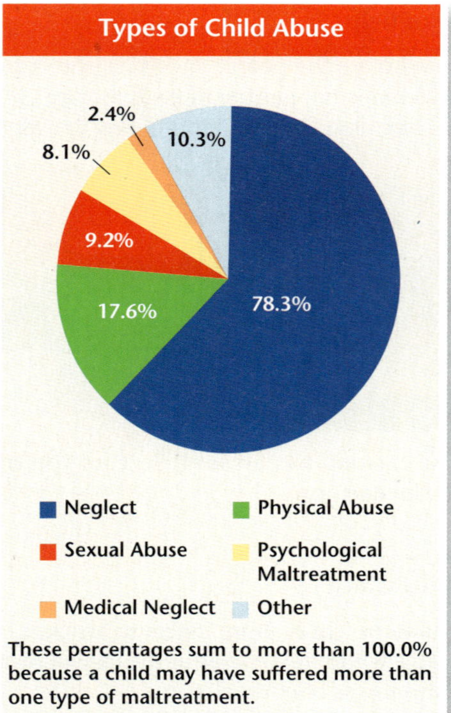

Yelling at children – Can it be usted as a parenting style?

Sometimes parents shout at their children. Some parents do this more often, they use it as a parenting style to show their children when they are misbehaving. Children disobey, say rude things, ignore their chores and parents, or have bad fights with their siblings. In these situations the most patient parent can end up yelling at their child. But in some households yelling at children has become common. It is seen as a normal measure of childrearing. Some yelling is normal, but too much combined with an aggressive tone can be abusive. Screaming something like "You damn idiot" at a child is a severe emotional abuse. It's an example of parents who not only raise their voice but combine their yelling with insults, criticism, or humiliation. This kind of yelling not only hurts children but may also give them the impression that this is how they can handle social interactions later on especially if parents use it as their usual parenting style. And is it really effective? A lot of parents have to realize that after a while their child will become immune and ignore their yelling.

Discussion

Task 4

Work on the following tasks.

a. Explain the negative effects yelling can have on children.
b. From your own experience, give reasons why parents might yell at their children.
c. Most often people think of hitting or misusing a child for sexual actions when they speak of child abuse. But those are only two forms of mistreatment. Look at the information on child abuse again, say why yelling can also be child abuse.

Writing

Task 5

There is nothing wrong with yelling. It's much better than hitting a child.

What do you think of this statement? Write a comment of about 150 words.

Activity

Task 6

You're doing a voluntary year in an American nursery school. Matthew, a boy of 5, is one of the children in your group. For the last two months you have noticed that Matthew is showing some kind of aggressive verbal behaviour and you believe that it is increasing. More than once a day Matthew shouts at the other children and uses a lot of rude words for minor reasons. Quite often when Matthew's parents fetch their son from nursery school you hear them yelling at their son using abusive words. When a girl sitting next to Matthew takes his red crayon he directly yells at her and hits her in the face. Because of this incident Matthew's parents are invited to come. Matthew's mother tells you, 'I sometimes don't know how to react to Matthew's misbehaviour. Then I start yelling at him.' And Matthew's father asks you, 'what's wrong with yelling? I don't slap him'. Now take up these answers and give advice to Matthew's parents showing them positive alternatives on how to handle their family situation.

Case study: Two cases of child abuse

Case 1

Susanna (42): My husband and eldest son of 13 are always at loggerheads. Mike can do no right in my husband's eyes. He seems to be watching him every minute. Even at the dinner table he can't leave him in peace 'Look at you! Sit straight up! You're looking like a monkey.' Those are only some of the abuses he shouts at him.

My son is becoming very withdrawn and sulky. Very often he doesn't know how to answer his father and sits dumb struck, which only infuriates my husband even more.

When I stop him from hitting my boy or kicking him, he turns at me. My husband is not like this with our other three children or me. I have tried to explain the damage he is doing but he won't listen.

Sometimes I feel that divorce is the only answer for the sake of my son.

Case 2

Henry (78): Two months ago a very young couple with three little children of 3, 5 and maybe 8 moved into the flat next to mine. Right from the beginning they kept to themselves and didn't search any contact. So I didn't try to start a conversation. But now I think there are some awful things happening in their flat. I'm a pensioner and I'm at home in the morning. More than once I heard the children crying desperately and I saw that both parents left the house in the morning. Obviously they go to work and leave the younger ones alone. Then the eight-year-old girl comes home from school in the early afternoon but the parents don't turn up before late evening. At night they have fierce arguments and then you can hear the children crying. I don't want to intervene in family affairs. I'm just a neighbour or should I do something?

Comprehension

Task 7

Here are short descriptions of both family situations. Fill in missing words from the letters.

Case 1

Susanna tells that her husband and **1** … son Mike live in a constant conflict. The boy's father treats his son badly. He not only hurts his son with verbal **2** … but also inflicts some physical power on the son like **3** … or **4** … him. As the son does not know how to react, he has become very **5** … and **6** … . Susanna believes that this family situation is doing a lot of **7** … to the boy.

Case 2

Henry is the neighbour of a family with three children. The children's parents are very **1** … . He believes that some **2** … things must be going on in his neighbours' flat. More than once Henry noticed that the parents **3** … their children alone. Very often he also hears a lot of **4** … from the children and during the night their parents have some loud **5** … . Nevertheless Henry does not want to do anything, since he believes he can't **6** … in **7** … .

Task 8

Now answer the following questions on the letters taking into account what you learnt about the different forms of child abuse.

a. Looking at the different forms of child abuse what kind of abuse do the children have to suffer from? Give examples from the text.
b. What could be the reasons for child mistreatment in these cases?
c. What effects does the child abuse have on the children?
d. What do you think about Henry? Does he behave correctly when he says he doesn't want to intervene? How should he behave?

Grammar

Web

Past Perfect

Bildung	**had + 3. Form des Verbs (= past participle)**
Anwendung	**Past Perfect** steht für Handlungen in der Vergangenheit, die zu einem bestimmten Zeitpunkt bereits abgeschlossen waren. Die „jüngere" Handlung steht dann im Past Tense, die „ältere" im Past Perfect.
Beispiel	*After her husband had injured her son, Susanna separated from him.* **Past Perfect** **Past Tense**
Anwendung	**Past Perfect** beschreibt auch Handlungen, die vor einem bestimmten Zeitpunkt in der Vergangenheit begannen und bis zu diesem oder über diesen hinaus andauerten.
Beispiel	*This mistreatment had already taken place for more than one year, before Susanna finally left her husband.*

Task 9

Fill in Past Tense or Past Perfect

The situation in Susanna's family escalated. Her husband attacked her eldest son and injured him severely. Mike was brought into hospital and the family separated. Two of Mike's teachers speak about the signs of mistreatment Mike had obviously shown but which they did not realise until then.

Mr Andrews: I saw something strange, but I did not react. During our sports lessons outside in summer, Mike **1 (leave)** his sweater on which he **2 (already wear)** when he **3 (arrive)** at school. And it **4 (be)** extremely hot all morning before we **5 (start)** our cross-country running, but neverthe-less he **6 (not want)** to put on a short-sleeved shirt then.

Mr Smith: Do you believe he **7 (do)** this because he **8 (be)** hit by his father?

Mr Andrews: Yes, I do now. I think he **9 (want)** to hide some bruises on that mor-ning, which his father **10 (inflict)** on him the day before.

Mr Smith: During the last weeks I remember him as a boy with a very low self-esteem. He **11 (not always be)** such an insecure boy.

But when we **12 (go)** on a class trip at the beginning of the year, Mike's behaviour **13 (totally change)**. By that time he **14 (become)** very timid and withdrawn from his classmates.

Mr Andrews: It's a pity to see what happened to Mike. Don't you think?

Activity

Case Study

Joanna Miller visits the family advice centre because she feels that she needs some help.

Task 10

Look at her account first and then give her some good advice.
Joanna: When we married my husband and I were sure we wanted to have children. And he was the happiest man when his son was born but suddenly he lost interest in us. He says he is too busy and can't spare any time for his son. I feel it's more, he ignores him. Thomas is suffering because he can't understand why his father turns away from him. Last month I asked my husband to fetch our son from nursery school and he forgot to do so. Thomas was desperate. He thought we both had given him up.
Since one of his projects at work failed, the situation has even become worse. He swears and shouts at us and sometimes he becomes so abusive that I start crying. He threatens and abuses Thomas. There is a permanent threat in our family. What can I do?

Task 11

Here are four parents who talk about the 'parenting style' they use. Comment on them.

A: Giving a slap is better than anything else. Whining children ask for it.
B: I don't slap my child. When my son Nick, aged 5, misbehaves, I just ignore him for some hours. This always works! Sooner or later he will give up misbehaving.
C: Miriam is 7 years now but she still shows some temper tantrums. I call her 'silly thing' because this is how she behaves in these situations. If I do this long enough, she will stop.
D: I promise Hannah, aged 6, an ice cream, a chocolate bar or I allow her to watch TV. But only if she shows that she is a well-behaved girl. This is how I always outwit her.

Task 12

in – on – at – up – from – for – against – with – to

Fill the gaps with one of these prepositions. Some prepositions can be used more than once.
Bringing **1** ... a child is not easy. Caring **2** ... a child does not only mean that you provide your child **3** ... food and clothes. Children need someone who sets rules but also someone who supports the child **4** ... developing her or his personality. The way parents treat their children has an impact **5** ... their later life as an adult. Setting rules is a problem and sometimes parents may yell **6** ... the child but using physical power **7** ... the child is absolutely wrong. Constant and fierce shouting is also a kind of mistreatment inflicted **8** ... the children and they suffer **9** ... it. Often people who are a witness to an obvious child mistreatment don't react **10** ... it. They say that they can't intervene **11** ... family affairs but that's a fatal mistake. Any kind of child mistreatment should be reported **12** ... the youth welfare department or the police.

UNIT 6: Food and health

Module 1: Keeping fit and healthy

There are lots of research results and guidelines on food and nutrition but one thing is always pointed out: to eat a wide variety of food is the key to a healthy diet, especially if you are a child or teenager, who is still growing. The food pyramid tries to give some help on how to make the best food choice to promote health. It outlines what you can eat each day to get all the nutrients you need and at the same time to avoid having an unbalanced diet.

Task 1

Study the food pyramid with your partner.

a. Prepare a talk in class on the topic: Food you should prefer and food you should avoid eating.
b. Imagine you live in a single household and there is no food left over. For the weekend, make a shopping list of food you should buy according to the food pyramid.

Eating habits

Task 2

Healthy and well-balanced diets prefer

- food which is low in fat, salt and sugar but
- high in natural fibre.
- products which are not highly processed.
- products with a high amount of vitamins.
- a daily eating plan which is a balanced mixture of proteins (e. g. in fish and meat), carbohydrates (all sorts of starchy products such as bread or cereals), fat (all sorts of dairy products), vitamins (vegetable and fruit).

Talk about your own eating habits.

a. What kinds of food do you prefer?
b. Is the food you like to eat healthy?
c. Do you eat fast food? When and why?
d. Do you eat different types of food on working days and at weekends or during free time?
e. Looking at the short information given on healthy eating, do you think you really eat a healthy diet? Give reasons.

Task 3

Now look at what the following families prefer to eat.

This is what Susan O'Brian bought for her family.

Both Susan and her husband Mike work full-time. For this reason Susan prefers to buy food which can be prepared easily and quickly.

This is what Carla White bought for her family. Carla stays at home to care for her family and spends quite a lot of time preparing meals.

a. What different kinds of food can you see in the pictures?
b. Do you think both families eat a healthy diet? Talk about their eating habits. You can make use of the phrases in the box below.

Helpful phrases

Your daily menu plan should include...
You shouldn't eat too much of.../too many of...
You ought to have enough...
Your body needs... which is mostly in...
You should choose to eat... instead of...
Rather prefer to eat...
Have some... rather than...
It's better to eat... because it is/they are low in.../high in ...
If you live on a diet of... this will lead to health problems because...
If you want to eat healthily, you need to...
A well-balanced diet supplies you with...

Healthy eating – Tips for kids and teenagers

Task 4

Read through the tips and try to fill in the missing words from the box below.

energy – pasta – vitamins – sugary drinks – snacks – enjoy – lean – rusty – bread – twice – whole-grain – variety – chips – exception – crisps – regularly – extra – active

Healthy eating – tips for kids and teenagers

1. ... your food! Take your time!
Don't hurry through your meals. Taste and enjoy your meal!

2. Breakfast is a very important meal!
Whether you set off for school or out for work, don't leave home without breakfast. For a good start to a new day, your body needs **2** ... and after a night's sleep your energy levels are low. Eat cereals with low-fat milk, fruit, yoghurt or **3** ... bread with **4** ... meats. These will offer your body plenty of carbohydrates which is the ticket for your day.

3. Eat lots of different foods!
To stay healthy eat a wide **5** ... of foods each day. No single food can offer you all nutrients which your body needs.

4. Base your food on carbohydrates!
Foods such as cereals, rice, **6** ..., potatoes and **7** ... contain carbohydrates. At least half of the calories in your diet should come from these foods. Include one of these at every meal time.

5. Eat fruit and vegetables at least five times a day!
Fruit and vegetables give you lots of **8** ..., minerals and fibre. For this reason you should try to eat five servings a day at each meal or as a snack.

6. Too much saturated fat is bad for your health!
Don't avoid eating fat, your body needs fats to get all the nutrients it needs. But it's wrong to eat too much of fatty foods like butter, fried meat, **9** ..., sausages, pastries and **10** ....

7. Eat 11 ... and eat little 12 ... between your meals!
Try to stick to regular meals each day. If you feel hungry during the day you can fill the gap between meal times with healthy snacks. But this snack should only be a little **13** ... and no full meal. Chips, chocolate bars, candies, cakes and biscuits should only be an **14** ... and small in portion. Prefer healthy snacks like fresh fruit, vegetables, some nuts or a small sandwich.

8. Don't forget to drink. Your body needs a lot of water!
Your body needs at least two litres of liquids each day, especially if you did some exercise, but don't quench your thirst with **15** .... Prefer still or sparkling water, tea, milk, fruit juices and soft drinks which are low in sugar or mix fruit juice with water.

9. Keep fit and stay 16 ...!

Doing some kind of sport **17** … a week is good for giving your body a workout. Just like any machine which becomes **18** … if you don't use it. Your muscles, bones and heart must be kept healthy by moving, too. So besides doing some sports include activity into your daily life, e. g. walk or cycle to school, don't use a lift but walk the stairs instead.

Task 5

There are six food groups you should choose your food from. Look at the table of food groups and the list below. First make sure you know what every word means.

a. Copy the table and fill in the different foods from the list.
b. Compare your table with your partner and try to add more food you know.

fat	dairy products	meat and fish	fruit	vegetables	starchy foods

peach – bread rolls – leg of lamb – Brussels sprouts – ice cream – yoghurt – peanut butter – biscuits – liver sausage – cauliflower – cereals – cheese – herring – pork chop – plum – potato – courgette – cod – doughnut – olive oil – beef steak – peas – raspberry – plaice – margarine

Task 6

Look at the different people and their eating habits. Explain why they don't live on a healthy diet and how they should change their eating habits.

a. Timothy (16) is very sporty. For this reason he thinks he should eat food with a lot of proteins. He eats lots of meat and eggs, for example he starts his day with a large portion of scrambled eggs and throughout the day he eats a lot of meat like pork chops, sausages and steaks, most often with only a slice of bread but no other side dish.

b. Your friend Sheila (17) is fascinated by supermodels and would like to look like one. She wants to become extremely slim. Sheila is in no way overweight, she is just normal. But now she is obsessed by the idea of slimming down to a skinny body in a short time. One week ago she went on a diet of apples and lettuce leaves with a bit of cottage cheese.

c. Louise (15) likes sweets. There is no day without a chocolate bar. Quite often she replaces her lunch or dinner with chocolate, cake or sweets. As soon as she feels she put on weight, she tries to get rid of it with a tough diet and fierce exercise.

What are useful measures against a fast food society?

In 2000 a government study on Britain's nutrition found out that the majority of British people were surviving on hamburgers, pizzas and chips all washed down with fizzy drinks while many households to a large extent or completely ignored fresh vegetables, fruit, salad and healthy drinks. This study set off a vehement discussion and for the first time aroused a wide interest in British eating habits. It also revealed that eight out of ten young people aged between four and eighteen were almost constantly eating junk food. And some of four-year-olds were consuming more salt than recommended levels for adults. Britain's school dinners were in a deep crisis. In 2005 Jamie Oliver, famous as a TV chef, cookery writer and restaurant owner, started working with schools. With his campaign 'Feed me better' he tried to transform British school dinners, a poor diet of fatty processed junk food, into healthy meals because for some children this is their only proper meal of the day. Jamie Oliver's campaign drove the government to bring in tough nutritional guidelines. Junk food and sweetened drinks were banned from school canteens and vending machines. School canteens are only allowed to serve fried food twice a week and have to serve at least two portions of fruit and vegetables per child. But many children who eat healthy lunches at primary school stop when they go to senior school. It seems that if teenagers have the choice, hamburgers with chips will win and not the healthy school meal. Large numbers of secondary school pupils shun their school meals since the healthy menus were introduced and stick to their unhealthy eating habits. In 2007 the BBC questioned 59 local authorities in England and found that 35 have seen a decrease in the number of secondary pupils taking school meals.

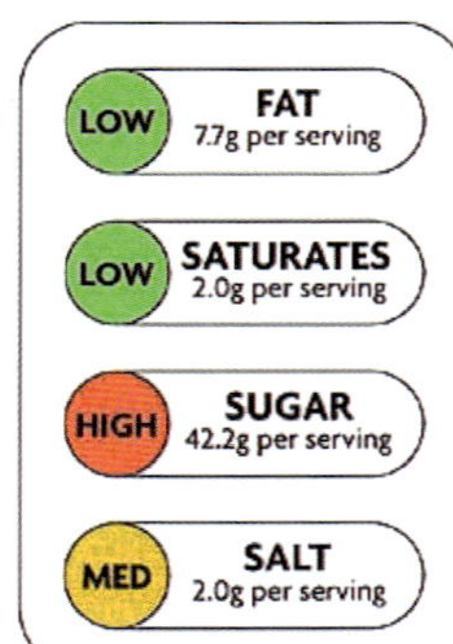

New numbers of an OECD (= Organisation for Economic Co-operation and Development) study focusing on Europe's obesity rates show that Britain could stop the increase of obesity rates among adults and children, although it still holds one of the highest rates in Europe. But this does not mean that the British people now prefer healthy food. Unhealthy foods or beverages are still their favourites. Several countries introduced taxes on unhealthy foods and beverages in 2011 as part of their efforts to counter malnutrition and obesity. This is one example of many European 'Fit not fat' campaigns which try to improve health by changing eating habits. Denmark introduced a tax on foods containing more than 2.3% saturated fats, Hungary a tax on foods with a high sugar, salt or caffeine content, Finland on confectionery products like biscuits, buns and pastries, France on sugary soft drinks. Britain among other countries still discusses taxation of unhealthy foods or beverages but introduced a traffic light labeling. Packed foods have a nutrition label on the back usually giving information on calories, protein, carbohydrate and fat. They may provide additional information on saturated fat, sugars, sodium, salt and fibre. All nutrition information is provided per 100 grams, sometimes per portion of the food. The traffic light labeling now demands that manufacturers put a labeling on the front of the package which clearly shows the levels of fat, saturated fat, sugar and salt, using traffic light colours to show how high the amount is, green for low, yellow for medium and red for high. These labels are meant to help people to choose a more balanced diet.

Adapted from OECD: Health Data 2012 [Information and statistical figures], www.oecd.org/health [01.10.2012]

Comprehension

Task 7

Are the following statements true or false? Give reasons for your decision.

a. The 2000 study on Britain's nutrition was one of many which did not arouse any attention.
b. New studies show that the British people have completely changed their eating habits.
c. During the last years Britain's obesity rate has not increased.
d. Despite lots of campaigns most British people did not change their eating habits.
e. Whereas British grown-ups stick to their unhealthy nutrition, British school kids changed their eating habits for the better.

Language

Task 8

Explain in your own words what the following words taken from the text mean.

a. survive on hamburgers, pizza and chips
b. junk food
c. nutritional guidelines
d. banned from canteens and vending machines
e. shun a school meal
f. malnutrition

Task 9

Discuss with your partner about Jamie Oliver's 'Feed me better' campaign and answer the questions below.

a. What could he change about Britain's school meals?
b. Do you think the whole campaign was a success or not? Give reasons.

Task 10

Also have a close look at the traffic light labeling.

a. Explain how it works.
b. Find out about saturated and unsaturated fat. Which one is more dangerous?
c. Do you think traffic light labelling can be successful in combating bad eating habits?

Writing

Task 11

What do you think of extra taxes on unhealthy foods? Write your comment of about 150 words.

Activity

Task 12

Sit in small groups and search the Web to gather some more information on healthy eating projects. Choose one of the following tasks.

a. Find out more about Jamie Oliver and his projects. Give your class a report.
b. Is or are there famous chefs in your country who also do campaigns to teach children in healthy eating? What do they do? Find out and tell your class.
c. Find out about other healthy eating campaigns in your country, area or town. Give your class a report.

What happens when the British school children come home? What do they prefer to eat then? The British government also launched several campaigns to inform parents of a healthy nutrition. But did all this really bring about a positive change in eating habits? Read the following article and find out.

Authentic reading

Only 12 % of Britons meet 'five a day' target for fruit and veg

Most Britons are not eating the daily recommended amount of fruit and vegetables, and most adults and youngsters are not eating enough fibre, research has found.

The Department of Health advises that people should eat at least five portions of fruit or vegetables a day to help reduce the risk of cancer, heart disease or chronic conditions. But a study of the marketing group TNS found that only 12 % of the population are adhering to the target, and another 12 % eat no fruit and veg at all. On average Britons are consuming just 2.5 daily portions of fruit and vegetables. Less well-off households fail the target. More affluent households are more likely to meet the guidelines.

Giles Quick, managing director of TNS, said: 'While the need for five a day seems to be common knowledge, the number of us who actually achieve this is shockingly low.' However, almost half of the people questioned claimed to be trying to increase their fruit and vegetable intake. Maybe an evidence that Britain is waking up to the importance of nutrition.

Indicating the huge obesity problem Britain is facing, the research also found that larger clothing sizes are now more common. People aged under 25 made up 5 % of the group wearing size 18 clothes (in German 48) and larger.

Most adults and children are failing to meet the government's recommended daily intake of 18 gm of fibre. A third of males and half of females are eating 12 gm fibre a day, only a minimum amount. Better news on eating habits includes the decline of 11 % in the eating of sweet and savoury snacks. And the majority of the households in the UK also bought less salt. Parents were cracking down on children's poor eating habits. Only 27 % of parents now buy their children what they want all the time – down from 41 % in 2005 – and compared with 2007, there are 8 % more packed lunches being taken to school. These meals are likely to contain 32 % more yoghurt, 25 % more vegetables and 16 % more fruit than a year ago.

Source: Fallon, Amy: Only 12 % of Britons meet 'fire a day' target for fruit and veg, in: The Guardian, 15.09.2008

Comprehension

Translation/Writing

Task 13

Work with your partner and try to understand the newspaper article.

a. With the help of bilingal dictionary work through the text again.
b. Write a short summary in English.

Task 14

Now work on questions a to c.

a. Take up each word from the list and talk about changes in eating habits.
fruit – vegetables – fibre – salt – sweets – savoury snacks – yoghurt
b. What could the reason be why children from less well-off households live on worse diets?
c. Describe what parents do to support their children's healthy nutrition?
d. What else could they do to establish healthy eating habits?

Activity

Task 15

Imagine you are an au pair in a British family with two children, Kevin 7 years old and Mary 11 years old. Both children take a packed lunch with them instead of eating a school meal. You are asked to pack their lunch boxes. What do you want to put in? Give reasons for your choice.

Task 16

Imagine you are doing a practical year in a British primary school as a social assistant. Every morning you sit in a circle with your pupils and talk. From these meetings you get to know that there are quite a lot of them who come to school without breakfast or who have just some sweets or crisps on the bus with coke or lemonade as a drink. For this reason you convince your colleagues to organise a breakfast club. For the next staff meeting you're asked to present your ideas. Present your proposal on a flip chart poster.

a. What kind of healthy breakfast do you want to offer to your pupils?
b. How do you want to teach your pupils to eat healthily?
c. How do you want to encourage them to get some more exercise?

Task 17

Design an advertising poster which invites the pupils to come to your breakfast club. Remember that you want to arouse the pupils' interest and make them feel your club is something they should join in.
First present your posters. Then compare your results in class. Which poster do you think does the best job?

Listening

Listen to an interview of a group of teenagers at Queen Burgers – a fast food chain. They talk about fast food and why they like to eat it.

Task 18

Who says what? Match the sentences and the persons.

Robert: No, not me. I don't eat fast food that often.
Tim: I'm sincere enough to tell the truth.
Laura: I like to eat the hamburgers, chips and apple tarts they offer you here.
Henry: It's great to be here.
Kim: It's better to sit here than hang around the streets.

Task 19

Listen to the dialogue again. Take notes and summarise its main aspects.

Selecting food for a healthy meal plan

For those who suffer from a chronic disease food and meal planning is most important. Food can offer your body a certain nutrient it is in need of. A special diet may help to keep you healthier for a longer time or to reduce symptoms of a disease. For example, those people who suffer from heart disease should eat a diet low in saturated fat and cholesterol but rich in fibre. A diet rich in fruits, vegetables and grain products that contain fibre may help to reduce the risk of coronary heart disease.

Activity

Task 20

Now look at what Nora, Peter, and Hanna are suffering from and try to work out a daily menu plan which fits to their special needs. What else can they do to keep fit? You may choose one of them and work in small groups. Present your results in class. Before you start working on a menu plan, make sure you clearly know what kind of disease they are suffering from. If necessary try to gather some further information.

Case 1

Peter (53) works as a lorry driver and he mostly eats in fast food restaurants when he is able to have a break. He is overweight. His cholesterol levels are high and his doctor told him that he suffers from arteriosclerosis, a hardening of the arteries, which means that his arterial walls are thickening and losing their elasticity. Peter has to change his life and eating habits because there is a high risk for him of having a heart attack.

Menu Plan

Name: ______________

- Breakfast:
- Mid morning snack:
- Lunch:
- Mid afternoon snack:
- Dinner:
- Evening snack:
- Some further tips/ how to keep fit:

Case 2

Hanna is 12 and she suffers from diabetes which means that there is far too much sugar in her blood. Every food intake affects her body's need for insulin which she sometimes must inject to keep her sugar levels low. It's hard for Hanna to see other kids eating sweets and chocolate and quite often she asks her parents for something sweet. Can you help her?

Case 3

Nora is now 60 years old and she suffers from osteoporosis. Bones in a healthy body are constantly regenerating but in Nora's case her bones lost density and strength. During the last year Nora suffered from several fractures. Now her doctors told her to live on a diet which provides her with calcium and vitamins, especially vitamin D and K.

Grammar

Web

If-clauses

Type 1:

If John doesn't eat so much fatty food, he will/can surely lose some weight.

- **If + Present Tense, will + Infinitiv (Future I)**
- **Die Bedingung ist erfüllbar, sie wird also wahrscheinlich eintreffen.**

Type 2:

John just can't say 'No' to hamburgers and chips. If he didn't eat so much of them, he would/ could lose some weight.

- **If + Past Tense, would + Infinitiv (Conditional I)**
- **Die Bedingung ist zwar nicht völlig unerfüllbar, es ist jedoch eher unwahrscheinlich, dass sie eintreffen wird.**

Task 21

When you want to give some advice you frequently make use of if-clauses. The following sentences present if-clauses type 1 and 2.

Transform the verb in brackets into its correct form.

a. If you (not live) on a well-balanced diet, you will surely suffer from various diseases later in your life.
b. If you stopped eating that much chocolate, you (lose) some weight.
c. You can do something against your high cholesterol levels, if you (avoid) hidden fat in food.
d. Percy suffers from a wheat allergy, if he eats any food which contains wheat, he (react) allergic against it.
e. If Sandra (eat) more vitamins instead of her beloved pasta and hamburgers, she (not be) ill that often. But she is still a fast food fan.
f. If you (eat) more vitamins instead of fast food, I'm absolutely sure you (not catch) a flu or a cold that often in winter.

Much/many – little/few

much = viel
*Is there **much** fat in a doughnut?*
→ unzählbare Nomen

many = viele
*Today **many** children suffer from allergies.*
→ zählbare Nomen/Nomen in der Pluralform

little = wenig
*There is only **little** soup left over.*
→ unzählbare Nomen

few = wenige
*Only a **few** of my friends don't like garlic.*
→ zählbare Nomen/Nomen in der Pluralform

Task 22

Fill in much or many, little or few.

a. How ... are these tomatoes? I can't buy ... because I didn't take ... money with me.
b. There are only a ... London restaurants which are excellent. I spent ... time reading ... different restaurant guides.
c. It will take ... effort to prepare a four course meal for our friends.
d. I only drink very ... coffee because I don't like it.
e. There was only a ... cream left over in the fridge. Tom likes to put ... cream onto his strawberries.

Module 2: Obesity

Children aged 5-17 who are overweight (including obese)

Girls (% of children aged 5-17 years)

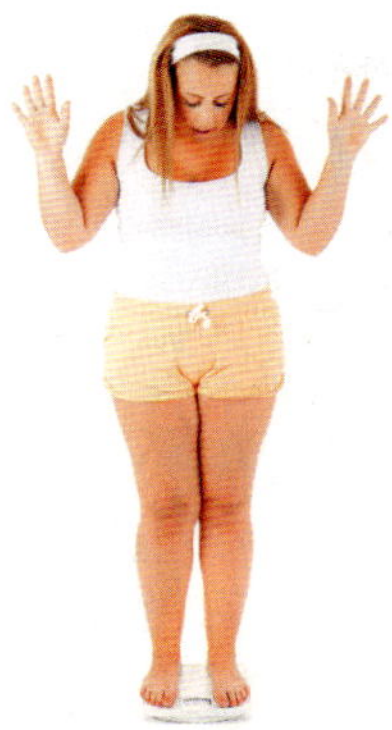

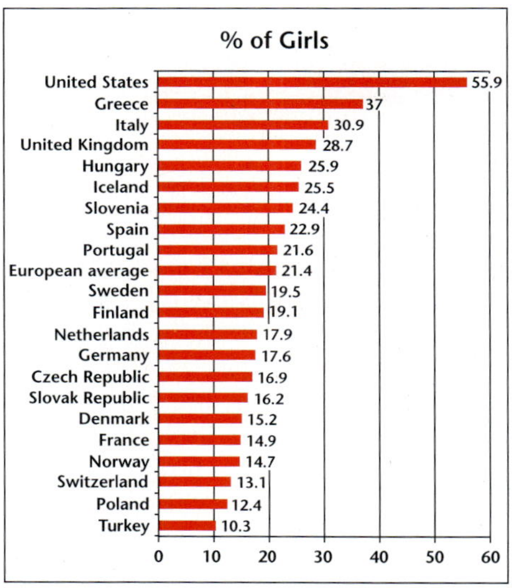

Boys (% of children aged 5-17 years)

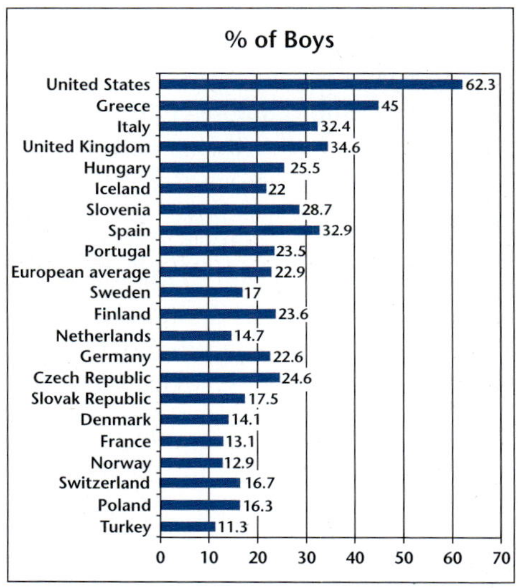

Adapted from OECD: Health Policy and Data, OECD Indicators (International Association for the Study of Obesity), 2011, www.oecd.org/els/healthpoliciesanddata/49716427.pdf [01.10.2012]

Task 1

Study these statistics on children who are overweight and comment on the statements below. Are they correct interpretations of the statistical figures?

a. Britain still is the European country with the highest rate of overweight children.
b. Looking at all countries, there are more boys than girls who have weight problems.
c. Compared to Europe America is not outstanding.
d. Britain now lies under the European average.
e. Mediterranean countries have a much lower overweight or obesity rate than the other European countries.
f. German boys and girls stay under the European average.

Writing

Task 2

Looking at the statistics, sum up your main results in about 150 words. For help look at the skills box 'analysing charts' on page 67–68.

Britain's obesity problem

In May 2004 British people were shocked to hear about the death of a three-year-old from heart failure because of extreme overweight. It was a girl of East London who should have weighed around 2 st (= stones) 4 lb (pounds) which is 14.5 kilograms, but instead this girl weighed 6 st (38 kilograms) and had a Body Mass Index of more than 40. Sadly this case is not a shocking exception.

What's BMI?

The Body Mass Index looks at weight in relationship to height. Weight in kilograms is divided by height in metres squared (kg/m²). For example, someone is 65 kilograms and 1,70 m high. Now divide 65 by 1.7 m² (1.7 × 1.7) and the result should be 22.5 which is normal weight. BMI from 18.5 to 24.9 is said to be normal weight. BMI less than 18.5 is underweight. Overweight starts with an BMI of 25. A person with a BMI of 30 or even more is said to be obese unless the person is very athletic. People with lots of trained muscles can have a high BMI, but they're not obese but healthy.

The little girl's death and the high number of obese children were highlighted in a Government report which warns that today's generation of obese children could be the first generation to die before their parents. Doctors at hospitals reported that many young patients have abnormally high sugar levels, an indicator of diabetes, which they directly relate to obesity. More and more children suffer from a heart condition. There are obese children who need breathing assistance to avoid death because of blocked airways during sleep. Doctors say that otherwise they could be 'choked by their fat'.

Dr Tim Barrett of Birmingham Children's Hospital told the BBC, 'Our clinics are currently being flooded with overweight children. At the moment, we haven't got adequate treatments at all. We need to set up specialist clinics for them.'

But why are there growing numbers of obese children and teenagers? Food specialists point out that it is becoming more and more difficult to stay fit and healthy in today's society. Fast food is not the only problem. Of course there are lots of fast food restaurants which offer you cheap king-sized or even supersized portions of hamburgers and chips soaked with fat and pizzas with mountains of fatty cheese and salami.

But fast food and lack of exercise are not the only reasons. Most experts think that obesity is at first hand a 'lifestyle' problem and that buying, preparing and eating food should be given more respect. Today everyone seems to be short of time. For those who do not want to prepare a real meal, supermarkets offer plenty of packaged meals which only need to be put into the microwave but which are laden with fat and sugar. To prepare a meal from natural ingredients and sit together with the family to enjoy it while you are talking things over has become very rare. Food intake must be quick, but this is a lifestyle which promotes obesity to a huge extent.

Comprehension

Task 3

Here are some statements on food and obesity. On the basis of the text say whether they are true or false. Give reasons for your decision.

a. The death of a three-year-old girl because of her extreme overweight is just an exception.
b. It's okay to eat packaged meals from the supermarket because you can have meals with meat, potatoes or rice and some kind of vegetable which is much healthier than eating a pizza.
c. The obesity problem is also a problem for the medical system.
d. Today people prefer to cook a meal with natural ingredients because everywhere you can buy lots of fresh vegetables and fruit.
e. Most people who eat a meal in a fast food restaurant eat much more than they want and need to.

Task 4

Answer the following questions on the text.

a. Why are obese children running a high risk of dying before their parents?
b. Why is obesity 'at first hand a life style problem'?

Discussion/Writing

Task 5

In line 33–35 of the text it says that 'food specialists point out that it is becoming more and more difficult to stay fit in today's society'. What's your opinion? Looking at your own daily life, do you believe this statement is true or false? Write a comment. Don't write less than 150 words.

Language

Task 6

Look at the list of nouns and say

what adjective fits to	what verb fits to
obesity	weight
health	assistance
comparison	treatment
youth	lack

Authentic reading

Obese Children – what role do parents play?

Case Study

Maria Hailstone and her daughters Nicola (9) and Sarah (8) are overweight. Here is what Maria told the press about how they got into the 'obesity trap'.

'I split up from my husband three years ago and started comfort eating. I became a bit of a shopaholic.

'For the sheer hell of it I tended to buy more and more. I shot up the best part of 3st (3 stones = 19 kilograms).

'I was eating huge bars of chocolate, crisps – anything, really. The girls would have it with me because it was there.

'I've never told them they should ask to take food – I wouldn't deny them having something to eat.

'I'd buy lots of convenience foods – pizzas and the like in the chilled section. Sainsbury's Chicken Kievs were quick and easy with chips, but also packed with calories. We used to have lots of stodge in the house – tins full of biscuits and cake. [...]

'I have the girls with me when I'm shopping – they want the Cadbury chocolate they see in the adverts, the Coco Pops and those Lunchables that are plugged in kids' programmes.

'I used to get big bags of crisps as well and they'd have a couple of bags each a day.'

Six months ago Maria realised she had to take drastic action. [...]

'I ditched the convenience foods and started cooking meals with fresh ingredients [...].

'The fresh meat and fresh ingredients don't cost any more than the convenience foods I was buying before.

But she remains critical of the big food companies. She said: 'The TV adverts still cause us problems – only recently the girls asked for Coco Pops when we were in the supermarket and I said, 'You're not having chocolate for breakfast.' [...] I'd like to kick all the adverts for unhealthy foods like that off the telly at times when children are watching.'

Source: Yates, Charles: Mum fights obesity trap, in: The Sun, 28.05.2004

Comprehension

Task 7

Explain why Maria Hailstone and her daughters got into the 'obesity trap'. Work through the questions first.

a. Maria talks about 'comfort eating'. What is that and when did it start?
b. What did Maria prefer to eat after her divorce? Did this have an influence on her girls?
c. What kind of convenience food did the girls prefer?
d. Did Maria try to control what the girls were eating or tell them about what is good or bad for them?
e. How did Maria finally change their eating habits?

Writing

Task 8

Sum up the main aspects of Maria Hailstone's case in a short essay. Make use of the skills training box. There is also an essay map and a helpful phrases box which show you how to structure your essay.

Skills Training

Summarising important aspects and issues in an essay

Essays are structured in the following way:

1. **Introduction:** What is the topic of your essay? Do you refer to a certain source, text or case study? If you talk about an issue which is not taken from a text, you may use an 'attention grabber' to arouse interest in your essay, e.g. give some important information on your issue or start with a startling information, or maybe a short example or story sounds interesting, or just start with the question you like to answer. But make sure that your attention grabber is short, only one or two sentences, maybe add two more sentences that will lead the reader to the main part, the body of your essay.
2. **Body:** Here you present your main arguments or the main aspects of your issue. Try to present each argument or aspect in one paragraph and do not forget to give explanations and reasons. If possible add an example to some of your arguments.
3. **Conclusion:** This is the last summarising paragraph of your essay. Here you should try to point out the most important aspect of your issue or you should give the reader your final statement or answer to the problem but in short. All the conclusion needs is three or four strong sentences.

Here is an example of an essay map to show you how to structure your essay.

Why are the rates of overweight or even obese children rising? The story of Maria Hailstone and her daughters may give an answer to this question. In my essay I am going to look at her case from different points of view.
One of the most important aspects is that ..., for example when Maria Hailstone got divorced she ... So the main reason for her comfort eating in this period of her life is that ...
One of the main reasons for her daughters' wrong eating habits is ... because...
One side of the problem is that Maria herself ... but there is also the problem that she does not .... .
Therefore I think that her behaviour is part of the problem because as a mother she should ...
On the other hand, Maria argues that ... and she blames ... for ... Her argument seems to be ... because when you look at her children ...
The main reason for believing ... is that ... One good illustration of this is ...
But the end of her story clearly shows that there is a possibility to get out of the obesity trap, she finally .... Her example shows that it is possible to ...
Summing up it can be said that this case ... It very clearly shows that the obesity problem has more than just one reason, but in this case I believe that it is most important that ...

Helpful phrases: Structuring your essay

First of all I think …	Zuerst einmal denke ich …
Not only that, but also …	Nicht nur, dass .. , sondern auch …
There are more reasons for …	Es gibt mehrere Gründe für …
First …/Firstly …	Erstens …
Second, …/Secondly …	Zweitens …
Moreover …/Furthermore …/In addition …	Außerdem …
Another important reason is that …	Ein anderer wichtiger Grund für … ist, dass …
On the one hand/On the other hand ….	Einerseits… Andererseits …
One side of the problem is that …	Eine Seite des Problems ist, dass …
In contrast to this …	Im Gegensatz dazu …
That is why …	Deshalb …
The result of all this is that …	Das Ergebnis davon ist, dass…
It is because …	Das liegt daran, weil …
Because of …	Wegen …
Take for example …	Nimmt man …/Nehmen wir zum Beispiel …
Look at …	Betrachtet man…/Betrachten wir …
Let me give an example …	Lassen Sie/Lasst mich ein Beispiel geben …
One good illustration of this argument is that …	Ein gutes Beispiel/ein guter Beleg für dieses Argument ist, dass …
Finally …	Schließlich …
All in all I believe …	Alles in allem glaube ich …
Summing up it can be said that …	Zusammenfassend kann man sagen, dass …
In other words …	Mit anderen Worten …
It appears to be …	Es scheint … zu sein …
Most important …	Am wichtigsten …
Most probable …	Am wahrscheinlichsten …

Task 9

Choose one of the following questions and write a comment.

a. Some people say parents are responsible for what their children eat and therefore responsible for their child's obesity. Others say if a child is demanding food it's very difficult to refuse it. What's your opinion?
b. Should there be a TV ban for unhealthy food, especially during children's programmes?

Food coaching – one way of tackling obesity

Amanda Wayn works as a nutritionist in a clinic for obese children. About her work she says:

"Kicking bad habits – that's the idea behind everything we do with the children. We tell them to become active, take exercise and to eat healthily, but we don't set the children on a harsh diet. This wouldn't work. Of course, they eat a healthy diet here and most often it's much different from what they used to eat. It's not only that the portions they eat here are smaller. The food is different. We want them to become more conscious about their intake of food. I'm their food coach who helps them to find their own healthy way. On their first day here I ask them about their favourite food and their 'normal eating day'. We then try to work out an eating plan which is well-balanced and healthy but which also allows them to have some of their favourites. The eating plan contains small extras or we show them how to prepare their favourite food without too much fat or sugar. I also go shopping with them and tell them to put everything into the trolley which they preferred to eat. Then we have a look at the labels and see whether the ingredients are good or bad for them. It's alarming to see that children's food often is of poorer quality than adults' food. It contains more additives, preservatives, colour and cheaper ingredients. There are some sorts of breakfast cereals especially designed for kids which have a healthy image but which are in reality packed with high levels of sugar, salt and fat and which are helping to make children dangerously podgy. If something is more than 10 grams of sugar, 20 grams of fat or 5 grams of saturated fat – I tell them to look at another food. We teach them to read the labels and then choose the right food for them."

Language

Task 10

Explain what these words and expressions from the text mean.

a. l. 1 kicking bad habits
b. l. 3 harsh diet
c. l. 16 additive
d. l. 16 preservative
e. l. 18 packed with
f. l. 19 podgy

Comprehension

Task 11

Answer the following questions on the text.

a. How does Amanda Wayn help children to 'kick bad habits'?
b. Why is it important to teach children to look at the labels of products?
c. What does Amanda Wayn point out about breakfast cereals?

Activity

Imagine that on their food coaching day Maria Hailstone's daughters put the following 'favourite food' into the supermarket trolley:
Tweenies Chocolate Spread, which they like to eat on white bread in the morning or Kids Choco Honey Lumps with milk. As a snack Happy Crocodiles Jellies, Kid's Milk Chocolate Bars and Teddy Bear Crisps. As a lunch both girls prefer fish fingers or Happy Dinosaur Steaks with chips, which is a kind of hamburger in the shape of a dinosaur.

Task 12

Take over Amanda Wayn's role and talk with Nicola and Sarah about their favourite food. What kind of advice do you want to give?

Task 13

Do you know food especially designed for children in your country?
Make a list of the different products you know.

Task 14

As homework: study some of the labels of food you find at home. Looking at what Amanda Wayn said about children's food, are the products you chose healthy? Present your results in class in your next lesson.

Module 3: Eating disorders

Audio

When eating becomes hell

Claudia and Alicia suffered from eating disorders when they were teens. Even today their eating habits are still abnormal. Here is how they describe this period of their life.

Case Study 1: The story of an anorexic:

Claudia, 21: When I was 13 we moved to another town and I had to attend a new class. I thought the others didn't like me. I became a bit of an outsider. The only thing I loved to do in my free time was to look through fashion magazines and I adored some of the supermodels. I thought if I were much slimmer, the girls in my class would accept me. There was some kind of bullying going on and I believed it was because of my figure. I lost some weight but then at 15 a kind of fear of eating arose in me. I entered puberty and my body changed. Not only my period started, my breasts became much bigger. But I didn't want all that. I started to hate myself and I felt ashamed of my own body. I wanted to stop getting any bigger, so I almost stopped eating. It took some time before my mother got suspicious of what I was doing. She started to control my eating. But it was already too late. Everything in me refused to eat. I had serious rows with my mother because I thought she wanted to make me fat again. It's strange, although I didn't want to eat, all my thoughts and talks circled around eating. I started collecting recipes and my mother got convinced that I had given up my starving. I put lots of food on my plate, cut it into tiny pieces but did not swallow a little bite. When I was able to cheat the others I felt happy. I loved my skinny body and was excited each time I lost more weight. I wore two or three layers of clothes just to cheat my family.

At 16 I lost control. I looked like a skeleton. I had bruises on my hips and ribs and sleeping on them became painful. I finally collapsed because of an overdose on laxatives and was brought into hospital. I had absolutely lost the ability to eat. I had to be tube-fed for a few days. Then I was sent into a clinic for a therapy and I slowly learnt to eat again. But I'm not absolutely cured. Now and then, if I feel deeply sad, insecure or unloved I sometimes show anorexic tendencies but now I am strong enough to get over them.

Case Study 2: The story of a bulimic and yo-yo-dieter:

Alicia, 24: Today I know that dieting is dangerous, even life-threatening. Those who have never had an 'issue' about food can't understand the vicious circle – emotionally and physically – that a yo-yo dieter can get trapped in. You eat too much, so you gain weight. You get depressed because you have gained weight, so you cheer yourself up with a small bowl of ice-cream or perhaps three or four because you are so depressed, which lets you just swell up like a balloon. Then you get even more depressed and you sure start your next fierce diet until you break it again. This had been my normal life style since I was 14. Sometimes I managed to eat less and healthily for about two or three months. I lost weight then and I led a real healthy life without eating chocolate or fatty cheese. I went out for a run regularly, even before breakfast, sometimes about three or four times a day. What an amazing feeling, I really lost weight. But then something crossed my way. A friendship broke up or I was worried about school exams or just small incidents happened which made me nervous. I lost my balance and as a consequence I went into the next supermarket and bought tons of chocolate or huge sacks with crisps and I swallowed everything in one or two hours. The thing about being overweight is that you feel different, excluded. I wanted to be like one of those girls pressed in mega small jeans and dressed with a tiny top. But I looked like a porky 17-year-old hidden in oversized shirts. Once in my life I wanted to succeed. This was when I went to the toilet for the very first time and put my finger into my mouth and managed to vomit. The vomiting was horrible, but when I saw everything before me in the toilet I felt great. Now each time I ate too much or felt that I had eaten something too fat or sweet I went to the toilet. Soon this habit took over, after every dinner, even after breakfast I tried to get rid of everything. Suddenly on a shopping trip I felt my heart racing and I had a black out. This incident changed my life. I had to stay in a clinic and here I worked out a healthy eating routine with a qualified nutritionist and I joined a self-help-group. Now I feel okay, although I am still chubby, but I learnt to accept myself.

Comprehension

Task 1

Here are some sentences which describe Claudia's and Alicia's stories. Reconstruct them by matching the sentence parts.

1. Claudia gets the idea to start a diet...	a. ...because she believes that her classmates don't like her outer appearance.
2. When she reaches puberty her eating disorder takes over...	b. ...when she overdoses on laxatives and finally collapses.
3. Her mother's attempt to control her daughter fails...	c. ...because Claudia is very clever in cheating her whole family.
4. At last her anorexia reaches a climax...	d. ...because she can't accept her body becoming more womanly.
5. Alicia believes that a yo-yo-dieter is caught in a vicious circle...	e. ...when she develops normal eating habits with the help of a nutritionist and a self-help-group.
6. Each time Alicia is confronted with a negative experience...	f. ...for this reason she eagerly wants to be one of the 'it-girls' who fit into extra small sizes.
7. Very often Alicia feels excluded because of her overweight and...	g. ...she tries to cheer herself up with binge eating of comfort food like sweet, soft or fat food which is high in calories like chocolate, ice cream and crisps.
8. Alicia manages to break out of her eating disorder...	h. ...because there is a constant change of fierce diets and binge eating.

Task 2

Have a close look at Claudia's and Alicia's stories again and answer the following questions.

a. Looking at the typical signs of anorexia and bulimia, do you think Claudia and Alicia show them? Give examples from the text!
b. Can you find reasons why both fall into an eating disorder?
c. How could both girls hide their eating disorder from others?

What is anorexia?

Most often anorexia occurs with teenage girls. Those people who suffer from anorexia are obsessed with being extremely thin. Anorexic people believe themselves to be fat when in reality they are extremely thin. They lose a lot of weight in a very short time and are almost terrified to gain weight. This starving is often used to deal with an emotional problem in a totally wrong way.

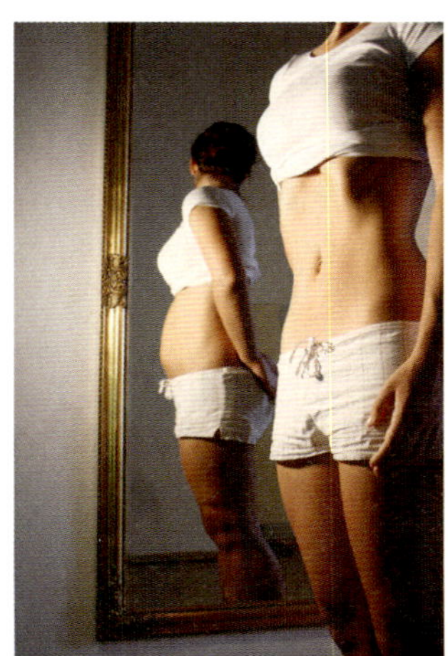

Frequent warning signs of anorexia:

- Deliberate self-starving and denial of hunger
- High weight loss in a short time
- Fear of gaining weight
- Refusal to eat
- Constant exercising
- Sensitivity to cold temperatures
- Absent or irregular periods
- Laxative abuse

What is bulimia?

In contrast to anorexic people who starve themselves and avoid any kind of high-calorie food, bulimic people eat huge amounts of food, but try to get rid of everything soon after dinner by vomiting or taking laxatives or water pills. Usually bulimia does not go hand in hand with a high weight loss.

What is a good treatment for an eating disorder?

Audio

Treatment for an eating disorder is always difficult, because those who suffer from it don't believe that there is anything wrong with them. Most often treatment starts after someone has a breakdown and is admitted to hospital. A treatment should always include psychotherapy and nutritional counselling. Psychotherapy is necessary to become aware of underlying reasons and nutritional counselling to develop normal eating habits. But for a successful treatment, patients must want to change. Some prefer an individual psychotherapy, others join a self-help-group. Nora Winters chose a different form of therapy. She went to live in a therapeutic group with two other girls who suffered from anorexia.

Reporter: Nora, when did you come to live in this group?

Nora: Well, after my complete body breakdown I first went into a clinic for people with eating disorders and I started therapy there, but I soon realised that this isn't the right therapy for me.

Reporter: Why?

Nora: Well, a stay in a clinic tears you out of your life. Of course, in some way it's good to have a break and leave your family and former life for some time. Sometimes only distance can help you to see what's wrong in your life. But this didn't really work for me. I wanted to keep up some kind of normal life. For example, the breakdown came only some months before my final school exams and I didn't want to chuck them. So to live here in this therapeutic group gave me the chance to go to school and live my life.

Reporter: Isn't there any professional help?

Nora: Yes, there is. Everyone of us receives individual counselling. Maren, our psychotherapist, visits us regularly and Thomas, our nutritionist, helped us to find a way back to normal eating. We went shopping together and he showed us how to cook healthily.

Reporter: How does living in a group help?

Nora: It's really good to see that there is someone with the same fate. You talk to someone who knows. This helps a lot. We grew very close. The group gives you security and we somehow take care of each other. Let's say there is some kind of positive control. It's funny, but last week we wanted to go out on Saturday evening. As always time ran short, so we didn't sit down for our evening meal. But just as we wanted to step out we stopped right in front of the door and we looked at each other knowing that we were doing something wrong. We decided to have a quick meal before leaving. This is what I mean when I speak of positive control.

Comprehension

Task 3

Read the interview with Nora again and try to complete the following sentences.

a. A treatment for an anorexic or bulimic person isn't easy because...
b. Every person who suffers from an eating disorder should undergo psychotherapy because...
c. A successful treatment should also include nutritional counselling because...
d. Sometimes a stay in a clinic away from friends and family can be good because...
e. Nora prefers to live in a therapeutic group because...

Task 4

Answer the questions on the text.

a. Nora says the group 'grew close'. Can you think of reasons for their close relationship?
b. Explain what Nora wants to express when she talks about 'positive control'.

Task 5

Copy and expand this mind map with the following words from this module. If you can, add more words which you believe to be important.

nutritional counselling – self-starving – binge eating – fear of gaining weight – therapeutic group – psychotherapy counselling – vomiting food – high weight loss – self-help group – laxative abuse – stay in special clinic – constant exercising – refusal to eat

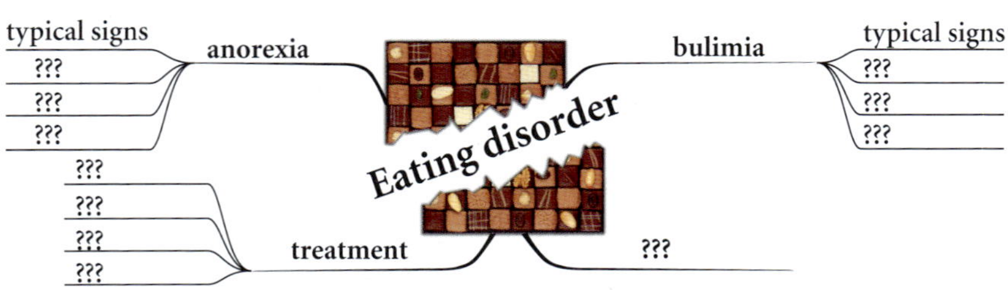

Skills Training

Making a mind map

Making a mind map can help you to collect ideas and remember the most important facts on a topic. With a mind map you can find out about the relationship of those words and facts you collected. Besides a mind map is helpful to learn the vocabulary on a certain topic more easily.

How to create a mind map?

a. Start with a main keyword which is the central idea/topic of your mind map in the centre of your paper.
b. Find keywords (not too many, perhaps three or four) which describe some main aspects of your central idea and link them to your central idea/topic.
c. Add further ideas to these main aspects.

In this way your ideas are summarised in a kind of hierarchy.

Tips

- Connect different ideas/aspects with lines and arrows to create a kind of network.
- Use different colours for different aspects or pictures and symbols to clearly show the relationship between different aspects and to stress important facts or ideas.

Helpful phrases: Presenting a mind map

I would like to present you my mind map with the topic …	Ich präsentiere Ihnen/euch meine Mindmap („Gedankenlandkarte") zum Thema …
This mind map deals with …	Diese Mindmap befasst sich mit …
Right in the middle/centre of the mind map you can see the overall topic which is …	Direkt in der Mitte der Mindmap kann man das übergeordnete Thema sehen, dieses ist …
The main topic has (number) subdivisions which are …	Das Hauptthema hat (Zahl) Unterteilungen, diese sind …
The main topic is split up in to/divided in to the following aspects …	Das Hauptthema ist in die folgenden Aspekte unterteilt …
All these aspects are linked to the main topic because …	Alle diese Aspekte verknüpfen sich mit dem Hauptthema, weil …
With regard to the main topic these aspects are important because …	In Bezug auf das Hauptthema sind diese Aspekte wichtig, weil …
(Topic) is an important aspect of the main topic because ….	(Thema) ist ein wichtiger Aspekt des Hauptthemas, weil …
Here you see one further link which is (topic).	Hier sieht man eine weitere Verknüpfung, diese ist (Thema).
There are (number) branch lines connected to the main topic which are …	Es gibt (Zahl) Zweiglinien, die sich mit dem Hauptthema verknüpfen, diese sind …
The aspects (topic) branch out from the overall topic …	Die Aspekte (Thema) verzweigen sich von dem übergeordneten Thema …

Task 6

Choose one of the following topics and create a mind map. Present your mind map in class. Possible topics are fast food, obesity and healthy eating.

Discussion/Writing

Task 7

Up till today the fashion industry has been working with extremely slim models. Again and again you see them in fashion magazines or even ultra-skinny models on the catwalks. There are also examples of famous actresses who are not much more than skin and bones which seems to be the ideal of beauty propagated by the film industry. A lot of people think that these actresses and the fashion models are dangerous for teenage girls.
What is your opinion? Take notes for the discussion with a partner.

Task 8

Here is what some people think of anorexia and bulimia. In pairs pick out two statements and say what you think of them.

a. Anorexia and bulimia are a typical girls' and women's problem.
b. Anorexia is not a disease. It is just a foolish temper which teenage girls show.
c. Anorexia and bulimia are serious addictions.
d. A lot of girls and women feel pressurized into being thin because they want to suit today's ideal of beauty.

Writing

Task 9

Imagine that you are Sheila's classmate. You regularly train in a fitness club and three months ago you met her at the club for the very first time. You get friends because from now on you meet her regularly and every time you take a break Sheila stops her training to have a chat. Sheila tells you that she trains almost every day. Some weeks later you notice that her exercising has become very intensive. She trains really hard and from that time on she does not stop to have a chat. Then two weeks later you see that she pauses more than once during her training, stepping on the scales to check her weight. But she does not talk to you, she tells you that she has to train. Later you have the chance to throw a short glance at Sheila under the shower and you are shocked to see that she has become extremely slim. You did not notice before because Sheila always wears much too large pullovers telling you that she feels cold. Now it comes into your mind that Sheila did not come into the school canteen for a real long period of time. In former times she used to sit at the table with you and the other girls of your class having a school dinner. But now you cannot remember having her seen eating something. All this worries you. Since Sheila seems to avoid talking to you, you decide to write her a letter telling what you are worried about. **Write this letter.**

UNIT 7:
Coping with illness and special needs

Module 1: Coping with illness

Lorna Baker works as a project manager in a computer company. Here is what she says about illness and prevention.

These days I try to do something to stay healthy. If possible I try to eat some vitamins. Most often I prefer to eat a salad. If I can spare some time, I do some walking. But I can't do all this regularly, I'm just too busy at work. I must admit I'm kind of a workaholic. I get stuck into my work and during the 'hot phase' of a project I work till late at night. In this time I can't bother about healthy eating. I eat in a restaurant or buy something and I drink a lot of coffee to stay awake. Last year I was in charge of two projects and during that time I caught almost any infectious disease which was circling around in our firm. I suffered from a persistent cough and had to see a doctor quite often. Above all sleeplessness made me feel deeply exhausted. But in summer I went on a three-week-holiday and I was able to relax. Now I feel better and up till now I have managed to take regular breaks despite all the work. In autumn I started to squeeze oranges and lemons to drink fresh juice. I'm sure this time I will stay healthy.

Comprehension

Task 1

a. What does Lorna do to stay healthy?
b. Can you find reasons why she had health problems?
c. Do you believe that Lorna has a good chance to stay fit this year?
d. What do you do to stay fit and healthy?

Task 2

Make sure you understand the meaning of the words in the two boxes. Then match them. Sometimes there is more than one possibility.

Example:

Whooping cough is a childhood disease.

allergy, chronic disease, heart disease, infection, fracture, injury, wound, genetic defect, disability/ special need, eating disorder, childhood disease, mental illness, neurological disease

cold, hay fever, cerebral palsy, chicken pox, anorexia, broken leg, heart attack, sprained wrist, bruise, burn, whooping cough, bronchitis, German measles, migraine, arachnophobia, Down Syndrome, cardiac disrhythmia

Task 3

Fill the gaps with words from the list below.

sprained · stretcher · bruise · surgery · convalescence · aircast splint · physiotherapy · crutches · plaster · swollen · ambulance · pain · ankle · fracture · x-ray

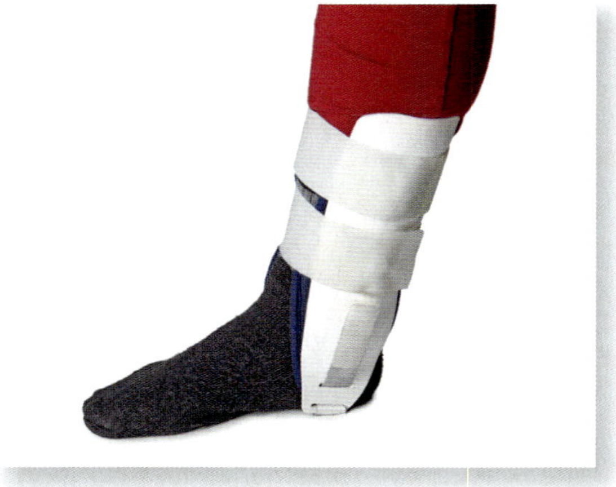

Three months ago when we wanted to go to the canteen during our midday break I noticed that I had forgotten to take my purse with me. So I turned around, ran back to my office and fetched my purse. Since the others had already gone into the canteen, I wanted to hurry up the stairs. But when I took the last step, I twisted my left 1 … . Immediately I felt a very sharp 2 … . When I looked down at my ankle, it was 3 … and there was already a deep blue 4 … . One of my colleagues came to help me to stand up. I tried to walk, but I absolutely couldn't. By that time I still hoped it was just a 5 … ankle. Our secretary called the 6 … and they carried me on a 7 … because I wasn't able to walk. In hospital they told me they presumed it was a 8 … but no sprain. To be sure they took an 9 … which showed what they had presumed. My left ankle was fractured. Worst of all, it could not be treated with a 10 … , I had to undergo 11 … and I stayed in hospital for seven days. I left hospital on 12 … and my ankle was fixed in an 13 … . During the first weeks I wasn't allowed to put more than half of my own weight onto my ankle. But I did not just sit still six to eight weeks until the fracture was healed, already two weeks after surgery I started a 14 … to support 15 … . The exercises I did strengthened the muscles around my ankle and six weeks after my accident I was able to walk without the help of crutches. What a splendid feeling! I was really glad to be back at work!

Teddy consulting hours

Not every indisposition must be treated by a doctor, but when you feel bad and worn-out you should see a doctor and of course when you suffer from an illness. No one likes to go to a doctor, in particular children. Here is one way of releasing anxiety.

'It won't hurt'. That's the usual thing parents tell their children when they have to see a doctor. But does this take away their fear? A child who is ill usually feels weak and frightened and a medical practice is full of special equipment which is even more scary. Dr Christine Poleman is a general practitioner and she does something unusual to take away children's worries and fears. Several times a year children can come to her practice with their 'ill' teddy bear or doll. Lots of 'soft toy parents' come to her and tell her their worries about their favourite toy's illness. This idea was taken up from Sweden. Here it's quite common at hospitals to arrange a 'teddy hospital' three or four times a year and nursery school classes are invited to visit hospital.

Dr Poleman offers teddy consulting hours to her patients' children, 'The teddy bears and dolls suffer from sometimes highly imaginative wounds and illnesses. It's not only headaches, a fever, a sprained ankle or a fractured leg but also the bite of a shark or a bad stomach ache because of a pizza which naughty teddy swallowed in one piece. Some of the dearly beloved soft toys suffer from an acute hair loss or the loss of an eye. These are only some of the illnesses and wounds we have to treat during our consulting hours. After all this time we are now well trained in replacing lost eyes. But that's only one of many things we do. We always take the pulse and the blood pressure first. We also put on bandages, but quite often the patient must have some kind of an injection or we have to take some blood. We do this because most children are afraid of injections and we hope they will get familiar with this kind of treatment.

Everything we do is attentively watched by the children. Then we talk about the diagnosis and a treatment. I always tell the children in simple words what I do and why I have to do it. In this way they get used to the idea of being ill and having to see a doctor. I'm convinced that our teddy consulting hours give children the possibility to swap roles. Here they see what may be happening to them in a medical practice but in a passive role. This will surely take away a lot of fear. Next time the children are patients themselves, they will know what everything looks like, what will happen to them and that 'it won't hurt' or at least not that much.'

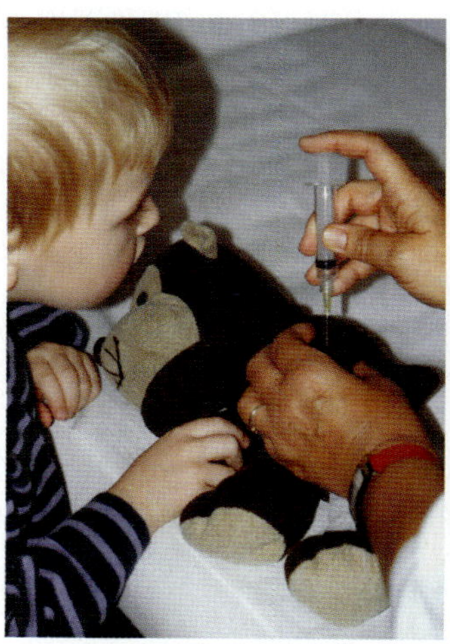

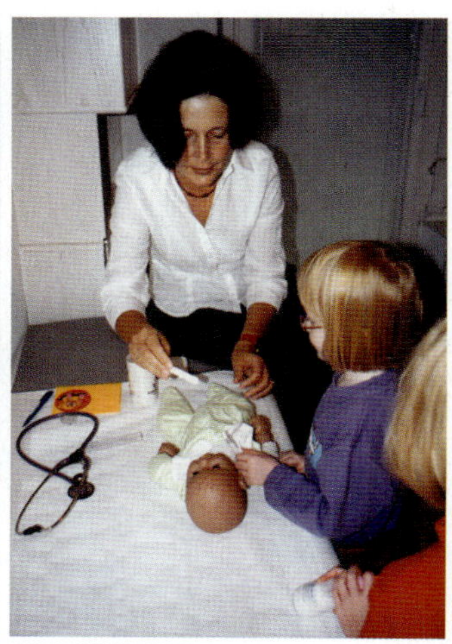

Comprehension

Language

Task 4

Follow the text and find words which belong to these definitions.

a. someone who goes to see a doctor
b. feel extremely exhausted
c. arousing fear
d. organise
e. a disease at point of crisis

Task 5

Here are some common words connected to the work of a doctor. Explain these expressions in your own words.

a. general practitioner
b. practice
c. consulting hours
d. diagnosis
e. treatment

Task 6

Because of her experience with her teddy consulting hours Christine Poleman comes to the following conclusions. Can you find reasons and examples in the text which back up her point of view?

a. Teddy consulting hours take away children's fears of doctors.
b. It's the best way to make children familiar with a doctor's practice and the typical medical treatment.
c. Teddy consulting hours improve the communication between doctors and children. They can both learn how to speak to each other and be understood.

Activity

Task 7

Imagine you are doing your placement in a nursery school. One of your group children suffers from different kinds of allergies and has to see a doctor quite often or even sometimes stay in a hospital. Every morning you sit in a circle with your children and you talk. Tony, the boy with the allergies, tells the other children about his visit to a doctor. Since the other children seem to be very interested in his story, you think of organising a visit to Dr Christine Poleman's teddy consulting hours. But first you have to talk to the parents and ask them for permission.

a. Prepare your speech to the parents. Give your speech in class. Don't read it out.
b. As a listener take over the role of the parent and say whether the speech was convincing or not. Give reasons.

Listening

Task 8

One morning Mrs Johnson wakes up her son Clive, 5 years, to get ready for nursery school. But Clive does not want to get up. That's quite unusual for him, because normally he loves to go to nursery school. He looks very pale and he has a fever. At breakfast he first refuses to eat and then only eats a bit of bread with butter. That's unusual again, since Clive is a good eater. All these things worry Mrs Johnson, so she decides to see a doctor right away.

Listen to the dialogue at the doctor's practice and try to fill in the gaps of these sentences with the missing words. Before listening look at the vocabulary help on page 243.

a. Clive has already got a 1 … because his finger had to be stitched in summer.
b. The assistant asks Mrs Johnson to sit down in the 2 … .
c. Clive says his head is 3 … .
d. In the morning Mrs Johnson took his 4 … which was 38,5 degrees.
e. The doctor believes Clive has 5 … because of his temperature and his 6 … tongue.
f. But Clive doesn't have a 7 … , yet.
g. The doctor prescribes some 8 … , which he has to take in the morning and early evening and some 9 … medicine for his temperature.

Grammar

Talking about accidents or illnesses someone has to suffer from, you will have to make use of the passive voice quite often.

For Example:

In case of a serious infection antibiotics are prescribed.
His fractured fingers were fixed with a plaster.
Tina was transferred to a specialist.

Passive Voice – das Passiv

<table>
<tr><td rowspan="2">Bildung</td><td colspan="2">Das Passiv wird mit einer Form von „be" und der 3. Form des Verbs (=past participle) gebildet. Von wem die Handlung ausgeführt wird, kann mit „by" angehängt werden. Da der Ausführende im Passiv jedoch in den Hintergrund rückt, wird der „by-agent" nur angehängt, wenn dies als sinnvoll erscheint.</td></tr>
<tr><td>Present Tense
am/is/are + 3. Form des Verbs</td><td>Past Tense
was/were + 3. Form des Verbs</td></tr>
</table>

Umwandlung eines Aktiv-Satzes in einen Passiv-Satz:

An ambulance	*takes*	*John*	*to hospital.*	*(aktiv)*
Subject	Verb	Object		

John	*is taken*	*to hospital*	*by an ambulance.*	*(passiv)*
Subject	Verb		by-agent	

Task 9

Transform these active sentences into passive sentences. Take the word in italics as the subject of your passive sentence and decide whether it makes sense to add a by-agent or not.

Example:

They show *the new nurse* around the ward.
***The new nurse* is shown around the ward.**

a. After his accident a lot of people visited *John* in hospital.
b. Two years ago Peter had a heart attack. Now doctors give *him* a check up every year.
c. Wrong eating habits cause *a lot of illnesses*.
d. Usually after a fracture people start *physiotherapy* to support convalescence.
e. After six weeks in hospital they transferred *my father* to a rehabilitation centre.
f. Today an appendectomy is a routine operation and people can leave the *hospital* after a week.
g. Some years ago, it was a serious operation and they did not discharge *people* that early.

Translation

Task 10

Translate the following sentences into English. Exchange your results with your partner.

a. Jedes Jahr werden Patientenkinder zu einer Teddybären-Sprechstunde eingeladen.
b. Mit Teddybären-Sprechstunden wird den Kindern ihre Angst vor dem Arzt genommen.
c. Alles wird von den Kindern genau beobachtet.

Surviving cancer and the importance of regular medical check-ups

To avoid severe or chronic diseases it is important to do something for prevention. Especially when people pass a certain age, cancer prevention becomes very important. Here is an example of someone who survived cancer.

Case Study

Shortly after her 36th birthday Tania Weathers had never felt better. She was full of energy and her smile was radiant because half a year before she had given birth to a boy. She was the happiest woman in the world.
So when she felt a small lump in her right breast as she showered one morning, she was not really worried. She considered herself to be in good health and assumed it was just a natural and harmless change in her body because she was a nursing mother.
But when she told her mother Louise about the lump two weeks after first noticing it, her mother did not react calmly but insisted to have it checked out.

Without her mother Tania might have paid a terrible price for ignoring what her body was telling her. Less than two weeks after that conversation with her mother, Tania and her husband David sat in a cancer specialist's practice and they were informed that she had breast cancer.

In a six-hour operation doctors removed Tania's breast and lymph nodes, which were, thankfully, clear of cancer. Since Tania acted quickly and after her early detection the cancer was not wide-spread. To further improve her chances of survival Tania decided to have chemotherapy.

Today, six years after that morning when she first felt the lump in her breast, Tania can look back positively at her experience. Cancer may not be a death sentence: if detected early, the survival rate can be as high as 85 to 90 %.

More than 30 000 women a year are diagnosed with breast cancer in Britain. It is the most common cause of deaths in women aged 35 to 54. Health authorities and gynaecologists distribute informative brochures about cancer in which they ask women to have regular medical check-ups and mammography if they belong in one of the age groups which run a high risk of cancer. Specialists point out that women do have a chance to survive breast cancer and go on to lead full lives. A key element to improving the chances of survival is early detection. No woman should ignore a lump, even if the chances of it being cancerous are very low.

Comprehension

Task 11

Exchange one word in each sentence to transform these false statements into true statements.

a. Shortly before her 36th birthday Tania Weathers felt a small lump in her breast.
b. Tania believed herself to be in bad health.
c. She presumed that this lump was harmful.
d. Tania's lymph nodes were already affected by cancer.
e. Tania started a chemotherapy to reduce her chances of survival.
f. Cancer surely is a death sentence.
g. Women aged 35 to 54 run a low risk of cancer.

Task 12

Now answer the following questions.

a. What might have been the reasons why Tania wasn't worried when she felt a lump in her right breast?
b. How did Tania combat cancer?
c. Cancer may not be a death sentence, if... ? How would you finish this sentence? Give some advice to women on how to prevent cancer.

Activity

Task 13

Imagine Tania reads her daily newspaper. An article about a woman who was able to survive cancer and some letters to the editor on this topic arouse her interest. There is one letter which Tania spontaneously decides to answer. Take over Tania's role and write an answer to the following letter.

I think most women are much too worried about cancer. I'm 36 and I feel just fine. I love my job, I have a nice and loving husband and lots of friends. I lead a happy life, so why should I be worried about cancer? I think as long as you lead a full life, nothing can really happen. Most of those people who suffer from cancer have some kind of family or personality problem and are deeply dissatisfied with their life. I'm not. I'm happy, strong and healthy, so there is no need to spend my time sitting in the waiting room of a medical practice. I believe, if you spend too much time with thinking about illness and prevention and see a doctor too often, he or she will surely find something!

Angela from Brighton

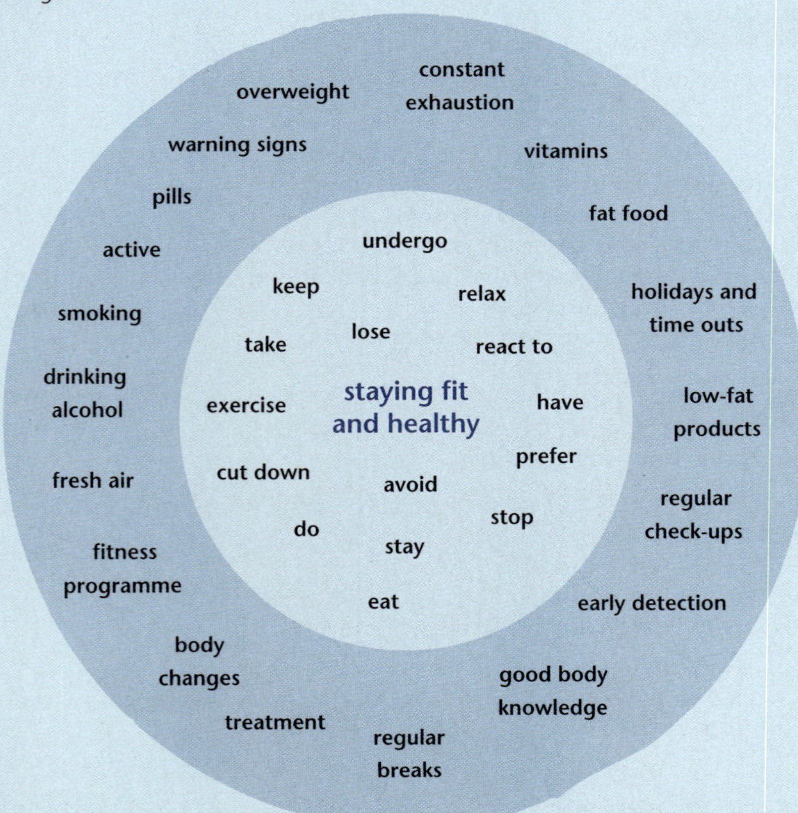

Task 14

What can someone do to stay fit and healthy?

Look at the two circles on the left for three minutes. They may give you some idea of how to answer this question. Then close your book and talk about this topic as long as possible.

Task 15

Imagine you are asked to make a presentation on the topic: 'How can we stay fit and healthy?' Considering all the different aspects of illness and staying healthy you learnt about in this module, what would you like to tell your audience and how do you want to present your results? Work through the skills training box on presentation and prepare your presentation.

Skills Training

Presentation

What makes a good presentation?

Visuals are always important. Each presentation should be supported with visuals. Mainly visuals should be used to give an overview of the topic and your main results. So only take down your most important points or headlines! And make sure your visuals go with your presentation – they should not give information before you've mentioned it or present information you talked about some minutes ago!

There is one exception: handouts and flyposters can contain some more information. They usually function as a summary of the whole presentation. Therefore some people offer handouts to their audience at the end of their presentation.

Some possible visuals which you can use to follow your presentation are: overhead-transparency, flip chart, poster, handout, flyposter, computer-presentation such as power point presentations

How to become a good presenter - some basic rules

- **Be well prepared!**
  Take down keynotes (no full sentences) perhaps on little cards as a reminder. Those who are very nervous can take down the opening sentences of their presentation. This will help to have a good start.
- **Don't waste time!**
  Know exactly how you want to start and name your topic clearly. Don't start with long and boring introductions without saying what your main topic is.
- **Talk to your audience!**
  Keep eye-contact and always remember that you want to speak to your audience, not to yourself.

- **Use short and simple language!**
  It's important that your audience understands what you are talking about.
- **Take your time!**
  Don't rush through your presentation. Pause when you need to. For example: if you make a very important point, give some time to your audience to understand.
- **Use visuals!**
  A good visual presents the most important information at first glance, so don't take down long sentences or text passages which are difficult to read through. Try to design your visuals in such a way that they catch your audience's attention. Don't hurry! Show your visual and give people a chance to look at it. Sometimes it's helpful to point to those headlines you are talking about.
- **Speak freely and clearly!**
  Don't read out your handout, that sounds boring. Use your voice for highlighting important facts. Besides use your body language. People who don't move or don't show any mimics are going to lose their listener's attention.
- **Welcome questions**
  Show interest in your audience and answer questions in a friendly way.

Helpful phrases: Presentation

I/We would like to tell you something about …	Ich/ Wir würde(n) Ihnen/euch gerne etwas über … erzählen.
I/We want to give you a short presentation about …	Ich/Wir möchte(n) eine kurze Präsentation über … halten.
I/We have chosen this topic because …	Ich/Wir habe(n) dieses Thema gewählt, weil …
I have worked on this topic in a group with …/ my partner(s) is/ are …	Ich habe zu diesem Thema in einer Gruppe mit … gearbeitet/ mein(e) Partner ist/ sind …
… That is why I/ we like to tell you more about …	… Dies ist, warum ich/wir Ihnen/ euch mehr über … erzählen möchten.
… That is why I/ we chose the topic for my/ our presentation.	… Dies ist, warum ich/ wir dieses Thema für meine/ unsere Präsentation gewählt habe(n).
Did you know that …/why …?	Wussten Sie, dass.../ warum …?
In my/ our presentation I/ we will give you an answer on the question …	In meiner/ unserer Präsentation werde ich/ wir Ihnen/ euch eine Antwort auf die Frage … geben.
In my/ our presentation you will find out about …	In meiner/ unserer Präsentation werden Sie/ ihr etwas über … erfahren.
Pay attention!	Passen Sie auf! / Passe auf!
Maybe take some notes during my/our presentation.	Vielleicht sollten Sie/ solltest du während der Präsentation Notizen machen.
All important facts will be visualized on transparencies/ with the help of a Power Point presentation.	Alle wichtigen Fakten werden auf Folie/ mit der Hilfe einer Power Point Präsentation visualisiert.

Let me begin by explaining why …/ how …	Lassen Sie mich/ Lasst mich damit anfangen zu erläutern, warum …/ wie …
Now (person) will talk about …	Nun wird (Name) über … sprechen.
Let's now move to …	Lassen Sie uns/ Lasst uns nun weiter gehen zu…
Another aspect is that …	Ein andere Aspekt ist, dass …
One can say that …	Man kann sagen, dass …
I have read that …	Ich habe gelesen, dass …
Hardly anyone knows that …	Kaum einer weiß, dass …
In the end of the presentation you will have the chance to ask questions.	Am Ende der Präsentation werden Sie/ ihr die Möglichkeit haben, Fragen zu stellen.
I/We prepared a paper for you with the most important facts …	Ich/ Wir habe(n) ein „Handout" (eine Zusammenstellung) mit den wichtigsten Fakten für Sie/euch vorbereitet.
Next I/we will present you some facts on (topic).	Als nächstes werde ich/ wir einige Fakten präsentieren zu/zum (Thema).
As you see on the transparency…	Wie man auf der Folie sieht …
The next transparency shows …	Die nächste Folie zeigt …
The chart shows that …	Die Statistik zeigt, dass …
The following picture shows that …	Das folgende Bild zeigt, dass.
Look at these pictures/ charts. They will speak for themselves.	Schauen Sie/ schaut auf diese Bilder/Statistiken. Sie sprechen für sich selber.
I think the picture/ chart perfectly shows that …	Ich denke, das Bild/ die Statistik zeigt sehr gut, dass …
This chart proves that …	Diese Statistik beweist, dass …
With regard to the topic it is interesting to know that …	Mit Blick auf das Thema ist es interessant zu wissen, dass …
It was not easy to …	Es war nicht leicht …
There were some problems with …	Es gab Probleme mit …
Thank you for listening!	Vielen Dank für das Zuhören!
Are there any questions left over?	Sind Fragen offen geblieben?
Don't hesitate to ask questions.	Zögern Sie/ zögert nicht, Fragen zu stellen.

Module 2: Being fatally ill

Studies clearly show that the majority of terminally ill people would prefer to die at home. But statistics still draw another picture. The British NHS System (=National Health System) wants to improve and provide more money for hospices which are mostly private and home care. The care for the dying should change in a way that terminally ill patients have the choice where they wish to die, in hospital, a hospice or at home. Specially trained nursing teams are able to give care to those who wish to die at home, surrounded by their loved ones. But it's still hard for patients, nurses and doctors to talk about the planning for death. Medical staff are to be trained in how to broach the delicate subject of a patient's prognosis. Teresa Tate reports about her feelings and experience on this topic.

Case Study – We need to be frank and honest: The doctor

Teresa Tate has an 18-year-experience in treating terminally ill people and telling patients the worst:

Teresa: Some people walk into the room and say that they don't want to hear any bad news about how long is left. We have to wait until that person comes around and is brave enough to ask the questions and we can make the appropriate arrangements. There may be reasons why it is impractical to send people home even if they wish it – for example, if they have only an elderly partner who might not be able to cope.

Predicting when patients will die can be difficult, but both symptoms and doctor's intuition play a part. Doctors and experienced nurses are relatively good picking up the clinical signs when someone is entering the last phase of life.

From my own experience in sending people home, most patients who can have access to 24-hour-nursing feel very comfortable discussing the options of dying at home, but we have to inform them early enough that they are beginning to die. In hospital we do not give dying patients the opportunity to say 'actually, I'd rather not be here', and often if we do not ask, they do not say anything. It is much better to have the conversation about what might happen before they enter the terminal phase of their illness, when they can consider things rationally, think about and record their wishes. We need to be frank and honest!

Place of death
Where people want to die

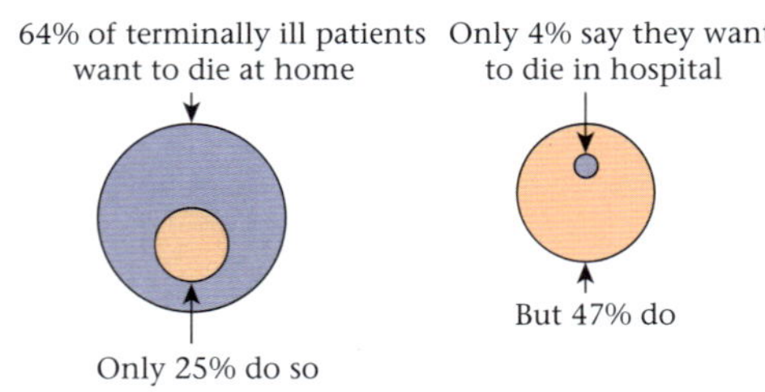

Example London; Where people die ....

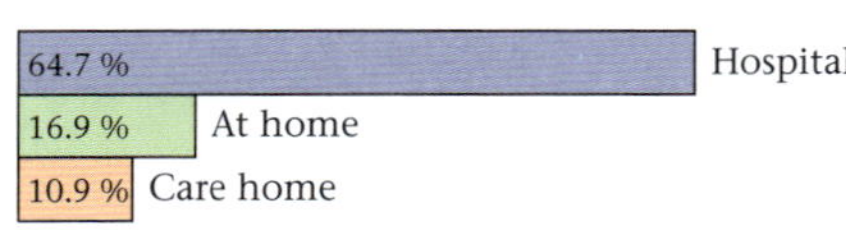

National comparisons
Deaths in hospital

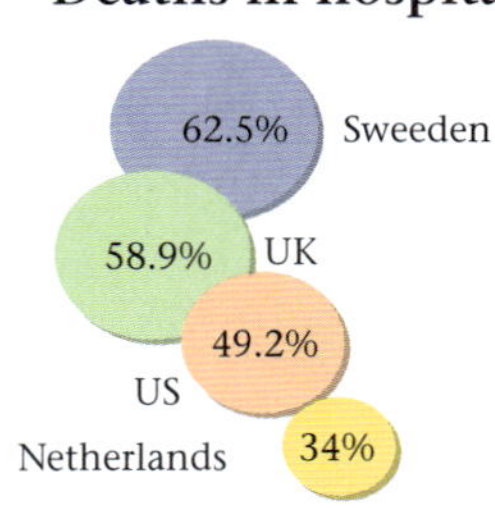

Adapted from 'The Times', 07.07.2008 (statistics)

Comprehension

Language

Task 1

Read through the text again and find words which fit these definitions. You can follow the order of the text to find them.

a. having a fatal disease
b. a place where e.g. terminal cancer patients can stay until they die
c. people who e.g. work in a hospital or nursing service
d. start talking about a certain topic

e. proving to be bad or wrong
f. here: symptoms that show you that someone is going to die

Task 2

Have a close look at the statistics and compare them. Where do people want to die and where do they actually die? Talk about your findings with your partner before you present them in class.

Task 3

Look at Teresa Tate's report and try to find reasons...

a. why it can be hard to tell terminally ill people that they are going to die soon.
b. why a lot of people still die in hospital.
c. How does Teresa Tate want to deal with terminally ill patients?

Case Study – Stating my wishes is liberating: The patient

Doreen Horton, 62, was used to encountering the onset of death in her former career as a nurse caring for terminally ill patients. But after an incurable cancer she has had to make her own preparations for future care:

Doreen: I haven't been given the prognosis but there may not be much time left. It's just a matter of when, not if. I'm realistic about the future and I've written a will with my lawyer, a living will about who should care for me, an advance directive that states I do not want to be resuscitated and another statement that hopefully explains my preferences. I will give this to my doctor and cancer specialist.

I wish to die in a hospice rather than at home because of the burden it could place on my husband, Bernard, 65. We have a son but he lives in Australia so because of that, when the time comes, I think I'd want to be somewhere to minimise the problems and fuss.
I'm not frightened of dying but I'm a woman of 62 and feel like I should have lots of time left. No one wants to die, but being given the chance to perhaps read about the options and then be invited for a discussion could make the end of life that much easier – for the patient and the patient's family. Everyone has to accept that the time comes, sooner or later. But bizarrely it has been liberating to be able to think about this and express wishes properly. I feel like everything is all arranged and I'm free to enjoy life; collecting memories, seeing friends and taking each day as it comes.

Comprehension

Task 4

Work on the following questions.

a. Describe Doreen Horton's situation.
b. What arrangements did she make in view of her death?
c. Explain why she prefers to die in a hospice.
d. Why does Doreen Horton think that it is much better to know about her coming death?

A visit at a hospice

You can't directly drive to the clinic. It's an old but freshly made up villa which is surrounded by a small park. While I was walking through it, I was somehow puzzled how green the grass is and how colourful the flowers are. There is a lake with some ducks. A peaceful atmosphere is lying on everything out here. Again I was astonished, because on that day there were some little ducks. But why was I astonished? Perhaps it's difficult to understand that there can be something so very young and lively around here. I visited my best friend Mabel. She is only 37, but she is going to die. Mabel is lying in Saint Barbara's Hospice.

When I came to the terrace of the house, there were two sick-beds standing outside in the midday sun under a sunshade. It's unusual. In a hospital sick-beds are only taken out of the hospital room for treatment but not to lie in the sun. Both patients seemed to be asleep. I threw a short glance at one patient's face and it had a calm and happy expression. Why not take sick people out? It's pleasant outside in the sun. 'Fresh air is good for your health', came into my mind. I winced when I realised that those patients won't recover. They are going to die.

Crossing the terrace someone called after me. 'Who are you looking for?' It was a nurse. 'My friend Mabel Harris.' – 'She's in her room. Do you know the way?' – 'Yes, I was here at the beginning of the week.' – 'You will find your way then. Dr Jennings and Dr Michaels are with her.' – 'Oh, I better stay outside then.' – 'Oh, no, just step in, all doors are open.' I suddenly understood the difference. In a hospice no one needs to hide the truth, it's so very clear and everyone here seems to have accepted it.

'This openness takes away a lot of stress', Mabel told me on Monday. 'We all know what is going to happen. Nothing to lie about.' In a brochure of Saint Barbara's Hospice which was lying on her desk, I read: 'Our task is to do everything so that our patients feel comfortable and free of pain. We want to give them a chance to take leave of their life, family and friends in a human and peaceful way. And of course, their relatives and friends should have the same chance.'

One way of managing this is to allow visitors and above all relatives to come and go whenever they like. There are extra beds in the patient's room and some extra-rooms for relatives to stay close to the dying patient. Everyone is given a chance to say goodbye and to stay with the patient holding her or his hand when time has come. Those patients who come here know their end is near and they need a medical care which they can't manage alone at home.

When I entered Mabel's room her husband and both doctors were sitting around her bed. From my hospital stay I remember doctors standing in front of my bed only for a short time during their daily round. Again there is a difference, but perhaps it was just because I only had an appendectomy. I stepped in and Mabel gave me a short smile, her husband and the doctors nodded at me. They were talking about some stronger drugs which take away her pain but also about its influence on her mind. The drug will take away her pain for some time but it will have a mind-numbing side effect. Does she want that? No, not yet, she wants to talk some things over with her husband and see her children. But then, when time has come and pain becomes unbearable, she wants to take it.

Comprehension

Task 5

Answer the questions on the text.

a. Explain what a hospice is.
b. Why do you think the speaker of the text is astonished when he or she walks through the park of Saint Barbara's Hospice?
c. What 'unusual' things and differences to a 'normal' hospital does the speaker mention and realise?
d. Mabel says that the 'openness' in a hospice takes away a lot of stress. What 'openness' does she mean? Why can this take away stress? Explain.

Discussion

Task 6

Do you believe that a hospice like Saint Barbara's Hospice gives patients a chance to take their leave of life in a human way? Give reasons for your opinion.

Grammar

Web

The speaker of the text uses Past Tense Simple and Past Tense Continuous.

Example:

While I was walking through it, I was somehow puzzled how green the grass was.

When I entered Mable's room, her husband and both doctors were sitting around her bed.

Past Tense Continuous

Bildung	was/were + 1. Verbform + 'ing'
Anwendung	– Die Verlaufsform betont den Ablauf bzw. die Dauer einer Handlung bzw. kennzeichnet Handlungen, die zu einem bestimmten Zeitpunkt in der Vergangenheit bereits „im Gange" waren. – Im Vergleich zur Past Tense Simple werden mit der Verlaufsform Handlungen gekennzeichnet, die bereits „im Gange waren" als eine andere Handlung „neu" einsetzte (= Simple Past). – Signalwörter: when, while

Make sure you know when to use the Past Tense Continuous form and work on the following sentences.

Task 7

Fill in Past Tense Simple or Past Tense Continuous.

a. While doctors (send) Mr Johnson to have an x-ray, his wife (wait) in the waiting room.
b. Some weeks ago an old lady (cross) the street, when suddenly a car (come) around the corner and (hit) her.
c. While she (lie) on the street, someone (call) the ambulance.
d. I (want) to make a doctor's appointment yesterday, but each time I (phone) the number I (not get) through because someone (speak) all the time.
e. While Mrs Hardy (stay) in hospital, some of her neighbours (come) to visit her.

Audio

Module 3: Having special needs

This is who I am

'My right arm does a lot of crazy stuff. Like the other day, I thought someone had stolen my wallet.' This is a joke but it's funny only if you know that the comedian Mr Blue has cerebral palsy. Blue won a comedian television contest with jokes like this one which shows that nowadays something has changed in society's attitude towards people with a disability.
The public image of people with disabilities has often hinged on the heroic or the tragic side of the story. Parents of children with a disability were praised for their engagement for their child and said to be 'the real heroes of our time' or they were pitied for the tragedy they had to go through. Talking about and depicting disabilities in public were said to be too difficult and unpleasant. So this topic was mostly excluded from public viewing. Fortunately these attitudes are out-dated. Mr Blue represents the broader portrait of disability in television, film and the print media. This new, sometimes confrontational depiction reflects a wide acceptance but also a higher expectation of many members of the disabled population to be treated as people who happen to have a disability rather than people defined by their disability. More people are saying, 'This is who I am. If you have a problem with it, that's your problem.'
Lawrence Carter-Long who is working for the Disabilities Network in New York City says, 'The frank depiction of disabilities in the media goes hand in hand with a change in people's minds. For example, more and more prosthetic patients show their legs or arms openly and more and more people say 'that's really cool!'. Ms. Haddad, whose right leg

was amputated below the knee after a car accident, says she has no problem wearing shorts when she goes shopping. Neither does she shy from removing the prosthesis to swim at the swimming pool. She says that sometimes people stare and there were a few who tapped her on the shoulder to ask her to put her leg back on telling her 'It is upsetting my child'. But she ignores such incidents and still refuses to hide. 'You either accept me as I am', she says, 'or you don't have to look at it'.

There is a change in the language usage as well. Words like, for example, 'the invalid', 'the disabled', 'the blind', 'the handicapped'... should be avoided because they discriminate against those who live with a disability. You can easily be negative in your language. Always think of the individual and their personality first, not of their impairment. So it's better to say 'the disabled person' or 'the blind person'. Don't use the word handicap because it comes from the image of a person begging for help, their cap in hand. Talk about 'people with a special need', this treats people with a disability as equal partners. Everyone has some kind of a need, don't you have one as well?

based on: Embracing the difference, in: The New York Times, 21.05.2007

Comprehension

Task 1

Look at the photo on page 162. With your partner, talk about the situation and the idea of disability it wants to come up with. Present your opinion in class.

Task 2

Describe the changing attitudes towards disability the text talks about.

a. How did the attitude of TV, film and the print media change?
b. How did people's minds change? Think of the statement 'This is who I am. If you have a problem with it, that's your problem.'
c. How did the language usage change?

Discussion/Writing

Task 3

Choose one of the following statements and comment on it. You may prepare a talk in class or write a comment of about 100 words.

Here are some questions which might help you to write your comment: What does the statement want to express? Do you agree with it or do you reject it? Why?

a. To pity someone for a special need is an act of discrimination.
b. Children should be kept away from disabilities like an amputated leg as long as possible, it's too shocking for them.
c. It's good to promote all kinds of shared education projects. Inclusion helps to accept disability as one aspect of someone's personality.
   Look at the next page. Here you will find some information about what inclusion means.

Inclusion

Today 'inclusion' is the word which tries to summarise the aim of shared education projects. The word 'inclusion' wants to refer to a universal human right, offering all people, irrespective of race, gender or special needs, equal access and opportunities. This idea is seen as a chance to get rid of discrimination and intolerance. With regard to educational programmes it means that children and students with special needs are placed in the same regular classrooms as able-bodied children, providing all children the opportunity to learn from and tolerate each other. Children with disabilities follow the same lessons as non-disabled, thus encouraging friendship and understanding in both groups. Students with disabilities can receive their education and job training in regular classes and environments when appropriate. They are placed in the same schools they would attend if they do not have special needs. Individualized educational programmes for every student try to support everyone in developing their individual strength and abilities.

Task 4

All these statements make use of discriminating language. Transform them into positive language.

a. In this nursery school project normal and disabled children join in one group.
b. The traffic lights are combined with a sound for the blind.
c. The equipment of our hotel is especially designed to meet the demands of handicapped people.
d. Our hotel has lifts and ramps for the wheelchair bound.
e. For the deaf we offer a subtitle.
f. Our special training programmes help children who are mentally retarded.

Language

positive words	avoid
people with disabilities/with special needs disabled people	the disabled the handicapped victims, sufferers
impairment	handicap illness, disease
have learning difficulties	mentally handicapped/ retarded
people who use a wheelchair	wheelchair bound
able-bodied non-disabled	normal

Activity

Task 5

Phab is one of many British charity programmes which encourage young people with and without a special need to come together on equal terms, to share experiences and gain some understanding for the other. One way of achieving this is to spend a holiday together in holiday centres in the Lake District or Devon. For this programme you need to be over 16 years old.
Imagine that you decided to apply for the holiday programme. Now you want to convince your classmates to join in. Prepare a talk in class or write a notice for your information board.

Caring for a disabled child alone – bordering on the limits?

Andrea Gallop is 26 years old and she has got an able-bodied daughter, Niomi, aged 5, and her son Adrian, aged 3, who has a birth defect. Here is what she relates about her first year with Adrian.

Case Study

Andrea: Shortly after his birth Adrian was diagnosed as having a disability. He has brain damage and a cleft palate. When I learnt about it only some hours after his birth I was struck by a tremendous blow. I was devastated and so confused that I recall little else from those first days other than the heartbreak I felt. It was like having a knife stuck in my heart. One of the first reactions was denial. 'This cannot be happening to me, to my child'. The next day there was a feeling of guilt. I was totally sure that I caused Adrian's problem. I believed I didn't take enough care when I was pregnant. Because of this feeling of guilt I refused to take any help in caring for Adrian, although doctors told me it would be too much and too complicated for someone not being trained in medical care. Even when someone from social service visited me in hospital to tell me about constructive help I could make use of, I refused again. I don't know why, but despite all these offers, I felt deeply isolated and separated from the outer world and even from my own family. There was only Adrian and me and I was convinced that only I knew what Adrian needed.

After Adrian's stay in hospital I hardly slept. I always had to be around him. Adrian had to be tube-fed because of his cleft palate and there was a constant threat that he could suffocate. During the first months there was a high risk that Adrian wouldn't survive. But because of my care his condition stabilised. I was proud but totally exhausted because of a constant lack of sleep. After a second operation doctors told me I could start feeding Adrian with semi-solid food, because he should learn to swallow. But to teach him how to do it, was hard work. It took hours to feed him because he could only swallow very small portions and there was a constant risk that he could swallow the wrong way and suffocate. I was nervous and exhausted.

My husband, relatives and friends were worried about me and told me how bad I looked. I ignored them. Each time they tried to convince me to put Adrian in a nursing home or at least day care for children with special needs, I reacted even more stubbornly. Finally I avoided any contacts with others. I preferred to stay with Adrian. But I felt a deep exhaustion. Adrian can't eat alone, he can't sit, speak, walk, crawl or even support himself with his hands.

Then suddenly, Adrian's condition worsened. He got an infection and was transferred into hospital. I felt my life breaking apart again, when doctors told me that he needed intensive care because this time his lungs had stopped working alone. Suddenly I started to tremble. It was the beginning of a nervous breakdown. But this time I realised that the care for Adrian had taken all of my energy and nerves.

Because of the intensive care in hospital and later in a nursing home Adrian's condition stabilised again. Now he is in a day care for children with special needs. Here he receives all the care he needs from professional people. After my experiences I know that only a professionally trained carer has the specialised knowledge and medical equipment my child needs. Sure I still feel that I have a very intimate knowledge of my child, but I must admit Adrian makes better progress in his day care.

Comprehension

Task 6

Work on the following questions.

a. Describe the different kinds of feelings Andrea went through when she heard about Adrian's birth defect.
b. How did she react towards the people around her?
c. Why do you think she decided to care for her son alone?
d. What were the difficulties Andrea had to cope with while caring for Adrian? Describe.

Task 7

According to the text all these statements are true. Explain why.

a. Caring for a disabled child alone without the help of a professional carer is more than one can take.
b. Andrea's wish to care for Adrian alone almost destroyed the family and isolated her from the people around her.
c. Caring for Adrian alone was also a high risk for the boy.

Activity

Task 8

Andrea relates that everyone around her was worried but she ignored her family's and friends' warnings. Imagine you are one of her best friends and you tried to talk to her but she didn't want to listen to you. Now you decided to write a letter to her.

Take down this letter.

UNIT 8:
Being addicted

Module 1: Alcohol – a soft drug?

A & E: accident and emergency unit

Task 1

a. First look at the poster and describe what you see.
b. What different aspects and consequences of drinking alcohol does the poster hint at?

Drinking habits

Task 2

Talk about your own drinking habits.

a. Do you drink alcohol? What kind of alcohol?
b. When do you drink alcohol? At weekends? During the week? With friends etc.?
c. Do you believe there are special occasions and events which go hand in hand with drinking alcohol? Which ones?

Task 3

Teenage drinking habits

a. Do you think teenagers prefer some special kind of alcohol?
b. Why do they drink alcohol? Can you think of situations and reasons for teenage drinking?

Drinking until you drop

A weekend barbecue or disco evening with beer, wine or champagne at a birthday party, one or two alcoholic drinks with some colleagues on your way home – these are just normal every day situations. No one at a birthday party or in a pub thinks of the dangers of becoming addicted or of health problems caused by drinking alcohol. Some medical reports seem to support the idea that moderate drinking is good for the heart. They speak of three glasses of wine which help to avoid heart diseases, but they let people forget about the damages it can do to their liver. It's a fact that it only takes ten minutes until more than 50 % of the alcohol will be in your bloodstream. If you keep on drinking, your speech becomes slurred, vision is blurred and you lose your balance. Heavy drinking may also cause a loss of memory. Dependence upon alcohol damages your liver, reduces your mental ability and may lead to cancer and strokes.

Despite all these dangers there is an alarming rise in drinking alcohol among teenagers and young professional women. Karen Hunter, 27, who works in a bank says, 'I live in London, a high-powered city, and I have a stressful job – drinking is a way to release tension for me.' Donna Barry, a 31-year-old single parent admits, 'At weekends I sometimes drink until I drop. I don't think it's too bad for my health because through the week I only drink water and Coke light. But once a week I have to enjoy myself. I need to get out.'

Dr John Raynor, who is the head of a clinic for alcoholics, points out that this kind of weekend drinking culture is dangerous. Drinking the full week's quota in one night is extremely harmful.

Even among teenagers having fun seems to go hand in hand with drinking high amounts of alcohol. By the time they reach their 16th birthday the vast majority of British youngsters have experimented with alcohol. Three quarters have been drunk. Binge drinking is on the increase. Often excessive drinking leads to conflicts with the law. High levels of alcohol in your blood may contribute to violence and anti-social behaviour. Police report that the number of late-night vandalising, rampage or fights of drunken teenagers is also rising. Young people usually start experimenting with alcohol and cigarettes, which is in some way quite normal. It's every parent's nightmare that their child is going to get involved with drugs. Rosie Bocklehunt, director of a drug and alcohol charity, tells parents to react quickly if their teenage child turns up drunk after a weekend party or disco more than once. She warns, 'for those who drink and smoke regularly or have even tried cannabis it's no big step to move on to hard drugs. Parents should not forget that alcohol leads to addiction as well. It's a problem that alcohol is still more socially accepted than drug taking, but it can be just as dangerous.'

How much alcohol is good for your body?

Over the years the recommended levels of alcohol have varied between 14 and 21 units a week for women and 21 to 28 units for men. One unit equals half a pint (= about 280 ml) of beer, one small glass of wine or one measure of spirit. But today a lot of medical reports say that this recommended quota is much too high. They advise to drink only very limited amounts of alcohol or much better no alcohol at all!

Language

Task 4

Find words or phrases in the text which are similar in meaning to the following words and phrases.

a. something very normal or usual
b. people you work with
c. to depend on
d. limited, not excessively
e. addiction to e. g. alcohol
f. find a way to relax from stress
g. dangerous/damaging health
h. drinking excessively until you drop

Comprehension

Task 5

Discuss the following questions with your partner before you talk about your answers in class.

a. John Barton works in a bank. Quite often there are weeks with a lot of stress. Then John drinks two or sometimes three pints of beer in a pub on his way home to find some relaxation after work. At weekends he likes to meet friends in a pub on Friday and Saturday evening. Each time he comes home drunk.
   1. According to what you learnt from the text, is what John does okay or wrong? Say why.
   2. What do you think about the common habit to find some release through alcohol?
b. Can you explain why excessive drinking often ends in a conflict with the law?
c. Why is there a high risk for those who are used to smoking and drinking to become dependent on hard drugs?

Discussion

Task 6

In lines 40–41 Rosie Bocklehurst says that 'it's a problem that alcohol is still more socially accepted than drug taking, but it can be just as dangerous'.

a. What does she mean? What kind of situations does she probably think of?
b. Do you think she is right or wrong? What's your opinion?

Activity

Task 7

Imagine you are working in a youth club. Normally you don't serve alcohol to the youngsters but they keep on asking to be allowed to drink some beer. Now you and your colleagues are discussing to make an exception when there is a party or disco on Saturdays. Some of you think of allowing 16-year-olds to drink at least two bottles of beer.

a. Go through the text again and sort out the most important facts which you believe could help you to find a decision. Prepare a flip chart poster.
b. One of your colleagues believes that most articles which talk about the dangers of alcohol overdo their warning. Try to convince your colleague that there are dangers in drinking alcohol.
c. After considering the different aspects, what would you suggest to your colleagues? Should the youngsters be allowed to drink two bottles of beer? Present your statement in class.
d. Imagine you decided not to serve any alcohol. How could the discussion with the teenagers of your youth club look like? How would you justify your attitude towards the teenagers? How might the teenagers react? Choose either the role of a teenager or a social worker and carry out a role play in class. Perhaps divide your class into four to six groups and prepare the social worker's or teenager's point of view by taking down some keywords before you start your discussion. Try to keep up the discussion for about 15 to 20 minutes!

Writing

Task 8

Imagine that you are the parent of a teenage girl or boy. You know that the supermarket in your neighbourhood sells soft alcohol like beer and beer-lemonade mixtures or breezers like lemonade mixtures with rum, vodka or tequila to teenagers. This makes you angry and you decide to write an open letter of protest. Write this letter.

What are the reasons for teenage drinking?

Britain's teenagers are among the heaviest drinkers and drug users in Europe, research has found.

Studies show that binge drinking is a growing problem in city centres in the UK. They point out that about 1.9 million binge drinking 'events' take place across the country each week. A frightening fact is that girls are drinking till they drop more than boys – 21 percent of girls and 18.8 percent of boys. Young people are turning away from softer drinks, such as beer or lemonade-alcohol mixtures to hard spirits like pure vodka and tequila.

Paul Omerod, one of the leading scientists says, 'Vomiting, collapsing in the street, shouting and chanting loudly, intimidating passers-by and fighting, children turning up in hospital because of excessive drinking are now regular night-time features of many British towns and cities.' Astonishingly the problem of excessive drinking now seems worst among girls. But why has this behaviour spread so rapidly? Researcher Professor Martin Plant points out: 'One of the biggest problems is that most young people who drink excessively think they are completely invunerable. They don't have any concept that there is a real health risk.'
Professor Plant says, many parents do not know where their teenage children go to in their spare time and do not try to impose any kind of restrictions on their behaviour. 'I know raising teenagers can be extremely tough, but my impression is that most British parents have just given up trying.'
Today teenagers have more money than in the past and they also have a greater choice of establishments in which they are easily served drinks. During the last years a lot of large 'drinking establishments' have opened their doors especially designed for young people who feel 'chic' while sitting there drinking. 'Happy hours' or 'all you can drink' offers in pubs and discos make people drink more than they can take. In addition, alcohol measures have increased in size. 'Low pricing and missing age controls make it easy for unscrupulous retailers to sell alcohol to underage kids', Martin Plant adds.
Paul Omerod has another idea. He thinks people, especially teenagers, like to follow certain behavioural patterns. It is striking that people with weight problems very often have overweight friends or a girl stops smoking because her friend stopped some weeks ago. To find out he asked 504 18–24 year-olds about their drinking patterns and those of their friends. 54% of binge drinkers think that 'all' or 'almost all' of their friends are binge drinkers and only 3% of binge drinkers have 'no' or 'hardly any' friends that binge drink.
The British government announced a number of measures to curb the alcohol intake. Among those are tougher controls of pubs and supermarkets, high fines for selling drink to under-18s, an information campaign on the dangers of drug use. Alcohol manufacturers will also be urged to include warnings on their products to encourage sensible drinking. As a consequence the advertisement for alcoholic drinks is seen as being 'irresponsible' and more and more people demand a general ban.

Adapted from Ormerod, Paul/Wiltshire, Greg: 'Binge' drinking in the UK: a social network phenomenon, june 2008, University of Durham, http://arxiv.org/ftp/arxiv/papers/0806/0806.3176.pdf [20.02.2013], Statistical figures taken from: CBS Interactive Network, 2012

Comprehension

Task 9

Are the following statements true or false? Give examples from the text which show that the statement is true or false.

a. Great Britain is one of the leading countries in Europe with regard to alcohol consumption.
b. Boys drink a lot more than girls.

c. Beer is still the most favourite drink in Britain.
d. Although British teenagers are heavy drinkers, collapsing teenagers who must be treated in hospital are still an exception.
e. Binge drinkers most often have friends who also drink excessively.
f. Most teenagers know about the health risk binge drinking has.

Task 10

Pick up the following keywords and explain why they represent a reason for teenage drinking.

no concept of health risk	lack of parental control	higher spending power	drinking establishments
happy hours and all-you-can-drink-offers	increase of alcohol measures	unscrupulous retailers	behavioural patterns

Task 11

Answer the following questions.

a. What are the consequences of binge drinking according to the text? Describe them.
b. Can you think of further consequences?
c. How does the British government try to reduce Britain's alcohol and drug abuse?
d. Which of the measures do you think has a chance to be successful? Why?

Underage drinking in cartoons

Task 12

Look at the cartoon description and fill in the gaps with the words from the box below.

pouring off – drunk – alcohol – party night – bottle of wine – skull – liquid – tossed over

www.CartoonStock.com

The cartoon shows a bottle which is lying on the floor. This could be a bottle with hard **1.** ... or maybe a **2.** ... . You could also imagine that this is the scene after a rough **3.** ... because the bottle is **4.** ... and seems to be left behind on the floor.
Maybe someone was too **5.** ... to pick it from the floor? There is still some **6.** ... in the bottle but the bottle top is missing. You can see that there is some of the alcohol **7.** ... from the neck of the bottle. But there is something striking about it. The drop which is running out of the bottle looks like a **8.** ... .

Task 13

A cartoon analysis always ends with its message. What does the cartoonist want to bring forward to us? Discuss with your partner the message of the cartoon and pick out one of the sentences below to take down your proposal. Present your message in class for discussion.

Helpful phrases: Expressing a cartoon message

I think with this cartoon the drawer wants to warn teenagers about … .
The cartoon arouses our interest/attention in …
With this cartoon the drawer wants to say that … /tell us that …
The cartoon especially addresses teenagers and makes clear to them that …
The cartoonist wants to criticise that …
The cartoon shows that its drawer rejects alcohol drinking/binge drinking at parties because …
The cartoon blames teenagers/us for …
The drawer brings forward to us that …

… because … Don't forget to give reasons!

Task 14

Look at the following three cartoons and discuss these questions. Present your results in class.

a. Which of the cartoons do you like best? Why?
b. Try to say who or what the cartoon wants to blame for underage drinking.
c. Say whether you think the cartoon has a chance to be successful in arousing interest. Give your reasons.

www.CartoonStock.com

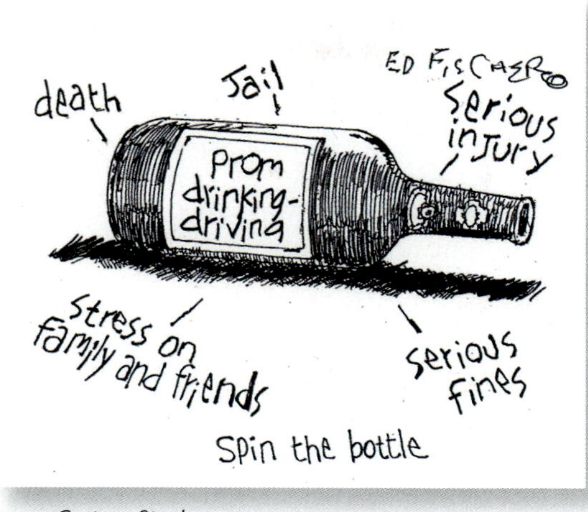

www.CartoonStock.com

prom = big party which takes place at the end of a student's college or high school time in the USA.
spin the bottle = a typical teenage party game, you spin the bottle and the one it points at has to do something or kiss someone

Writing

Task 15

Now choose one of the cartoons and write a full analysis. Use the skills training and helpful phrases boxes below.

Skills Training

Analysing cartoons

Step 1 **First look at the cartoon and make sure that you understand the situation it shows.**
Do you know all the vocabulary to describe the cartoon?

Step 2 **Cartoons usually show a situation which is somehow unrealistic or exaggerated, something that does not really depict reality or fit into a normal everyday situation.**
Is there anything striking or strange? Is there anything which arouses your attention (a so-called eye-catcher)?

Step 3 **Now describe the cartoon's situation but make sure to use the present continuous form. When you describe what you can see in the picture, you describe what is right then happening in the picture. For example, 'Some liquid is running out of the bottle'.**

Step 4 **What do you think is the message?**
What does the drawer/cartoonist want to bring forward with the cartoon? Why does he want to arouse interest with the cartoon? Does the drawer want to criticise a certain situation or attitude people seem to have?

Helpful phrases: Writing a cartoon analysis

The cartoon shows .../depicts ...	Das Cartoon zeigt .../stellt ... dar.
The cartoon shows a scene from ...	Das Cartoon zeigt eine Szene aus ...
In the picture you can see ...	Auf dem Bild sieht man ...
On the left/right there is/are ...	links/ rechts ist/sind ...
In the foreground/background of the picture you can see ...	im Vordergrund/ im Hintergrund des Bildes sieht man ...
In the upper part ...	im oberen Teil
In the lower part ...	im unteren Teil
In the middle ...	in der Mitte
It is striking that ...	Es ist auffallend, dass ...
The scene is unrealistic because ...	Die Szene ist unrealistisch, weil ...
The cartoon draws an exaggerated picture of ... because ...	Das Cartoon stellt ein übertriebenes Bild von ... dar, weil ...
The cartoon gives/arouses the impression that ...	Das Cartoon macht/erweckt den Eindruck, dass ...
The figures in the cartoon look as if ...	Die Figuren auf dem Bild sehen aus, als ob ...
The viewer has the impression that ...	Der Betrachter hat den Eindruck, dass ...
The cartoon shows a typical scene/untypical scene ...	Das Cartoon zeigt eine typische/untypische Szene ...
The most important elements of this picture are ...	Die wichtigsten Elemente des Bildes sind ...
The cartoonist/drawer uses exaggeration to express that ...	Der Cartoonist/Zeichner gebraucht Übertreibung, um damit auszudrücken, dass ...
The picture inspires the viewer to think about ...	Das Bild inspiriert den Betrachter über ... nachzudenken.
It is obvious that the cartoonist criticises/ wants to express that ...	Es ist offensichtlich, dass der Cartoonist kritisieren/ausdrücken möchte, dass ...
What the drawer wants to point out is that ...	Was der Zeichner herausstellen möchte, ist, dass ...
The problem illustrated here is that ...	Das Problem, das hier dargestellt/illustriert wird, ist, dass ...

Also use the helpful phrases box of task 13 to express the cartoon message!

Grammar

which/who

– Which → Bezug auf Dinge/Gegenstände *A breezer is a **drink which** contains lemonade mixed with rum, vodka or tequila.*
– Who → Bezug auf Personen *Those **people who** believe that alcopops are dangerous demand tougher controls in pubs and supermarkets.*

Task 16

Fill in which or who

a. Youngsters ... are younger than 16 aren't allowed to buy alcoholic drinks.
b. Are these orange, blue and red bottles some of these alcopops ... you talked about yesterday?
c. Drinking up to four pints of beer every evening is an alcohol quota ... is far too much and harmful.
d. When police stopped him for control he had an alcohol level ... was just over the limit.
e. Those ... drive a car should abstain from alcohol.
f. Everyone ... knows about a supermarket ... sells alcohol to teenagers should report this to the police.
g. The number of girls ... go on weekend binges is dramatically rising
h. There are more and more pubs or other drinking establishments ... are especially designed for young people ... like to spend an evening with drinking.

Module 2: Hard drugs – being caught in a vicious circle

Case Study: Sarah Hampton – the story of an addict

Sarah's life ended abruptly when she was only 24 years old. She is one of many heroin victims in Glasgow which is a drug capital. Here drugs are killing more young people than any other cause. Social workers in the Scottish city call it 'slaughter by needle'. Sarah's drug career was absolutely 'normal'. She was an alcoholic at 11, a junkie at 15 and finally killed herself with an overdose of heroin at 24.

Sarah grew up in one of Glasgow's council estates on the outskirts of the city. They are no real slum areas but a lot of people who are out of work live there.

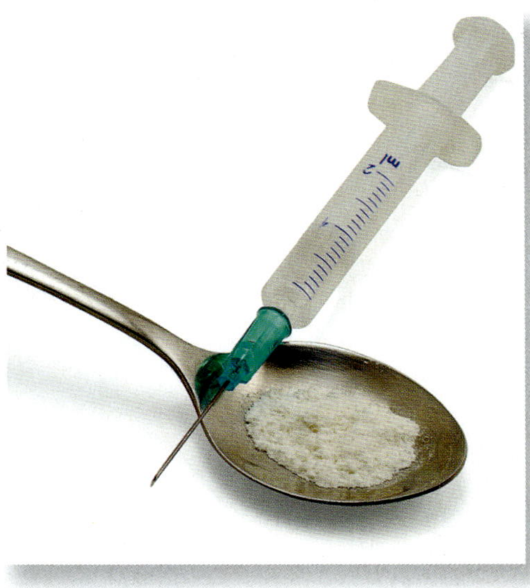

Sarah shared this fate. At 16 she had to leave school with no qualifications after being drunk at school and showing disorderly behaviour. There was no hope for her to find a job and soon she started to hang around and drink heavily, later she turned to drugs.

First Sarah began to steal to finance her alcohol. Later prison for theft, drug-dealing and prostitution followed. She managed to stop drinking and taking drugs for a short time when she found out that she was pregnant. But she didn't manage to stay clean and lost her baby. Finally she had her 'last shot'.

In an interview her mother describes Sarah's history of addiction:v

Sarah was only 11 when she came home drunk from a party. We didn't want to overreact because teenagers, even children, like to have a try. Sometimes at family parties and when we sat in front of the TV we allowed her to have some sparkling wine. We thought if we allowed her to do this under our control, she wouldn't bother to drink more. At 15 and later at 16 she came home from parties drunk and sometimes had a bad hang-over. Still I didn't believe she had a serious problem with alcohol. Every time she told us it was only by accident and it would never happen again. I wanted to trust her and I didn't question her answers. But then she was thrown out of school and when I tidied up her room I found three bottles of wine and cannabis. We had a serious row that day and Sarah ran away. She slept in the park, on a bench for a few days. During these days she must have come into contact with harder drugs. She was picked up by the police who took her home. I was alarmed, but I thought we could manage alone without professional help. What I didn't realise was that my daughter was a drug addict by that time. I locked her up in her room. I thought this would bring her away from drugs. Only one day later she showed withdrawal symptoms. She started trembling all over her body. Cold sweat was on her forehead and she had emotional outbursts during which she made awful whining noises and even smashed some of the furniture in her room. We should have brought her into a clinic because she soon took the chance to run away again. It was disgusting to see what she did to get money for drugs. It was not long before she got involved into prostitution. Again and again she was brought back by police but we couldn't hold her. We lost her. She was totally out of control. When she went on living in a run-down room with her 'friends' who were all on the needle, she tried all kinds of drugs. Last time I saw her alive she was looking filthy and worn out. But still she didn't want to give up drugs.

Comprehension

Task 1

Match the sentence parts according to Sarah's history of drug addiction.

1. Social workers call the way Sarah died 'slaughter by needle'	a. her mother played everything down as normal teenage behaviour.
2. Already at 11 Sarah came home drunk from a party	b. when Sarah was thrown out of school.
3. Even when Sarah returned home drunk more than once as a teenager	c. she tried to solve the problem alone by locking her daughter up in her room.
4. There was some kind of turning point in her mother's behaviour	d. because Sarah died of her 'last shot' which was an overdose of heroin.
5. Then her mother reacted and	e. therefore she escaped to get hold of drugs.
6. Soon Sarah suffered from withdrawal symptoms,	f. but her mother didn't react because she believed it to be a single case.
7. Finally Sarah decided to live together with other junkies	g. whose only aim in life was to have another heroin shot.

Task 2

Answer the following questions on the text.

a. Can you find reasons in the text why Sarah might have become a drug addict?
b. Most often a drug career is accompanied by drug-related crimes. What could this expression mean? Can you find examples of drug-related crimes in Sarah's life story?
c. How did her mother react to Sarah's early alcohol abuse?
d. Should she have reacted differently? How?
e. What do you think about her mother's attempt to solve the problem by locking Sarah up in her room?

Writing

Task 3

Sum up Sarah's history of addiction in a brief report. You may find the following leading questions and words useful.

Helpful phrases

How does her drug addiction start?
She is only ... when ...
At ... she consumes ... for the very first time.
Her drug addiction starts when ...
When she comes into contact with ...
She gets hooked when ...

How does it develop?
Her drug consumption becomes problematic/alarming when ...
At ... she develops an alcohol habit ...
Her dependence on ... increases gradually ...
Everything becomes worse when ...
At ... the amount of ... exceeds ...

When does she reach a point of serious addiction?
At ... /After ... years you can call her a serious drinker/addict because ...

At this point of her addiction she can't live without...
She is so deeply caught in her addiction that...
... shows that drinking and purchasing drink dominate her life.
The drug consumption has an impact on her daily life, for example...
She shows very typical symptoms of an addiction, such as...
Her addiction reaches a climax when...

How does her history of addiction end?
Her drug addiction comes to an end when...
When she realises that...
She manages to change her life when...
She accepts to undergo treatment when...
In the end she isn't able to see that...
The extensive drug consumption has already harmed her health, for example...
It comes to a total body/mental breakdown when...

Language

Task 4

Norma Stanly helps drug addicted young people who live on the street. Read her account first. Some words have been left out. After your first reading, look at the words given below and put them in the correct position.

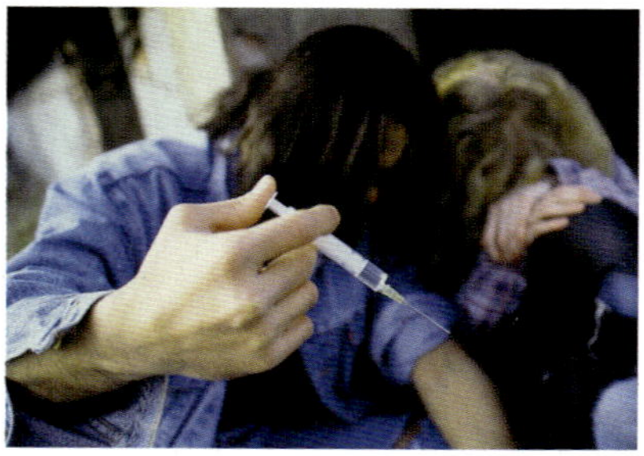

quit · drug scene · hooked · junkies · trip on · detox programme · self-help group · relapse · overdose · sterilised · depend on · take their mind off · undergo

Working on the streets to combat teenage drug abuse

Norma Stanly works as a street worker. Every evening till late at night she sets off in a small motor caravan with some medicine and **1** ... needles for those who can't reach one of the junkie's centres. Norma has a good insight into the Liverpool **2** ... . She knows where **3** ... meet and where they buy their booze or drugs.
'Some of them are serious bashers. They drink ale, cheap wine and any kind of booze they can get a hold of. They **4** ... drink. In winter it keeps them warm and of course they drink until they get high. Drink and drugs **5** ... their troubles and living situation. But most of the young people have already got **6** ... . They **7** ... heroin or cocaine. 'The only thing I can do, is to keep them away from infected needles and make sure they don't take an **8** ... . Just in case I always have some first aid equipment with me. But mainly I talk to them and show them my interest in their life and fate. There is only some hope and chance for them if they realise their situation. Only if they accept their addiction they have a chance to **9** ... drugs. Every therapy without the addict's consent or against his will is doomed to failure. The addict himself must see that he needs help and he must ask for it. Once they are on the needle only a **10** ... can help. I support and help them to find a place in a clinic where they can **11** ... treatment. I also help them to find another surrounding and place to live, far away from their former friends. We always separate them from their former living circumstances. During and after treatment they are asked to keep contact with me or another social worker. We also suggest that they join a **12** ... . This may prevent having a **13** ... because it keeps them under a certain control and they can meet other people with the same problem who they can talk to and gather some advice from. You can achieve a lot more when you are together with people who share the same experience.'

The vicious circle of drug addiction

People who depend on drugs are caught in a vicious circle which they can't escape. Any time they are confronted with a problem they will take drugs to overcome this moment of crisis. As soon as the dependence on a drug takes over, it will come to a crisis each time the addict feels that the drug loses its effect. He will need more drugs to feel some kind of release. As a 'side effect' the addict damages his health and most often the drug abuse is accompanied by a social decline.

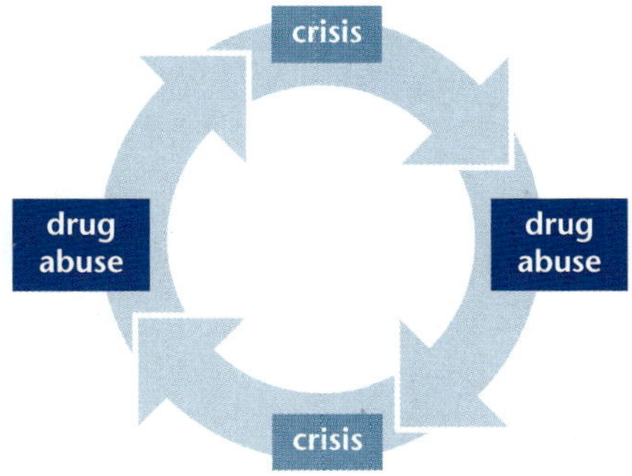

Task 5

The following pieces of a 'puzzle' describe typical stages of a 'drug career'. Reconstruct their correct order.

Addict relapses again and again. (1)	First drug consumption seemingly brings some kind of release. (2)	Each moment of crisis is followed by drug abuse in hope to find some further release. (3)
Something in the person's life happens which seems to be an insurmountable problem. (4)	The drug consumption reaches a point far beyond being normal. (5)	At next point of crisis addict turns to drug again. (6)
Mental and physical breakdown. (7)	High and repeated drug consumption shows first effects (e. g. health problems, addict becomes unreliable, failure at work, loss of social contacts). (8)	Drug dose increases. (9)
First contact with drug. (10)	Loss of life control, addict's daily life breaks down. (11)	Addict loses insight in his own life and behaviour and denies his dependence on drugs. (12)

Activity

Choose one of these two cases to work on.

Case 1

Melissa, 16, likes to go to raves. There she tried some ecstasy. Sometimes she smokes cannabis. Now Melissa has to work for her exam. At a disco someone offers her some speed.

She takes this to keep fit for learning but when she wants to find some sleep she needs sleeping pills. Although she learnt day and night Melissa fails on her final exam day. This is the starting point of a drug career.

Case 2

John Barton has some trouble at work. One of his projects failed. He himself feels like a failure. As a compensation he goes into the pub every evening. Now his evenings end up with binge drinking. But this only causes more problems at work because the next day he can't concentrate. Again some mistakes happen which John can't hide from his boss. When he finds a letter of caution in his letterbox, he decides to skip work and go straight into the pub although it's in the morning.

Task 6

Looking at the typical stages of an addiction, can you work out Melissa's and John's history of drug addiction? Try to outline a typical and realistic drug story. Work in small groups or in pairs and present 'your' story in class.

Listening

Audio

Task 7

Case Study

In an interview with a daily newspaper Tessa Corner talks about her first experiences with drugs and her later addiction to hard drugs.

Before you listen to the recording of her interview look into the vocabulary list. There you will find the translation of some words which are difficult to understand.

Then listen to Tessa's life story and with your partner decide which of the following answers is correct.

a. How did Tessa Corners' addiction start?
- (☐) As a girl of 16 she met some new friends in a disco who liked to experiment with drugs.
- (☐) Her friend's brother introduced her to cannabis when she was 14.

b. How did her drug career procede?
- (☐) She contacted drug dealers and tried speed and acid. Then at 16 she was going out with a drug dealer and took some cocaine. When this relationship broke up she got hooked on heroin to calm down.
- (☐) At 17 she already tripped on cocaine. Then she met a drug dealer who she started to work for. This is how she got hold on heroin and acid for free.

c. How could she finance her addiction?
- (☐) She was able to keep up her job but all her salary was spent on drugs. Besides she dated some dealers to get some drugs for free.
- (☐) She had a well-paid office job and she earned enough money to buy drugs.

d. Was there a turning point?

(☐) She was arrested by the police and had to undergo a drug-programme.

(☐) Police caught her with a week's supply of drugs and she had to confess everything to her parents, who insisted that she went into rehab.

e. Did she relapse?

(☐) With the help of her parents and regular meetings with a self-help-group she was able to undergo rehab and stay clean.

(☐) On her way to her self-help group she decided to contact her old dealer again.

f. How did her story end?

(☐) When she found out she was pregnant she was able to stay clean for a short time but now she's on the needle again.

(☐) She found out she was pregnant and decided to do a rapid detox programme to stay clean.

Writing

Task 8

Listen to Tessa's story again. Take down some more notes and sum up her history of drug addiction.

Should we be tough on cannabis?

Since Tessa believes that smoking cannabis was the starting point of her drug addiction, she took part in a TV discussion on the question whether cannabis should be legalised or not. Here are some of the participants' statements.

Tessa Corner: I was living in a filthy squat and was addicted to heroin. Now I'm sure it was a direct result of those first puffs I took on a cannabis joint when I was about 14. It felt like having fun but soon I was looking for another thrill. It seemed to be a very natural progression after cannabis to try heroin.

Alan Moffit: As a police officer, I know the damaging effects drugs have on society and I'm sick of hearing this nonsense about soft and harmless drugs. That's rubbish. There aren't any harmless drugs.

Judy Russel: I think, it's a good plan to inflict a real tough punishment on anyone in possession of cannabis no matter how much he carries with him. This will deter people from experimenting with cannabis.

Jason Butterfield: If we do so, we will maybe fine seriously ill people who use cannabis not for leisure but to help to control pain. There are a lot of cancer patients who are suffering severely. They need to take cannabis to cope with their pain.

Discussion

Task 9

Should cannabis be legalised? What's your opinion? Discuss. Maybe first talk about it with your partner and collect keywords for your discussion in class.

Grammar

Web

Direct speech and indirect speech

Direct speech	Indirect speech (main clause in Past Tense)
Present Tense: 'I take drugs.' →	**Simple Past:** Tessa said (that) she took drugs.
Simple Past: 'I took drugs.' →	**Past Perfect:** Tessa admitted (that) she had taken drugs.
Present Perfect: 'I have always taken drugs.' →	**Past Perfect:** Tessa told us (that) she had always taken drugs.
Future I: 'I will never take drugs again.' →	**Conditional I:** Tessa remarked (that) she would never take drugs again.
Future II: 'Next year I will have been clean for more than five years.' →	**Conditional II:** Tessa explained (that) she would have been clean for more than five years.

Task 10

The statements from Tessa and the other participants are reported as the most important and interesting arguments of the evening in a newspaper article about the discussion on cannabis. Take over the role of the reporter and transform the statements into reported speech.

Example:

In yesterday's discussion Tessa Corner said that she had been living in a filthy squat … Go on!

Audio

Module 3: The dangers of synthetic designer drugs

How dangerous are designer drugs?

In the 1990s Ecstasy became popular among teenagers who wanted to dance through a long rave night. There were some teenagers who died after taking Ecstasy because it raised their body temperature and after many hours of wild rave dancing they suffered from dehydration which led to a complete organ failure.

Today Ecstasy is an outdated drug compared to a large number of new synthetic drugs which have dangerous short-term and long-term effects. Agnes Thun and Bill Randall work in a drug advice centre for teenagers and parents and they know about the dangers of synthetic drugs. Here is an interview they gave to the newspaper reporter Beatrice Bright.

Beatrice Bright: Well, first of all, I think it will be interesting for parents and those who haven't heard about synthetic drugs to know what kind of drugs they are.

Agnes Thun: The names of these drugs change but right now there is a synthetic designer drug which is sold under the name Spice. The name Spice is used to describe the different herbal mixtures and shredded plants this drug contains.

Beatrice Bright: But this does not really sound dangerous.

Agnes Thun: This is the most common error. These seemingly harmless ingredients are mixed with all kinds of unknown ingredients, among those aspirin, caffeine or even heroin. These mixtures speed up the heart, raise the temperature and can in this combination lead to heart attacks or have mind-altering effects. Synthetic drugs are highly unpredictable.

Bill Randall: Yes, that's an emerging trend. Young people experiment with all kinds of substances they have free access to. For example, bath salts which everyone can legally buy. Most of them they can order from the Internet. Mixed together to a synthetic drug they have an effect similar to cocaine, amphetamines and Ecstasy. That's exactly the dangerous aspect of designer drugs. Teenagers can mix them themselves not knowing about the damage they do to their body and there are lots of Internet pages with synthetic drug recipes.

Beatrice Bright: But how dangerous are they? Do the teenagers feel sick or are the effects even worse?

Agnes Thun: Indeed they are. There are shocking numbers of emergency room visits and calls to the Poison Control Centre related to teenage drug experiments.

Bill Randall: Even worse, there are designer drug patients with an irreversible brain damage after trying a synthetic drug only once or twice. In contrast to Ecstasy most overdose victims survive but they may never fully recover mentally, they develop paranoia, show violent behaviour, some have suicidal thoughts. We already know that these drugs cause lasting brain damage.

Beatrice Bright: What can parents do?

Agnes Thun: Well, it's always the same story. Parents should discuss the dangers of drugs with their teenage children, but as a routine.

Bill Randall: Another problem is that teenagers are offered drugs in their drinks not knowing about them. Always remind your kid to be cautious when someone hands them something to eat or drink. Tell them that they should always make sure their drink isn't unguarded.

Beatrice Bright: But I think there is one big problem. How can parents know about what their children do? Most teenagers hide everything from them.

Agnes Thun: Never stop asking questions. If there are signs of drug taking, like depressive moods followed by aggressive behaviour, concentration problems, health problems for example, parents can come to our centre for help. We offer counselling with parents and children. There is also the possibility to do a drug testing to make sure what is going on.

Bill Randall: Well, if there is no doubt that the teenagers are already addicted to drugs we can discuss and help to find ways out of addiction like therapies with a psychologist, self-help groups for teenagers or therapies in teenage rehab clinics.

Comprehension

Task 1

Here are some statements on synthetic designer drugs of people who do not exactly know. Looking at the text again, explain why they are wrong.

a. Ecstasy is a harmless party drug. Maybe if you take too many Ecstasy pills they will keep you awake far too long and you will have a sleepless night. But that is all.
b. Spice only consists of herbs and plants. In a way it is completely organic and no risk at all.
c. Synthetic designer drugs may have a short-term effect. Wrong mixtures can make you sick for one or two days.
d. It is much too difficult for teenagers to mix their own designer drugs. They cannot get hold on their ingredients easily.

Task 2

In their interview Agnes Thun and Bill Randall use some phrases and words which are not easy to understand at first. Read the text passages in which these words are used again and explain in your own words what they express.

a. Agnes Thun talks about a *common error* (l. 9) about synthetic designer drugs. What is it?

b. She also says that these drugs are *highly unpredictable* (l. 13). What does she want to point out?

c. Bill Randall talks about an *emerging trend* (l. 14). What is it?

d. He also uses the word *irreversible* (l. 27). What does the word mean and what is irreversible?

e. What does Agnes Thun want parents to do when she underlines that this should be done as a *routine* (l. 35)?

f. Why should a drink never be *unguarded* (l. 39) as Bill Randall points out?

Task 3

With your partner or in small groups sum up the main aspects of synthetic designer drugs in a mind map! Draw your mind map on a flip chart poster or a transparency and present it in class.

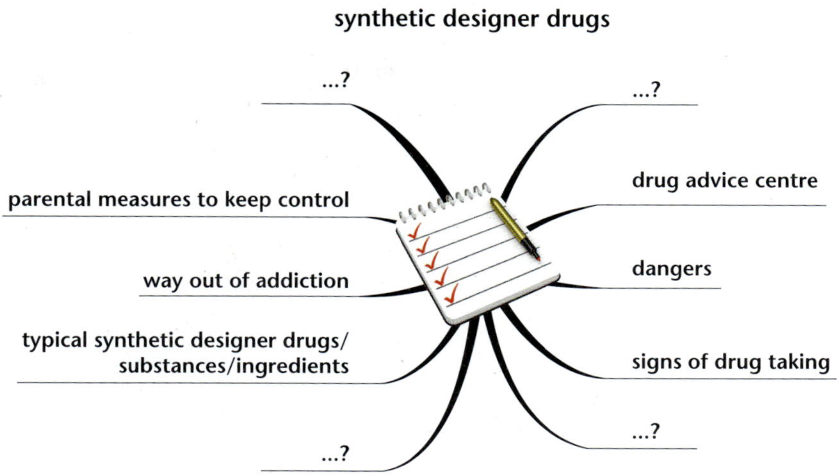

Teenage Drug Rehab – One way out of addiction?

Agnes Thun and Bill Randall already talked about teenage drug rehabs as one possibility to escape drug addiction. Rehab programmes can take place in residential rehab centres. They are like clinics the addicted teenager has to stay in for some weeks. But there is also the possibility to undergo therapy as outpatients who stay with their family and in their living environment and only visit the clinic for consultations and therapy sittings for some hours but then return to their family. Here are two controversial positions on residential drug rehabs for teenagers.

Only a stay in our rehab clinic can provide a safe and intensive therapeutic atmosphere which an addicted teenager needs to quit drugs.

Renée Walters: Teens become addicted because of a poor living situation at home and a disturbed communication between family members. High pressure at school and wrong friends circles have a great influence on them and support their drug habit. In case of addiction their old living environment is dangerous for them. This environment is full of problems and bad influence. There are several ways to prevent drug addiction, but I think once being hooked on drugs only a stay in a residential drug rehab can offer hope and the right help in curing the teenage drug addict. Here the teenager can break free from his old and wrong living circumstances. Any teenager who got involved into drugs needs safety and a dense programme of therapy in a group, individual psychological treatment, and a medical detoxification under supervision. All this has to go hand in hand. And this can only take place in a residential rehab. Here the teenager is under control surrounded by professionals who know what they do. Here he will also find other teenagers with the same personal story who can understand what he is going through. In the addict's situation our clinic staff and the other patients can be of greater help than an unknowing family who is overwhelmed with the problem.

My stay in a residential rehab only encouraged me to take hard drugs.

Thomas Mattison: Everything began when I experimented with marijuana and got caught together with a teenage drug dealer who sold a joint to me. My increasing alcohol use and my bad school performance seemed to speak for a drug treatment in a teenage residential rehab. I was only 14 and being cut from my parents and home was menacing for me. My self-confidence already broke into tiny pieces on my first rehab day, when they told me that I was a drug addict and alcoholic with no hope for the future. Again and again I was told how I would end but all this did not work as it should. For me it was no deterrence.

I was sure that being a drug addict was my fate. I also attended daily group therapy with older teens telling all kinds of stories about drugs which sometimes sounded like a great adventure. What's your drug of choice? This was the question everyone was asked and it was followed by 'What's the drug like?' I listened to stories of LSD trips which were so highly seductive that I promised myself that I would try myself if I got the chance. And I did, as soon as I left rehab. I think that the constant exposure to drug stories can especially be dangerous for impressionable youngsters.

Comprehension

Task 4

Each sentence carries wrong information. Transform the false sentences by giving the correct word or words from the different points of view.

a. Renée Walters thinks that in case of addiction the old environment is safe for the teenager.
b. This old environment can be full of positive support.
c. In rehab there will be other teenagers with different personal stories.
d. Being cut from his family was a positive experience for Thomas Mattison.
e. He felt that his self-confidence was already strengthened on his first rehab day.
f. For him the other drug stories sounded like a horror trip.
g. Listening to stories of LSD trips was highly deterring for him.

Task 5

First discuss the following questions with your partner before presenting your answers in class.

a. What reasons for drug addiction does Renée Walters point out?
b. Why does she prefer a stay in a residential rehab? What advantages does she refer to?
c. What are her reasons to think that the contact to other drug addicted patients can be of help?
d. What were the reasons to send Thomas Mattison into a residential rehab at the age of 14?

e. How did he feel at his first rehab day?
f. What problem does he see in a residential group therapy for teenagers?
g. What effect did the rehab experience have for him?

Writing

Task 6

Do residential teenage drug rehabs cure addiction or create it? Discuss this question.

The skills training and helpful phrases boxes on argumentative essay writing and discussion will give you some help.

Task 7

Pick out one of the statements and discuss it. Write an argumentative essay of about 200 words.

a. *Weak parents have weak children and teenagers. Parents should be positive role models. Those parents who sit in front of their children drinking and smoking are guilty of raising drug addicts.*

b. *Internet makes it impossible to control teenagers and prevent them from being seduced by synthetic designer drugs. As long as they can purchase all substances they need legally, no one can stop the rapid incline of synthetic drug abuse.*

c. *Our media are full of film, pop and rock stars who present drug taking as a very normal part of their life. It is shown as something cool, something you must do to be in and chic. These are dangerous images which convey a totally wrong idea about drugs.*

Skills Training

Writing an argumentative essay/discussing statements

Generally argumentative essays are structured in the following way.

1. **Introduction:** Say what the topic of your essay is or outline the question you would like to discuss. If you take up a given statement, explain how you understand it. If you refer to a text, e.g. newspaper article, summarise its main arguments first.
2. **Body:** Develop your own pro and con arguments adding more to the point of view given in the introduction. You can weigh the pros and cons. If you prefer, e.g. the con position, you should start with the pro arguments and then present your con arguments because they should be the strongest arguments. Most often people start with rather weak arguments and add the strongest at last because they are kept in mind. You should end the discussion with finally stating your personal point of view: Do you agree or disagree with the introductory statement or question?
3. **Examples:** It is always good to give examples which can support your point of view.
4. **Conclusion:** This should be a last, short paragraph in which you try to sum up your main argument and offer a final perspective on the statement, topic, or question you discussed in your argumentative essay.

Helpful phrases: Discussion

I think this statement wants to express that …	Ich denke, die Behauptung soll zum Ausdruck bringen, dass …
The main idea is that …	Der Hauptgedanke/die wesentliche Idee ist, dass …
This argument underlines/points out that …	Dieses Argument unterstreicht/hebt hervor, dass …
The writer hints at a general/an urgent/a crucial problem …	Der Verfasser verweist auf ein generelles/ein dringendes/ein wesentliches Problem …
I basically/partly agree/disagree …	Generell/zum Teil stimme ich zu/stimme ich nicht zu …
I personally believe …	Ich persönlich glaube …
I support the argument that … because …	Ich unterstütze das Argument, dass …, weil …
I can't understand how someone can support this argument …	Ich kann nicht verstehen, wie jemand dieses Argument unterstützen kann …
There are several reasons for my point of view.	Für meinen Standpunkt gibt es verschiedene Gründe.
I can't understand the writer's attitude because …	Ich kann die Meinung/Haltung des Verfassers nicht verstehen, weil …
I totally reject this point of view because …	Ich lehne diese Sichtweise völlig ab, weil …
I can't agree with this idea.	Ich kann diesem Gedanken nicht zustimmen.
I can't share this point of view because …	Ich teile diese Meinung/Ansicht nicht, weil …
Unlike (author) I think …	Im Gegensatz zu (Autor) denke ich …
This is a complete contradiction to …	Das steht völlig im Widerspruch zu …
Under certain circumstances …	Unter bestimmen Bedingungen …
It's not as simple as it seems because …	Es ist nicht so einfach, wie es aussieht, weil …
I would like to add that …	Ich würde gerne hinzufügen, dass …
In other words …	In anderen Worten …
I should like to repeat once again that …	Ich würde gerne noch einmal wiederholen, dass …
All in all I believe …	Alles in allem glaube ich, dass …
Weighing all the pros and cons, I come to the conclusion that …	Wenn man die Pro und Kontra-Argumente abwägt, kommt man zu dem Schluss, dass …

Activity

Task 8

Each year there are poster campaigns warning teenagers about the fatal consequences designer drugs have. This poster is an example of many different kinds of posters which you may see in a British disco or youth club. Sit in small groups and work on the following tasks.

a. First describe the poster.
b. Do you believe it could be successful in combating drug abuse among teenagers? Give reasons for your opinion and discuss them in class.
c. Design your own anti-drug poster and present it in class.

UNIT 9:
Violence and crime

Module 1: Young offenders

What does a typical offender look like?

As 13- and 14-year-old girls Ellen and Lara Moore joined a teenage girl gang who brings terror and crime into the city centres. Shoppers, workers and residents are intimidated and abused by the gang. Mobile phone thefts and violent assaults are their main deeds. While high on glue, the girls vandalise buses, bus shelters, or telephone boxes.
The girls' father, a lorry driver, left his family when they were toddlers. They live with their unemployed mother in a two-bedroom maisonette in an area where the houses are full of graffiti, have smashed windows and where lots of tins and empty fast food packagings lie on the stairs and around the houses.
With this family history and social background these girls fit into the image people have of teenage offenders. Many young criminals come from disturbed family situations with financial problems. They live in poor areas and have problems in school. Quite often they are truants. Nowadays statistics show that girls are becoming more and more violent. It's striking that they are increasingly involved in brutal muggings.
But teenagers in middle-class families in which parents still live together are just as likely to be involved in crime, drug taking and playing truant. So as a matter of fact there is no typical offender.

Comprehension

Task 1

Answer the following questions.

a. What kind of crimes do Ellen and Lara commit?
b. Looking at both girls' family and living situation, can you find reasons why they may have become criminal and violent towards people?
c. What does a criminal offender look like? Can you give an answer to this question?

Is it a crime?

John, 14:
My parents are very strict people. O boy, a bad mark is like a catastrophe. What else can I do but cheat in tests or forge my parents' signature under a bad class test?

Christine, 16:
My dad has been out of work since last year. Mom only works in a supermarket. You don't earn much filling shelves. We are short of money, but you can't turn up in school always wearing the same shabby and old-fashioned clothes. I think it's understandable that I have to go into shops and steal what I like to wear.

Tom, 15:
Last time I went to meet my girl I passed our public garden. When I saw all the roses I somehow got the idea to take some with me. I picked a whole bunch of flowers.

Ester, 13:
Mr Thompson, our English literature teacher, can be a real pest. 'Kill Mr Thompson' is written on almost every toilet door. I wrote his name on the seats and back rests in our school bus. Everyone does that, look at all the vandalised school busses, telephone boxes or bus shelters!

Suzanne, 17:
I love to be different. Last year I cut all my hair off. I wore a blue and pink mohican haircut and black clothes. I use swearwords in public, I laugh or sing at the top of my voice and listen to my favourite heavy metal music in public. Who wants to stop me? Perhaps people feel disturbed. I don't bother, why should I?

Comprehension

Task 2

Have a closer look at the statements. Do you believe the reported deeds are criminal acts or examples of deviant behaviour?
Look at the two boxes with ideas or words which may help you discussing the different deeds.

What do the youngsters do?

- provoke people
- offend someone
- disturb people
- break the law
- follow mean reasons
- inflict physical strength on someone
- take away someone else's property or destroy it
- show anti-social behaviour
- play bad jokes on people
- shock people with an abnormal appearance or abnormal performances
- do something which isn't widely accepted
- show different behaviour

These phrases may give you some help discussing the statements:

Helpful phrases: Discussion

I think a deed such as ... can be regarded as a crime because ...

I believe an offence like ... must be seen as a crime because ...

Doing something like ... is worse than ... because ...

I wouldn't call ... a (serious) crime because ...

It's exaggerated to say ... committed a crime because ...

Discussion

Task 3

Look at Christine's and Ester's statements. Do you believe their deeds are 'minor' or 'more serious' offences? Give reasons for your opinion.

Task 4

Look at the word box. All the words in the box below are criminal acts. Some of them are said to be typical teenage crimes. Make sure you understand what the different words mean and make a list of crimes which you believe to be typical teenage crimes. Read out your list in class and give reasons for your decision.

assault – robbery – arson – car theft – burglary – theft – shoplifting – disorderly conduct – drunk driving – drug abuse – drug dealing – mugging – vandalism – forgery of signatures – tax evasion – weapons possession – truancy – computer crimes – liquor law violations – prostitution – car crashing – tram or train surfing – murder

Task 5

Which words from the list match the following definitions?

a. to set fire to buildings
b. to attack someone in the street or another public place to take away their money
c. to destroy private or public property
d. steal things from other people's houses or flats
e. steal things from a shop
f. copy a signature to trick people

Language

Task 6

Any offence (or crime) is committed by an offender (or criminal). Now fill in the missing offence (crime) or offender (criminal). You may use a monolingual dictionary.

offence	offender
mugging	
	crashkid
	rapist
theft	
burglary	
murder	
shoplifting	
fraud	
vandalism	
computer crimes	

Task 7

The words below describe criminal actions. Try to explain what kind of crime they refer to. Explain in full sentences. If you can't give an explanation, try to give an example.

a. computer crimes
b. disorderly conduct

c. tram surfing
d. robbery

Task 8

Read through the text below and fill the gaps with words from the box. Before you start filling the gaps make sure you understand the words.

offences – committed – prison – borstal – fine – arrested – escape – sentenced – community service – police file – court – law – charge

What happens to young notorious offenders?

Ellen and Lara Moore are not just harmless teenagers who somehow come into a conflict with the **1** ..., they are notorious offenders and they have more than once been **2** ... by the police. At the age of 11 and 12 both girls had already had a **3** ... which was as thick as a telephone book. But since they were too young to bring a **4** ... against them, police could only take down a statement and hand them over to a social worker or take them home to their mother. As soon as they passed the age of 14 the situation changed. At this age youngsters can be brought into **5** ... for their **6** ... Teenagers can't be put into **7** ... but they can be charged with a **8** ... . Most often they have to do some **9** ... which is of benefit to the public. For example, young offenders clean public gardens or work in old people's homes for a certain number of hours according to the crime they **10** ... . Youngsters who again and again break the law and show outstanding anti-social behaviour can be sent into a **11** ... .
At age 14 and 15 Ellen and Lara abused and attacked some bus commuters who called the police. When police officers came to the scene Ellen could **12** ... but Lara couldn't because some of the people kept a firm hold of her. This time she was charged. For five years she is banned from entering the city centre, or taking a bus anywhere in the city, unless she is accompanied by her mother or a guardian. And she was **13** ... . to do 60 hours of community service.

Authentic reading

Mob of 30 teenagers attacked police officers who asked girl to pick up fast-food wrapper

Pair kicked to the ground in front of shoppers

Two police officers who asked a teenager to pick up some litter she had dropped were attacked by a mob in a suburban high street and punched, kicked, slapped and bitten. Witnesses said that the two male officers had to use batons to fight off about 30 teenagers who had kicked them to the ground. But two men then joined the attack, one of whom punched an officer in the face, as they shouted insults at the officers.

The extraordinary scene took place in the middle of the afternoon in a high street in Croydon, South London. Local shopkeepers said that the area was plagued by youths and gangs fighting and causing trouble.

The teenager picked up a fast-food wrapper when she was asked – but immediately dropped it on the ground again, the Metropolitan Police said. As the girl and a friend became aggressive towards the officers, a crowd of youths began to grow. [...]

Witnesses said that the crowd kicked the officers on the ground, and the police responded with batons. At this point, bystanders joined the attack, telling the officers that they 'should not attack little girls'. Then, 'one of these older men punched an officer in the face and knocked him to the ground', said Adeel Ramjaun. 'The crowd had made a semi-circle around the officers. It looked like a gladiatorial ring. They were shouting and swearing at the officer.' [...]

Police confirmed yesterday that a 15-year-old-girl had been arrested at the scene on suspicion of assault and had been bailed pending further inquiries. Two men aged 34 and 38 were also arrested on suspicion of assault and violent disorder. [...]

The two officers, aged 34 and 29, are on sick leave suffering from bruises and knee injuries. The 34-year-old officer required hospital treatment for a bite wound.

Speaking on BBC London Radio yesterday, he said that he had feared for his life and called for urgent assistance as the violence broke out. He said, 'She just threw litter on the floor and we asked if she could pick that up. As we walked away, she threw it at us. Then we went back to talk to her. You don't arrest these people for such minor offence; it is a complete waste of time.'

'It is amazing and it depresses you, the state of children today – the disrespect, not only for people who might not be in the police but anyone who is older.' [...]

Local people claimed that the area was plagued by gangs and that young people could identify which gang a youth was in by the colours they wore and the style of their trainers. Retailers said that they often faced trouble from youths milling around outside shops after school and fighting.

Handrit Kikay, 21, who works in Aldo clothes store said: 'We get loads of trouble here, especially on Thursdays, when there is late-night shopping. The main problem is the fighting between the different schools.'

Reza Joody, 36, who runs a local shoe shop, said: 'The kids come in the shop and damage and scratch the shoes. What can we say to them? They're kids.'

Source: Ahmed, Murad/Peach, James: Pair killed to the ground in front of shoppers, in: The Times, 19.07.2008, p. 29

Comprehension

Task 9

Before you have a closer look at the text, sum up in one sentence what impression this incident made on you. Choose one of the sentence beginnings.

a. I'm shocked about… because …
b. I can't understand that/how …
c. I'm astonished about …
d. Where I live I can/can't imagine that … because …

Task 10

The report below carries some pieces of wrong information. Try to find them out.

a. First read the report and say what is wrong. Then say what the correct information is.
b. Now write a short description of the deed.

Two police officers were attacked by teenagers in a side street in Croydon, North London. The incident took place in the late evening. Two police officers asked a teenage girl to bin some litter which she had picked up from the street. But she refused to do so and immediately started to attack the police officers with the help of two friends. Bystanders ignored the scene. Although the teenagers' attacks became very aggressive the officers soon had everything under control. The teenage girls were arrested. No one was seriously hurt. Retailers say that this shopping area is rarely visited by teenagers and that there have not been any problems up till now.

Task 11

The following questions help you to have a closer look at the case. Work on them with your partner and take down keywords for a discussion in class.

a. Look at the text again and try to find the reasons why the teenagers were ready to use violence.
b. Can you think of further reasons why youngsters seem to be increasingly aggressive and willing to use violence today?
c. What do you think of the bystanders' behaviour?
d. Discuss Reza Joody's opinion that she cannot say anything to kids who come into her shop damaging shoes.
e. Do you think the act of aggression against the police officers is just an isolated case or does it reflect more?

Discussion/Writing

Teenage gangs in Britain

In 2008 Britain suffered from a series of stabbings among teenagers. This appalling scale of knife crime seemed to be the result of gang wars. All this made Britain scared of its youth. Newspapers spoke of a 'nation living in the shadow of the knife and teenage crime'. In April 2008 the *Time* magazine had a title page and a leading article on the new generation of 'British teenage thugs' who are 'unhappy, unloved and out of control' and spoke about an epidemic of violence, drunkenness and street crime.

In July 2008 each week one youngster was murdered because of wars between street gangs or the so-called 'postcode gangs' and school gangs wearing the typical 'street uniform', pulled down hoodies combined with a special kind of trainers.
Nowadays teenage gangs who commit violent offences have become a norm in large cities, mainly in areas with a high unemployment rate.

Peer groups

Teenage gangs are a typical example of peer groups and peer group pressure. But what are peer groups?

A peer group is a group of people who are the same age and are united because they have something in common. In German 'peer' means „ein/eine Gleichrangige(r)/Gleichaltrige(r)".

Most teenagers follow certain trends in clothes or activities and only accept those in their group who follow the same trends. This means that this group sticks together because its members have mutual experiences and interests. But only as long as you represent the group's interests you belong to it. This is called 'peer group pressure'.

Task 12

Choose one of the statements and discuss it in an argumentative essay.

a. Today's children and teenagers are brought up to show a general disrespect.
b. As long as we do not give teenagers a perspective and, for example, solve our unemployment problem, we will not be able to reduce teenage crime.
c. The growing fear of teenagers and our suspicion will only isolate them and contribute to more acts of violence against our society.

Listening

Task 13

Audio

Find out about what happened to Anthony Brickwood in a London youth club on New Year's eve. Listen to the victim's account and pick out the correct sentence ending. Before you start listening, look at the vocabulary for some help.

1. The incident happened
(☐) right at the beginning of the party.
(☐) when the party was on for at least two hours.

2. Some boys turned up and
(☐) wanted to speak with Anthony.
(☐) tried to barge their way into the party.

3. Someone
(☐) called Anthony to the door for help.
(☐) asked Anthony for help because he was already standing at the door.

4. Parents
(☐) were at the party to supervise.
(☐) weren't there to look after the teenagers on that evening.

5. One of the gatecrashers
(☐) started an argument with Anthony and both got into a fight during which he injured Anthony.
(☐) suddenly pulled out an axe and swung it towards Anthony.

6. Anthony was
(☐) seriously hurt and brought into hospital. After his wound had been stitched he could leave hospital after some days.
(☐) seriously hurt. The injury was life-threatening and Anthony lay in a coma for some days.

Task 14

Listen to the recording again and try to answer the following questions.

a. Reconstruct in a couple of sentences what happened on that evening.
b. How does Anthony feel today?
c. Can you find reasons why all this might have happened?

Module 2: How can young offenders be punished?

Juvenile punishment at Chancery Juvenile Court

Justice Samual Mooreland serves at Chancery Juvenile Court in America. Teenagers and their families who have to appear before Juvenile Court will not only meet Justice Mooreland but come into contact with many people. Those people are for example a social worker, security officers, a lawyer, a state's attorney and some more court officers, who are mainly occupied with writing a transcript of the proceedings and helping to run the court session. All those people are important. Without them a decision could not be made.

In an interview Justice Mooreland and Annette Gleeve, the social worker at Chancery Juvenile Court, talk about their work.

Reporter: What are the most common sentences for young offenders?

Justice Mooreland: There are no common punishments but a wide range of possibilities. A person who is 15 years but not yet 18 years old at the time of the offence can be sentenced to juvenile punishment. Those who are 18 and older can't count on a milder punishment. They can be sentenced under adult law and even youngsters who are under 18 and commit a serious crime can be put under adult law.

Reporter: How do you make a decision?

Justice: All facts have to be considered which may give some explanation why the child or teenager has committed a crime. Then I have to decide whether I want to be strict, rehabilitate or punish. If there are no earlier offences punishment will be milder. Most often those youngsters are asked to do some hours of community service. Quite often I send them into a hospital or nursing home to work there. Youngsters can also be asked to pay a fine, for example to pay compensation if anyone got hurt or if property was destroyed.

Reporter: Do you have cases of serious crimes?

Justice: Unfortunately, yes. And the number of juvenile delinquents who commit serious crimes is increasing. Sometimes we are forced to realise that a mild punishment doesn't work. If youngsters committed earlier crimes and experience showed that a warning or milder punishment didn't work or in case of serious crimes such as aggravated assaults, drug dealing or even homicide, youngsters have to be charged with imprisonment. They can be sent into a juvenile prison or into an adult prison in case of a serious crime. Here in America we sometimes offer teenage delinquents the chance to go into a boot camp for six months. Many youngsters take the chance to change a long imprisonment in adult prison into six months of rigid boot camp drill. But it's a rather controversial way of punishment.

Reporter: Do you receive any help?

Justice: Yes of course, most decisive for my work is the social worker's report.

Comprehension

Task 1

Work through the interview again concentrating on the court work and the various possibilities of juvenile punishment. Then copy the mind map below and try to expand it as far as possible. Compare your results.

Task 2

Answer the following questions.

a. What role does the age of a delinquent play in finding a punishment?
b. What are mitigating or aggravating circumstances in finding a punishment for juvenile delinquents?

Language

Task 3

Fill the gaps with one of the connectors below.

in order to – because – since – before – on the basis of – which – whether – although

1 ... a juvenile delinquent appears in court, Justice Mooreland asks Annette Gleeve to write a report about this juvenile **2** ... find some kind of explanation for the deed. **3** ... there are always a lot of cases **4** ... have to be dealt with, Justice Mooreland spends a lot of time studying the case in detail, **5** ... he wants to be sure about what kind of person the criminal youngster is. **6** ... the delinquent's living circumstances and life story play an important role, the social worker's report is decisive. **7** ... this report Justice Mooreland decides **8** ... he has to be strict, rehabilitate or punish.

Annette Gleeve – a social worker at Chancery Juvenile Court

Audio

This is how Annette Gleeve describes her work during the interview.

Annette: First of all, I work together with the teenagers and the families to figure out the problems that brought them to court. I gather all pieces of information which seem to be important and hand them over in a detailed report to the court. This report can help to reach a clear and objective decision. Besides this, I supervise juveniles to make sure the orders of the court are followed, especially if there is some period of probation. Above all I believe that it is my main task to support the young persons in their life situation. I talk to their parents, teachers, friends and most intensively to the youngsters themselves to understand their background and living circumstances and at last to understand their criminal behaviour. Then I work out a plan for their reintegration. I accompany them to school and help them to take up a normal life again. Or I try to find some place for them to work or do vocational training which can be a solid basis for a better reintegration. Sometimes a young offender must first undergo a mental or a drug treatment. We also offer various courses and training programmes to aggressive juveniles. Here they can learn to manage their life situation without violence or breaking the law. The first and most important thing I want to achieve is to bring the delinquents to the point that they themselves understand why they committed the crime and what impact their offence had on the victims and their own life. Then I try to show them how they can behave differently in situations where they are tempted to commit a crime. Nevertheless there are notorious criminals who reject any attempt to help them. In this case a hard punishment is unavoidable. Still, I don't think of punishment at first hand. I want to achieve social goals!

Comprehension

Task 4

Work on the following questions.

a. Try to outline in your own words which different tasks a social worker at juvenile court has to carry out.
b. What does Annette Gleeve prefer to do with violent juveniles? What does she want to achieve?
c. Annette Gleeve says she wants to 'achieve social goals' (line 21). Can you explain what she tries to express using these words?

Discussion

Task 5

Justice Moorland calls Annette Gleeve's work 'most decisive'. Do you believe he is right or wrong? Give reasons for your opinion.

Three cases of juvenile crime

Case 1 – Mabel, 15

Mabel looks younger than she is and she behaves so childishly you wouldn't believe that she is a dangerous criminal. She started her criminal career with shoplifting, although she comes from a well-off family. Then she vandalised. More than once she was caught vandalising telephone boxes or setting fire to dustbins in public buildings. When she was 13 she ran along parked cars and scratched them with a key. In her first year in senior school she destroyed the windows of one of her teacher's cars with a baseball bat after having a row because of her disorderly behaviour in class. Under the supervision of a social worker she said that she sometimes can't find any rest until she smashes something or sets something on fire. Most often she damages those people's property she has some kind of conflict with. Now she has set fire to a youth club while there had been a party going on. She was sent out of the club because she had started a fist fight with another girl. During the fire one girl suffered serious burns which had to be treated in hospital.

Case 2 – Robert, 16

Robert plays truant a lot. Once police fetched him from his home and took him to school. But again and again Robert doesn't appear in school. He leaves home but then doesn't go to school but hangs around in the city centre. He likes to sit together with other youngsters who ran away from home and live on the streets or who play truant as well. Robert's parents separated because his father went to live with another woman. Now his mother has to look after him and his two brothers and one sister. Robert's mother depended on her husband financially and she was totally unprepared when he left her. She began drinking heavily and lost her grip on the family. Most of the time the children are left alone.

When Robert needs money he goes into the streets grabbing old ladies' handbags because they are usually too weak to struggle with him. But one of the old ladies was willing to fight for her money. He threw her down and kicked her violently with his heavy boots because her resistance made him angry. The lady was seriously injured and will continue to be a case for nursing.

Case 3 – Bill, 17

'We like to have a bit of fun, me and my friends, it's just fun. When you smash something up or hit someone it's a hell of fun. We laugh a lot then and I enjoy myself. Look, you've got to have a bit of fun. I need to do it. The feeling is great when you've just slapped someone right in the face and he or she looks so very puzzled. Since I did that and showed the pictures around, my classmates have become interested in me. They treat me with some respect. No one dares to boss me around. Perhaps they're afraid but the feeling is great. I love it'.

This is what Bill told the social worker who has to write a report about him. Bill is charged in court for 'happy slapping'. He and his friends walk amongst people in the streets or in the underground and suddenly slap them or kick them violently just for the fun of it. They pick out an innocent person for their arbitrary attacks and record their brutal assault with their mobile phones. The pictures are sent to their friends' mobile phones or they are put into the web. Bill is a single child. His parents run their own business. They want their son to perform well at school and later go to university to take over their family business.

Activity

Task 6

Imagine you are Annette Gleeve. Now one of the cases is handed over to you to state your opinion on the question of how hard the punishment should be.
Sit together in small groups and choose one of the cases. Prepare your advice for punishment and present it to your class for discussion.
Perhaps take down your main thoughts on a transparency or poster to present them to your class mates for a better discussion.

Study the following list of phrases which might help you to work out your advice.

Helpful phrases: Describing punishment

In this case we won't need a hard punishment because ...
The deed should (not) be followed with legal consequences because ...
With regard to ... I suggest/I propose to ...
The offender should be sentenced to ... hours community service, because ...
Instead of imprisonment the youngster should be fined with ... because ...
I think it is justified to...
His/her deed shows extraordinary brutality ... therefore the punishment should be tough/hard/severe for example ...
We should take into account that this is a first and single crime/that he/she planned the deed/committed a crime repeatedly/is a repeat offender
In this case age and living background should be considered ... because ...
Bad living circumstances explain why ...
He/she cannot fully be blamed for ... because ...
In this case it is reasonable to undergo psychological treatment/a therapy in order to ...
This sentence can have a signal for .../can prevent/deter the offender from ...

Task 7

Justice Mooreland talks about the possibility to send those youngsters who committed serious crimes into a 'boot camp' and calls it 'a rather controversial form of punishment'.

a. In order to understand what he wants to suggest, sit together with some of your classmates and try to summarise all information on boot camps you yourself have and which you can gather from the web. Then think of how you can inform your class on the topic.
b. Finally discuss your attitudes towards boot camps in class.

Grammar

Web

Conditional clauses Type 3 – impossible condition (unmögliche Bedingung)

	Nebensatz	Hauptsatz
Bildung	if + had + past participle (= 3. Verbform) ➔ Past Perfect	would/could/might + have + past participle (= 3. Verbform) ➔ Conditional II
Beispiel	*If I had known that there were some trouble makers at that party, I would not have allowed my son to join the party.* *If a social worker had known about Robert's living situation before, something could have been done to prevent him from committing crimes.*	
Gebrauch	Die oben aufgeführten Beispielsätze beziehen sich alle auf die Vergangenheit. Sie beschreiben eine unmögliche Bedingung, die der Sprecher vielleicht gewünscht hätte, die aber unerfüllbar geworden ist, da die Situation sich anders entwickelt hat und die Ereignisse bereits in der Vergangenheit abgeschlossen wurden.	

Task 8

Fill in the correct form of the verb in brackets (conditional clause type 3).

a. If the teenage girl (not drop) the litter on the street, the police officers would not have given her a lecture.
b. If the incident hadn't aroused any interest in the other teenagers, the situation (not escalate) in such a way.
c. The police officers might not have suffered from such serious bruises and knee injuries, if the bystanders (intervene) in the fight.

Task 9

Make up an if-clause type 3 to describe the situation in a – c.

Example:

The burglar got into our house because we didn't close the bathroom window.
If we had closed the bathroom window, the burglar would not have got into our house.

a. I suggested a hard punishment for this teenage offender, but I didn't know about the boy's terrible childhood.
b. Mary continued shoplifting, because her parents refused to give her any pocket money.
c. The juvenile criminal committed a second brutal mugging, because he didn't undergo an anti-aggression training.

Task 10

The following sentences are if-clauses of all three types. Transform the verb in brackets into the correct form. If you need to repeat the grammar rules for type 1 and 2, have a look at Unit 6 page 131.

a. If we tried to work out more anti-aggression programmes for juvenile criminals, the crime rate (decrease).
b. According to Annette Gleeve there is no doubt that juvenile criminals will be integrated more easily, if they (have) the chance to finish vocational training.
c. We wouldn't have such a high juvenile crime rate, if government (spend) more money on social workers.
d. If the Stevens hadn't forgotten to switch on their alarm system, a burglar (not break) into their house.

Module 3: School Crime

Bullying at school

Studies today show that almost every pupil will be bullied once in their school life. 98% suffer from bullying, mainly verbal abuses but also violent physical attacks. Nowadays there is a new kind of bullying which is called 'cyberbullying'. This can be not only verbal attacks in social networks but also short videos with violent, threatening or abusive content involving pupils

and teachers mostly secretly taken and made public. Their only aim is to expose and humiliate the person they show. In extreme cases this online bullying can drive a child or teen to deep depressions and even suicide. In America they now use a new word for this sad phenomenon. Here statistics speak of 'bullycide' with an estimated number of five suicides each month. Britain speaks of approximately 16 'suicidal cases' each year. Here are two typical cases.
Also read the info box on page 209 which gives you some detailed information on cyber-bullying.

Case 1

'You should go and kill yourself because you don't mean anything to anyone.'
This is one of the last Facebook messages Robert onar (15) read after a long time of cyber-bullying. And he felt in such a distress that he really began to harm himself. Robert received abusive messages on Facebook by a bully who presumably used the same strategy most bullies do. They create an account under a false name and pick out someone to start a long series of anonymous bullying.
Robert still remembers the first message:
One afternoon I read, 'You're nothing, "No one cares about you"'. At first I thought it was a joke and I just shrugged it off my shoulders. But right next day there was a new message, 'You nerd, no one wants you'. From now on the messages came in every day and they became more and more abusive. Normally I'm a 'happy go lucky' person, I laugh a lot and go out but when the cyberbullying took over, it started eating into my self-confidence. I stayed at home and I began feeling unsafe. I entered the school bus and saw my school mates laughing about something and I thought, 'They know about the messages and laugh about you'. During break time I avoided any group and one question kept on circling around in my head, 'Who is the bully?' After endless messages abusing me and sleepless nights and days full of doubts I finally got the message to kill myself, my feelings were blunted so much that I took a knife from our kitchen and started to cut my wrists.

Case 2

Grace Logan (16) was bullied by a boy of 17 both in person and online. She moved into a new town and right from the beginning of the school year she was harassed by that boy:
He came up to me right on the first day in our canteen, forcing his way beside me and telling me that he is going to be my lover. I was puzzled and told him that I'm not interested but this kicked off a huge wave of bullying. He called me names in school, getting dangerously close to me and whispering menacing words in my ears. Then on Facebook he posted daily messages using rude words for me and telling fantasy stories about my sex life. I got lots of abusive messages from people I didn't know. I told them to stop and one day I really begged them, telling them that I'm suicidal and in great distress. The only reaction was, 'Go, kill yourself! No one would care if you died!' But I did not kill myself, I told my parents about everything and they went to school with me next day. As a result the boy was suspended from school but was offered to reassign at an alternate school. School reported everything to the police. In my case it was easy to spot the bully and after what happened to me our headmaster gave a 15-minute-lecture about bullying, that it's not acceptable and that there will be legal consequences. But what about all the bullies who remain anonymous and go on bullying without consequences?

Comprehension

Task 1

These sentences sum up Robert's and Grace's story. Match the sentence parts.

a. When the first cyberbullying message entered Robert's computer …	1. one morning when he entered the school bus he thought that everyone was laughing about him.
b. But this first message was only the beginning …	2. he lost self-control and started harming himself with a knife.
c. More and more Robert lost his self-confidence so that …	3. sexually harassing her.
d. One further consequence of his lost trust in his fellow students was that he …	4. broke down begging the bullies to stop and honestly telling them about her suicidal feelings.
e. When a message came telling him to kill himself, …	5. he reacted in a relaxed way and did not really care.
f. The bullying Grace had to suffer from …	6. stopped joining any groups.
g. That boy directly started …	7. with telling invented stories about Grace's sex life.
h. This harassing was repeated on Facebook …	8. by telling her parents and school about the bully who was then suspended from school and recorded to the police.
i. Other joined in sending abusive messages and Grace finally …	9. started right on her first day in a new school with a boy she had not met before.
j. But her honest message …	10. of a multitude of abuses coming in daily.
k. But finally Grace succeeded in breaking through this vicious circle of cyberbullying …	11. was answered with a wave of messages telling to go on and commit suicide.

Language

Task 2

The definitions below describe words from the two cases. Try to find them.

a. verb: expressing that someone tries to taunt someone with calling him/her names, inventing stories, or even attacking the person physically
b. noun: person who carries out the harassing
c. noun: using the social network to abuse and harass someone
d. noun: expressing that someone killed himself because of being harassed via social networks
e. verb: doing something to your body which hurts, inflicting injuries to oneself
f. verb: telling something about a person which should be kept a secret, showing someone in a way that is humiliating
g. noun: act of killing oneself
h. verb: telling someone that he/she has to leave school
i. verb+noun: giving a speech to a group telling what is right or wrong
j. verb: finding out who is the wrongdoer

Task 3

Now it is your turn to explain what these words and phrases want to express. Take into consideration what they reveal about Robert's and Grace's emotional state.

a. In line 9 Robert says that he 'shrugged' the first abusive message 'off his shoulder'. What does he want to express about his first feelings?
b. In line 11. Here he says he is a 'happy go lucky' person. What kind of person is he?
c. After daily messages Robert says, that they were 'eating into his self-confidence' (l. 12). What does this phrase show you about his changed emotional state?
d. In line 17 Robert says, 'my feelings were blunted'. What does he want to express about his feelings shortly before harming himself? Does that explain why he reacted in such a way?
e. What do Grace's words that she 'begged' the bullies to stop because she felt to be 'suicidal' (l. 32) show about her emotional state after a long period of cyberbullying?

Discussion/Writing

Task 4

Discuss the following questions in class or pick out one and write an argumentative essay.

a. How can someone escape from cyberbullying? Looking at Grace's failed attempt and her final breakthrough, discuss the chances and possible escape strategies.
b. Talk about the term 'social network'. What image does the word convey? Is it really a 'social' communication technology?
c. What is your attitude towards cyberbullying? Is it severe bullying or just a harmless joke you play on someone?
d. Why do you think do people use social networks to start bullying? What could be the motivation for others to join in very often not knowing who the bullied person is?

What is cyberbullying?

Cyberbullying – the word is used when someone deliberately uses information and communication technologies to communicate false, embarrassing, or hostile information about or to another person.

Typical types of cyberbullying are:

- **Gossip:** Posting or sending cruel gossip to damage a person's reputation and relationships.
- **Exclusion:** Deliberately excluding someone from an online group.
- **Impersonation:** Breaking into someone's email or other online account and sending messages that will cause embarrassment or damage to the person's reputation.

- **Harassment:** Repeatedly posting or sending offensive, rude, and abusing messages.
- **Cyberstalking and cyberthreats:** Posting or sending unwanted or intimidating messages. Threatening someone or implying violent behaviour, displaying suicidal tendencies.
- **Flaming:** Online fights where scornful and offensive messages are posted on websites, forums, or blogs.
- **Outing and Trickery:** Tricking someone into revealing secrets or embarrassing information which is then shared online like posting unauthorized photos.

Steps against cyberbullying:

- Don't respond to the bullies!
- Keep evidence, record dates, times and instances when cyberbullying has occurred, save screenshots, emails, and text messages.
- Report bullies to the police.
- Block the bully.
- Inform the social media site about the cyberbullying. They should take action against bully.
- Speak about the cyberbullying with your school mentor. In many countries schools developed strategies to combat cyberbullying and they work together with educational psychologists and the police. Your report may also prevent someone else from being bullied.

Statistics

- A study says that 32% of online teens say they have been targets of a range of annoying or potentially menacing online activities. 15% of teens say someone has forwarded or posted a private message they've written, 13% say someone has spread a rumour about them online, 13% say someone has sent them a threatening or aggressive message, and 6% say someone has posted embarrassing pictures of them online.
- 38% of online girls report being bullied, 26% of online boys. In particular, 41% of older girls (15–17) — more than any other age or gender group.

Source: National Voices for Equality Education & Enlightenment (NVEEE): Cyber Bullying Statistics, www.nveee.org/statistics [01.10.2012]

Zero tolerance at American schools

Reading an American school crime statistic may sound like reading the file of a dangerous criminal. Maybe you think of school in the naïve way having in mind the image of children who sometimes misbehave, do some cheating in class tests, have arguments, maybe show disrespect and, at the extreme, have a fist fight. You are absolutely wrong with regard to public schools in the deprived areas of large cities. Here

you will read about criminal deeds like theft, vandalizing, serious violent assault, bullying, gang violence, sexual harassment, carrying a weapon, rape, drug dealing and even homicide. And, America still has the highest number of shootings in schools all over the world, although we should not forget that other European countries had to suffer from dreadful shootings as well. All this led to the American *zero tolerance* policy. *Zero tolerance* started out as a term that was used in combating drug trafficking in schools and after the Columbine school massacre[1] it became a popular school policy. There are schools with a shocking crime rate but most schools do not have to cope with serious threats of violence. As a measure to prevent possible criminal behaviour more and more US schools have police patrolling the corridors. Schools now have their own police force with officers in uniform who carry guns to keep order in school corridors and canteens, playgrounds and even during lessons. These police forces eat up the school budget which should be used for maintenance, school equipment, learning tools, books, computers etc. It is some kind of irony that schools with the most violent activities in deprived areas cannot afford these security services because the local communities already have to spend too much money for police in their town and school budgets are cut down.
Since schools have introduced police forces who strictly carry through the zero tolerance policy, each day hundreds of school children appear before courts charged for offences like swearing, misbehaving in class or on the school bus, getting into a punch-up on the playground, wearing 'inappropriate' clothes, being late for school, or showing offence gestures. For example a boy of 7 was charged because he held the fingers of his right hand like a gun. Pupils are sent to court for throwing paper planes and failing to pick up crumbs from the canteen floor. With regard to school shootings there are lots of teachers, parents and politicians who want to stick to the zero tolerance policy, but the number of those who question what is going on is growing.

Comprehension

Task 5

Add the missing reasons.

a. Some of the American school crime statistics sound like the file of a dangerous criminal because …
b. School shootings are not only a typical American problem because …
c. The shocking school crime rate is not an overall problem because …
d. Schools introduce police forces because …
e. Schools in deprived areas would need the help of a police force but cannot introduce them because …
f. Money for the maintenance of schools, learning tools and further school equipment is missing because …

Task 6

Sit in pairs and explain in your own words what the American *zero tolerance* is. Think of its origin, how it is carried out and the consequences it has on the school surrounding and atmosphere.

---

[1] *Look at the info box on the last worst school shooting on page 213 to gather further information.*

Zero tolerance – Two points of view

Ramona Baker and her daughter Jenny

Ramona: I think that this policy is an overreaction to behaviour that others would generally think of as just childish misbehaviour rather than being the criminal act of a deprived child who breaks the law once again. Why is our state criminalising normal childhood behaviour? My daughter was fined because she sprayed some perfume on her neck in class. Her classmates were taunting her with 'you smell' and she did not think of the consequences and used some perfume. The teacher called the police and they 'arrested' her, a girl of 9! She was scared. I was very upset at the teacher because he could have stopped everything, saying, 'Okay class, that's enough'. He could have told her that she behaved inappropriately and not to do that again. But he called the police. My daughter is a little girl who still has to learn what is good and bad behaviour. This perfume didn't harm anybody. Now she has a criminal file and all this had a traumatizing effect on her. She will never again speak in class and has become lethargic because she fears to do something wrong. But maybe, this is what teachers want, suppressing our children so that they will submissively obey them.

School principal Jonathan Downsend

Jonathan: It's an illusion that our today's kids only misbehave in school sometimes but in reality respect school rules, their classmates and teachers. Times have changed. Too many parents don't control their children. We can't be sure about our children today. Our school kids can be gang members who maybe carry weapons that kill. They can be criminals, even killers, but that's not written all over their face. Police control helps us to take measures in worst cases. Lots of students come into your classroom and they have no respect, no self-discipline. They're doing badly, they don't want to learn, they just want to disrupt and hinder those who want to learn in achieving something. They can be very threatening. Police get called because in that way our teachers can go on with teaching instead of wasting the lesson dealing with one child, and it sends a message to the other kids: 'We don't want any disruptive actions and troublemakers'. We need police in schools. You never know, any situation can get physical and turn out to be very bad. I don't want anybody to be hurt here or let those troublemakers take over and disturb our school atmosphere.

Comprehension

Task 7

Discuss these two points of view in class. But before you do this, try to understand both. The following questions will give you a help to look at most important text passages again. Work on them with your partner.

a. What does Ramona Baker want to express when she talks about an overreaction?
b. Why does she come to the conclusion that the American State is criminalizing normal childhood behaviour?
c. Why is she upset about teachers? What does she insinuate that teachers use, rather misuse the zero tolerance policy and police forces for?
d. What changes in children's behaviour does Jonathan Downsend point out?
e. What dangers does he see in gangs and troublemakers?
f. Why does he believe that police control is very helpful to establish a good learning atmosphere at his school?

Writing/Discussion

Task 8

Pick out one of the point of views and discuss it in an argumentative essay. If you need help, look at page 189/190. Here you will find a skills training and helpful phrases box on discussion.

Activity

This could be one of America's schools …

Right at the school entrance there is a security check point. Security officers control every student who wants to pass. They let them go through a security door system to detect weapons and they also control every school bag. Right with the beginning of lessons the school gate is closed, no one can come in or go out during lessons. Police patrols wander along the corridors. You can look into each class room through high windows. The school looks run-down. The class room furniture is old, walls need painting and the floor covering has got holes. The classes are large, 35 students in one class as a minimum. Specialist rooms are rare and with old equipment, for example the school only has 20 computers, most of them out of function and with a rather old technology.

Task 9

Sit together in groups and work on the following tasks.

a. Discuss the learning surrounding and atmosphere this school offers to its students. Sum up your results in a critical statement. Do not forget to give reasons for your opinion.
b. How do you wish the learning surrounding of a school to be? How would a perfect example look like?
c. Present your results in class for discussion.

School shooting – why do they happen?

First look at the table below, which sums up the worst school shootings.

United States, April 1999

Dylan Harris and Eric Klebold killed 12 of their classmates and a teacher at Columbine High School in Littleton, Colorado, before killing themselves.

United States, March 2000

A six-year-old boy came to school in Mount Morris Township with a gun and killed a girl the same age. The boy took the loaded gun from under blankets in his uncle's house where he lived after his father went to prison and his mother was evicted from their home. Police officers said that he did not understand what he had done but that he felt like being in a TV show. After the police interview he sat there drawing pictures.

Germany, April 2002

Seventeen people were killed after a gunman – a former pupil, Robert Steinhäuser – opened fire in a school in Erfurt. Finally he turned the gun on himself. Robert Steinhäuser failed his Abitur and was due to resit the exam but had been expelled some months before the shooting because of playing truant and falsifying doctor's notes. He was a member of a gun club and a trained marksman.

United States, March 2005

Jeff Weise, 16, killed grandfather and companion, then arrived at school where he killed a teacher, a security guard, five students and finally himself, leaving a total of ten dead.

United States, April 2007

A 23-year-old Virginia Technology student, Cho Seung-Hui, killed two in a dorm, then killed 30 more 2 hours later in a classroom building. His suicide brought the death toll to 33, making the shooting rampage the most deadly in US history; 15 others were wounded.

Finland, November 2007

18-year-old Pekka-Eric Auvinen, who was one of the secondary school's students killed nine people: five male students, (ages 16–18), one female student (age 25), the school principal (age 61), the school nurse (age 43); and himself. The morning of the incident Auvinen posted a video on YouTube announcing the massacre at the school.

United States, February 2008

Stephen P. Kazmierczak, a former graduate student, came back to his former school after one year and killed five students and then himself, and wounded 17 more when he opened fire on a classroom at Northern Illinois University.

Finland, September 2008

A 20-year-old male student shot and killed nine students and himself at a vocational college.

Germany, March 2009

Tim Kretschmer, 17, a graduate student opened fire in a classroom at his former secondary school in Winnenden, a small town near Stuttgart, killing nine students (eight girls and one boy) and three teachers, all women. He flew from the school building and killed more people. After being wounded by the police, he commited suicide, leaving a total of 15 killed people and 7 wounded students. He took the gun from his father, a member of a shooting club who owned legally registered weapons.

United States, December 2012

Twenty-year-old Adam Lanza, was carrying an arsenal of hundreds of rounds of deadly ammunition - enough to kill nearly every student in a school in Newtown. The gunman shot his mother four times in the head before going to the school and gunning down 26 victims before shooting himself when he heard police approaching the classroom. All the victims at the school were shot multiple times with a high-power rifle. All six adults were women. Of the 20 children, eight were boys and 12 were girls, helpless children of 6 or 7 years.

Task 10

After the school shooting at Columbine, Americans discussed why youngsters commit such violent crimes. The following statements summarise the main reasons which were supported in the public media. Discuss them with your partner first before you tell your class whether you believe them to be right or wrong. Give reasons or examples for your opinion.

a. You cannot be surprised about youngsters who run amok if you look at the brutality shown in TV programmes, horror videos or movies and shocking rock music performances which many of them like to watch and listen to.

b. Today's juvenile unemployment and bad future prospects put a lot of pressure on young people. They are told to be successful at school and in their life. But what if they aren't? Some of them cannot cope with the constant pressure to do well or with a failure and show aggressive behaviour.

c. Nowadays a lot of families are disturbed and family structures are volatile. Youngsters don't receive the care and security which they need and do not develop strong personalities.

d. The attitude towards guns must be blamed for school shootings. Gun possession is allowed within the law and Americans show a love for guns. There are about 300 million guns circulating in the country. In most US states it is legal to carry a gun in public and there is a gun in almost every household. About 90 people die at the hand of a gun each day, among those an estimated number of 15 children.

e. Our teacher staff is not trained for our today's children. At first hand they want to teach the yearly curriculum and do not see the social and psychological problems their students have. They do not want to or can not care for them because they are not trained in counselling students who have some kind of personality problem. Schools need psychological counselling. Instead of taking some time for those students they put them under pressure because they do not want them to disturb their daily routine. This pressure causes emotional outbursts, in the extreme school shootings.

Activity

Task 11

Pick out one of the school shootings and gather more information to analyse this individual case. Perhaps surf the Web. Mainly work on the following aspects.

a. What kind of person was or were the school shooters? Try to find out about their family or social background, about the life they were leading before the school shooting.
b. Does the school shooter's individual life story give you some hint why he committed the crime?

School shooting in Cartoons

Task 12

Look at the cartoon description and fill the gaps with the words from the box below.

convey – numb – subtitle – stuffed – closed – depict – blame – weapons – school shooters – skull

The cartoon shows a young man or teenager whose **1** ... is open right above his forehead. Lots of DVDs and film rolls are **2** ... into this open skull. The boy is carrying two **3** ... The boy is wearing a dark T-shirt. His eyes are **4** ... . They create a somehow **5** ... impression. Perhaps this should arouse the idea that he is numbed by the violent films or TV programmes which he watched or the violent music he listened to.
There is no **6** ... under the cartoon. But its title could be 'violence is cool' because these are the words the boy is saying. This may hint at the boy's attitude towards guns and violence. He seems to love guns and like to copy violent films and TV programmes.
With this cartoon the artist wants to **7** ... those TV programmes, video films and music which **8** ... violence. They **9** ... the idea that conflicts can be solved with violence. The artist wants to say that if youngsters are always confronted with violence they will surely react violently themselves. Maybe they will become **10** ... if they are confronted with a conflict they can't solve.

Task 13

Talk about the cartoons with your partner.

a. These cartoons do not have a subtitle. Can you think of one? Present your subtitle in class and say why you chose it.
b. Which of the cartoons do you think succeeds in depicting a typical aspect of school shooting? Tell your class why.

Writing

Task 14

Pick out one of the cartoons and write a full analysis. If you need help, look at page 175. There you will find a skills training and a helpful phrases box on analysing cartoons.

UNIT 10: Media

Module 1: Living in a media world

Media are just everywhere

Media are just everywhere. There are print media like newspapers, magazines and books but also ads, posters and fly-posters. And there is a multitude of digital media like computers, computer and console games, iPads, the Net and all kinds of social networks. Books are offered as e-books. And there is a huge market for mobile media like cellphones, smartphones, Black Berries and iPhones. Compared to the new technologies, watching TV or listening to the radio is rather old-fashioned. But despite the new technology trends TV still is the media children, teenagers and grown-ups spend most time with, very often not sitting in front of TV, but with a TV in the background while they are using another media. Compared to a lot of grown-ups, kids consume media all the time and are not afraid of new technology, they do not spend many years to get used to new media and do not hesitate at using them. They just grow up with the media. A lot of teenagers multi-task, using more than just one media is a quite common sight with this age group. Whereas the digital media consumption is going through the roof, the print media consumption is tiny and small. We wander through a constant flow of media messages which rain down on us, but mainly this flow consists of pictures or short verbal messages, the written word has become of minor importance. More and more children lose their interest in reading a book and literacy skills decline. A lot of parents show the same lack of love for books. Parents both do not read books themselves and do not read to their children. Lots of small children go to bed with the TV on in their bedroom or they listen to their iPod or MP3 player but without a bedtime story read to them. And, reading a daily newspaper seems to be something left to old people, teenagers very seldom take up a newspaper maybe left behind by their parents to have a look inside.

Task 1

Talk about your own media habits.

a. What media do you possess and use regularly?
b. Try to say how much time you spend with media during a day.
c. Do you multi-task? What media do you use when you multi-task? Give typical examples.
d. Describe your print media consumption. Do you read books, the daily newspaper?
e. Talk about your TV watching habits. How much time do you spend watching TV? What kind of programmes do you prefer?

the news – talk shows – game shows – reality shows – documentaries – political programmes – family series – crime stories – films – mystery series/films – science fiction series/films – comics – casting shows – comedies – soap operas

Task 2

Explain what the following statements want to point out about our today's media consumption. Also say whether you believe them to be true or not. Maybe discuss them with your partner first.

a. Today only visuals or visuals combined with verbal messages find their way into our kids' brains.
b. Catching up visuals is easier and faster; therefore teenagers shun the effort of reading.
c. We wander through a constant flow of media messages which rain down on us. (See l. 14–15.)
d. As soon as kids and teens are awake, they start consuming media. They consume all the time and multiple media at the same time.

Statistics on media consumption

The American Kaiser Family Foundation did the most comprehensive study on American children's and teenagers' media consumption in the last years. They surveyed more than 2,000 American families comparing changes in media habits and gathered all kinds of information about the media habits of 8 to 18-year-olds released in an extensive report. It confirms the high media consumption of children, which is a daily average of 10 hours and 45 minutes. Most of the 8 to 18-year-olds multi-task. They ignore print media, 75% of American households have more than one TV set and in 70% of American households, children and teenagers have their own TV set in their bedroom. Only one third of households have media-consumption rules. It is maybe no surprise that the media consumption among children and teenagers is that high because TV sets are always on, there are no rules and kids have them in their bedrooms. And there is something else, which does not surprise: kids who consume the most media have the worst school performance.

Among all 8 to 18-year-olds

... amount of time spent with each medium in a typical day:

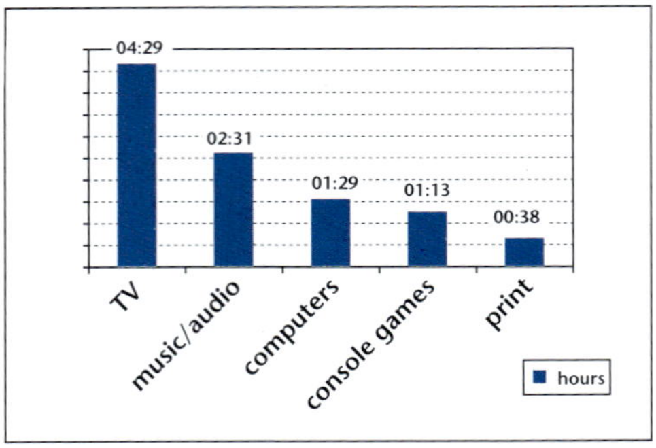

... total amount of media consumption in a typical day:

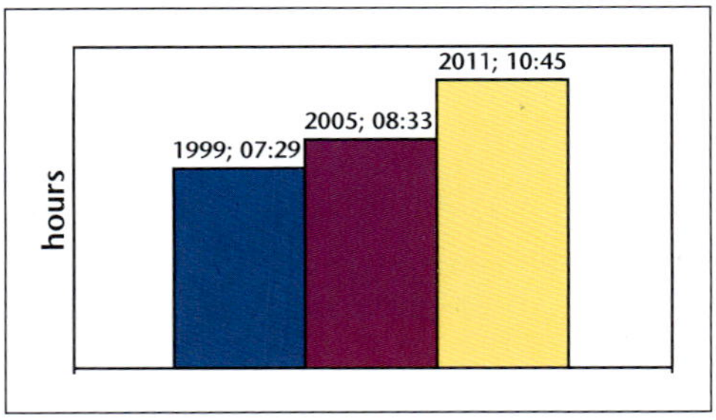

... computer time spent with various activities on a typical day:

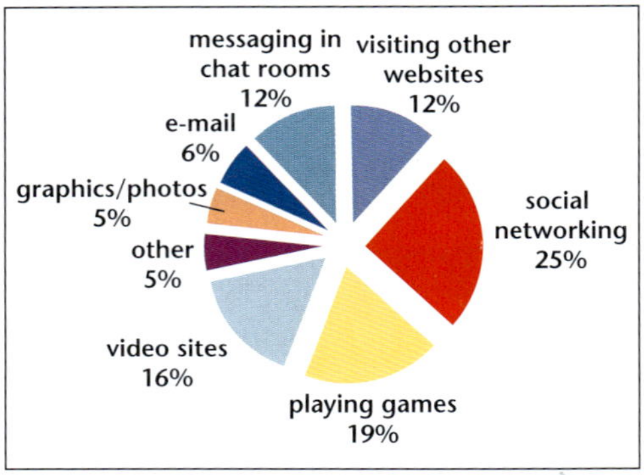

Writing

Task 3

Look at all statistical figures based on the Kaiser Family Foundation study. And compare and discuss them with your partner.

a. Are there figures and trends which surprise you? Or did you expect them? Give reasons.
b. Do you think there are alarming trends? Are these trends typical or rather surprising? Give reasons.
c. Compare your own media habits with the statistics. Do you think they fit to your own media consumption? Or do you think that your media consumption is (much) different?

Task 4

Take down your results in a written analysis.

If you need help, go back to pages 67 and 68. There you will find a skills training and a helpful phrases box on writing an analysis.

Children and watching TV

Today kids take part in the world of television long before they enter school. For example two-thirds of infants and toddlers watch a screen an average of 2 hours a day and kids under 6 years an average of 2 hours of primarily TV or DVDs. Kids older than 6 and teens watch TV an average of 4 hours and very often spend additional hours on the computer (outside of school-work) with playing games or doing console games. Paediatricians believe this to be an alarming trend and are sure that much screen time will have a bad impact on the children's development because the first two years of life are considered a critical time for the brain development. Therefore health experts recommend that kids under 2 years should not watch any TV or be exposed to a screen. They hint at research results which show that young children of households with a TV constantly on often show attention problems and learning difficulties.

But before totally condemning TV one should not forget that it is a source of information and it helps grown-ups as well as children to get some rest and entertainment, thus helping to release tension and relax. TV in moderation can be a good thing. It can help kids to learn about the world. There are children's programmes which are excellent educators, for example preschooler programmes which help to learn the alphabet. Other programmes for school kids give helpful information about wildlife on nature shows or scientific programmes explain physics experiments. There are problem-oriented films which help children to cope with their own problems and develop social skills.

But despite these advantages, as kids grow older, too much screen time can interfere with activities such as being physically active, reading, doing homework, playing with friends, and spending time with the family. Children who spend more than 4 hours a day watching TV are more likely to be overweight.

It is also alarming that families sit together for their evening meal in front of TV. While the family is having their meal, the children are fed with a diet of violence and sex. Experts are sure that children who view violent acts are more likely to show aggressive behaviour but also fear that the world is scary and that something bad will happen to them. TV characters very often depict risky behaviour, they do stunts, or show excessive drinking, and some of the TV programmes reinforce typical gender roles, or racial stereotypes. If children see and hear these kinds of messages again and again, they will take them in as being normal. In the end they cannot tell the difference between fact and fiction and they will, for example, use violence as the only way to 'handle' a conflict, or smoke and drink because they believe it to be appropriate and cool behaviour.

Comprehension

Task 5

Discuss the following statements with your partner and comment on them on the basis of the text and the information you could gather so far.

a. It is no problem to let infants and toddlers watch TV as long as the programme does not depict any violence.
b. Watching TV only makes our children stupid.
c. Watching too many hours screen media can cause serious health problems, especially to babies but also to older children.
d. Watching TV does not have any positive effects at all.
e. TV films and programmes can help children to develop skills.
f. The multitude of screen media destroys our children's literacy skills.
g. Watching evening programmes can be mentally harmful for children.
h. TV cannot take any influence on children under 6, because they are too young to understand and take up TV messages.
i. Children from 6 to 8 cannot be influenced by bad role models in TV programmes because they know that this is not the real world.

Task 6

Complete the following sentences by giving a reason mentioned in the text or adding your own personal opinion.

a. TV should not be used as a babysitter because …
b. Parents should make 'no-screen-time' a rule for their children, who are younger than two years, because …
c. You should not only condemn TV because …
d. It's totally wrong to have a TV set in children's bedrooms because …
e. Parents should not replace reading a bedtime story to their children with letting them watch TV because …
f. Setting up TV-watching rules is important because …
g. The rules should be screen-time and not only TV-watching rules because …

Activity

Task 7

Do some preparatory work as homework. Watch the news, read a daily newspaper for one week and collect news and articles which you think are the most interesting. Then sit in groups to work out a news survey.

a. Present your collection of news topics to your group.
b. Discuss these topics in your group and choose those you believe to be most interesting.
c. Prepare a 5-minute weekly news survey and choose a speaker of your group to read it out in class.

Grammar

Grammar revision

Task 8

Transform the verb in brackets into the Present Simple, Past Simple, Present Perfect or Future (I) Tense.

Despite the experts' advice to stick to a no-screen-time rule before a child's second birthday, there are DVDs and TV-for-babies programmes like the American 'Baby Einstein' and the British 'Teletubbies' which are especially designed to begin watching when two months old.
Who 1 (be) the Teletubbies? In 1996 BBC 2 (start) this children's programme in Great Britain and from there it 3 (spread) over to almost every European country. Its origin 4 (lie) in America. But what 5 (this children's programme/depict)? Mainly it 6 (show) four cuddly creatures looking like a children's soft toys. The red Teletubby is named Po, the purple Tinky Winky, the green Dipsy, and Laa-Laa is the yellow Teletubby. Each creature 7 (represent) a special character trait. For example Tinky Winky, the biggest Teletubby, 8 (love) walking and falling over; Dipsy, the second biggest, 9 (be) fond of dancing. Besides each Teletubby 10 (own) a special thing. Laa-Laa's favourite thing 11 (be) an orange ball and Po, the red and smallest Teletubby, always 12 (appear) with her pink and blue scooter which she 13 (ride) very fast. These favourite things and character traits 14 (never change) since the start of the series and the producers always 15 (point out) that this typical format 16 (not change) in future.
When the programme 17 (start), there 18 (be) quite a lot of people who 19 (criticise) the language the Teletubbies 'speak'. The Teletubbies' movements and language 20 (be) similar to that of a toddler. Up till now educators 21 (not stop) pointing out that this 22 (not stimulate) children to make a progress in learning a language. But the designers of the Teletubbies 23 (be) sure their programme 24 (encourage) curiosity and imagination which 25 (have) a positive impact on the very young children's future development.

Writing

Task 9

Do you know the Teletubbies or any kind of TV-for-babies programme? What do you think of these programmes? Write a comment of about 150 words.

Listening

Task 10

Michael Cooper, 46 years old – Rosalind Hardy, 62 – John, 14 – Emma, 10 – Mary Ryan, 34

Listen to those people talking about their attitude towards TV and favourite TV programmes. Try to understand what their opinions are and take down a short summary of their main ideas.

Discussion

Task 11

Choose one of these statements and say whether you support or reject the speaker's attitude. Support your attitude with at least two personal reasons.

Kathleen Johnson, 78:
Looking at today's programmes like those talk shows, I think TV makes people stupid and teaches them bad manners.

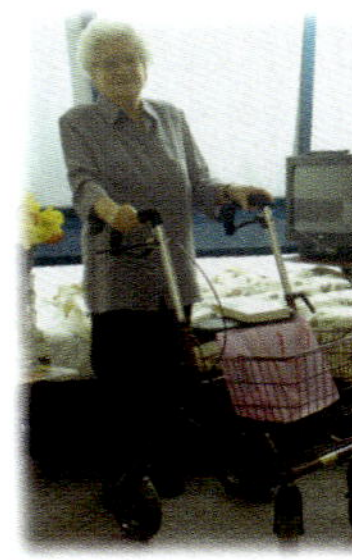

Suzanna Oliver, 42:
Everyone knows about the bad influence TV has on us and our children, but does anyone turn off? It's already too late, we have all lost the ability to sit together and talk. TV kills our ability to talk and be sociable.

Thomas McArthur, 34:
We always sit around dinner or supper with our children and watch TV. Why not? Otherwise I would never have a chance to watch the news and hear about what's going on?

Activity

Task 12

Sit in groups and do your own media research. Maybe ask about what media people use and prefer, or ask about TV habits. What kind of programmes do people prefer? You could compare the new media consumption with the consumption of print media. And, do people multi-task? These are different possibilities. Discuss in your group what you really want to find out about media consumption and work on a questionnaire. Ask pupils and/or students of your school, teachers and maybe family members to gather figures from different age groups.

Sum up your results and present them in class.

Case study: Mary Goldsmith and her two sons

Mary Goldsmith and her two sons aged 9 and 11 are living in Manchester. They took part in research on the role TV plays in British families. Dr Caroline Bowler led this research and she visited Mary for an interview. Here is what she remembered:

'When we entered the living room the television set was on and the children were sitting in front of it not watching any programme but playing with their computer games. Obviously Mary was ironing while she was watching a talk show. We sat down for the interview and Mary kept the TV on but then noticed that it was disturbing us and switched it off.

For Mary Goldsmith and her two sons television is the constant 'background noise' in their household. During the interview Mary said, 'when I get up I go down into the kitchen and first switch on the telly before I go on making coffee. We've got a telly in every room, not a fixed one in the bathroom, but we've got a small portable which I take with me when I take a bath or stay in the bathroom for longer. The telly is still on while we are having our meals and also during the time the children do their homework.'

When Mary had her babies she turned on the TV while she was nursing them and kept it on when she was together with the kids. Now the TV stays on the whole day. There is always some kind of nervous energy which electrifies the household and perhaps as a result her eldest son Benjamin has serious attention problems and suffers from ADD – attention deficit disorder. Mary went on telling us: 'Sometimes he sits on the sofa with the computer on his lap and the TV is still on, but I think the TV calms him in some way. But of course in the next moment he jumps up and runs through the house. He can't stick to one thing for long.' But although both her sons suffer from attention problems Mary still believes that the telly has a lot of good aspects. 'I couldn't get my day done without the telly, of course it's a kind of babysitter and children can learn about life from it. But sometimes there is a part of me that thinks on some level I have done something wrong.'

Comprehension

Task 13

Work on the following questions and find out why Mary's son suffers from attention problems.

a. Describe the atmosphere in Mary Goldsmith's home in Manchester. Why does Caroline Bowler speak of a 'nervous energy which electrifies the household'?
b. What role does TV play for Mary?
c. How does Benjamin's ADD become noticeable? How does Benjamin behave?
d. Why do you think does Mary's son Benjamin suffer from ADD? Take into consideration what you learnt about TV and the impact it has on children.

Activity

Task 14

At the end of the interview Mary says she thinks that 'on some level she has done something wrong'. Imagine Mary feels that she has to change her own and her children's dealing with TV. If she asked you for some advice, what would you tell her to change?

Module 2: Media education

What are media education basics for parents?

Audio

Kate Jordan works for the British magazine 'Parents and Kids'. The topic 'media and children' aroused her attention and she worked on a report for her magazine. One part of her report is an interview with Dr Michael Little who is a leading child psychologist. He is especially interested in the impact media has on children and specialised on media education. Here is the interview:

Kate Jordan: How deep is the impact of media on our children? Some say children catch up what they see and hear very quickly and easily, others say it's exaggerated to claim that children always react to media. What do you believe?

Dr Little: It's naive to think that children don't react to what they see or hear from the media around them or won't take media messages up. Sometimes it's startling. Maybe the radio is on and although your child isn't really listening to the radio and surely will not be able to understand what the topic is, suddenly he or she starts singing an advertising jingle or your child suddenly mimics a TV character. Sadly, this may be the jingle of a popular brand of beer, or a fighting scene which somehow must have got stuck in the child's memory. That's the problem, children can take in those media messages much easier than grown ups but they can't see the difference between good or bad.

Kate Jordan: Let's stick to TV. Some parents believe children should be kept away from TV, others don't see any dangers and even use the TV set as a babysitter.

Dr Little: You mustn't stick to the 'absolutely-no-TV-strategy', if your child is older than two, but using the TV as a babysitter without knowing what the child is watching is irresponsible. Not everything shown on TV is bad for your child. You must set limits with regard to the hours of watching TV, a DVD, or playing a computer game, and surfing the web. And make sure the TV programme or computer game is of good quality.

Kate Jordan: What time limits would you recommend?

Dr Little: I recommend no more than one to two hours of TV or screen media a day for older children and absolutely no screen time for children under two.

Kate Jordan: I think this is sometimes quite difficult to manage. You always have to keep an eye on the time and perhaps sometimes the child wants to watch a children's series and later play computer games but this won't fit in the set time limit.

Dr Little: Well, it's hard work, I know. But parents have to be strict. Only if you show your child that you are serious about it, he or she will understand how serious the matter is. Sometimes we suggest parents to use a timer. When the timer goes off, your child's media time is up, no exceptions.

Kate Jordan: I remember my eight-year-old son coming home from school and asking me to watch a mystery series which obviously wasn't appropriate for him. But he eagerly insisted on it, because 'all the other kids in class are allowed to watch it'. The other thing is that he wants to have a TV set in his bedroom. We have quite some rows about these questions.

Dr Little: These kind of conflicts aren't avoidable, but think of the negative side effects wrong media consumption can have. Research results show that children who watch TV far too much and who are fed with the wrong messages for their young brain may show poor school performance. Those who prefer watching violent TV programmes, mystery or horror films start reacting aggressively towards other kids and adults. Smaller children may have nightmares. Some parents underestimate the influence of commercial spots. Today experts are sure that obesity among young children can partly be put down to wrong advertisement messages children pick up. Keep TV sets, video games and computers out of children's bedrooms. Children must be supervised!

Kate Jordan: So it's important to know what the children are watching.

Dr Little: Yes, absolutely. Parents should set clear guidelines. They have to make clear to their children what they want them to watch. Help children to choose shows, DVDs and video games that are appropriate for their age and interest. Don't let them go into a shop and spend their pocket money on rubbish.

Kate Jordan: That's a lot of checking up. Can you give parents some more practical advice?

Dr Little: Parents should make media a family activity. On the one hand you can sit around a table with your family and set up rules together with the children. Maybe take down the rules on a poster and pin it up as a reminder. On the other hand, whenever possible, use media with your children and discuss what they see, hear and read. When you share your children's media experiences, you can help them to analyse the media messages themselves and find out what is real or unreal, good or bad. That's what we call 'media education'. Try to provoke your child's sense of realism. Question what your child sees. Can someone really be run over by a car and get up and run down the street again? Is this realistic? Then encourage your child to ask their own questions. This will help your child to become a critical media consumer.

Kate Jordan: I think these are a lot of useful ideas parents can work with. Thanks a lot for the interview.

Comprehension

Task 1

Answer the following questions on the text.

a. Do children always react towards media messages?
b. Why does Kate Jordan think it will be difficult for parents to get their children to agree to certain rules?
c. Why should parents be very strict about time limits and what can they do to be in control?
d. What can be possible negative side effects of excessive media consumption?
e. What should media consumption as a family activity look like? What practical advice does Dr Little give?

Task 2

Try to explain what Dr Michael Little talks about when he uses the expression.

a. the absolutely-no-TV-strategy (l. 27)
b. media education (l. 74–75)
c. make media a family activity (l. 68)

Task 3

Match the following sentences on the basis of the information the interview offers you.

1. It's dangerous to use a TV set as a babysitter...
2. Crime series and horror films...
3. Parents should never underestimate...
4. TV research results show that excessive media consumption...
5. Children who watch violent TV programmes or DVDs...
6. If small children watch any kind of film which stirs up fear in them...
7. Advertisement for unhealthy food such as chocolate bars may lead to obesity...

a. ...often show aggressive behaviour towards others.
b. ...because not every programme is appropriate for children.
c. ...the influence TV has on the child's psyche.

d. ...they won't be able to sleep because of nightmares.
e. ...because it suggests to the children that they must buy and eat this chocolate bar to be 'in'.
f. ...may teach the child to use violence against others.
g. ...will cause negative side effects.

Language

Task 4

Can you find words in the interview which are opposites to the following words?

a. play things down
b. stay unmoved
c. similarity
d. break limits
e. passivity
f. sweet dreams

Task 5

Try to change these words from the interview into words of opposite meaning.

a. unhealthy
b. appropriate
c. realistic
d. critical
e. encourage
f. useful

Listening/Writing

Task 6

When Kate Jordan came back to her office she once more listened to the recording of the interview and then took down main ideas as a memory note. What do you think could she have written down? Listen to the interview again or read through it in silence, close the book and try to summarise the main ideas in about 150 words. (If you need help, turn back to Unit 5. Here you will find a skills training and helpful phrases box on writing a summary.)

Activity

Task 7

a. Dr Michael Little suggested sitting around a table and setting up media rules as a family activity. Imagine you are parent of Robert, aged four, and Theresa, aged six. Now sit together in groups and try to set up rules for them and take them down on a poster. Give reasons for your rules. Present your results in class.

1. Robert's watching time is... and Theresa is allowed to...
2. ...
3. ...

b. Dr Michael Little speaks of quality TV for children. What do you believe to be appropriate children's programmes for Robert and Theresa? Look at the media landscape around you. Which children's programmes would you recommend? Are there international programmes which you would regard as quality programmes? Perhaps surf the Web and present your results in class, saying what the programme deals with and giving reasons for your choice.

c. There is a discussion in nursery school about watching TV. Imagine that you are the nursery nurse and you read Kate Jordan's report on the topic. What would you answer to the following questions and statements? Perhaps work on the answers in a group and present the whole discussion in class as a role play.

A: I don't allow my child to watch everything, only some children's programmes. But Mike always tries to argue with me because his friends are allowed to watch just any programme.

B: How many hours is my daughter of 5 allowed to watch? Two, three or even more? What's your suggestion?

C: Sandra always watches the news together with us – why not? It's reality and I can't hide the truth from her? Can I?

D: Honestly sometimes it's the best solution to let Anna sit in front of the TV while I'm ironing or cooking.

E: I don't think it's some kind of catastrophe if my son of 5 sometimes watches an afternoon detective series. Reality can even be more brutal – so what's wrong about letting him watch some of the afternoon programmes?

F: John's older brother Theo has got his own TV set in his bedroom. Now John wants to have one, too. We told him he will have to wait until his eighth birthday as well. Then he will also have his own TV. I myself had my own TV when I was young. This kept a lot of trouble away from my parents.

G: I'm very strict about television. Sheila, my daughter of 6, is only allowed to watch Sesame Street – anything else is just forbidden. I want to keep her away from any kind of brutality. I also read all the children's books myself before she is allowed to have them. If there is anything which might cause any kind of bad feeling or fear, I throw them away.

Module 3: What are the dangers of a media world?

Case study

There is a golden rule in class: All mobiles have to be switched off. Although Julia knows perfectly well about this rule, she breaks it every day because she cannot do without having a glance at the display of her mobile. This is why Julia is lacking in concentration in class and cannot follow her teacher Mrs Hollander. Of course she urges her to be more attentive and switch off her mobile. But Julia only pretends to do so because she wants to keep contact to her friends. Someone is texting her and she cannot resist to answer. It is now the third time that Mrs Hollander urged her to switch off her mobile which means that she has to hand it over. Julia knows that the consequence now is that her mobile will be locked away until next school day. That is the school rule. But Julia does not want to do without her mobile, therefore she starts a fierce argument with her teacher that she needs it, and will not get over the day without her cellphone. She does not want to be 'disconnected from the world' for one single day. But Mrs Hollander does not want to make an exception and asks her again to give her the mobile. Now Julia panics, she vehemently refuses to hand her cellphone over to Mrs Hollander and finally jumps up and runs out of her classroom with her mobile leaving anything else behind.

Task 1

Talk about Julia's behaviour.

a. Describe Julia's attitude towards her mobile.
b. Can you understand her feelings and behaviour?

Task 2

'Our today's teenagers are addicted to mobile phones'. Discuss this statement with your partner.

a. Do you think this statement is true or false? Give your reasons.
b. Looking at Julia's behaviour again, do you think it reflects typical symptoms of addiction?

Task 3

Talk about your own mobile media habits.

a. Do you possess a mobile phone? What kind? And, what do you use it for?
b. How often do you use it? Do you stay in contact all the time? Why yes or no?
c. What does the mobile phone mean to you?

Are today's teenagers addicted to mobile and digital media?

Mobile phones are not only a problem in school classes. Everywhere mobiles are left on. They intrude on most private moments. Teenagers admit using their device in class, in the toilet and would even answer their phone if it woke them up late at night. And who has not experienced situations like these, sitting in a cafe for a quiet moment but being disturbed by a mobile, listening to most private stories or watching a film in the cinema with all kinds of mobile phone tunes as a kind of background music. Not to forget the long arguments parents have with their teen daughter or son because they refuse to switch it off over dinner.
Today smartphones and iPhones are a 'must-have'. Smartphone sales have long outstripped sales of regular mobiles because the teenage yearning for Facebook and social networks has driven a huge demand for these phones.

Many teenagers are fanatical about being always available and are extremely uneasy to contact their friends countless times a day. They not only make calls but also use their devices to send millions of text messages to friends each day. All this arouses the impression that they are addicted to this media.

Experts believe this to be a rather alarming trend because it shows that teenagers will soon be incapable of forming and maintaining relationships without the help of a mobile and staying in touch seems to matter more than actually leading a communication which has some kind of content. Teenagers invest more time with sending messages, sitting in front of their computer and contacting people on social networks than actually being physically active in a group. They hate to feel as if they are not in a group, and think that without a smartphone they will be left out. Frequent e-mailing takes time which they should spend for reading, studying or recreating. The only spare time left over is often spent on a job financing their mobile. But speaking on the phone and sending lots of text messages, or posting messages in a social network, can in reality not replace a real talk and real friendship. Having lots of acquaintances in a social network is rather showing that you are socially isolated. A lot of teenagers mix up quantity with quality.

Comprehension

Task 4

Look through the text again and find the words which fit the following definitions.

a. expression for equipment, here it is used for any kind of mobile phone.
b. disturb
c. be a lot better than something or someone else
d. easy to get or buy
e. to be unable to do something
f. keep something in a good condition
g. relaxing
h. people you know, friends

Task 5

Answer the questions on the text.

a. What typical symptoms of an addiction to mobile and digital media do teenagers show?
b. Why have smart phones become popular in the recent years?
c. How do the new mobile and digital media influence teenage friendship? How did the character of friendship change?
d. What consequences do the new mobile media have for a teenager's private life?

Task 6

Here are some statements taken from the text. Explain in your own words what they want to express and point out.

a. They (= mobiles) intrude on most private moments. (l. 3)
b. ... staying in touch seems to matter more than actually leading a communication which has some kind of content. (l. 28–29)

c. Having lots of acquaintances in a social network is rather showing that you are socially isolated. (l. 37–38)
d. A lot of teenagers mix up quantity with quality. (l. 38–39)

Language

Task 7

Do you know the nouns which fit to the following verbs?

a. intrude	b. sell	c. demand	d. replace
e. isolate	f. contact	g. impress	h. matter
i. refuse	j. communicate	k. admit	l. maintain

Task 8

Translate the following sentences into English.

a. Mein Mobiltelefon ist eingeschaltet, weil ich immer erreichbar sein möchte.
b. Ich investiere in das Versenden von Nachrichten viel Zeit, um meine Bekanntschaften im sozialen Netz aufrecht zu erhalten.
c. Ich habe keine Freizeit mehr übrig, weil ich sehr viel Zeit mit meinen Mailkontakten verbringe.
d. Ich arbeite, um mein Smartphone zu finanzieren.

Violence in screen media – What influence does it have on young children?

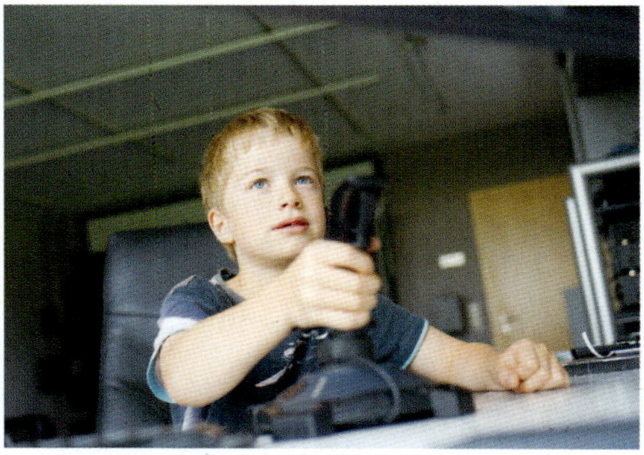

1 The average American child will witness 200,000 violent acts on TV by age 18. But that is not the only violence they may meet. There are lots of computer games glorifying violence. Psychologists think that the digital world these computer games build up in front of the children's eyes can be dangerous. Children immerse in this fictional world losing their grip to reality. And the violence which they can actively inflict on their fictional enemy may desensitize them and make them more aggressive.

Violent acts shown on TV invite children to imitate them because they are very often promoted as fun and the best way to get what you want. Many TV series present violent acts which are perpetrated by the 'good guys'. And kids admire them. Parents telling that it is not okay to hit someone are forgotten as soon as the good guy bites, hits, kicks, or even shoots someone and is rewarded for that.

Today psychologists are sure that children with emotional and behavioural problems are more easily influenced by TV. The impact TV violence has on children may immediately become evident, small children directly suffer from nightmares and difficulties in going to sleep. With older children the exposure to violence may surface years later in aggressive behaviour towards others.

Task 9

Discuss the following statements with your partner.

a. Do you think they are true or false? Give reasons.
b. Do you know examples which support your point of view?

A: It's no wonder that some of the school shooters spent a lot of time with violent computer games before they finally went into schools to kill.
B: Today more and more people quit the real world to live an artificial life in a digital world because they don't want to be confronted with their own frustrating and boring reality.
C: The digital world is a world full of fighting. Computer games very often depict worlds which are full of enemies you can only combat with brutality.
D: Most TV heroes and those of computer games are dangerous for kids.

Task 10

Work through the next case study.

a. First make sure that you understand the text. Maybe make use of a bilingual dictionary.
b. Sum up the main facts in about 100 words.

Case study: Robert Thompson and Jon Venables

Although the following case of Robert Thompson and Jon Venables already happened years ago, psychologists still refer to it as an example for the impact televised violence can have on children.
Robert Thompson and Jon Venables took James Bulger, a two-years-old boy, from a shopping centre where he had gone with his mother. In a short moment in which his mother left James out of her sight they marched him two miles away to a railway line where they battered him with bricks, punched, kicked and finally killed him. The killers were each aged ten and six months at the time.
Both Thompson and Venables came from broken homes. Venables's parents were separated but cooperated in a friendly way for the sake of their children. They had two other children, one with learning difficulties. Jon was also put back a year in school although he was considered to be intelligent enough. Like Venables, Thompson had been relegated to a younger class, not because he was stupid, but because he played truant. In a single term he had missed half of the lessons. Thompson was one of a family of seven children aged between 8 and 20. His father left the family when Thompson was only 5. He was apparently knocked about by his older brothers. Some of the children had been taken into care. His mother was known to be 'fond of drinking'. Seven months before the murder she had a baby by another man.

Both murderers and the victim lived in Kirkby, a town north-east of Liverpool with a bad reputation by that time. It was a crime-ridden town with the most vandalized phone boxes and the worst truancy rate in Britain. In Country Road, the 'home ground' of Thompson and Venables, the boys were known as notorious troublemakers, vandals and shoplifters. They spent much of their spare time in video shops.
Police investigation found evidence that in one of the boy's homes there had been over 400 videos in only a couple of years, 64 of which contained violence or soft pornographic material.
The last video rented by Jon Venables's father before James was killed was the adult horror video 'Child's Play 3'. Neil Venables denied letting his son watch the film, but there were startling parallels between its plot and little James Bulger's fate.
The video depicts a doll called Chucky dressed in toddler's clothes. This doll comes to life. In a fight Chucky is splashed with blue paint and during the film's final scene the doll's head is mutilated and he is chopped to death on a funfair ghost train railway line. The boys splashed James's head with blue paint before battering his skull and placing his body on the railway line.

(Robert Thompson and Jon Venables were sentenced to life-long imprisonment on November 24th, 1993)

Comprehension

Task 11

Find out why both boys might have become brutal murderers by working on the following questions.

a. Describe Robert Thompson's and Jon Venables's family situation and social environment.
b. How did both boys spend most of their days?
c. Which aspects of their story and deed underline the conclusion that their liking for certain horror videos can be an explanation for their deed?
d. Do you think that their exposure to horror videos is the only explanation for their deed? Are there other reasons which can be found in their social situation?

Task 12

Now write an essay on the question why the two boys became Britain's youngest killers.

If you need some help on essay writing, look at Unit 6, page 137. There you will find a skills training and a helpful phrases box on essay writing.

Cartoons on TV violence and children

Talking about the cartoons

Task 13

Work on the cartoons with your partner.

a. Find a subtitle or title for each of the cartoons and tell your class why you choose them for the cartoons.
b. Which of the cartoons do you like best? Why?
c. What is the message each cartoon tries to bring forward? Give reasons for your opinion.

Writing

Task 14

Choose one of the cartoons and write an analysis. (If you need some help, turn back to Unit 8, page 175. There you will find a skills training and a helpful phrases box on analysing cartoons.)

Vocabulary

English – German

Starter

introduce oneself to – sich vorstellen
productive conversation – gelungenes Gespräch
be responsible for – verantwortlich sein für
skills – Fähigkeiten, (berufl.) Fertigkeiten
common – allgemein
sit in a circle – im Kreis sitzen
join a group – sich einer Gruppe anschließen
achieve – erreichen
in any case – auf jeden Fall
strange face – fremdes Gesicht
majority – Mehrheit
cautious – vorsichtig
intimidated – eingeschüchtert
result in – hier: führen zu
health Gesundheit care – Pflege, Betreuung
care work – Sozial- und/oder Gesundheitspflege/arbeit
social worker – Sozialarbeiter
child care worker – Sozial- und Gesundheitspfleger/in für Kinder
job training – Berufsausbildung
placement – Praktikum
university entrance qualification – Zulassung zur Universität/Fachschule, vgl. mit (Fach)Abitur
childminder – Kinderbetreuerin, auch: Tagesmutter
mind children – Kinder betreuen
participant – Teilnehmerin/Teilnehmer
nursery school – Kindergarten
colleague – Kollege/Kollegin
staff meeting – Mitarbeiterbesprechung
exchange student – Austauschschülerin/Austauschschüler
host – hier: Animateur
hostess – hier: Animateurin
formal gathering – formale Zusammenkunft, hier: Besprechung im Berufsleben
depend on – abhängen von
work experience – Berufserfahrung
icebreaker – Eisbrecher, hier: gemeinsame Aktivität zum Kennenlernen/zur Stimmungsauflockerung
personality – Persönlichkeit
cooperation – Zusammenarbeit
understanding –Verständnis
preparation – Vorbereitung
blackboard – Tafel
description – Beschreibung
repetition –Wiederholung
reflect – reflektieren, wiedergeben, überdenken, darstellen
sign – unterschreiben
pen name – Pseudonym, erfundener Name
add – hinzufügen
subdivide – unterteilen
goal – Tor, hier: Ziel
heroine – Heldin
hero – Held
category – Kategorie, hier: Oberbegriff für Unterteilung
proposal – Vorschlag
invent – erfinden

Unit 1
Care worker– a job with a difference

care worker – Sozial- und/oder Gesundheitspfleger
care assistant – Sozialassistent
special need – hier: Behinderung
assist – helfen, assistieren
residential setting – Heim
include – beinhalten
personal care – Persönlichkeitsfürsorge
social care – Sozialfürsorge
medical care – Gesundheitsfürsorge
first aid – erste Hilfe
domestic care – Haushaltsfürsorge
professional – hier: ausgebildet
educator – Erzieher/in
medical assistant – medizinische(r) Assistent(in)
nursery nurse – Kinderpfleger(in)/Kindergärtner(in)
dietician – Diät–/Ernährungsberater(in)
occupational therapist – Beschäftigungstherapeut(in)
education worker – Erziehungspfleger für schulische oder Ausbildungsbelange
old people's nurse – Altenpfleger (in)
child care home –Kinderpflegeheim
old people's home – Altenpflegeheim
day care – Tagespflege

change dressings – Verbände wechseln
lift – heben
patient – Patient
homeless people – Obdachlose
counsel – beraten
distribute – verteilen, austeilen
supervise – beaufsichtigen
do handcraft – basteln
look after – sich kümmern um, pflegen, für jmd. sorgen
care for – sich kümmern um, pflegen, für jmd. sorgen
support – unterstützen, auch: stützen
watch – beobachten, beaufsichtigen
supply with – versorgen mit
night shift – Nachtschicht
ward – Krankenhausstation
outing – Ausflug
attentive – aufmerksam
district – hier: Verwaltungsbezirk
sick – krank
exam – Examen, Abschlussprüfung
take responsibility – Verantwortung übernehmen
result – Ergebnis
excellent – hervorragend
patient file – Krankenakte
examine – untersuchen
worry s.o. – jmd. beunruhigen
emergency case – Notfall
emergency call – Notruf
bathe – baden
carefully – vorsichtig
child care – Kinderpflege
chat – Gespräch, Plauderei
lonesome – einsam
maternal clinic – Geburtsklinik
ambulance – Krankenwagen
be contented – zufrieden sein
genuine interest – echtes, aufrichtiges Interesse
unpleasant – unerfreulich
good listener – guter Zuhörer
properly – ordentlich, sorgsam
safe – sicher
be in charge of – zuständig sein für, hier: die Leitung haben
employee – Mitarbeiter(in)
trust – Vertrauen
be responsible for – verantwortlich sein für
education – Erziehung
constant – fortwährend, stets, konstant
sort things out – hier: die Dinge klären
stabilise – (sich) stabilisieren
qualification – Qualifikation, auch: Berufs-oder Schulabschluss
high school diploma – Hochschul/ Universitätsabschluss
voluntary – freiwillig
apply for – sich bewerben für
degree – hier: Abschluss
requirements – Voraussetzungen, Bedingungen
fulfil – erfüllen
necessary – notwendig
flexible – flexibel
tolerant – tolerant, aufgeschlossen
share – teilen
pass – hier: bestehen
GCSE – Abschluss der Sekundarstufe II
A–level – vergleichbar mit Fachhochschulreife
College of Further Education – Berufskolleg
careers adviser – Berufsberater
school–leaver – Schulabsolvent(in)
indecisive – unentschlossen
register at – sich an der Hochschule einschreiben
mention – erwähnen
future prospects – Zukunftsaussichten
suggest – vorschlagen
offer – Angebot
provide – hier: zur Verfügung stellen, ausschreiben
compulsory – obligatorisch, Pflicht- . . .
curriculum vitae (CV) – Lebenslauf
resumé – Lebenslauf
references – hier: Referenzen
attend – hier: (eine Schule) besuchen
gain – hier: (Berufserfahrung) sammeln
graduate from – eine Schule absolvieren/mit einem Abschluss verlassen
produce – hier: vorlegen
neat final version – eine saubere Endversion
body of the letter – Hauptteil des Briefes
complementary close – Schlusszeile
subject matter – Betriffzeile
salutation – Anrede
inside address – Adresse des Empfängers auf dem Brief
date – Datum
advertised – annonciert
enclose – hier: beifügen
attention – hier: zu Händen
avoid – vermeiden

confusions – Verwechslungen
signature – Unterschrift
enclosure – Anlage (eines Briefes)
deafblind – taub und blind
work conditions – Arbeitsbedingungen
spare time – hier: Zeit aufbringen
disability – Behinderung
advantageous – von Vorteil, vorteilhaft
reliability – Zuverlässigkeit
patience – Geduld
vital – hier: wichtig, entscheidend
job interview – Vorstellungsgespräch
exchange programme – Austauschprogramm
social gap year – freiwilliges soziales Jahr
agency – Agentur
assessment centre – Auswahlzentrum, auch: Prüfungszentrum
assessment board – Auswahlgremium, auch: Prüfungsausschuss
allocation – Verteilung
be fed up with – etwas satt haben, die Nase voll haben von
invite – einladen
casual clothes – hier: Alltagskleidung
convey the impression – den Eindruck vermitteln
outward appearance – äußeres Erscheinungsbild
consist of – bestehen aus
personnel manager – Personalchef
awkward – seltsam
unpleasant – unangenehm
purposely – aus Absicht, absichtlich
avoid – vermeiden
failure – Fehlschlag
be out to make the impression – einen Eindruck hinterlassen wollen
interaction – Interaktion, kommunikativer Austausch
facial expression – Gesichtsausdruck
posture – Körperhaltung
defensive – verteidigend, in einer Verteidigungshaltung
barrier – Barriere, Hinternis
folder – Aktenordner
trust – vertrauen
mistrust – mistrauen
eye contact – Blickkontakt
fidget – zappeln
wring hands – Hände ringen
crossed – verschränkt, über Kreuz
be aware – hier: sei vorsichtig!
be concerned – sich um etwas sorgen, hier: an etwas interessiert sein
lean towards – sich lehnen/neigen (nach), anlehnen
colleague – Kollege/Kollegin
canteen kitchen – Großküche
common rooms – Gemeinschaftsräume
caretaker – Hausmeister
staff – Personal
be equipped with – ausgestattet sein mit
training – hier: Schulung, Fortbildung
lecture – Vortrag
blackboard – Tafel
interrupt – unterbrechen
volunteer – Freiwillige(r)
storage room – Lagerraum
staff room – Personalraum
first aid room – Sanitätsraum
transparency – Overheadfolie
trainee – Auszubildende(r)
child sized – kindgerechte Größe
sink – Spüle
play carpet – Spielteppich
cloakroom – Garderobe
quiet corner – Kuschelecke
blanket – Decke
mattress – Matratze
block – Spielblöcke, Spielklötze
cutlery – Besteck
dishes – Geschirr
notice board – Pinnwand
wall bars – Sprossenwand
climbing frame – Klettergerüst
sick bed – Krankenbett
wheelchair – Rollstuhl
sick room/hospital room – Patientenzimmer
treatment room – Behandlungszimmer
operation theatre – Operationssaal
day room – Aufenthaltsraum

Unit 2
Working World

unemployed – arbeitslos
night shift – Nachtschicht
surgery – Operation, chirurgischer Eingriff
emergency – Notfall
lose a job – einen Job/die Arbeit verlieren
serious – ernst, ernsthaft
pay off – abbezahlen
bank loan – Bankkredit

unemployment – Arbeitslosigkeit
rate of unemployment – Arbeitslosenrate
high – hoch
low – niedrig
as … as – so … wie
almost the same – fast gleich
than – als
less … than – weniger .. als
angel – Engel
white coat – hier: Schwesterntracht, auch Arztkittel
ironed – gebügelt
fatally ill – unheilbar erkrankt
energetic – voller Engergie, „energiegeladen"
human being – menschliches Wesen
insight – Einblick
shortage – Kürzung
immense – immens, gewaltig
strain – Stress, Belastung
be inspired to do sth. – inspiriert/motiviert sein etwas zu tun
gratitude – Dankbarkeit
tiredness – Müdigkeit
vigour – hier: Schwung, Elan
exhausted – erschöpft
enthusiasm – Enthusiasmus, Begeisterung
reward – belohnen
independent – unabhängig
day care – hier: Ganztagseinrichtung
short of breath – kurzatmig
oxygen – Sauerstoff
treatment – Behandlung
accompany s.o. – jmd. begleiten
privileged – priviligiert, heausragend
privileged thing – hier: etwas Besonderes
consoling words – tröstende Worte
efficient – effizient, wirtschaftlich
occupied – belegt
physical – körperlich
emotional – psychisch, emotional
racial discrimination – Diskriminierung von Ausländern, Ausländerfeindlichkeit
sexual harassment – sexuelle Belästigung
outdated – hier: veraltet
drained – ausgelaugt
equal share – gleiche Beteiligung, gleicher Anteil
gradually – allmählich
overwhelmed – überfordert
guilty – schuldig
lack of time – Zeitmangel
childminder – Kinderbetreuer(in)
interactive – interaktiv, in einem gemeinsamen aktiven Austauch sein
irresponsible – unverantwortlich
personality – Persönlichkeit
vulnerable – verletzlich
weak – schwach
rely on – abhängen von, abhängig sein von
income – Einkommen
particularly – besonders, insbesonders
attitude – Haltung, Meinung
strength – Stärke
weakness – Schwäche
survey – Umfrage
questionnaire – Fragebogen
voluntary social year – freiwilliges soziales Jahr
clue – Idee, Vorstellung von etwas
face – hier: konfrontiert sein mit, gegenüber treten/stehen
gap year – ein Jahr Auszeit
university graduate – Universitätsabsolvent(in)
volunteer – Freiwillige(r), Voluntär(in)
lend a hand – mit anpacken, zupacken
cope with a situation – mit einer Situation umgehen
demanding – anspruchsvoll
introduction – Einführung, hier auch: Einweisung
challenge – Herausforderung
secure – sicher

Unit 3
Living in a family

decrease – abnehmen
raise a family – eine Familie gründen
cancer – Krebs (Krankheit)
nag at s.o. – (umgangssprachl) jmdn. eine Standpauke halten, jmdn. kritisieren
supply s.o. with – jm. mit etwas versorgen
introduce into society – in die Gesellschaft einführen
primary school – Grundschule
divided into – eingeteilt in/aufgeteilt in
extended family – Großfamilie
nuclear family – Kleinfamilie
patchwork family – Familie, die sich aus zwei Familien neu zusammensetzt
single-parent family – Familie mit nur einem Elternteil
stepmother – Stiefmutter
stepfather – Stiefvater

stepchildren – Stiefkinder
divorce – Scheidung
loss – Verlust
stem from – stammen von
master a problem – ein Problem meistern
working–class area – Arbeiterviertel
run a restaurant – ein Restaurant betreiben
emigrate – auswandern, emigrieren
family party – Familienfeier
marriage market – "Heiratsmarkt"
be promised to s.o. – jmd. versprochen werden
have the impression that – den Eindruck haben, dass
lead on – weiterführen
get divorced – sich scheiden lassen, geschieden werden
feel ashamed – sich schämen
keep up a marriage – eine Ehe aufrecht erhalten
stick together – zusammen halten
witness – Zeuge, hier: Trauzeuge
spoil a child – ein Kind verwöhnen
self–centred – egoistisch
siblings – Geschwister
pamper – verwöhnen, verhätscheln
strict – streng
adopt – adoptieren
adoption – Adoption, auch: übernehmen
extra-large family – Großfamilie mit mehr als 4 Kindern
education – Erziehung
survey – Studie, auch: Überblick
professional – hier: berufstätig
wealthy – wohlhabend
peaceful – friedlich
operation – hier: (Militär)Einsatz
minority – Minderheit
majority – Mehrheit
occupation – Ein-/Übernahme, Besetzung, hier: Nutzung
chores – Haushaltspflichten
range from… to – reichen von … bis
fend for oneself – sich selber helfen/versorgen
yell – schreien, rufen
cliché – Klischee, voreingenommene Meinung
respond to – reagieren auf
sibling – Geschwisterkind
entrance examination – Aufnahmeprüfung
intellectual development – intelektuelle/geistige Entwicklung
challenge – Herausforderung
minor – unbedeutend, unwichtig
mentally exhausted – geistig erschöpft
face – konfrontiert werden mit, sich einer Sache stellen/gegenübertreten
prejudices – Vorurteile
meet with – stoßen auf
disapproval – Missbilligung
take precautions – hier: verhüten
associate with – in Verbindung bringen mit, assoziieren mit
disadvantaged – benachteiligt
s.o. lacks s.th. – jm. mangelt es an etwas
lack of – Mangel an …
raise a child – ein Kind großziehen
feeling of inferiority – Minderwertigkeitsgefühl
family advice centre – Familienberatung
controversial – kontrovers, umstritten
draw the conclusion – zu dem (Ab)Schluss kommen, eine Schlussfolgerung ziehen aus
point out – herausstellen
health insurance – Krankenversicherung
provision for old age – Altersvorsorge

Unit 4
Growing up

argue – hier: verbal streiten
puberty – Pubertät
pass a time – eine Zeit durchlaufen/durchmachen
rebellion – Rebellion, Widerspruch
arising sexuality – erwachende Sexualität
appearance – Erscheinung, äußeres Erscheinungsbild
bad temper – schlechte Laune
lack of understanding – mangelndes Verständnis
withdrawal – Rückzug, Sich-Zurückziehen
spots – Pickel
wrinkles – (Gesichts)Falten
hint at – weisen auf
hormone changes – hormonelle Veränderungen
experiment – experimentieren, ausprobieren
contraception – Verhütung
the pill – die Pille
condom – Kondom
guy (slang) – Kerl, Typ
secretly – heimlich
behaviour – Verhalten
influence – Einfluss
dye – färben
nearby – in der Nähe
weird – verdreht, komisch

forbid, forbade, forbidden – verbieten
hurt, hurt, hurt – verletzen
be upset – enttäuscht/traurig sein
make a fuss about – etwas übertreiben
refuse – ablehnen, sich weigern
bombard s.o. with – jmd. mit etwas bombardieren
reproach – Vorwurf
reproach s.o. for sth. – jmd. etwas vorwerfen
best manners – beste Manieren
Middle Ages – Mittelalter
handle sth. – mit etwas umgehen
advice corner – Ratschlagecke/Rubrik mit Briefen ratsuchender Leser
agony aunt – Kummerkastentante
Comprehensive sex education – gemeinsame (Jungen+Mädchen) Sexualerziehung
wink at – jmd. zuzwinkern
flatter – schmeicheln
cause – verursachen, hier: dazu bewegen
conception – Empfängnis
escort – begleiten
fall pregnant – schwanger werden
integral parts – (integrale) Bestandteile
enter a relationship – eine Beziehung eingehen
muddle through – sich durchschlagen
pressure – Druck
figure – hier: Figur
blossom – erblühen, sich entfalten, zu etwas heranwachsen
pass for – hier: als ... durchgehen
virginity – Jungfräulichkeit
physically – körperlich
motherhood – Mutterschaft
morning sickness – morgendliche Übelkeit
reflect – überdenken, reflektieren
blame for – beschuldigen
tell s.o. the facts of life – jmd. aufklären
chubby – pummelig, rundlich
creche – Kinderkrippe
veer off – abdrehen, hier: einem Gespräch eine Wendung geben
salvation – Rettung, Heil
mortification – äußerste Verlegenheit, Demütigung
judgemental – hier: anklagend, verurteilend
baby-flap – Babyklappe
distress – Bedrängnis, verzweifelte Lage
sex education – Sexualerziehung
take into consideration – in Erwägung ziehen
act on – reagieren auf
be aware about – sich bewusst sein über
unwanted pregnancy – ungewollte Schwangerschaft
raise the subject – das Thema ansprechen
nursery school age – Kindergartenalter
switch off – hier: nicht mehr zuhören
French kiss – Zungenkuss
at first hand – zuerst, an erster Stelle
encourage – hier: ermutigen
sex organs – Sexualorgane
'babies aren't found under the gooseberry bush' – Babys werden nicht vom Klapperstorch gebracht
sex act – Sexualakt
scientific – wissenschaftlich
concept – Konzept, Plan
present so. with sth. – jm. etwas übergeben/überreichen
launch – anlaufen lassen, herausbringen
depict – darstellen
transmitted disease – Übertragungskrankheit, Infektionskrankheit
be infected – infiziert sein
sexual intercourse – Geschlechtsverkehr
semen – Sperma
vaginal fluid – Vaginalflüssigkeit
share needles – Nadeln miteinander teilen
haemophiliac – Bluter
act of procreation – Zeugungsakt
be barred from – ausgeschlossen/ausgesperrt sein

Unit 5
When a family breaks apart

trouble kids – Problemkinder
misbehave – sich schlecht benehmen, ungezogen sein
temper tantrums – Wutanfall, Trotzreaktion
rude – grob, hier: ungezogen, unverschämt, unhöflich
yell – schreien, yell at s.o. – jmd. anschreien
drive s.o. insane – jmd. in den Wahnsinn treiben
disturb (a relationship) – (eine Beziehung/Verhältnis) zerstören
impact on – Einfluss auf
parenting programme – Erziehungskurs ("Elternführerschein")
troubleshooter – „Problemfinder", Supervisor/in
settle an argument – einen Streit beilegen

provoke – provozieren
impulsive – impulsiv
damage – zerstören, beschädigen
wilfully – absichtlich, mit voller Absicht
set rules – Regeln aufstellen/setzen
feedback – Rückmeldung
praise – Lob
feel pushed aside – sich zur Seite geschoben fühlen/sich übergangen fühlen
bad conscience – schlechtes Gewissen
put pressure on – unter Druck setzen/Druck ausüben auf
refuse – sich weigern, verweigern
parenting styles – Erziehungsstile
authoritative – entschieden, verlässlich, hier: demokratischer Erziehungsstil
interfere in – sich einmischen in
authoritarian – autoritär, dominant, beherrschend
best perfomances – hier: beste Noten und bestes Betragen
educational methods – Erziehungsmethoden
threatening – hier: Drohung, Angst–Einflößen
punishing – Bestrafen
keep discipline – die Disziplin aufrecht erhalten
indulgent – nachsichtig, (zu) nachgiebig
attentively – aufmerksam
uninvolved – gleichgültig
at the extreme – im Extremfall
neglect – Vernachlässigung
desperate – verzweifelt
transform – umwandeln
viewer – hier: Fernsehzuschauer
down–to–earth – bodenständig, praktisch, realistisch
psychologist – Psychologe/in
behavioral scientist – Verhaltenswissenschaftler
day–to–day – täglich
demonstrate – vorführen, demonstrieren
implement – durchführen, ausführen, hier: in die Tat umsetzen
make an effort – sich anstrengen, sich bemühen
particularly – insbesondere
time out – Auszeit
naughty – ungezogen
distraction – hier: Ablenkung
conform to – entsprechen, sich anpassen
decisive – entschieden, „durchgreifend"
give an account – einen Bericht geben, berichten
choose as a topic – zum Thema wählen
subdivide – unterteilen
introductory sentence – Einleitungssatz
depict – zeigen, abbilden
expose – entblößen, zur Schau stellen
high chair/child seat – Kinderhochsitz
grab – greifen (nach)
fooling around – Unsinn machen
tear down/tore/torn – herunterreißen
vehemently – vehement, heftig
divorce – Scheidung
divorce rate – Scheidungsrate
persuade – überreden
irrevocable – unumstößlich, unabänderlich
socially accepted – gesellschaftlich anerkannt
financially dependent on – finanziell abhängig von
stigma – Brandmal, Stigma, Stigmatisierung
blame – Schuld
blame s.o. for – jmd. die Schuld an etwas geben
attach to sb./sth – an jmd./an etwas hängen
nevertheless – trotzdem, dennoch
distress – Verzweiflung, Kummer, Sorge
victimless – opferlos, ohne Opfer
tend to – neigen zu
family advice centre – Familienberatungsstelle
behavioural science – Verhaltensforschung
family law – Familienrecht
Youth Welfare Department – Jugendamt
psychic strain – psychische Belastung
leave its mark on sb./sth – seine Spuren auf jmd./etwas hinterlassen
arrangements about – Absprachen über
visiting days – Besuchstage
get noticed – hier: auffällig werden
grant sth. to sb – jmd etwas zusprechen
custody – hier: Sorgerecht
maintenance – hier: Unterhalt
disobey – nicht gehorchen, sich widersetzen
yell – schreien, hier auch: jmd. anschreien
inevitable – unvermeidlich
emotional abuse – emotioneller Missbrauch
insult – Beleidigung
ridicule – sich lächerlich machen, hier: das Lächerlichmachen
humiliation – Demütigung
blaming – anklagend, verantwortlich machend
shaming – beleidigend
vent – hier: seinen Gefühlen freien Lauf lassen
social interaction – sozialer Umgang/ Kommunikation

inflict on – zufügen
deliberately – absichtlich
impel so to do sth – jmd. nötigen etwas zu tun
physical power – hier: körperliche Gewalt
take a risk – ein Risiko eingehen
injure – verwunden, eine Wunde zufügen
child abuse – Kindes-missbrauch
child mistreatment – Kindes-misshandlung
beat – schlagen
shake – schütteln
push – stoßen, schupsen
choke – drosseln, würgen
burn – verbrennen
kick – treten
attack s.o. with a weapon – jmd. mit einer Waffe angreifen
fondling – schmusen, streicheln
rape – Vergewaltigung
prostituting s.o. – jmd. prostituieren
shelter – Obdach
threat – Drohung
intimidation – Einschüchterung
be at loggerheads – sich in den Haaren liegen, einen Streit haben
sulky – schmollend, beleidigt
dumb struck (slang) – stumm, sprachlos/„mit Stummheit geschlagen"
infuriate – zornig machen
fierce – hier: heftig
intervene in – sich einmischen in
family affairs – Familienangelegenheiten

Unit 6
Food and Health

guidelines – Richtlinien, Grundsätze
nutrition – Ernährung
wide variety – breite Vielfalt
diet – 1. Ernährung, 2. Diät
promote health – Gesundheit fördern
nutrients– Nährstoffe
unbalanced diet – unausgewogene Ernährung
well–balanced – ausgewogene Ernährung
eating habits – Essgewohnheiten
menu – Speiseplan
menu plan – Essensplan
ought – sollte
lean meat – mageres Fleisch
rusty – rostig, verrostet
whole–grain – Vollkorn
chips – Pommes Frittes
crisps – Chips
cereal – Getreide, hier: Cornflakes, Müsli etc.
level – Anteil, Grad, Niveaux
carbohydrates – Kohlenhydrate
minerals – Mineralien
fibre – Balaststoffe
servings – hier: Portionen
chocolate bar – Schokoriegel
candies – Bonbons, Süßigketen
biscuit – Keks
nuts – Nüsse
liquid – Flüssigkeit
quench thirst – Durst stillen
still water – stilles Mineralwasser
sparkling water – sprudelndes Mineralwasser
workout – hier: körperliche Belastung/Training
muscles – Muskeln
bones – Knochen
cycle – Rad fahren
dairy products – Milchprodukte
starchy products – stärkehaltige Produkte
bread rolls – Brötchen
lamb – Lamm
Brussels sprouts – Rosenkohl
peanut – Erdnuss
liver sausage – Leberwurst
cauliflower – Blumenkohl
chop – Kotelett
courgette– Zucchini
cod – Kabeljau
peas – Erbsen
raspberry – Himbeere
plaice – Scholle
sporty – sportlich
protein – Protein
scrambled eggs – Rührei
side dish – Beilage
overweight – übergewichtig
be obsessed by – besessen sein von
slim – abnehmen
slim down – „herunter hungern"
lettuce leaf – Salatblatt
cottage cheese – Hüttenkäse
replace with – ersetzen durch, austauschen mit
put on weight – Gewicht zulegen
a tough diet – eine strenge Diät
fierce – wild, hier: übertrieben
fizzy drinks – hier: Limonaden, süße Getränke
cookery writer – Kochbuchautor
nutritional guidelines – Ernäherungsrichtlinien

vending machine – Automat
shun – hier: versäumen, auslassen
beverages – Getränke
introduce – hier: einführen
taxes – Steuern
malnutrition – Fehlernährung
caffeine – Koffein
confectionery – Konditorwaren, Süßwaren
bun – Brötchen, auch/hier: süßes Teilchen
pastry – Pastete
label – Produktetikett, Aufkleber
labeling – Etikettierung
nutrition label – Etikett-Information über Inhaltsstoffe
additional information – Zusatzinformation
manufacturer – Hersteller
obesity – Fettleibigkeit
heart failure – Herzversagen
triple – verdreifachen
measure – messen, hier: wiegen
relate to – hier: in Verbindung bringen mit
breathing assistance – Atemhilfe
blocked airways – blockierte Atemwege
kingsized/supersized – extra große Portionen
soaked with – durchtränkt mit
lack of exercise – Bewegungsmangel
packaged meals – Fertiggerichte
laden with – überladen mit
obese – fettleibig
trap – Falle
split from – sich trennen von
comfort eating – „Frustessen"
shopaholic – jemand, der viel und gerne einkauft
'for the sheer hell of it' (Slang) – einfach so, einfach aus Spaß
deny – hier: verweigern
convenience food – Fertiggerichte
chilled section – Kühlregal, Kühlwarenabteilung
stodge (Slang) – Gebäck
ditch – in den Abfall werfen
kick off (Slang) – herauswerfen, hier: aus dem Programm nehmen
food coaching – „Esstraining", Ernährungsberatung
harsh – hart, streng
conscious – bewusst
trolley – Einkaufswagen
additives – Zusätze, Zusatzstoffe
preservatives – Konservierungsstoffe
podgy – rundlich, pummelig
chocolate spread – Schokoladenbrotaufstrich
jellies – Fruchtgummibonbons
fish fingers – Fischstäbchen
issue – Thema, Streitfrage, Problemstellung
anorexic – Magersüchtige(r)
anorexia – Magersucht
skeleton – Skelett
bruise – blauer Fleck
hip – Hüfte
ribs – Rippen
be tube-fed – künstlich ernährt werden
cured – geheilt
bulimic – Bulimiekranke
bulimia – Bulimie
life-threatening – lebensbedrohlich
have an issue about – ein Thema für jmd. sein
cheer oneself up – sich aufmuntern
bowl – Schüssel
swell up – aufquillen
exclude s.o. – jmd. ausschließen
porky – pummelig
vomit – erbrechen
race – rasen
nutritionist – Ernährungsberater(in)
climax – Höhepunkt
binge eating – im Überfluss essen, „Fressattacke"
terrify – verängstigen, einschüchtern
deliberate – bewusst, mit Absicht
denial – Leugnen
sensitivity – Empfindlichkeit
periods – hier: Menstruation (Monatsblutung)
be admitted to hospital – in das Krankenhaus eingewiesen werden
nutritional counselling – Ernährungsberatung
become aware of s.th. – sich einer Sache bewusst werden
underlying reasons – tiefer liegende Probleme, versteckte Probleme
therapeutic group – hier: therapeutische Wohngemeinschaft
chuck – „hinschmeißen", Schluss machen

Unit 7
Coping with illness and special needs

prevention – Vorsorge
stay healthy – gesund bleiben
infectious disease – Infektionskrankheit
circle around – kreisen, kursieren
persistent – beständig, hartnäckig
cough – Husten

sleeplessness – Schlaflosigkeit
relax – entspannen
squeeze – auspressen
allergy – Allergie
chronic disease – chronische Erkrankung
infection – Infektion
fracture – Fraktur, Knochenbruch
injury – Verletzung
wound – Wunde
genetic defect – genetischer Defekt
disability/special need – Behinderung
childhood disease – Kinderkrankheit
mental illness – mentale Erkrankung, psychische Erkrankung
neurological disease – neurologische Erkrankung, Nervenerkrankung
cold – Schnupfen
hay fever – Heuschnupfen
cerebral palsy – zerebrale Lähmung
chicken pox – Windpocken
heart attack – Herzanfall, Herzinfakt
sprained – verstaucht
wrist – Handgelenk
bruise – blauer Fleck, Hämathom
burn – Brandwunde
whooping cough – Keuchhusten
bronchitis – Bronchitis
German measles – Masern
migraine – Migräne
arachnophobia – Spinnenphobie, Angst vor Spinnen
cardiac disrhythmia – Herzrythmusstörungen
stretcher – Trage
convalescence – Genesung
aircast splint – Aircast Schiene
physiotherapy – Physiotherapie
crutches – Gehhilfen
plaster – Gippsverband
swollen – geschwollen
pain – Schmerz
ankle – Knöchel
x–ray – Röntgenuntersuchung
twist – verdrehen
fractured – gebrochen
undergo – hier: sich (einer Behandlung/ Operation) unterziehen
fixed – fixiert, fest
heal – heilen
consulting hours – Sprechstunden
indisposition – Unpässlichkeit, Unwohlsein
medical practice – Arztpraxis
equipment – Ausstattung, Apparatur, Geräte
general practitioner – allgemeiner Arzt/Ärztin
soft toy – Kuscheltier
imaginative – hier: phantasievoll
stomach ache – Bauchschmerzen
acute – akut
take some blood – Blut entnehmen
get familiar with – sich gewöhnen an, vertraut werden mit
attentive – aufmerksam
diagnosis – Diagnose
swap roles – Rollen tauschen
temperature – Temperatur, hier: Fieber
prescribe – verschreiben
antibiotics – Antibiotika
transfer s.o. to – hier: jmd. überweisen an
rehabilitation centre – Reha, Rehabilitationszentrum
appendectomy – Blinddarmoperation
discharge – hier: aus dem Krankenhaus entlassen
survive – überleben
medical check-ups – medizinische Kontrolluntersuchungen
radiant – strahlend
lump – Knoten
assume – vermuten
harmless – harmlos, ungefährlich
nursing mother – stillende Mutter
insist to – insistieren auf, bestehen auf
breast cancer – Brustkrebs
remove – entfernen
lymph nodes – Lymphknoten
detection – Entdeckung, Erkennung
wide–spread – weit verbreitet
survival – Überleben
chemotherapy – Chemotherapie
death sentence – Todesurteil
detect – entdecken, aufdecken
survival rate – Überlebensrate
most common cause – hier: Hauptursache
gynaecologist – Gynäkologe, Frauenarzt
mammography – Mammografie
cancerous – mit Krebs befallen, bösartig
combat – bekämpfen
prevent – vermeiden, hier: Vorsorge treffen
exhaustion – Erschöpfung
warning signs – Warnsignale

visuals – visuelle Vorlagen
overview – Überblick
handout – Handreichung
flyposter – Flugblatt, Handzettel
audience – Zuhörer, Zuhörerschaft
presenter – Referent, der/die Vortragende
reminder – Erinnerung
opening sentences – hier: dier ersten Referatsätze
waist time – Zeit verschenken/verschwenden
eye–contact – Blickkontakt
rush through – durch etwas hindurcheilen
pause – pausieren
at first glance – auf den ersten Blick
highlight sth. – hier: etwas hervorheben
terminally ill – unheilbar krank
hospice – Sterbehospiz
planning for death – sich auf den Tod einstellen, hier auch: die letzte Lebensphase planen
broach – hier: ein Thema anschneiden
patient's prognosis – hier: Lebenserwartung eines Patienten
frank – offen, ehrlich
impractical – unpraktisch
predict – vorausschauen, voraussagen
intuition – Eingebung, hier: Gefühl für den nahenden Tod
options – Möglichkeiten
rational – rational, vernunftbestimmt
liberating – befreiend
incurable – unheilbar, hier auch: bösartig
will – letzter Wille
advance directive – hier: Patientenverfügung, Anweisungen für die letzte Lebensphase
resuscitate – wieder beleben
preferences – Vorlieben, hier: Patientenwünsche für die letzte Lebensphase
bizarre – bizarr, seltsam
puzzled – verwirrt, irritiert
terrace– Terasse
sunshade – Sonnenschirm
start back – zurückschrecken
recover – sich erholen, gesund werden
nod at s.o. – jmd. zunicken
mind–numbing – betäubend, empfindungslos machend
side–effect – Nebenwirkung
unbearable – unerträglich
wallet – Brieftasche
hinge on – hier: jmd./einer Sache etwas anhängen, etwas mit jmd./einer Sache verbinden
heroic – heldenhaft
engagement – hier: elterliche Fürsorge
pity – bemitleiden
confrontational – auf Konfrontation abzielend
prosthetic patient – Patient mit einer Prothese
amputate – amputieren
shy from – hier: zurückschrecken vor
tap on the shoulder – auf die Schulter klopfen
discriminate – diskriminieren, benachteiligen
impairment – Beeinträchtigung
equal partners – gleichgestellte Partner
awareness – Bewusstsein
barrier – Barriere, Hindernis
prejudice – Vorurteil
inclusion – Inklusion, Zusammenführung
universal human right – allgemeines Menschenrecht
shared education – gemeinsame Erziehung
irrespective of – ungeachtet von
equal access – gleicher/gleichgerechtigter Zugang
individualized educational programmes – individuelle Erziehungs-/Förderprogramme
border on the limits – an die Grenzen stoßen
birth defect – Geburtsfehler
brain damage – Hirnschaden
cleft palate – offene Gaumenspalte
be devastated – am Boden zerstört sein, sehr verzweifelt sein
confused – verwirrt, durcheinander
recall s.th. – etw. erinnern
denial – Verweigerung, Ablehnung
guilt – Schuld
refuse – ablehnen
social service – Sozialdienst
constructive – konstruktiv
be tube-fed – künstlich ernährt werden
suffocate – ersticken
lack of sleep – Schlafmangel
semi–solid food – Brei
swallow the wrong way – sich verschlucken
stubborn – stur
crawl – kriechen
support oneself with the hands – sich mit den Händen abstützen
intensive care – Intensivpflege
nervous breakdown – Nervenzusammenbruch
intimate – intim, hier: besonders eng, privat

Unit 8
Being Addicted

poison – Gift
Poison Control Centre – Giftzentrale
A & E unit – Notaufnahme
prat – Verrückter
drink until you drop – bis zum Umfallen trinken
alcoholic – alkoholisch
moderate – gemäßigt
liver – Leber
bloodstream – Blutkreislauf
slurred – undeutlich
vision – Sehvermögen
blurred – verschwommen
lose balance – Gleichgewicht verlieren
loss of memory – Gedächtnisverlust
mental ability – geistige Fähigkeit
stroke – Schlaganfall
release tension – Spannungen/Anspannung abbauen
week's quota – wöchentliche Ration
vast – gewaltig, riesig
drunk – betrunken
binge drinking – Saufgelage
excessive – übermäßig, übertrieben
anti–social behaviour – asoziales Verhalten
vandalising – Vandalismus, Zerstörungswut
rampage – Randalieren
get involved into – verwickelt werden in, sich einlassen auf
socially accepted – gesellschaftlich anerkannt
spirits – Alkohol, Spirituosen, Branntwein
rapid – sehr schnell
invulnerable – unverletzbar
concept – hier: Vorstellung
impose – auferlegen, verhängen
restrictions – Beschränkung, Einschränkung
unscrupulous – skrupellos, gewissenlos
retailer – Einzelhändler/in
behavioural patterns – Verhaltensmuster
announce – ankündigen
curb – einschränken, hier: bekämpfen, eindämmen
fine – Geldstrafe
manufacturer – Hersteller
urge s.o. to do sth. – jmd. zwingen/dazu drängen etwas zu tun
irresponsible – verantwortungslos
lack of parental control – mangelnde elterliche Kontrolle/Mangel an elterlicher Fürsorge
spending power – Kaufkraft
skull – Schädel, Totenschädel
vicious circle – Teufelskreis
physical decline – körperlicher Zerfall
skinny – knochig
deeply lined face – durchfurchtes Gesicht
slaughter – Abschlachten
share fate with – das Schicksal teilen mit
disorderly – unordentlich, undiszipliniert
last shot – der letzte Schuss (hier: an einer letzten Drogeninjektion sterben)
withdrawal symptoms – Entzugserscheinungen, Symptome des Entzugs
emotional outburst – Gefühlsausbruch
whining – wimmernd, jaulend
filthy – dreckig, verschmutzt
worn out – ausgemergelt
letter of caution – Abmahnung
skip work – die Arbeit „schwänzen"
be hooked on – abhängig sein von
detox programme – Entzug, Entgiftung
relapse – Rückfall, auch rückfällig werden
overdose – Überdosis
take the mind off – hier: Kummer vergesssen lassen, ablenken von
legalise – legalisieren, gesetzlich erlauben
inflict a fine on s.o. – jemandem eine Geldstrage auferlegen
deter from – abschrecken von
long–term effects – Langzeiteffekt, hier: Langzeitschäden
short-term effect – Kurzzeiteffekt, hier: zeitlich begrenzte gesundheitliche Reaktion
drug advice centre – Drogenberatungsstelle
spice – Gewürz, hier: Name für neue Designerdroge
herbal – Kräuter-.../aus Kräutern bestehend
shredded plants – gehackte Pflanzen
seemingly – offenbar
harmless – ungefährlich, gesundheitlich unbedenklich/ungefährlich
speed up – antreiben, hoch treiben
mind-altering – den Geist/Verstand verändernd
unpredictable – nicht vorhersehbar, unberechenbar
emerging trend – aufkommender/neuer Trend
substance – Bestandteil, Substanz
free access to – freier Zugriff auf/Zugang zu
amphetamines – Aufputschmittel, Amphitamine
damage – Schaden

emergency room – Notaufnahme
irreversible – unabänderlich, nicht mehr umkehrbar
brain damage – Hirnschaden
fully recover – hier: gesundheitlich völlig genesen
mentally – geistig
paranoia – Wahnvorstellung
suicidal thoughts – Selbstmordgedanken
lasting – bleibend, anhaltend
cautious – vorsichtig
unguarded – unbewacht
depressive mood – niedergeschlagene/depressive Stimmung
drug testing – Drogentest
self-help group – Selbsthilfegruppe
rehab clinic – hier: Drogenentzugsklinik
friends circle – Freundeskreis
environment/living circumstances – hier: (soziales) Umfeld, Lebensumfeld/ Lebensumstände
cure – kurieren, heilen
dense – dicht, hier: intensiv, in kurzen Abständen
individual psychological treatment – psychologische Einzelbehandlung
medical detoxification – medizinischer Entzug
under supervision – unter Aufsicht
overwhelmed – überfordert
drug treatment – Drogenbehandlung, Drogenentzug
menacing – bedrohlich, Angst einflößend
self-confidence – Selbstvertrauen
deterrence – Abschreckung
group therapy – Gruppentherapie
adventure – Abenteuer
seductive – verführend, verführerisch
exposure – Ausgesetztsein
impressionable – beeindruckbar, hier: leicht beeinflussbar
purchase – kaufen
rapid incline – rapider/sprunghafter Anstieg
intensive care unit - Intensivstation
dehydration – Austrocknung, Dehydration
failure of organs – Organversagen
caffeine – Koffein
intensive care unit – Intensivstation

Unit 9
Violence and Crime

offender – Angreifer, hier: Straftäter
offence – Angriff, hier: Straftat
violence – Gewalt
violent – gewalttätig
crime – Kriminalität, auch: Straftat
resident – Bewohner
intimidate – einschüchtern
abuse – hier: beschimpfen, „anpöbeln"
theft – Diebstahl
assault – Angriff, hier: Körperverletzung
deed – Tat, hier: Straftat
glue – Klebstoff
vandalise – mutwillig beschädigen, verwüsten
vandalism – Vandalismus, mutwillige Beschädigung
bus shelter – überdachte Bushaltestelle
smashed – hier: zerschlagen
mugging – Straßenraub, Überfall auf offener Straße
commit a crime – eine Straftat begehen
notorious offender – Wiederholungstäter
commuter – Pendler
ban s.o. from – jmd. verbannen
guardian – Bewacher, Begleiter
fraud – hier: betrügen
forge – fälschen
steal – stehlen, entwenden
swearwords – Flüche
bunch – Bündel, hier: (Blumen)strauß
back rest – Rückenlehne
offend – angreifen, auch: verletzen, schädigen
mean – gemein, hintertrieben, bösartig
inflict on – zufügen
property – Eigentum
performance – hier: Benehmen
exaggerated – übertrieben
robbery – Raub
arson – Brandstiftung
car theft – Autodiebstahl
burglary – Einbruch
shoplifting – Ladendiebstahl
disorderly conduct – Erzeugung eines öffentlichen Ärgernisses
drunk driving – Trunkenheit am Steuer
forgery of signatures – Unterschriftenfälschung
tax evasion – Steuerhinterziehung
weapons possession – Waffenbesitz
truancy – Schulschwänzen
liquor law violation – unerlaubter Alkoholkonsum/-besitz
tram – Straßenbahn
murder – Mord

borstal – Erziehungsheim
fine – Geldstrafe
arrest – festnehmen
escape – flüchten
sentence s.o. – jmd. verurteilen
community service – gemeinnützige Arbeit
police file – Polizeiakte
court – Gericht
charge – Anklage
mob – Meute
wrapper – Verpackung
witness – Zeuge
baton – Schlagstock
extraordinary – außergewöhnlich
be plagued by – geplagt sein von, leiden unter
respond – antworten, reagieren auf
bystander – Schaulustige(r)
semi–circle – Halkreis
gladiatorial ring – Kampfarena
on suspicion – unter Verdacht
be bailed – auf Kaution frei
be on sick leave – krank geschrieben sein
bite wound – Bisswunde
minor – weniger wichtig, weniger schwerwiegend
disrespect – Respektlosigkeit
claim – hier: behaupten
mill around – hier: sich herumtreiben
juvenile punishment – Jugendstrafe
juvenile court – Jugendgericht
Justice – Richter
security officers – Sicherheitsbeamte
lawyer – Rechtsanwalt
state's attorney – Staatsanwalt
court officers – Justizbeamte
transcript – protokollieren
proceedings – hier: Geschehen im Gerichtssaal
court session – Gerichtsverhandlung
sentence – Urteil
range – Reichweite
count on – sich verlassen auf
adult law – Erwachsenenrecht
rehabilitate – rehabilitieren, wieder eingliedern
juvenile delinquent – jugendlicher Straftäter
be forced to – gezwungen sein zu
aggravated assault – schwere Körperverletzung
homicide – Mord
imprisonment – Inhaftierung
juvenile prison – Jugendgefängnis
adult prison – Erwachsenengefängnis
mitigating circumstances – mildernde Umstände
aggravating circumstances – erschwerende Umstände
figure out – herausfinden, herausarbeiten
objective – objektiv
orders – hier: gerichtliche Auflagen
probation – Bewährung
reintegration – Reintegration, Wiedereingliederung
goal – Tor, hier: Ziel
scratch – kratzen
bat – hier: Schläger
be willing to – willens sein etwas zu tun
resistance – Widerstand
case for nursing – Pflegefall
puzzled – verwirrt
dare – sich wagen
arbitrary – willkürlich
legal consequences – gerichtliche Folgen/ Maßnahmen
justified – gerechtfertigt
extraordinary – außergewöhnlich
tough – hart
severe – schwer
take into account – in Erwägung ziehen
living circumstances – Lebensumstände
prevent s.o. from – jmd. schützen vor/abhalten von
deter s.o. from – jmd. von etwas abschrecken
boldness – Mut
bullying – Mobbing
be bullied – gemobbt werden
bully – mobben, auch: Mobber
cyberbullying – Mobbing durch das Internet
social networks – soziale Netzwerke
abusive – pöbelnd, diffamierend
expose – bloßstellen
humiliate – demütigen
depression – Niedergeschlagenheit, Depression
suicide – Selbstmord
suicidal – selbstmörderisch
bullycide – Selbstmord ausgelöst durch Cybermobbing
estimated – geschätzt
distress – Verzweiflung
harm oneself – sich selbst verletzen
anonymous – anonym
shrug sth off the shoulder – etwas(von den Schultern) abschütteln
nerd – Schwachkopf

eat into self-confidence – das Selbstvertrauen "anfressen"/zerstören
blunted – abgestumpft, empfindungslos
harass s.o. – (sexuell) belästigen
harassment – (sexuelle) Belästigung
kick off – auslösen, lostreten
call so. names – jemanden mit Schimpfworten versehen, beschimpfen
menacing – bedrohlich
rude words /language – Beschimpfungen
suspend so. – jemanden suspendieren, hier: von der Schule verweisen
reassign – sich wieder eintragen, erneut anmelden
alternate – alternativ
give a lecture – hier: eine Standpauke halten, Grundsätze klären
taunt – verspotten
deliberately – absichtlich, mit Absicht
hostile – feindlich
gossip – Klatsch, Tratsch
reputation – Ansehen
exclude so. – jmd. ausschließen
exclusion – Ausschluss
impersonation – hier: (unfreiwillige) Freigabe persönlicher Daten
imply – andeuten
stalking – Verfolgung
display – hier: zur Schau stellen
flaming – jmd. verfluchen, angreifen
scornful – verächtlich, höhnisch
offensive – angreifend
outing – Bloßstellung
trickery – Betrug, Hereinlegen
keep evidence – hier: Beweise sammeln/ festhalten
combat – bekämpfen
educational psychologist – Schulpsychologe/in
spread a rumour – ein Gerücht verbreiten
deprived – heruntergekommen
homicide – Mord
school shooting – Schießerei an einer Schule
zero tolerance – keine Toleranz (hier für Straftaten)
drug trafficking – Drogenhandel
police force – Polizeieinheit
budget – Budget, finanzielle Mittel
maintenance – Instandhaltung
school equipment – Schulausstattung
learning tools – Lernmittel, Lernwerkzeuge
local communities – hier: Verwaltungen der Kommunen
carry through – durchführen, auch: durchsetzen
disrupt – stören
disruptive – störend, auch: zerstörerisch
hinder so. – jemanden hindern, behindern
insinuate – unterstellen
security door system – Sicherheitsschleuse
detect – aufspüren, entdecken
high windows – Oberlichter
specialist room – Fachraum
learning surrounding – Lernumgebung
curriculum – Lehrplan
deny – leugnen
initiate – initiieren, auslösen
soar – aufsteigen
education authority – hier: Schulbehörde
take action – Maßnahmen ergreifen
harassment – Belästigung
put arm in a vice – den Arm umdrehen
tie to – festbinden an
concrete – massiv
metal-edged – mit Metalkanten versehen
MP – Member of Parliament = Parlamentsabgeordnete(r)
school shooting – Schießerei an der Schule
shoot s.o. dead – jmd. erschießen
evict – jmd. zur Räumung zwingen
expell s.o. from school – jmd. der Schule verweisen
resit – hier: wiederholen
falsifying doctor's notes – Fälschung von ärztlichen Attesten
marksman – Schütze
dorm – Schlafsaal
suicide – Selbstmord
rampage – Herumwüten, Wutausbruch
failure – Versagen
volatile – unsicher, schwankhaft
protect – beschützen
deterrent – Abschreckung
be armed – bewaffnet sein
shape – hier: formen, erziehen
state – äußern, vorbringen
convey – vermitteln
numb – dumpf, leer
subtitled – mit Untertitel, untertitelt
stuff with – vollstopfen mit
depict – zeigen, darstellen

school shooter – jmd. der an Schulen eine Schießerei begeht
bullet – Kugel
skull – Schädel

Unit 10
Media

media – Medien
ads = advertisment – Werbung/Werbeanzeige
hesitate at – zögern bei
multitask – viele Dinge auf einmal tun
movies – Kinofilme
wander through – wandern durch
flow – Flut, Strom
minor – hier: gering(er)
multitude – Vielzahl
multiple – viel(zählig), zahlreich
gather information – Informationen sammeln/ beschaffen
released – hier: veröffentlicht
extensive – umfangreich
infant – Kleinkind (ca. bis 2 Jahre)
toddler – Kleinkind (ca. 2-3 Jahre)
paediatrician – Kinderärztin/-arzt
brain development – Hirnentwicklung
be exposed to – ausgesetzt sein
attention problems – Konzentrationsprobleme
learning difficulties – Lernschwierigkeiten, Lernschwächen
condemn – verurteilen
source of information – Informationsquelle
in moderation – in Maßen
educator – Erzieher
preschooler – Vorschulkind
problem-oriented – problembezogen, problemorientiert
interfere – (sich) einmischen, hier: kollidieren mit, behindern
view – sehen
risky behaviour – riskantes/gefährliches Verhalten
do stunts – gefährliche Dinge tun/vorführen
excessive – ausschweifend, exzessiv
reinforce – bestärken
gender-roles – Geschlecherrollen
racial – rassisch, Rassen-…
stereotypes – Stereotypen, Cliché
fiction – Vorstellung, Fiktion
appropriate – geeignet
lack – Mangel
children's programme – kinderprogramm
unsupervised – unbeaufsichtigt
paediatrician – Kinderarzt
brain development – Hirnentwicklung
attention problems – Konzentrationsprobleme
learning disability – Lernbehinderung
fiction – Vorstellung, Fiktion
portable – tragbares Fernsehgerät
nurse – hier: stillen
ADD (attention deficit disorder) – Aufmerksamkeitsdefizitsyndrom, Hyperaktivität, ADS
lap – Schoß
media education – Medienerziehung
startling – auffällig
jingle – hier: Werbemelodie
timer – Zeitmesser, Stoppuhr
be appropriate for – geeignet sein für
side effects – Nebeneffekt, Nebenwirkung
media consumption – Medienkonsum
commercial spot – Werbespot/kurzer Werbefilm
media experience – Medienerfahrung
media message – Medienbotschaft
sense of realism – Realitätssinn
media consumer – Medienkonsument
be switched off – ausgeschaltet
have a glance at – einen Blick haben/werfen auf
lack concentration – an Konzentration mangeln
urge s.o. – jmd. ermahnen
pretend – vorgeben, vorspielen
text s.o. – jmd. eine Nachricht schicken
refuse – hier: sich weigern
intrude on – eindringen in, stören bei
device – Gerät
sales – Verkauf
outstrip – überholen, übertreffen
yearning for – Verlangen nach
drive – hier: antreiben, hochtreiben
demand – Nachfrage
fanatical – fanatisch
be available – hier: erreichbar sein
be uneasy – unruhig sein, hier: beschäftigt sein mit
be incapable of – unfähig sein zu
maintain relationships – Beziehungen pflegen/ aufrecht halten
content – Inhalt
invest – investieren, hier: (Zeit) verbringen
recreating – Erholung
aquaintances – Bekanntschaften
isolated – isoliert/ausgegrenzt sein

glorify – glorifizieren, überhöhen
immerse – eintauchen
inflict on – ausüben auf, auch: zufügen
enemy – Feind
desensitize – desensibilisieren, abstumpfen
imitate – imitieren, nachahmen
perpetrate – hier: ausüben
admire – bewundern
reward s.o. – jmd. belohnen
become evident – offensichtlich/sichtbar werden
surface – hier: an die Oberfläche kommen
leave out of sight – aus den Augen/Blick lassen
march s.o. to – hier: jmd hinführen zu
batter s.o. – auf jmd. einschlagen
bricks – Ziegelsteine
learning difficulties – Lernschwierigkeiten, Lernstörung
relegate – jmd. degradieren, hier: in eine untere Klasse zurück setzen
term – hier: Schuljahr
be knocked about – hier: verprügeln, schlagen
crime–ridden – von Kriminalität betroffen
truancy – Schulschwänzen
notorious – notorisch
suspect – hier: vermuten, auch: verdächtigen
police investigation – polizeiliche Untersuchung
deny – leugnen
plot – Handlung
splash – bespritzen
mutilate – entstellen, verstümmeln
chop – hacken
funfair – Jahrmarkt, Kirmes
ranking – Rangliste
plunge from ... to – („abtauchen"), heruntergehen von .. zu ...
literacy/reading skills – Lesefähigkeiten
scheme – hier: Unterstüzungsprogramm
make available – zur Verfügung stellen
radical reforms – einschneidende Reformen
questionnaire – Fragebogen
„buzz" of reading – hier: Freude am Lesen, Lesespaß
reputation – Ruf

Vokabelhilfen zu den Hörverständnisübungen

Unit 1 – Module 2

assemble	[ə'sembl]	(sich) versammeln
consequences	['kɒnsɪkwənsɪz]	Konsequenzen, hier: Maßnahmen
first-aid room	[ˌfɜːst 'eɪd ˌrʊm]	Sanitätsraum
injured	['ɪndʒəd]	verletzt
share	[ʃeə]	(miteinander) teilen
sick	[sɪk]	krank
switch on	[ˌswɪtʃ 'ɒn]	an/einschalten

Unit 2 – Module 1

boring	['bɔːrɪŋ]	langweilig
bottom	['bɒtəm]	Hintern
chain	[tʃeɪn]	hier: (Hotel- und Restaurant) Kette Vokabelhilfen zu den Hörverständnisübungen
chef	[ʃef]	(gelernter) Koch
insurance company	[ɪn'ʃʊərəns ˌkʌmpəni]	Versicherungsgesellschaft
kitchen porter	['kɪtʃən ˌpɔːtə]	Küchenhilfe
prejudices	['predʒədɪsɪz]	Vorurteile
repetitive	[rɪ'petətɪv]	hier: sich stets wiederholende Arbeiten
suit skills	[ˌsjuːt 'skɪlz]	den Fähigkeiten entsprechen
urgent(ly)	['ɜːdʒənt(li)]	dringend

Unit 5 — Module 1

ability	[ə'bɪləti]	Fähigkeit
clench fists	[ˌklenʃ 'fɪsts]	Fäuste ballen
company	['kʌmpəni]	hier: die Gesellschaft anderer Menschen
doubt	[daʊt]	bezweifeln
envious/jealous	['enviəs / 'dʒeləs]	neidisch
"I've done my bit"	[ˌaɪv 'dʌn maɪ ˌbɪt]	„Ich habe meinen Beitrag geleistet"
make sth. plain to someone	['meɪk ˌsʌmθɪŋ 'pleɪn tu ˌsʌmwʌn]	jmdn. etwas deutlich sagen/klar machen
mash	[mæʃ]	hier: Kinderbrei

Unit 7 — Module 1

prescribe	[prɪ'skraɪb]	verschreiben
prescription	[prɪ'skrɪpʃən]	Rezept
rash	[ræʃ]	Ausschlag
Scarlet fever	['skɑːlət ˌfiːvə]	Scharlach

Unit 8 — Module 2

affluent	['æfluənt]	im Überfluss
allowance	[ə'laʊəns]	finanzielle Unterstützung, Unterhalt
anaesthetised	[ə'niːsθətaɪzd]	betäubt
be devastated	[bi 'devəsteɪtɪd]	sehr verzweifelt sein
bear	[beə]	ertragen
catatonic with grief	[ˌkætə'tɒnɪk ˌwɪð 'griːf]	vor Kummer erstarren
fund	[fʌnd]	hier: (Drogen) finanzieren
junction	['dʒʌŋkʃn]	Kreuzung
kid oneself	['kɪd wʌnˌself]	sich selbst etwas vormachen
live a life on the edge	[ˌlɪv ə 'laɪf ɒn ˌði 'edʒ]	„auf der Überholspur leben"
property developer	['prɒpəti dɪˌveləpə]	Immobilienmakler
reach rock bottom	['riːtʃ ˌrɒk 'bɒtəm]	am Boden liegen, ganz unten landen
squat	[skwɒt]	Absteige, Unterschlupf
stack shelves	[ˌstæk 'ʃelvz]	Regale auffüllen
suburb	['sʌbɜːb]	Vorort
weird	[wɪəd]	verrückt

Unit 9 — Module 1

axe	[æks]	Axt
barge	[bɑːdʒ]	hier: sich einen Weg bahnen, erkämpfen
consciousness	['kɒnʃəsnəs]	Bewusstsein
drift	[drɪft]	hier: gleiten
duck	[dʌk]	sich ducken, sich bücken
gatecrasher	['geɪtkræʃə]	Eindringling, Störenfried
housing estates	[ˌhaʊzɪŋ ɪ'steɪts]	Wohngegend
huge	[hjuːdʒ]	riesig, gewaltig (in der Anzahl/Größe)
launch a search	[ˌlɔːnʃ ə 'sɜːtʃ]	hier: eine Suchaktion beginnen
lawyer	['lɔːjə]	Rechtsanwalt/ Rechtsanwältin
recover	[rɪ'kʌvə]	sich erholen, genesen
skull	[skʌl]	Schädel
upper	['ʌpə]	gehoben

Summary		Vokabelhilfen
Connectors		
als	[wen]	when
angesichts	[ˌɪn ˈvjuː ˌɒf]	in view of
auf Grund	[ˈdjuː ˌtu]	due to
Aus diesem Grund (Satzanfang)	[ˌfɔː ðɪs ˈriːzən / ˈðæt ɪz ˌwaɪ]	For this reason/That is why
außerdem	[bɪˈsaɪdz]	besides
damit	[ˈsəʊ ˌðæt]	so that
danach	[ˈɑːftə]	after
davor	[bɪˈfɔː]	before
Da/Weil (Satzanfang)	[æz]	As
Da/Weil (Satzanfang)	[sɪns]	Since
deshalb	[ˈðeəfɔː]	therefore
falls	[ɪf]	if
obwohl	[ɔːlˈðəʊ / ˌiːvən ˈðəʊ]	although/even though
seit	[sɪns]	since
sobald	[ˌæz ˈsuːn ˌæz]	as soon as
trotzdem, dennoch	[ˌnevəðəˈles]	nevertheless
um zu	[ɪn ˈɔːdə tu]	in order to
während	[waɪl]	while
was auch immer	[wɒˈtevə]	whatever
weil (Nebensatz)	[bɪˈkɔːz]	because
zuerst/zunächst – dann –schließlich	[fɜːst - ðen - ˈfaɪnəli]	first - then - finally
Zusammenfassend (Satzeinleitung)	[ˌsʌmɪŋ ˈʌp]	Summing up

Möglichkeiten "say" mit einem anderen Verb zu ersetzen:

behaupten	[kleɪm]	claim
berichten	[rɪˈleɪt / rɪˈpɔːt]	relate/report
beschreiben	[dɪˈskraɪb]	describe
erläutern	[ɪkˈspleɪn]	explain
hervorheben	[ˌpɔɪnt ˈaʊt]	point out
informieren	[ɪnˈfɔːm]	inform
schließen, folgern	[kənˈkluːd]	conclude
unterstreichen	[ˌʌndəˈlaɪn]	underline
zum Schluss kommen/ eine (Schluss) Folgerung ziehen	[ˌkʌm tu ðə kənˈkluːʒən]	come to the conclusion
zusammenfassen	[ˈsʌməraɪz / ˌsʌm ˈʌp]	summarise/ sum up

Vocabulary chronological

A & E unit	[ˌeɪ ənd ˈiː (ˌæksɪdənt ænd ɪˈmɜːdʒənsi) ˌjuːnɪt]	Notaufnahme
a tough diet	[ə ˌtʌf ˈdaɪət]	eine strenge Diät
abuse	[əˈbjuːz]	hier: beschimpfen, „anpöbeln"
abusive	[əˈbjuːsɪv]	pöbelnd, diffamierend
accompany so.	[əˈkʌmpəni ˌsʌmwʌn]	jmd. begleiten

achieve	[ə'tʃiːv]	erreichen
act of procreation	[ˌækt əf ˌprəʊkri'eɪʃən]	Zeugungsakt
act on	['ækt ɒn]	reagieren auf
acute	[ə'kjuːt]	akut
add	[æd]	hinzufügen
ADD (attention deficit disorder)	[ˌeɪ diː 'diː (ə'tenʃən ˌdefɪsɪt dɪ'sɔːdə)]	Aufmerksamkeitsdefizitsyndrom, Hyperaktivität, ADS
additional information	[ə'dɪʃənəl ɪnfəˌmeɪʃən]	Zusatzinformation
additives	['ædətɪvz]	Zusätze, Zusatzstoffe
admire	[əd'maɪə]	bewundern
adopt	[ə'dɒpt]	adoptieren, auch: übernehmen
adoption	[ə'dɒpʃən]	Adoption
ads = advertisment	[ædz]	Werbung/ Werbeanzeige
adult law	[ˌædʌlt 'lɔː]	Erwachsenenrecht
adult prison	[ˌædʌlt 'prɪzən]	Erwachsenengefängnis
advance directive	[əd'vɑːns dɪˌrektɪv]	hier: Patientenverfügung, Anweisungen für die letzte Lebensphase
advantageous	[ˌædvən'teɪdʒəs]	von Vorteil, vorteilhaft
adventure	[əd'ventʃə]	Abenteuer
advertised	['ædvətaɪzd]	annonciert
advice corner	[əd'vaɪs ˌkɔːnə]	Ratschlagecke, Rubrik mit Briefen ratsuchender Leser
agency	['eɪdʒənsi]	Agentur
aggravated assault	[ˌægrəveɪtɪd ə'sɔːlt]	schwere Körperverletzung
aggravating circumstances	[ˌægrəveɪtɪŋ 'sɜːkəmstænsɪz]	erschwerende Umstände
agony aunt	['ægəni ˌɑːnt]	Kummerkastentante
aircast splint	['eəkɑːst ˌsplɪnt]	Aircast Schiene
alcoholic	[ælkə'hɒlɪk]	alkoholisch
A-level	['eɪlevəl]	vergleichbar mit Fachhochschulreife
allergy	['ælədʒi]	Allergie
allocation	[ælə'keɪʃən]	Verteilung
almost the same	['ɔːlməʊst ðə ˌseɪm]	fast gleich
alternate	[ɔːl'tɜːnət]	alternativ
ambulance	['æmbjələns]	Krankenwagen
amphetamines	[æm'fetəmiːnz]	Aufputschmittel, Amphitamine
amputate	['æmpjəteɪt]	amputieren
angel	['eɪndʒəl]	Engel
ankle	['æŋkl]	Knöchel
announce	[ə'naʊns]	ankündigen
anonymous	[ə'nɒnɪməs]	anonym
anorexia	[ˌænə'reksiə]	Magersucht
anorexic	[ˌænə'reksɪk]	Magersüchtige(r)
antibiotics	[ˌæntɪbaɪ'ɒtɪks]	Antibiotika
anti-social behaviour	[ˌæntɪ'səʊʃəl bɪˌheɪviə]	asoziales Verhalten
appearance	[ə'pɪərəns]	Erscheinung, äußeres Erscheinungsbild
appendectomy	[ˌæpen'dektəmi]	Blinddarmoperation
apply for	[ə'plaɪ fɔː]	sich bewerben für
appropriate	[ə'prəʊpriət]	geeignet
aquaintances	[ə'kweɪntənsɪz]	Bekanntschaften

arachnophobia	[əˌræknəʊˈfəʊbiə]	Spinnenphobie, Angst vor Spinnen
arbitrary	[ˈɑːbɪtrəri]	willkürlich
argue	[ˈɑːgjuː]	hier: verbal streiten
arising sexuality	[əˈraɪzɪŋ ˌsekʃuˈæləti]	erwachende Sexualität
arrangements about	[əˈreɪndʒmənts əˌbaʊt]	Absprachen über
arrest	[əˈrest]	festnehmen
arson	[ˈɑːsən]	Brandstiftung
as ... as	[æz ... æz]	so ... wie
assault	[əˈsɔːlt]	Angriff, hier: Körperverletzung
assessment board	[əˈsesmənt ˌbɔːd]	Auswahlgremium, auch: Prüfungsausschuss
assessment centre	[əˈsesmənt ˌsentə]	Auswahlzentrum, auch: Prüfungszentrum
assist	[əˈsɪst]	helfen, assistieren
associate with	[əˈsəʊʃieɪt wɪð]	in Verbindung bringen mit, assoziieren mit
assume	[əˈsjuːm]	vermuten
at first glance	[ˌæt ˈfɜːst ˌglɑːns]	auf den ersten Blick
at first hand	[ˌæt ˈfɜːst ˌhænd]	zuerst, an erster Stelle
at the extreme	[ˌæt ði ɪkˈstriːm]	im Extremfall
attach to sb./sth	[əˈtætʃ tu ˌsʌmbədi/ˌsʌmθɪŋ]	an jmd./an etwas hängen
attack so. with a weapon	[əˈtæk ˌsʌmwʌn wɪð ə ˈwepən]	jmd. mit einer Waffe angreifen
attend	[əˈtend]	hier: (eine Schule) besuchen
attention	[əˈtenʃən]	hier: zu Händen
attention problems	[əˈtenʃən ˌprɒbləmz]	Konzentrationsprobleme
attentive	[əˈtentɪv]	aufmerksam
attentively	[əˈtentɪvli]	aufmerksam
attitude	[ˈætɪtjuːd]	Haltung, Meinung
audience	[ˈɔːdiəns]	Zuhörer, Zuhörerschaft
authoritarian	[ˌɔːθɒrɪˈteəriən]	autoritär, dominant, beherrschend
authoritative	[ɔːˈθɒrɪtətɪv]	entschieden, verlässlich
avoid	[əˈvɔɪd]	vermeiden
awareness	[əˈweənəs]	Bewusstsein
awkward	[ˈɔːkwəd]	seltsam
babies aren't found under the gooseberry bush	[ˈbeɪbis ɑːnt faʊnd ˌʌndə ðə ˈgʊzbəri bʊʃ]	(Redewendung) Babys werden nicht vom Klapperstorch gebracht
baby-flap	[ˈbeɪbiflæp]	Babyklappe
back rest	[ˈbæk rest]	Rückenlehne
bad conscience	[ˌbæd ˈkɒnʃəns]	schlechtes Gewissen
bad temper	[ˌbæd ˈtempə]	schlechte Laune
ban so. from	[ˈbæn ˌsʌmwʌn frɒm]	jmd. verbannen
bank loan	[ˈbæŋk ˌləʊn]	Bankkredit
barrier	[ˈbæriə]	Barriere, Hindernis
bat	[bæt]	hier: Schläger
bathe	[beɪð]	baden
baton	[ˈbætɒn]	Schlagstock
batter so.	[ˈbætə ˌsʌmwʌn]	auf jmd. einschlagen
be admitted to hospital	[bi ədˈmɪtɪd tu ˌhɒspɪtəl]	in das Krankenhaus eingewiesen werden

be at loggerheads	[bi ˌæt ˈlɒgəhedz]	sich in den Haaren liegen, einen Streit haben
be available	[bi əˈveɪləbl]	hier: erreichbar sein
be aware	[bi əˈweə]	hier: sei vorsichtig!
be aware about	[bi əˈweər əˌbaʊt]	sich bewusst sein über
be bailed	[bi ˈbeɪld]	auf Kaution frei
be barred from	[bi ˈbɑːd frɒm]	ausgeschlossen/ausgesperrt sein
be bullied	[bi ˈbʊlid]	gemobbt werden
be concerned	[bi kənˈsɜːnd]	sich um etwas sorgen, hier: an etwas interessiert sein
be contented	[bi kənˈtentɪd]	zufrieden sein
be devastated	[bi ˈdevəstetɪd]	am Boden zerstört sein, sehr verzweifelt sein
be equipped with	[bi ɪˈkwɪpt wɪð]	ausgestattet sein mit
be exposed to	[bi ɪkˈspəʊzd tu]	ausgesetzt sein
be fed up with	[bi ˌfed ˈʌp wɪð]	etwas satt haben, die Nase voll haben von
be forced to	[bi ˈfɔːst tu]	gezwungen sein zu
be hooked on	[bi ˈhʊkt ɒn]	abhängig sein von
be in charge of	[bi ˌɪn ˈtʃɑːdʒ ɒf]	zuständig sein für, hier: die Leitung haben
be incapable of	[bi ɪnˈkeɪpəbl ɒf]	unfähig sein zu
be infected	[bi ɪnˈfektɪd]	infiziert sein
be inspired to do sth.	[bi ɪnˈspaɪəd ˌtu ˈduː ˌsʌmθɪŋ]	inspiriert/motiviert sein etwas zu tun
be knocked about	[bi ˈnɒkt əˌbaʊt]	hier: verprügeln, schlagen
be obsessed by	[bi əbˈsest baɪ]	besessen sein von
be on sick leave	[bi ɒn ˈsɪk ˌliːv]	krank geschrieben sein
be out to make the impression	[bi ˌaʊt tu meɪk ði ɪmˈpreʃən]	einen Eindruck hinterlassen wollen
be plagued by	[bi ˈpleɪgd baɪ]	geplagt sein von, leiden unter
be promised to so.	[bi ˈprɒmɪst tu ˌsʌmwʌn]	jmd. versprochen werden
be responsible for	[bi rɪˈspɒnsəbl fɔː]	verantwortlich sein für
be switched off	[bi ˌswɪtʃt ˈɒf]	ausgeschaltet
be tube-fed	[bi ˈtjuːbfed]	künstlich ernährt werden
be uneasy	[bi ʌnˈiːsi]	unruhig sein, hier: beschäftigt sein mit
be upset	[bi ʌpˈset]	enttäuscht/traurig sein
be willing to	[bi ˈwɪlɪŋ tu]	willens sein etwas zu tun
beat	[biːt]	schlagen
become aware of s.th.	[bɪˌkʌm əˈweər ɒf ˌsʌmθɪŋ]	sich einer Sache bewusst werden
become evident	[bɪˌkʌm ˈevɪdənt]	offensichtlich/sichtbar werden
behavioral scientist	[bɪˈheɪvjərəl ˌsaɪəntɪst]	Verhaltenswissenschaftler
behaviour	[bɪˈheɪvjə]	Verhalten
behavioural patterns	[bɪˈheɪvjərəl ˌpætənz]	Verhaltensmuster
behavioural science	[bɪˈheɪvjərəl ˌsaɪəns]	Verhaltensforschung
best manners	[ˌbest ˈmænəz]	beste Manieren
best perfomances	[ˌbest pəˈfɔːmənsɪz]	hier: beste Noten und bestes Betragen
beverages	[ˈbevərɪdʒɪz]	Getränke
binge drinking	[ˈbɪndʒ ˌdrɪnkɪŋ]	Saufgelage
binge eating	[ˈbɪndʒ ˌiːtɪŋ]	im Überfluss essen, „Fressattacke“
birth defect	[ˌbɜːθ dɪˈfekt]	Geburtsfehler

biscuit	['bɪskwɪt]	Keks
bite wound	['baɪt ˌwuːnd]	Bisswunde
bizarre	[bɪ'zɑː]	bizarr, seltsam
blackboard	['blækbɔːd]	Tafel
blame	[bleɪm]	Schuld
blame for	['bleɪm fɔː]	beschuldigen
blame so. for	['bleɪm ˌsʌmwʌn fɔː]	jmd. die Schuld an etwas geben
blaming	['bleɪmɪŋ]	anklagend, verantwortlich machend
blanket	['blæŋkɪt]	Decke
block	[blɒk]	Spielblöcke, Spielklötze
blocked airways	[ˌblɒkt 'eəweɪz]	blockierte Atemwege
bloodstream	['blʌdstriːm]	Blutkreislauf
blossom	['blɒsəm]	erblühen, sich entfalten, zu etwas heranwachsen
blunted	['blʌntɪd]	abgestumpft, empfindungslos
blurred	['blɜːd]	verschwommen
body of the letter	['bɒdi ɒf ðə ˌletə]	Hauptteil des Briefes
boldness	['bəʊldnəs]	Mut
bombard so. with sth.	[bɒm'bɑːd ˌsʌmwʌn wɪð ˌsʌmθɪŋ]	jmd. mit etwas bombardieren
bones	[bəʊnz]	Knochen
border on the limits	[ˌbɔːdə ɒn ðə 'lɪmɪts]	an die Grenzen stoßen
borstal	['bɔːstəl]	Erziehungsheim
bowl	[bəʊl]	Schüssel
brain damage	['breɪn ˌdæmɪdʒ]	Hirnschaden
brain development	['breɪn dɪˌveləpmənt]	Hirnentwicklung
bread rolls	['bred ˌrəʊlz]	Brötchen
breast cancer	['brest ˌkænsə]	Brustkrebs
breathing assistance	['briːðɪŋ ə'sɪstəns]	Atemhilfe
bricks	[brɪks]	Ziegelsteine
broach	[brəʊtʃ]	hier: ein Thema anschneiden
bronchitis	[brɒŋ'kaɪtɪs]	Bronchitis
bruise	[bruːz]	blauer Fleck, Hämatom
Brussels sprouts	[ˌbrʌsəlz 'spraʊts]	Rosenkohl
budget	['bʌdʒɪt]	Budget, finanzielle Mittel
bulimia	[bʊ'lɪmiə]	Bulimie
bulimic	[bʊ'lɪmɪk]	Bulimiekranke
bullet	['bʊlɪt]	Kugel
bully	['bʊli]	mobben, Mobber
bullycide	['bʊlɪsaɪd]	Selbstmord ausgelöst durch Cybermobbing
bullying	['bʊliɪŋ]	Mobbing
bun	[bʌn]	Brötchen, auch/hier: süßes Teilchen
bunch	[bʌnʃ]	Bündel, hier: (Blumen)Strauß
burglary	['bɜːgləri]	Einbruch
burn	[bɜːn]	verbrennen
burn	[bɜːn]	Brandwunde
bus shelter	['bʌs ˌʃeltə]	überdachte Bushaltestelle
bystander	['baɪˌstændə]	Schaulustige(r)
caffeine	['kæfiːn]	Koffein

call so. names	['kɔːl ˌsʌmwʌn 'neɪmz]	jmd. mit Schimpfwörtern versehen, beschimpfen
cancer	['kænsə]	Krebs (Krankheit)
cancerous	['kænsərəs]	mit Krebs befallen, bösartig
candies	['kændiz]	Bonbon, Süßigkeit
canteen kitchen	[kæn'tiːn ˌkɪtʃən]	Großküche
car theft	[kɑː θeft]	Autodiebstahl
carbohydrates	[ˌkɑːbəʊ'haɪdreɪts]	Kohlenhydrate
cardiac disrhythmia	[ˌkɑːdiæk dɪs'rɪθmiə]	Herzrythmusstörungen
care	[keə]	Pflege, Betreuung
care assistant	['keər əˌsɪstənt]	Sozialassistent
care for	['keə ˌfɔː]	sich kümmern um, pflegen, für jmd. Sorgen
care work	['keə ˌwɜːk]	Sozial- und/oder Gesundheitspflege/arbeit
care worker	['keə ˌwɜːkə]	Sozial- und/oder Gesundheitspfleger/-in
careers adviser	[kə'riəz ədˌvaɪzə]	Berufsberater
carefully	['keəfəli]	vorsichtig
caretaker	['keəteɪkə]	Hausmeister
carry through	[ˌkæri 'θruː]	durchführen, auch: durchsetzen
case for nursing	[ˌkeɪs fɔː 'nɜːsɪŋ]	Pflegefall
casual clothes	[ˌkæʒuəl 'kləʊðz]	hier: Alltagskleidung
category	['kætəgəri]	Kategorie, hier: Oberbegriff für Unterteilung
cauliflower	['kɒlɪˌflaʊə]	Blumenkohl
cause	[kɔːz]	verursachen, hier: dazu bewegen
cautious	['kɔːʃəs]	vorsichtig
cereal	['sɪəriəl]	Getreide, hier: Cornflakes, Müsli etc.
cerebral palsy	[ˌserəbrəl 'pɔːlzi]	zerebrale Lähmung
challenge	['tʃæləndʒ]	Herausforderung
change dressings	[ˌtʃeɪndʒ 'dresɪŋz]	Verbände wechseln
charge	[tʃɑːdʒ]	Anklage
chat	[tʃæt]	Gespräch, Plauderei
cheer oneself up	[ˌtʃɪə wʌnˌself 'ʌp]	sich aufmuntern
chemotherapy	[ˌkiːməʊ'θerəpi]	Chemotherapie
chicken pox	['tʃɪkɪn ˌpɒks]	Windpocken
child abuse	['tʃaɪld əˌbjuːs]	Kindesmissbrauch
child care	['tʃaɪld ˌkeə]	Kinderpflege
child care home	['tʃaɪld ˌkeə 'həʊm]	Kinderpflegeheim
child care worker	['tʃaɪld ˌkeə 'wɜːkə]	Sozial- und Gesundheitspfleger/in für Kinder
childminder	['tʃaɪldˌmaɪndə]	Kinderbetreuer/-in, auch: Tagesmutter
child mistreatment	['tʃaɪld mɪsˌtriːtmənt]	Kindesmisshandlung
child sized	['tʃaɪld ˌsaɪzd]	kindgerechte Größe
childhood disease	['tʃaɪldhʊd dɪˌziːz]	Kinderkrankheit
chilled section	[ˌtʃɪld 'sekʃən]	Kühlregal, Kühlwarenabteilung
chips	[tʃɪps]	Pommes Frittes
chocolate bar	['tʃɒklət ˌbɑː]	Schokoriegel
chocolate spread	['tʃɒklət ˌspred]	Schokoladenbrotaufstrich
choke	[tʃəʊk]	drosseln, würgen

choose as a topic	['tʃuːz ˌæz ə 'tɒpɪk]	zum Thema wählen
chop	[tʃɒp]	Kotelett
chop	[tʃɒp]	hacken
chores	[tʃɔːz]	Haushaltspflichten
chronic disease	[ˌkrɒnɪk dɪ'ziːz]	chronische Erkrankung
chubby	['tʃʌbi]	pummelig, rundlich
chuck	[tʃʌk]	„hinschmeißen", Schluss machen
circle around	[ˌsɜːkl ə'raʊnd]	kreisen, kursieren
claim	[kleɪm]	hier: behaupten
cleft palate	[ˌkleft 'pælət]	offene Gaumenspalte
cliché	['klɪːʃeɪ]	Klischee, voreingenommene Meinung
climax	['klaɪmæks]	Höhepunkt
climbing frame	['klaɪmɪŋ ˌfreɪm]	Klettergerüst
cloakroom	['kləʊkrʊm]	Garderobe
clue	[kluː]	Idee, Vorstellung von etwas
cod	[kɒd]	Kabeljau
cold	[kəʊld]	Schnupfen
colleague	['kɒliːg]	Kollege/Kollegin
College of Further Education	[ˌkɒlɪdʒ əf 'fɜːðər ˌedʒʊ'keɪʃən]	Berufskolleg
combat	['kɒmbæt]	bekämpfen
comfort eating	['kʌmfət ˌiːtɪŋ]	„Frustessen"
commercial spot	[kə'mɜːʃəl ˌspɒt]	Werbespot/ kurzer Werbefilm
commit a crime	[kə'mɪt ə ˌkraɪm]	eine Straftat begehen
common	['kɒmən]	allgemein
common rooms	['kɒmən ˌruːmz]	Gemeinschaftsräume
community service	[kə'mjuːnəti ˌsɜːvɪs]	gemeinnützige Arbeit
commuter	[kə'mjuːtə]	Pendler
complementary close	[ˌkɒmplɪ'mentəri ˌkləʊz]	Schlusszeile
comprehensive sex education	[ˌkɒmprɪ'hensɪv ˌseks edʒʊ'keɪʃən]	gemeinsame Sexualerziehung von Jungen und Mädchen
compulsory	[kəm'pʌlsəri]	obligatorisch, Pflicht-…
concept	['kɒnsept]	Konzept, Plan, Vorstellung
conception	[kən'sepʃən]	Empfängnis
condemn	[kən'dem]	verurteilen
condom	['kɒndɒm]	Kondom
confectionery	[kən'fekʃənəri]	Konditorwaren, Süßwaren
conform to	[kən'fɔːm tu]	entsprechen, sich anpassen
confrontational	[ˌkɒnfrʌn'teɪʃənəl]	auf Konfrontation abzielend
confused	[kən'fjuːzd]	verwirrt, durcheinander
confusions	[kən'fjuːʒənz]	Verwechslungen
conscious	['kɒnʃəs]	bewusst
consist of	[kən'sɪst ɒf]	bestehen aus
consoling words	[kən'səʊlɪŋ ˌwɜːdz]	tröstende Worte
constant	['kɒnstənt]	fortwährend, stets, konstant
constructive	[kən'strʌktɪv]	konstruktiv
consulting hours	[kən'sʌltɪŋ ˌaʊəz]	Sprechstunden
content	['kɒntent]	Inhalt
contraception	[ˌkɒntrə'sepʃən]	Verhütung
controversial	[ˌkɒntrə'vɜːʃəl]	kontrovers, umstritten

convalescence	[ˌkɒnvəˈlesəns]	Genesung
convenience food	[kənˈviːniəns ˌfuːd]	Fertiggerichte
convey	[kənˈveɪ]	vermitteln
convey the impression	[kənˌveɪ ði ɪmˈpreʃən]	den Eindruck vermitteln
cookery writer	[ˈkʊkəri ˌraɪtə]	Kochbuchautor
cooperation	[kəʊˌɒpəˈreɪʃən]	Zusammenarbeit
cope with a situation	[ˈkəʊp wɪð ə ˌsɪtjuˈeɪʃən]	mit einer Situation umgehen
cottage cheese	[ˌkɒtɪdʒ ˈtʃiːz]	Hüttenkäse
cough	[kɒf]	Husten
counsel	[ˈkaʊnsəl]	beraten
count on	[ˈkaʊnt ɒn]	sich verlassen auf
courgette	[kɔːˈʒet]	Zucchini
court	[kɔːt]	Gericht
court officers	[ˈkɔːt ˌɒfɪsəz]	Justizbeamte
court session	[ˈkɔːt ˌseʃən]	Gerichtsverhandlung
crawl	[krɔːl]	kriechen
creche	[kreʃ]	Kinderkrippe
crime	[kraɪm]	Kriminalität, auch: Straftat
crime–ridden	[ˈkraɪmrɪdən]	von Kriminalität betroffen
crisps	[krɪsps]	Chips
crossed	[krɒst]	verschränkt, über Kreuz
crutches	[ˈkrʌtʃɪz]	Gehhilfen
curb	[kɜːb]	einschränken, hier: bekämpfen, eindämmen
cure	[kjʊə]	kurieren, heilen
cured	[kjʊəd]	geheilt
curriculum	[kəˈrɪkjələm]	Lehrplan
curriculum vitae (CV)	[kəˌrɪkjələm ˈviːtai (ˌsiː ˈviː)]	Lebenslauf
custody	[ˈkʌstədi]	hier: Sorgerecht
cutlery	[ˈkʌtləri]	Besteck
cyberbullying	[ˈsaɪbəˌbʊliɪŋ]	Mobbing durch das Internet
cycle	[ˈsaɪkl]	Rad fahren
dairy products	[ˈdeəri ˌprɒdʌkts]	Milchprodukte
damage	[ˈdæmɪdʒ]	Schaden
damage	[ˈdæmɪdʒ]	zerstören, beschädigen
dare	[deə]	sich wagen
date	[deɪt]	Datum
day care	[ˈdeɪ ˌkeə]	Tagespflege; hier: Ganztagseinrichtung
day room	[ˈdeɪ ˌruːm]	Aufenthaltsraum
day-to-day	[ˌdeɪtəˈdeɪ]	täglich
deafblind	[ˈdefblaɪnd]	taub und blind
death sentence	[ˈdeθ ˌsentəns]	Todesurteil
decisive	[dɪˈsaɪsɪv]	entschieden, „durchgreifend“
decrease	[dɪˈkriːs]	abnehmen
deed	[diːd]	Tat, hier: Straftat
deeply lined face	[ˈdiːpli laɪnd ˌfeɪs]	durchfurchtes Gesicht
defensive	[dɪˈfensɪv]	verteidigend, in einer Verteidigungshaltung
degree	[dɪˈgriː]	hier: Abschluss
dehydration	[ˌdiːhaɪˈdreɪʃən]	Austrocknung, Dehydration

deliberate	[dɪˈlɪbərət]	bewusst, mit Absicht
deliberately	[dɪˈlɪbərətli]	absichtlich, mit Absicht
demand	[dɪˈmɑːnd]	Nachfrage
demanding	[dɪˈmɑːndɪŋ]	anspruchsvoll
demonstrate	[ˈdemənstreɪt]	vorführen, demonstrieren
denial	[dɪˈnaɪəl]	Leugnen, Verweigerung, Ablehnung
dense	[dens]	dicht, hier: intensiv, in kurzen Abständen
deny	[dɪˈnaɪ]	hier: verweigern
deny	[dɪˈnaɪ]	leugnen
depend on	[dɪˈpend ɒn]	abhängen von
depict	[dɪˈpɪkt]	zeigen, darstellen, abbilden
depression	[dɪˈpreʃən]	Niedergeschlagenheit, Depression
depressive mood	[dɪˈpresɪv ˌmuːd]	niedergeschlagene/depressive Stimmung
deprived	[dɪˈpraɪvd]	heruntergekommen
description	[dɪˈskrɪpʃən]	Beschreibung
desensitize	[ˌdiːˈsentɪsaɪz]	desensibilisieren, abstumpfen
desperate	[ˈdespərət]	verzweifelt
detect	[dɪˈtekt]	entdecken, aufdecken, aufspüren
detection	[dɪˈtekʃən]	Entdeckung, Erkennung
deter from	[dɪˈtɜː frɒm]	abschrecken von
deter so. from	[dɪˈtɜː ˌsʌmwʌn frɒm]	jmd. von etwas abschrecken
deterrence	[dɪˈtɜːrəns]	Abschreckung
detox programme	[ˈdiːtɒks ˌprəʊgræm]	Entzug, Entgiftung
device	[dɪˈvaɪs]	Gerät
diagnosis	[ˌdaɪəˈnəʊsɪs]	Diagnose
diet	[ˈdaɪət]	1. Ernährung, 2. Diät
dietician	[ˌdaɪəˈtɪʃən]	Diät–/Ernährungsberater/-in
disability	[ˌdɪsəˈbɪləti]	Behinderung
disability/special need	[ˌdɪsəˈbɪləti / ˈspeʃəl ˌniːd]	Behinderung
disadvantaged	[ˌdɪsədˈvɑːntɪdʒd]	benachteiligt
disapproval	[ˌdɪsəˈpruːvəl]	Missbilligung
discharge	[dɪsˈtʃɑːdʒ]	hier: aus dem Krankenhaus entlassen
discriminate	[dɪˈskrɪmɪneɪt]	diskriminieren, benachteiligen
dishes	[ˈdɪʃɪz]	Geschirr
disobey	[ˌdɪsəˈbeɪ]	nicht gehorchen, sich widersetzen
disorderly	[dɪˈsɔːdəli]	unordentlich, undiszipliniert
disorderly conduct	[dɪˌsɔːdəli ˈkɒndʌkt]	Erzeugung eines öffentlichen Ärgernisses
display	[dɪˈspleɪ]	hier: zur Schau stellen
disrespect	[ˌdɪsrɪˈspekt]	Respektlosigkeit
disrupt	[dɪsˈrʌpt]	stören
disruptive	[dɪsˈrʌptɪv]	störend, auch: zerstörerisch
distraction	[dɪˈstrækʃən]	hier: Ablenkung
distress	[dɪˈstres]	Bedrängnis, verzweifelte Lage
distress	[dɪˈstres]	Verzweiflung, Kummer, Sorge
distribute	[dɪˈstrɪbjuːt]	verteilen, austeilen
district	[ˈdɪstrɪkt]	hier: Verwaltungsbezirk
disturb (a relationship)	[dɪˈstɜːb (ə rɪˈleɪʃənʃɪp)]	(eine Beziehung/ein Verhältnis) zerstören
ditch	[dɪtʃ]	in den Abfall werfen
divided into	[dɪˈvaɪdɪd ɪnˌtu]	eingeteilt in/aufgeteilt in
divorce	[dɪˈvɔːs]	Scheidung

divorce rate	[dɪ'vɔːs ˌreɪt]	Scheidungsrate
do handcraft	[ˌduː 'hændkrɑːft]	basteln
do stunts	[ˌduː 'stʌnts]	gefährliche Dinge tun/vorführen
domestic care	[də'mestɪk ˌkeə]	Haushaltsfürsorge
down to earth	[ˌdaʊn tu 'ɜːθ]	bodenständig, praktisch, realistisch
drained	['dreɪnd]	ausgelaugt
draw the conclusion	[ˌdrɔː ðə kən'kluːʒən]	zu dem (Ab)Schluss kommen, eine Schlussfolgerung ziehen aus
drink until you drop	['drɪŋk ʌnˌtɪl juː 'drɒp]	bis zum Umfallen trinken
drive	[draɪv]	hier: antreiben, hochtreiben
drive so. insane	['draɪv ˌsʌmwʌn ɪn'seɪn]	jmd. in den Wahnsinn treiben
drug advice centre	[ˌdrʌg əd'vaɪs ˌsentə]	Drogenberatungsstelle
drug testing	['drʌg ˌtestɪŋ]	Drogentest
drug trafficking	['drʌg ˌtræfɪkɪŋ]	Drogenhandel
drug treatment	['drʌg ˌtriːtmənt]	Drogenbehandlung, Drogenentzug
drunk	[drʌŋk]	betrunken
drunk driving	[ˌdrʌŋk 'draɪvɪŋ]	Trunkenheit am Steuer
dumb struck (slang)	['dʌm ˌstrʌk]	stumm, sprachlos, „mit Stummheit geschlagen"
dye	[daɪ]	färben
eat into self-confidence	['iːt ˌɪntə ˌself'kɒnfɪdəns]	das Selbstvertrauen „anfressen"/ zerstören
eating habits	['iːtɪŋ ˌhæbɪts]	Essgewohnheiten
education	[ˌedʒʊ'keɪʃən], [ˌedjʊ-]	Erziehung
education worker	[ˌedʒʊ'keɪʃən ˌwɜːkə], [ˌedjʊ-]	Erziehungspfleger für schulische oder Ausbildungsbelange
educational methods	[ˌedʒʊ'keɪʃənəl ˌmeθədz], [ˌedjʊ-]	Erziehungsmethoden
educational psychologist	[ˌedʒʊ'keɪʃənəl ˌsaɪ'kɒlədʒɪst], [ˌedjʊ-]	Schulpsychologe/-in
educator	['edʒʊkeɪtə], ['edjʊ-]	Erzieher/-in
efficient	[ɪ'fɪʃənt]	effizient, wirtschaftlich
emergency	[ɪ'mɜːdʒənsi]	Notfall
emergency call	[ɪ'mɜːdʒənsi ˌkɔːl]	Notruf
emergency case	[ɪ'mɜːdʒənsi ˌkeɪs]	Notfall
emergency room	[ɪ'mɜːdʒənsi ˌrʊm]	Notaufnahme
emerging trend	[ɪ'mɜːdʒɪŋ ˌtrend]	aufkommender/neuer Trend
emigrate	['emɪgreɪt]	auswandern, emigrieren
emotional	[ɪ'məʊʃənəl]	psychisch, emotional
emotional abuse	[ɪˌməʊʃənəl ə'bjuːs]	emotionaler Missbrauch
emotional outburst	[ɪˌməʊʃənəl 'əʊtbɜːst]	Gefühlsausbruch
employee	[ɪm'plɔɪiː], [ˌemplɔɪ'iː]	Mitarbeiter/-in
enclose	[ɪn'kləʊz]	hier: beifügen
enclosure	[ɪn'kləʊʒə]	Anlage (eines Briefes)
encourage	[ɪn'kʌrɪdʒ]	hier: ermutigen
enemy	['enɪmi]	Feind
energetic	[enə'dʒetɪk]	voller Engergie, „energiegeladen"
engagement	[ɪn'geɪdʒmənt]	hier: elterliche Fürsorge
enter a relationship	[ˌentər ə rɪ'leɪʃənʃɪp]	eine Beziehung eingehen
enthusiasm	[ɪn'θjuːziæzm]	Enthusiasmus, Begeisterung

entrance examination	['entrəns ɪgˌzæmɪ'neɪʃən]	Aufnahmeprüfung
environment/living circumstances	[ɪn'vaɪərənmənt / 'lɪvɪŋ ˌsɜːkəmstænsɪz]	hier: (soziales) Umfeld, Lebensumfeld/ Lebensumstände
equal access	[ˌiːkwəl 'ækses]	gleicher/gleichgerechtigter Zugang
equal partners	[ˌiːkwəl 'pɑːtnəz]	gleichgestellte Partner
equal share	[ˌiːkwəl 'ʃeə]	gleiche Beteiligung, gleicher Anteil
equipment	[ɪ'kwɪpmənt]	Ausstattung, Apparatur, Geräte
escape	[ɪ'skeɪp]	flüchten
escort	[ɪ'skɔːt]	begleiten
estimated	['estɪmeɪtɪd]	geschätzt
exaggerated	[ɪg'zædʒəreɪtɪd]	übertrieben
exam	[ɪg'zæm]	Examen, Abschlussprüfung
examine	[ɪg'zæmɪn]	untersuchen
excellent	['eksələnt]	hervorragend
excessive	[ɪk'sesɪv]	übermäßig, übertrieben, übermäßig, übertrieben
exchange programme	[ɪks'tʃeɪndʒ ˌprəʊgræm]	Austauschprogramm
exchange student	[ɪks'tʃeɪndʒ ˌstjuːdənt]	Austauschschülerin/Austauschschüler
exclude so.	[ɪks'kluːd ˌsʌmwʌn]	jmd. ausschließen
exclusion	[ɪks'kluːʒən]	Ausschluss
exhausted	[ɪg'zɔːstɪd]	erschöpft
exhaustion	[ɪg'zɔːstʃən]	Erschöpfung
experiment	[ɪk'sperɪmənt]	experimentieren, ausprobieren
expose	[ɪk'spəʊz]	entblößen, zur Schau stellen, bloßstellen
exposure	[ɪk'spəʊʒə]	Ausgesetztsein
extended family	[ɪkˌstendɪd 'fæməli]	Großfamilie
extensive	[ɪk'stensɪv]	umfangreich
extra-large family	['ekstrə ˌlɑːdʒ 'fæməli]	Großfamilie mit mehr als vier Kindern
extraordinary	[ɪk'strɔːdɪnəri]	außergewöhnlich
eye contact, eye-contact	[aɪ'kɒntækt]	Blickkontakt
face	[feɪs]	hier: konfrontiert sein mit, gegenüber treten/stehen
facial expression	[ˌfeɪʃəl ɪk'spreʃən]	Gesichtsausdruck
failure	['feɪljə]	Fehlschlag
failure of organs	['feɪljər əv ˌɔːgənz]	Organversagen
fall pregnant	[ˌfɔːl 'pregnənt]	schwanger werden
family advice centre	[ˌfæməli əd'vaɪs ˌsentə]	Familienberatung, Familienberatungs-stelle
family affairs	['fæməli əˌfeəz]	Familienangelegenheiten
family law	[ˌfæməli 'lɔː]	Familienrecht
family party	['fæməli ˌpɑːti]	Familienfeier
fanatical	[fə'nætɪkəl]	fanatisch
fatally ill	[ˌfeɪtəli 'ɪl]	unheilbar erkrankt
feedback	['fiːdbæk]	Rückmeldung
feel ashamed	[ˌfiːl ə'ʃeɪmd]	sich schämen
feel pushed aside	[ˌfiːl ˌpʊʃt ə'saɪd]	sich zur Seite geschoben fühlen/sich übergangen fühlen
feeling of inferiority	['fiːlɪŋ ɒf ɪnˌfɪəri'ɒrəti]	Minderwertigkeitsgefühl
fend for oneself	[ˌfend fɔː wʌn'self]	sich selber helfen/versorgen

fibre	['faɪbə]	Ballaststoffe
fiction	['fɪkʃən]	Vorstellung, Fiktion
fidget	['fɪdʒɪt]	zappeln
fierce	['fiəs]	hier: heftig
fierce	['fiəs]	wild, hier: übertrieben
figure	['fɪgə]	hier: Figur
figure out	[ˌfɪgər 'aʊt]	herausfinden, herausarbeiten
filthy	['fɪlθi]	dreckig, verschmutzt
financially dependent on	[faɪˌnænʃəli dɪ'pendənt ɒn]	finanziell abhängig von
fine	[faɪn]	Geldstrafe
first aid	[ˌfɜːst 'eɪd]	erste Hilfe
first aid room	[ˌfɜːst 'eɪd ˌrʊm]	Sanitätsraum
fish fingers	['fɪʃ ˌfɪŋgəz]	Fischstäbchen
fixed	['fɪkst]	fixiert, fest
fizzy drinks	['fɪzi ˌdrɪŋks]	hier: Limonaden, süße Getränke
flaming	['fleɪmɪŋ]	jmd. Verfluchen, angreifen
flatter	['flætə]	schmeicheln
flexible	['fleksɪbl]	flexibel
flow	[fləʊ]	Flut, Strom
flyposter	['flaɪˌpəʊstə]	Flugblatt, Handzettel
folder	['fəʊldə]	Aktenordner
fondling	['fɒndlɪŋ]	schmusen, streicheln
Food coaching	['fuːd ˌkəʊtʃɪŋ]	„Esstraining“, Ernährungsberatung
fooling around	[ˌfuːlɪŋ ə'raʊnd]	Unsinn machen
forbid, forbade, forbidden	[fə'bɪd, fə'beɪd, fə'bɪdən]	verbieten
forge	[fɔːdʒ]	fälschen
forgery of signatures	[ˌfɔːdʒəri ɒf 'sɪgnətʃəz]	Unterschriftenfälschung
formal gathering	[ˌfɔːməl 'gæðərɪŋ]	formale Zusammenkunft, hier: Besprechung im Berufsleben
'for the sheer hell of it' (Slang)	[fɔː ðə ʃɪə 'hel əf ɪt]	einfach so, einfach aus Spaß
fractured	['fræktʃəd]	gebrochen
frank	[fræŋk]	offen, ehrlich
fraud	[frɔːd]	hier: betrügen
free access to	[ˌfriː 'ækses tu]	freier Zugriff auf/Zugang zu
French kiss	[ˌfrenʃ 'kɪs]	Zungenkuss
friends circle	['frendz ˌsɜːkl]	Freundeskreis
fully recover	[ˌfʊlɪ rɪ'kʌvə]	hier: gesundheitlich völlig genesen
funfair	['fʌnfeə]	Jahrmarkt, Kirmes
future prospects	[ˌfjuːtʃə 'prɒspekts]	Zukunftsaussichten
gain	[geɪn]	hier: (Berufserfahrung) sammeln
gap year	['gæp ˌjɪə]	ein Jahr Auszeit
gather information	[ˌgæðər ɪnfə'meɪʃən]	Informationen sammeln/beschaffen
GCSE	[ˌdʒiː siː es 'iː]	Abschluss der Sekundarstufe II
gender-roles	['dʒendə ˌrəʊlz]	Geschlechterrollen
general practitioner	[ˌdʒenərəl præk'tɪʃənə]	allgemeiner Arzt/Ärztin
genetic defect	[dʒəˌnetɪk dɪ'fekt]	genetischer Defekt
genuine interest	[ˌdʒenjuɪn 'ɪntrəst]	echtes, aufrichtiges Interesse

German measles	[ˌdʒɜːmən ˈmiːzlz]	Masern
get divorced	[ˌget dɪˈvɔːst]	sich scheiden lassen, geschieden werden
get familiar with	[ˌget fəˈmɪliə wɪð]	sich gewöhnen an, vertraut werden mit
get involved into	[ˌget ɪnˈvɒlvd ɪnˌtu]	verwickelt werden in, sich einlassen auf
get noticed	[ˌget ˈnəʊtɪst]	hier: auffällig werden
give a lecture	[ˌgɪv ə ˈlektʃə]	hier: eine Standpauke halten, Grundsätze klären
give an account	[ˌgɪv ən əˈkaʊnt]	einen Bericht geben, berichten
gladiatorial ring	[ˌglædiəˈtɔːriəl ˌrɪŋ]	Kampfarena
glorify	[ˈglɔːrɪfaɪ]	glorifizieren, überhöhen
glue	[gluː]	Klebstoff
goal	[gəʊl]	Tor, hier: Ziel
good listener	[ˌgʊd ˈlɪsənə]	guter Zuhörer
gossip	[ˈgɒsɪp]	Klatsch, Tratsch
grab	[græb]	greifen (nach)
gradually	[ˈgrædʒuəli]	allmählich
graduate from	[ˈgrædjueɪt frɒm]	eine Schule absolvieren/mit einem Abschluss verlassen
grant sth. to sb.	[ˈgrɑːnt ˌsʌmθɪŋ tu ˌsʌmbədi]	jmd. etwas zusprechen
gratitude	[ˈgrætɪtjuːd]	Dankbarkeit
group therapy	[ˌgruːp ˈθerəpi]	Gruppentherapie
guardian	[ˈgɑːdiən]	Bewacher, Begleiter
guidelines	[ˈgaɪdlaɪnz]	Richtlinien, Grundsätze
guilt	[gɪlt]	Schuld
guilty	[ˈgɪlti]	schuldig
guy	[gaɪ]	(umgangssprachl.) Kerl, Typ
gynaecologist	[ˌgaɪnəˈkɒlədʒɪst]	Gynäkologe, Frauenarzt
haemophiliac	[ˌhiːməˈfɪliæk]	Bluter
handle sth.	[ˈhændl ˌsʌmθɪŋ]	mit etwas umgehen
harass so.	[ˈhærəs ˌsʌmwʌn]	(sexuell) belästigen
harassment	[ˈhærəsmənt]	(sexuelle) Belästigung
harm oneself	[ˈhɑːm wʌnˌself]	sich selbst verletzen
harmless	[ˈhɑːmləs]	ungefährlich, gesundheitlich unbedenklich/ungefährlich
harmless	[ˈhɑːmləs]	harmlos, ungefährlich
harsh	[hɑːʃ]	hart, streng
have a glance at	[ˌhæv ə ˈglɑːns æt]	einen Blick haben/werfen auf
have an issue about	[ˌhæv ən ˈɪʃuː əˌbaʊt]	ein Thema für jmd. sein
have the impression that	[ˌhæv ði ɪmˈpreʃən ðæt]	den Eindruck haben, dass
hay fever	[ˈheɪ ˌfiːvə]	Heuschnupfen
heal	[hiːl]	heilen
health	[helθ]	Gesundheit
health insurance	[ˈhelθ ɪnˌʃʊərəns]	Krankenversicherung
heart attack	[ˈhɑːt əˌtæk]	Herzanfall, Herzinfakt
heart failure	[ˈhɑːt ˌfeɪljə]	Herzversagen
herbal	[ˈhɜːbəl]	Kräuter-.../aus Kräutern bestehend
hero	[ˈhɪərəʊ]	Held
heroic	[hɪˈrəʊɪk]	heldenhaft
heroine	[ˈherəʊɪn]	Heldin

hesitate at	['hezɪteɪt æt]	zögern bei
high	[haɪ]	hoch
high chair/child seat	['haɪ ˌtʃeə / 'tʃaɪld ˌsiːt]	Kinderhochsitz
high school diploma	['haɪ ˌskuːl dɪ'pləʊmə]	Hochschul-/Universitätsabschluss
high windows	[ˌhaɪ 'wɪndəʊz]	Oberlichter
highlight sth.	['haɪlaɪt ˌsʌmθɪŋ]	hier: etwas hervorheben
hinder so.	['hɪndə ˌsʌmwʌn]	jmd. hindern, behindern
hinge on	['hɪndʒ ˌɒn]	hier: jmd./einer Sache etwas anhängen, etwas mit jmd./einer Sache verbinden
hint at	['hɪnt ˌæt]	weisen auf
hip	[hɪp]	Hüfte
homeless people	[ˌhəʊmləs 'piːpl]	Obdachlose
homicide	['hɒmɪsaɪd]	Mord
hormone changes	[ˌhɔːməʊn 'tʃeɪndʒɪz]	hormonelle Veränderungen
hospice	['hɒspɪs]	Sterbehospiz
host	[həʊst]	hier: Animateur
hostess	['həʊstɪs]	hier: Animateurin
hostile	['hɒstaɪl]	feindlich
human being	[ˌhjuːmən 'biːɪŋ]	menschliches Wesen
humiliate	[hjuː'mɪlieɪt]	demütigen
humiliation	[hjuːˌmɪli'eɪʃən]	Demütigung
hurt, hurt, hurt	[hɜːt]	verletzen
icebreaker	['aɪsbreɪkə]	Eisbrecher, hier: gemeinsame Aktivität zum Kennenlernen/zur Stimmungsauflockerung
imaginative	[ɪ'mædʒɪnətɪv]	hier: phantasievoll
imitate	['ɪmɪteɪt]	imitieren, nachahmen
immense	[ɪ'mens]	immens, gewaltig
immerse	[ɪ'mɜːs]	eintauchen
impact on	[ɪm'pækt ˌɒn]	Einfluss auf
impairment	[ɪm'peəmənt]	Beeinträchtigung
impel so. to do sth.	[ɪm'pel ˌsʌmwʌn tu 'duː ˌsʌmθɪŋ]	jmd. nötigen etwas zu tun
impersonation	[ɪmˌpɜːsən'eɪʃən]	hier: (unfreiwillige) Freigabe persönlicher Daten
implement	['ɪmplɪmənt]	durchführen, ausführen, hier: in die Tat umsetzen
imply	[ɪm'plaɪ]	andeuten
impose	[ɪm'pəʊz]	auferlegen, verhängen
impractical	[ɪm'præktɪkəl]	unpraktisch
impressionable	[ɪm'preʃənəbl]	beeindruckbar, hier: leicht beeinflussbar
imprisonment	[ɪm'prɪzənmənt]	Inhaftierung
impulsive	[ɪm'pʌlsɪv]	impulsiv
in any case	[ɪn 'eni ˌkeɪs]	auf jeden Fall
in moderation	[ɪn ˌmɒdə'reɪʃən]	in Maßen
include	[ɪn'kluːd]	beinhalten
inclusion	[ɪn'kluːʒən]	Inklusion, Zusammenführung
income	['ɪnkʌm]	Einkommen
incurable	[ɪn'kjʊərəbl]	unheilbar, hier auch: bösartig
indecisive	[ˌɪndɪ'saɪsɪv]	unentschlossen

independent	[ˌɪndɪ'pendənt]	unabhängig
indisposition	[ˌɪndɪspə'zɪʃən]	Unpässlichkeit, Unwohlsein
individual psychological treatment	[ˌɪndɪ'vɪdʒuəl ˌsaɪkə'lɒdʒɪkəl ˌtriːtmənt]	psychologische Einzelbehandlung
individualized educational programmes	[ˌɪndɪ'vɪdʒuəlaɪzd ˌedʒʊ'keɪʃənəl ˌprəʊgræmz]	individuelle Erziehungs-/Förderprogramme
indulgent	[ɪn'dʌldʒənt]	nachsichtig, (zu) nachgiebig
inevitable	[ɪ'nevɪtəbl]	unvermeidlich
infant	['ɪnfənt]	Kleinkind (ca. bis 2 Jahre)
infection	[ɪn'fekʃən]	Infektion
infectious disease	[ɪnˌfekʃəs dɪ'ziːz]	Infektionskrankheit
inflict a fine on so.	[ɪnˌflɪkt ə 'faɪn ɒn ˌsʌmwʌn]	jemandem eine Geldstrage auferlegen
inflict on	[ɪn'flɪkt ɒn]	ausüben auf, auch: zufügen
influence	['ɪnfluəns]	Einfluss
infuriate	[ɪn'fjʊərieɪt]	zornig machen
injure	['ɪndʒə]	verwunden, eine Wunde zufügen
injury	['ɪndʒəri]	Verletzung
inside address	[ˌɪnsaɪd ə'dres]	Adresse des Empfängers auf dem Brief
insight	['ɪnsaɪt]	Einblick
insinuate	[ɪn'sinjueɪt]	unterstellen
insist to	[ɪn'sɪst tu]	insistieren auf, bestehen auf
insult	['ɪnsʌlt]	Beleidigung
integral parts	[ˌɪntəgrəl 'pɑːts]	(integrale) Bestandteile
intellectual development	[ˌɪntə'lektjuəl dɪˌveləpmənt]	intellektuelle/geistige Entwicklung
intensive care	[ɪnˌtensɪv 'keə]	Intensivpflege
intensive care unit	[ɪnˌtensɪv 'keə ˌjuːnɪt]	Intensivstation
interaction	[ˌɪntər'ækʃən]	Interaktion, kommunikativer Austausch
interactive	[ˌɪntər'æktɪv]	interaktiv, in einem gemeinsamen aktiven Austauch sein
interfere	[ˌɪntə'fɪə]	(sich) einmischen, hier: kollidieren mit, behindern
interfere in	[ˌɪntə'fɪər ˌɪn]	sich einmischen in
interrupt	[ˌɪntə'rʌpt]	unterbrechen
intervene in	[ˌɪntə'viːn ˌɪn]	sich einmischen in
intimate	['ɪntɪmət]	intim, hier: besonders eng, privat
intimidate	[ɪn'tɪmɪdeɪt]	einschüchtern
intimidated	[ɪn'tɪmɪdeɪtɪd]	eingeschüchtert
intimidation	[ɪnˌtɪmɪ'deɪʃən]	Einschüchterung
introduce	[ˌɪntrə'djuːs]	hier: einführen
introduce into society	[ˌɪntrə'djuːs ˌɪntu sə'saɪəti]	in die Gesellschaft einführen
introduce oneself to	[ˌɪntrə'djuːs wʌnˌself tu]	sich vorstellen
introduction	[ˌɪntrə'dʌkʃən]	Einführung, hier auch: Einweisung
introductory sentence	[ˌɪntrə'dʌktəri ˌsentəns]	Einleitungssatz
intrude	[ɪn'truːd]	eindringen in, stören bei
intuition	[ˌɪntju'ɪʃən]	Eingebung, hier: Gefühl für den nahenden Tod
invent	[ɪn'vent]	erfinden
invest	[ɪn'vest]	investieren, hier: (Zeit) verbringen
invite	[ɪn'vaɪt]	einladen

invulnerable	[ˌɪnˈvʌlnərəbl]	unverletzbar
ironed	[ˈaɪənd]	gebügelt
irrespective of	[ˌɪrɪˈspektɪv ɒf]	ungeachtet von
irresponsible	[ˌɪrɪˈspɒnsəbl]	unverantwortlich
irresponsible	[ˌɪrɪˈspɒnsəbl]	verantwortungslos
irreversible	[ˌɪrɪˈvɜːsəbl]	unabänderlich, nicht mehr umkehrbar
irrevocable	[ˌɪrɪˈvəʊkəbl]	unumstößlich, unabänderlich
isolated	[ˈaɪsəleɪtɪd]	isoliert/ausgegrenzt sein
issue	[ˈɪʃuː]	Thema, Streitfrage, Problemstellung
jellies	[ˈdʒeliz]	Fruchtgummibonbons
jingle	[ˈdʒɪŋgl]	hier: Werbemelodie
job interview	[ˌdʒɒb ˈɪntəvjuː]	Vorstellungsgespräch
job training	[ˌdʒɒb ˈtreɪnɪŋ]	Berufsausbildung
join a group	[ˌdʒɔɪn ə ˈgruːp]	sich einer Gruppe anschließen
judgemental	[dʒʌdʒˈmentəl]	hier: anklagend, verurteilend
Justice	[ˈdʒʌstɪs]	Richter
justified	[ˈdʒʌstɪfaɪd]	gerechtfertigt
juvenile court	[ˌdʒuːvənaɪl ˈkɔːt]	Jugendgericht
juvenile delinquent	[ˌdʒuːvənaɪl dɪˈlɪŋkwənt]	jugendlicher Straftäter
juvenile prison	[ˌdʒuːvənaɪl ˈprɪzən]	Jugendgefängnis
juvenile punishment	[ˌdʒuːvənaɪl ˈpʌnɪʃmənt]	Jugendstrafe
keep discipline	[ˌkiːp ˈdɪsəplɪn]	die Disziplin aufrecht erhalten
keep evidence	[ˌkiːp ˈevɪdəns]	hier: Beweise sammeln/festhalten
keep up a marriage	[ˌkiːp ˈʌp ə ˌmærɪdʒ]	eine Ehe aufrecht erhalten
kick	[kɪk]	treten
kick off	[ˌkɪk ˈɒf]	auslösen, lostreten
kick off (Slang)	[ˌkɪk ˈɒf]	herauswerfen, hier: aus dem Programm nehmen
kingsized/supersized	[ˈkɪŋsaɪzd / ˈsuːpəsaɪzd]	extra große Portionen
label	[ˈleɪbəl]	Produktetikett, Aufkleber
labeling	[ˈleɪbəlɪŋ]	Etikettierung
lack concentration	[ˈlæk ˌkɒnsənˈtreɪʃən]	an Konzentration mangeln
lack of	[ˈlæk ˌɒf]	Mangel an ...
lack of exercise	[ˌlæk ɒf ˈeksəsaɪz]	Bewegungsmangel
lack of parental control	[ˌlæk ɒf pəˈrentəl kənˈtrəʊl]	mangelnde elterliche Kontrolle/Mangel an elterlicher Fürsorge
lack of sleep	[ˌlæk ɒf ˈsliːp]	Schlafmangel
lack of time	[ˌlæk ɒf ˈtaɪm]	Zeitmangel
lack of understanding	[ˌlæk ɒf ʌndəˈstændɪŋ]	mangelndes Verständnis
laden with	[ˈleɪdən ˌwɪð]	überladen mit
lamb	[læm]	Lamm
lap	[læp]	Schoß
last shot	[ˌlɑːst ˈʃɒt]	der letzte Schuss (hier: an einer letzten Drogeninjektion sterben)
lasting	[ˈlɑːstɪŋ]	bleibend, anhaltend
launch	[lɔːntʃ]	anlaufen lassen, herausbringen
lawyer	[ˈlɔːjə]	Rechtsanwalt
lead on	[ˌliːd ˈɒn]	weiterführen
lean meat	[ˌliːn ˈmiːt]	mageres Fleisch
lean towards	[ˌliːn tʊˈwɔːdz]	sich lehnen/neigen (nach), anlehnen

learning difficulties	['lɜːnɪŋ ˌdɪfɪkəltiz]	Lernschwierigkeiten, Lernschwächen, Lernstörung
learning surrounding	['lɜːnɪŋ səˌraʊndɪŋ]	Lernumgebung
learning tools	['lɜːnɪŋ ˌtuːlz]	Lernmittel, Lernwerkzeuge
leave its mark on sb./sth	[ˌliːv ɪts 'mɑːk ɒn ˌsʌmbədi/ ˌsʌmθɪŋ]	seine Spuren auf jmd./etwas hinterlassen
leave out of sight	['liːv ˌaʊt ɒf 'saɪt]	aus den Augen/Blick lassen
lecture	['lektʃə]	Vortrag
legal consequences	[ˌliːgəl 'kɒnsɪkwənsɪz]	gerichtliche Folgen/Maßnahmen
legalise	['liːgəlaɪz]	legalisieren, gesetzlich erlauben
lend a hand	[lend ə hænd]	mit anpacken, zupacken
less ... than	[les ðæn]	weniger .. als
letter of caution	[ˌletər ɒf 'kɔːʃən]	Abmahnung
lettuce leaf	['letɪs ˌliːf]	Salatblatt
level	['levəl]	Anteil, Grad, Niveau
liberating	['lɪbəreɪtɪŋ]	befreiend
life-threatening	['laɪfˌθretənɪŋ]	lebensbedrohlich
lift	[lɪft]	heben
liquid	['lɪkwɪd]	Flüssigkeit
liquor law violation	['lɪkə ˌlɔː ˌvaɪə'leɪʃən]	unerlaubter Alkoholkonsum/ -besitz
liver	['lɪvə]	Leber
liver sausage	['lɪvə ˌsɒsɪdʒ]	Leberwurst
living circumstances	['lɪvɪŋ ˌsɜːkəmstænsɪz]	Lebensumstände
local communities	[ˌləʊkəl kə'mjuːnətis]	hier: Verwaltung der Kommunen
lonesome	['ləʊnsəm]	einsam
long-term effects	'lɒŋtɜːm ɪˌfekts	Langzeiteffekt, hier: Langzeitschäden
look after	[ˌlʊk 'ɑːftə]	sich kümmern um, pflegen, für jmd. Sorgen
lose a job	[ˌluːz ə 'dʒɒb]	einen Job/die Arbeit verlieren
lose balance	[ˌluːz 'bæləns]	Gleichgewicht verlieren
loss	[lɒs]	Verlust
loss of memory	[ˌlɒs ɒf 'meməri]	Gedächtnisverlust
low	[ləʊ]	niedrig
lump	[lʌmp]	Knoten
lymph nodes	['lɪmf ˌnəʊdz]	Lymphknoten
maintain relationships	[meɪnˌteɪn rɪ'leɪʃənʃɪps]	Beziehungen pflegen/aufrecht halten
maintenance	['meɪntənəns]	Instandhaltung, Unterhalt
majority	[mə'dʒɒrəti]	Mehrheit
make a fuss about	[ˌmeɪk ə 'fʌs əˌbaʊt]	etwas übertreiben
make an effort	[ˌmeɪk ən 'efət]	sich anstrengen, sich bemühen
malnutrition	[ˌmælnjuː'trɪʃən]	Fehlernährung
mammography	[mæm'ɒgrəfi]	Mammografie
manufacturer	[ˌmænjə'fæktʃərə]	Hersteller
march so. to	['mɑːtʃ ˌsʌmwʌn tu]	hier: jmd hinführen zu
marriage market	['mærɪdʒ ˌmɑːkɪt]	"Heiratsmarkt"
master a problem	[ˌmɑːstər ə 'prɒbləm]	ein Problem meistern
maternal clinic	[məˌtɜːnəl 'klɪnɪk]	Geburtsklinik
mattress	['mætrəs]	Matratze
mean	[miːn]	gemein, hintertrieben, bösartig
measure	['meʒə]	messen, hier: wiegen

media	['mi:diə]	Medien
media consumer	['mi:diə kən,sju:mə]	Medienkonsument
media consumption	['mi:diə kən,sʌmpʃən]	Medienkonsum
media education	['mi:diə ˌedʒʊ'keɪʃən]	Medienerziehung
media experience	['mi:diə ɪk,spɪəriəns]	Medienerfahrung
media message	['mi:diə ˌmesɪdʒ]	Medienbotschaft
medical assistant	[ˌmedɪkəl ə'sɪstənt]	medizinische/-r Assistent/-in
medical care	[ˌmedɪkəl 'keə]	Gesundheitsfürsorge
medical check-ups	[ˌmedɪkəl 'tʃekʌps]	medizinische Kontrolluntersuchungen
medical detoxification	[ˌmedɪkəl di:ˌtɒksɪfɪ'keɪʃən]	medizinischer Entzug
medical practice	[ˌmedɪkəl 'præktɪs]	Arztpraxis
meet with	['mi:t ˌwɪð]	stoßen auf
menacing	['menəsɪŋ]	bedrohlich, Angst einflößend
mental ability	[ˌmentəl ə'bɪləti]	geistige Fähigkeit
mental illness	[ˌmentəl 'ɪlnəs]	mentale Erkrankung, psychische Erkrankung
mentally	['mentəli]	geistig
mentally exhausted	[ˌmentəli ɪg'zɔ:stɪd]	geistig erschöpft
mention	['menʃən]	erwähnen
menu	['menju:]	Speiseplan
menu plan	['menju: ˌplæn]	Essensplan
Middle Age	['mɪdl ˌeɪdʒ]	Mittelalter
migraine	['mi:greɪn]	Migräne
mill around	[ˌmɪl ə'raʊnd]	hier: sich herumtreiben
mind children	[ˌmaɪnd 'tʃɪldrən]	Kinder betreuen
mind-altering	['maɪnd ˌɔ:ltərɪŋ]	den Geist/Verstand verändernd
mind-numbing	['maɪnd ˌnʌmɪŋ]	betäubend, empfindungslos machend
minerals	['mɪnərəlz]	Mineralien
minor	['maɪnə]	unbedeutend, unwichtig, gering(er)
minor	['maɪnə]	weniger wichtig, weniger schwerwiegend
minority	[maɪ'nɒrəti]	Minderheit
misbehave	[ˌmɪsbɪ'heɪv]	sich schlecht benehmen, ungezogen sein
mistrust	[mɪ'strʌst]	misstrauen
mitigating circumstances	[ˌmɪtɪgeɪtɪŋ 'sɜ:kəmstænsɪz]	mildernde Umstände
mob	[mɒb]	Meute
moderate	['mɒdərət]	gemäßigt
morning sickness	['mɔ:nɪŋ ˌsɪknəs]	morgendliche Übelkeit
mortification	[ˌmɔ:tɪfɪ'keɪʃən]	äußerste Verlegenheit, Demütigung
most common cause	[ˌməʊst 'kɒmən ˌkɔ:z]	hier: Hauptursache
motherhood	['mʌðəhʊd]	Mutterschaft
muddle through	[ˌmʌdl 'θru:]	sich durchschlagen
mugging	['mʌgɪŋ]	Straßenraub, Überfall auf offener Straße
multiple	['mʌltɪpl]	viel(zählig), zahlreich
multitask	[ˌmʌltɪ'tɑ:sk]	viele Dinge auf einmal tun
multitude	['mʌltɪtju:d]	Vielzahl
murder	['mɜ:də]	Mord
muscles	['mʌsəlz]	Muskeln
mutilate	['mju:tɪleɪt]	entstellen, verstümmeln

nag at so.	['næg æt ˌsʌmwʌn]	(umgangsprachl.) jm. eine Standpauke halten, jm. kritisieren
naughty	['nɔːti]	ungezogen
nearby	[ˌnɪə'baɪ]	in der Nähe
neat final version	[ˌniːt 'faɪnəl ˌvɜːʃən]	eine saubere Endversion
necessary	['nesəsəri]	notwendig
neglect	[nɪ'glekt]	Vernachlässigung
nerd	[nɜːd]	Schwachkopf
nervous breakdown	[ˌnɜːvəs 'breɪkdaʊn]	Nervenzusammenbruch
neurological disease	[ˌnjʊərə'lɒdʒɪkəl dɪˌziːz]	neurologische Erkrankung, Nervenerkrankung
nevertheless	[ˌnevəðə'les]	trotzdem, dennoch
night shift	['naɪt ˌʃɪft]	Nachtschicht
nod at so.	['nɒd æt ˌsʌmwʌn]	jmd. zunicken
notice board	['nəʊtɪs ˌbɔːd]	Pinnwand
notorious	[nəʊ'tɔːriəs]	notorisch
notorious offender	[nəʊˌtɔːriəs ə'fendə]	Wiederholungstäter
nuclear family	[ˌnjuːkliə 'fæməli]	Kleinfamilie
numb	[nʌm]	dumpf, leer
nurse	[nɜːs]	hier: stillen
nursery nurse	['nɜːsəri ˌnɜːs]	Kinderpfleger/-in/Kindergärtner/-in
nursery school	['nɜːsəri ˌskuːl]	Kindergarten
nursery school age	['nɜːsəri ˌskuːl 'eɪdʒ]	Kindergartenalter
nursing mother	['nɜːsɪŋ ˌmʌðə]	stillende Mutter
nutrients	['nuːtriənts]	Nährstoffe
nutrition	[nuː'trɪʃən]	Ernährung
nutrition label	[nuː'trɪʃən ˌleɪbəl]	Etikett-Information über Inhaltsstoffe
nutritional counselling	[nuː'trɪʃənəl ˌkaʊnsəlɪŋ]	Ernährungsberatung
nutritional guidelines	[nuː'trɪʃənəl ˌgaɪdlaɪnz]	Ernäherungsrichtlinien
nutritionist	[nuː'trɪʃənɪst]	Ernährungsberater(in)
nuts	[nʌts]	Nüsse
obese	[əʊ'biːs]	fettleibig
obesity	[əʊ'biːsəti]	Fettleibigkeit
objective	[əb'dʒektɪv]	objektiv
occupation	[ˌɒkjə'peɪʃən]	Ein-/Übernahme, Besetzung, hier: Nutzung
occupational therapist	[ˌɒkjə'peɪʃənəl ˌθerəpɪst]	Beschäftigungstherapeut/-in
occupied	['ɒkjəpaɪd]	belegt
offence	[ə'fens]	Angriff, hier: Straftat
offend	[ə'fend]	angreifen, auch: verletzen, schädigen
offender	[ə'fendə]	Angreifer, hier: Straftäter
offensive	[ə'fensɪv]	angreifend
offer	['ɒfə]	Angebot
old people's home	[ˌəʊld 'piːplz ˌhəʊm]	Altenpflegeheim
old people's nurse	[ˌəʊld 'piːplz ˌnɜːs]	Altenpfleger/-in
on suspicion	[ˌɒn sə'spɪʃən]	unter Verdacht
opening sentences	['əʊpənɪŋ ˌsentənsɪz]	hier: dier ersten Referatsätze
operation	[ˌɒpə'reɪʃən]	hier: (Militär)Einsatz
operation theatre	[ˌɒpə'reɪʃən ˌθɪətə]	Operationssaal
options	['ɒpʃənz]	Möglichkeiten
orders	['ɔːdəz]	hier: gerichtliche Auflagen

ought	[ɔːt]	sollte
outdated	[ˌaʊtˈdeɪtɪd]	hier: veraltet
outing	[ˈaʊtɪŋ]	Ausflug, hier auch: Outing, Bloßstellung
outstrip	[ˌaʊtˈstrɪp]	überholen, übertreffen
outward appearance	[ˌaʊtwəd əˈpɪərəns]	äußeres Erscheinungsbild
overdose	[ˈəʊvədəʊz]	Überdosis
overview	[ˈəʊvəvjuː]	Überblick
overweight	[ˈəʊvəweɪt]	übergewichtig
overwhelmed	[ˌəʊvəˈwelmd]	überfordert
oxygen	[ˈɒksɪdʒən]	Sauerstoff
packaged meals	[ˌpækɪdʒd ˈmiːlz]	Fertiggerichte
paediatrician	[ˌpiːdiəˈtrɪʃən]	Kinderärztin/-arzt
pain	[peɪn]	Schmerz
pamper	[ˈpæmpə]	verwöhnen, verhätscheln
paper	[ˈpeɪpə]	Handout, Handreichung
paranoia	[ˌpærəˈnɔɪə]	Wahnvorstellung
parenting programme	[ˈpeərəntɪŋ ˌprəʊgræm]	Erziehungskurs ("Elternführerschein")
parenting styles	[ˈpeərəntɪŋ ˌstaɪlz]	Erziehungsstile
participant	[pɑːˈtɪsɪpənt]	Teilnehmerin/Teilnehmer
particularly	[pɑːˈtɪkjələli]	besonders, insbesondere
pass	[pɑːs]	hier: bestehen
pass a time	[ˌpɑːs ə ˈtaɪm]	eine Zeit durchlaufen/durchmachen
pass for	[ˈpɑːs ˌfɔː]	hier: als ... durchgehen
pastry	[ˈpeɪstri]	Pastete
patchwork family	[ˈpætʃwɜːk ˌfæməli]	Familie, die sich aus verschiedenen Familien neu zusammensetzt
patience	[ˈpeɪʃəns]	Geduld
patient	[ˈpeɪʃənt]	Patient
patient file	[ˈpeɪʃənt ˌfaɪl]	Krankenakte
patient's prognosis	[ˈpeɪʃənts prɒgˌnəʊsɪs]	hier: Lebenserwartung eines Patienten
pause	[pɔːz]	pausieren
pay off	[ˌpeɪ ˈɒf]	abbezahlen
peaceful	[ˈpiːsfʊl]	friedlich
peanut	[ˈpiːnʌt]	Erdnuss
peas	[piːz]	Erbsen
pen name	[ˈpen ˌneɪm]	Pseudonym, erfundener Name
performance	[pəˈfɔːməns]	hier: Benehmen
periods	[ˈpɪəriədz]	hier: Menstruation (Monatsblutung)
perpetrate	[ˈpɜːpətreɪt]	hier: ausüben
persistent	[pɜːˈsɪstənt]	beständig, hartnäckig
personal care	[ˌpɜːsənəl ˈkeə]	Persönlichkeitsfürsorge
personality	[ˌpɜːsəˈnæləti]	Persönlichkeit
personnel manager	[pɜːsəˈnel ˌmænɪdʒə]	Personalchef
persuade	[pəˈsweɪd]	überreden
physical	[ˈfɪzɪkəl]	körperlich
physical decline	[ˌfɪzɪkəl dɪˈklaɪn]	körperlicher Zerfall
physical power	[ˌfɪzɪkəl ˈpaʊə]	hier: körperliche Gewalt
physically	[ˈfɪzɪkəli]	körperlich
physiotherapy	[ˌfɪziəʊˈθerəpi]	Physiotherapie
pill	[pɪl]	Pille (Verhütungsmittel)

pity	['pɪti]	bemitleiden
placement	['pleɪsmənt]	Praktikum
plaice	[pleɪs]	Scholle
planning for death	[ˌplænɪŋ fə 'deθ]	sich auf den Tod einstellen, hier auch: die letzte Lebensphase planen
plaster	['plɑːstə]	Gipsverband
play carpet	['pleɪ ˌkɑːpɪt]	Spielteppich
plot	[plɒt]	Handlung
podgy	['pɒdʒi]	rundlich, pummelig
point out	[ˌpɔɪnt 'aʊt]	herausstellen
poison	['pɔɪzən]	Gift
Poison Control Centre	[ˌpɔɪzən kən'trəʊl ˌsentə]	Giftzentrale
police file	[pə'liːs ˌfaɪl]	Polizeiakte
police force	[pə'liːs ˌfɔːs]	Polizeieinheit
police investigation	[pə'liːs ɪnˌvestɪ'geɪʃən]	polizeiliche Untersuchung
porky	['pɔːki]	pummelig
portable	['pɔːtəbl]	tragbares Fernsehgerät
posture	['pəʊstʃə]	Körperhaltung
praise	[preɪz]	Lob
prat	[præt]	Verrückter
predict	[prɪ'dɪkt]	vorausschauen, voraussagen
preferences	['prefərənsɪz]	Vorlieben, hier: Patientenwünsche für die letzte Lebensphase
prejudice	['predʒədɪs]	Vorurteil
prejudices	['predʒədɪsɪz]	Vorurteile
preparation	[ˌprepə'reɪʃən]	Vorbereitung
preschooler	['priːˌskuːlə]	Vorschulkind
prescribe	[prɪ'skraɪb]	verschreiben
present so. with sth.	[prɪ'zent ˌsʌmwʌn wɪð ˌsʌmθɪŋ]	jm. etwas übergeben/überreichen
presenter	[prɪ'zentə]	Referent, der/die Vortragende
preservatives	[prɪ'zɜːvətɪvz]	Konservierungsstoffe
pressure	['preʃə]	Druck
pretend	[prɪ'tend]	vorgeben, vorspielen
prevent	[prɪ'vent]	vermeiden, hier: Vorsorge treffen
prevent so. from	[prɪ'vent ˌsʌmwʌn frɒm]	jmd. schützen vor/abhalten von
prevention	[prɪ'venʃən]	Vorsorge
primary school	['praɪməri ˌskuːl]	Grundschule
privileged	['prɪvəlɪdʒd]	priviligiert, herausragend
privileged thing	[ˌprɪvəlɪdʒd 'θɪŋ]	hier: etwas Besonderes
probation	[prə'beɪʃən]	Bewährung
problem-oriented	['prɒbləm ˌɔːrientɪd]	problembezogen, problemorientiert
proceedings	[prə'siːdɪŋz]	hier: Geschehen im Gerichtssaal
produce	[prə'djuːs]	hier: vorlegen
productive conversation	[prə'dʌktɪv ˌkɒnvə'seɪʃən]	gelungenes Gespräch
professional	[prə'feʃənəl]	hier: ausgebildet, auch berufstätig
promote health	[prəˌməʊt 'helθ]	Gesundheit fördern
properly	['prɒpəli]	ordentlich, sorgsam
property	['prɒpəti]	Eigentum
proposal	[prə'pəʊzəl]	Vorschlag

proposely	Lautschrift fehlt	aus Absicht, absichtlich
prosthetic patient	[prɒsˈθetɪk ˌpeɪʃənt]	Patient mit einer Prothese
prostituting so.	[ˈprɒstɪtjuːtɪŋ ˌsʌmwʌn]	jmd. prostituieren
protein	[ˈprəʊtiːn]	Protein
provide	[prəˈvaɪd]	hier: zur Verfügung stellen, ausschreiben
provision for old age	[prəˈvɪʒən fər ˌəʊld ˈeɪdʒ]	Altersvorsorge
provoke	[prəˈvəʊk]	provozieren
psychic strain	[ˌsaɪkɪk ˈstreɪn]	psychische Belastung
psychologist	[saɪˈkɒlədʒɪst]	Psychologe/-in
puberty	[ˈpjuːbəti]	Pubertät
punishing	[ˈpʌnɪʃɪŋ]	Bestrafen
purchase	[ˈpɜːtʃəs]	kaufen
purposely	[ˈpɜːpəsli]	aus Absicht, absichtlich
push	[pʊʃ]	stoßen, schupsen
put on weight	[ˌpʊt ˈɒn ˌweɪt]	Gewicht zulegen
put pressure on	[ˌpʊt ˈpreʃə ˌɒn]	unter Druck setzen, Druck ausüben auf
puzzled	[ˈpʌzəld]	verwirrt, irritiert
qualification	[ˌkwɒlɪfɪˈkeɪʃən]	Qualifikation, auch: Berufs-oder Schulabschluss
quench thirst	[ˌkwenʃ ˈθɜːst]	Durst stillen
questionnaire	[ˌkwestʃəˈneə]	Fragebogen
quiet corner	[ˌkwaɪɪt ˈkɔːnə]	Kuschelecke
race	[reɪs]	rasen
racial	[ˈreɪʃəl]	rassisch, Rassen-…
racial discrimination	[ˈreɪʃəl dɪˌskrɪmɪˈneɪʃən]	Diskriminierung von Ausländern, Ausländerfeindlichkeit
radiant	[ˈreɪdiənt]	strahlend
raise a child	[ˌreɪz ə ˈtʃaɪld]	ein Kind großziehen
raise a family	[ˌreɪz ə ˈfæməli]	eine Familie gründen
raise the subject	[ˌreɪz ðə ˈsʌbdʒɪkt]	das Thema ansprechen
rampage	[ˈræmpeɪdʒ]	Randalieren
range	[reɪndʒ]	Reichweite
range from… to	[reɪndʒ frɒm … tu]	reichen von … bis
rape	[reɪp]	Vergewaltigung
rapid	[ˈræpɪd]	sehr schnell
rapid incline	[ˌræpɪd ɪnˈklaɪn]	rapider, sprunghafter Anstieg
raspberry	[ˈrɑːzberi]	Himbeere
rate of unemployment	[ˌreɪt ɒf ˌʌnɪmˈplɔɪmənt]	Arbeitslosenrate
rational	[ˈræʃənəl]	rational, vernunftbestimmt
reassign	[ˌriːəˈsaɪn]	sich wieder eintragen, erneut anmelden
rebellion	[rɪˈbeliən]	Rebellion, Widerspruch
recall s.th.	[rɪˈkɔːl ˌsʌmθɪŋ]	etw. erinnern
recover	[rɪˈkʌvə]	sich erholen, gesund werden
recreating	[ˈrekrieɪtɪŋ]	Erholung
references	[ˈrefərənsɪz]	hier: Referenzen
reflect	[rɪˈflekt]	reflektieren, wiedergeben, überdenken, darstellen
refuse	[rɪˈfjuːz]	ablehnen, verweigern, sich weigern
register at	[ˈredʒɪstə ˌæt]	sich an der Hochschule einschreiben
rehab clinic	[ˈriːhæb ˌklɪnɪk]	hier: Drogenentzugsklinik

rehabilitate	[ˌriːhə'bɪlɪteɪt]	rehabilitieren, wieder eingliedern
rehabilitation centre	[ˌriːhəˌbɪlɪ'teɪʃən ˌsentə]	Reha, Rehabilitationszentrum
reinforce	[ˌriːɪn'fɔːs]	bestärken
reintegration	[ˌriːɪntɪ'greɪʃən]	Reintegration, Wiedereingliederung
relapse	[rɪ'læps]	Rückfall, auch rückfällig werden
relate to	[rɪ'leɪt tu]	hier: in Verbindung bringen mit
relax	[ɪ'læks]	entspannen
release tension	[rɪˌliːs 'tenʃən]	Spannungen/Anspannung abbauen
released	[rɪ'liːzd]	hier: veröffentlicht
relegate	['relɪgeɪt]	jmd. degradieren, hier: in eine untere Klasse zurück setzen
reliability	[rɪˌlaɪə'bɪləti]	Zuverlässigkeit
rely on	[rɪ'laɪ ˌɒn]	abhängen von, abhängig sein von
reminder	[rɪ'maɪndə]	Erinnerung
remove	[rɪ'muːv]	entfernen
repetition	[repə'tɪʃən]	Wiederholung
replace with	[rɪ'pleɪs ˌwɪð]	ersetzen durch, austauschen mit
reproach	[rɪ'prəʊtʃ]	Vorwurf
reproach so. for sth.	[rɪ'prəʊtʃ ˌsʌmwʌn fɔː ˌsʌmθɪŋ]	jmd. Etwas vorwerfen
reputation	[ˌrepjə'teɪʃən]	Ansehen
requirements	[rɪ'kwaɪəmənts]	Voraussetzungen, Bedingungen
resident	['rezɪdənt]	Bewohner
residential setting	[ˌrezɪ'denʃəl ˌsetɪŋ]	Heim
resistance	[rɪ'zɪstəns]	Widerstand
respond	[rɪ'spɒnd]	antworten, reagieren auf
respond to	[rɪ'spɒnd tu]	reagieren auf
restrictions	[rɪ'strɪkʃənz]	Beschränkung, Einschränkung
result	[rɪ'zʌlt]	Ergebnis
result in	[rɪ'zʌlt ɪn]	hier: führen zu
resumé	['rezjuːmeɪ]	Lebenslauf
resuscitate	[rɪ'sʌsɪteɪt]	wieder beleben
retailer	['riːteɪlə]	Einzelhändler/in
reward (so.)	[rɪ'wɔːd ˌsʌmwʌn]	(jmd.) belohnen
ribs	[rɪbz]	Rippen
ridicule	['rɪdɪkjuːl]	sich lächerlich machen, hier: das Lächerlichmachen
risky behaviour	[ˌrɪski bɪ'heɪvjə]	riskantes, gefährliches Verhalten
robbery	['rɒbəri]	Raub
rude	[ruːd]	grob, hier: ungezogen, unverschämt, unhöflich
rude words/language	[ˌruːd 'wɜːdz / 'læŋgwɪdʒ]	Beschimpfungen
run a restaurant	[ˌrʌn ə 'restərɔ̃ːŋ]	ein Restaurant betreiben
rush through	[ˌrʌʃ 'θruː]	durch etwas hindurcheilen
rusty	['rʌsti]	rostig, verrostet
safe	[seɪf]	sicher
sales	[seɪlz]	Verkauf
salutation	[ˌsæljə'teɪʃən]	Anrede
salvation	[sæl'veɪʃən]	Rettung, Heil
school equipment	['skuːl ɪˌkwɪpmənt]	Schulausstattung
school shooter	['skuːl ˌʃuːtə]	jmd. der an Schulen eine Schießerei begeht

school shooting	['sku:l ʃu:tɪŋ]	Schießerei an einer Schule
school-leaver	['sku:l ˌli:və]	Schulabsolvent/-in
scientific	[ˌsaɪən'tɪfɪk]	wissenschaftlich
scornful	['skɔ:nfʊl]	verächtlich, höhnisch
scrambled eggs	[ˌskræmbld 'egz]	Rührei
scratch	[skrætʃ]	kratzen
skull	[skʌl]	Schädel, Totenschädel
secretly	['si:krətli]	heimlich
secure	[sɪ'kjʊə]	sicher
security door system	[sɪˌkjʊərəti 'dɔ: ˌsɪstəm]	Sicherheitsschleuse
security officers	[sɪˌkjʊərəti 'ɒfɪsəz]	Sicherheitsbeamte
seductive	[sɪ'dʌktɪv]	verführend, verführerisch
seemingly	['si:mɪŋli]	offenbar
self-centred	[ˌself'sentəd]	egoistisch
self-confidence	[ˌself'kɒnfɪdəns]	Selbstvertrauen
self-help group	['selfhelp ˌgru:p]	Selbsthilfegruppe
semen	['si:mən]	Sperma
semi-circle	['semɪˌsɜ:kl]	Halkreis
semi-solid food	['semɪˌsɒlɪd 'fu:d]	Brei
sense of realism	[ˌsens ɒf 'rɪəlɪzm]	Realitätssinn
sensitivity	[ˌsensɪ'tɪvəti]	Empfindlichkeit
sentence	['sentəns]	Urteil
sentence so.	['sentəns ˌsʌmwʌn]	jmd. verurteilen
serious	['sɪəriəs]	ernst, ernsthaft
servings	['sɜ:vɪŋz]	hier: Portionen
set rules	[ˌset 'ru:lz]	Regeln aufstellen/setzen
settle an argument	[ˌsetl ən 'ɑ:gjəmənt]	einen Streit beilegen
severe	[sɪ'vɪə]	schwer
sex act	['seks ˌækt]	Sexualakt
sex education	['seks ˌedjʊ'keɪʃən]	Sexualerziehung
sex organs	['seks ˌɔ:gənz]	Sexualorgane
sexual harassment	[ˌsekʃʊəl 'hærəsmənt]	sexuelle Belästigung
sexual intercourse	[ˌsekʃʊəl 'ɪntəkɔ:s]	Geschlechtsverkehr
shake	[ʃeɪk]	schütteln
shaming	[ʃeɪm]	beleidigend
share	[ʃeə]	teilen
share fate with	[ˌʃeə 'feɪt ˌwɪð]	das Schicksal teilen mit
share needles	[ˌʃeə 'ni:dlz]	Nadeln miteinander teilen
shared education	['ʃeəd ˌedʒʊ'keɪʃən]	gemeinsame Erziehung
shelter	[ʃeltə]	Obdach
shopaholic	[ˌʃɒpə'hɒlɪk]	jemand, der viel und gerne einkauft
shoplifting	['ʃɒplɪftɪŋ]	Ladendiebstahl
short of breath	[ˌʃɔ:t ɒf 'breθ]	kurzatmig
shortage	['ʃɔ:tɪdʒ]	Kürzung
short-term effect	[ˌʃɔ:tˌtɜ:m ɪ'fekt]	Kurzzeiteffekt, hier: zeitlich begrenzte gesundheitliche Reaktion
shredded plants	[ˌʃredɪd 'plɑ:nts]	gehackte Pflanzen
shrug sth. off the shoulder	['ʃrʌg ˌsʌmwʌn 'ɒf ðə ˌʃəʊldə]	etwas (von der Schulter) abschütteln
shun	[ʃʌn]	hier: versäumen, auslassen

shy from	['ʃaɪ ˌfrɒm]	hier: zurückschrecken vor
sibling	['sɪblɪŋ]	Geschwisterkind
siblings	['sɪblɪŋz]	Geschwister
sick	[sɪk]	krank
sick bed	['sɪk ˌbed]	Krankenbett
sick room/hospital room	['sɪk ˌrʊm / 'hɒspɪtəl ˌrʊm]	Patientenzimmer
side dish	['saɪd ˌdɪʃ]	Beilage
side effects	['saɪd ɪˌfekts]	Nebeneffekt, Nebenwirkung
side-effect	['saɪd ɪˌfekt]	Nebenwirkung
sign	[saɪn]	unterschreiben
signature	['sɪgnətʃə]	Unterschrift
single-parent family	['sɪŋgl ˌpærənt 'fæməli]	Familie mit nur einem Elternteil
sink	[sɪŋk]	Spüle
sit in a circle	[ˌsɪt ɪn ə 'sɜːkl]	im Kreis sitzen
skeleton	['skelɪtən]	Skelett
skills	[skɪlz]	Fähigkeiten, (berufl.) Fertigkeiten
skinny	['skɪni]	knochig
skip work	[ˌskɪp 'wɜːk]	die Arbeit „schwänzen“
skull	[skʌl]	Schädel
slaughter	['slɔːtə]	Abschlachten
sleeplessness	['sliːpləsnəs]	Schlaflosigkeit
slim	[slɪm]	abnehmen
slim down	[ˌslɪm 'daʊn]	„herunter hungern“
slurred	['slɜːd]	undeutlich
smashed	['smæʃt]	hier: zerschlagen
so. lacks s.th.	[ˌsʌmwʌn 'læks ˌsʌmθɪŋ]	jm. mangelt es an etwas
soaked with	['səʊkt ˌwɪð]	durchtränkt mit
social care	[ˌsəʊʃəl 'keə]	Sozialfürsorge
social gap year	[ˌsəʊʃəl 'gæp ˌjɪə]	freiwilliges soziales Jahr
social interaction	[ˌsəʊʃəl ɪntər'ækʃən]	sozialer Umgang/Kommunikation
social networks	[ˌsəʊʃəl 'netwɜːks]	soziale Netzwerke
social service	[ˌsəʊʃəl 'sɜːvɪs]	Sozialdienst
social worker	['səʊʃəl ˌwɜːkə]	Sozialarbeiter
socially accepted	[ˌsəʊʃəli ək'septɪd]	gesellschaftlich anerkannt
soft toy	['sɒft ˌtɔɪ]	Kuscheltier
sort things out	['sɔːt ˌθɪŋz 'aʊt]	hier: die Dinge klären
source of information	[ˌsɔːs əf ɪnfə'meɪʃən]	Informationsquelle
spare time	[ˌspeə 'taɪm]	hier: Zeit aufbringen
sparkling water	[ˌspɑːklɪŋ 'wɔːtə]	sprudelndes Mineralwasser
special need	[ˌspeʃəl 'niːd]	hier: Behinderung
specialist room	['speʃəlɪst ˌrʊm]	Fachraum
speed up	[ˌspiːd 'ʌp]	antreiben, hoch treiben
spending power	['spendɪŋ ˌpaʊə]	Kaufkraft
spice	[spaɪs]	Gewürz, hier: Name für neue Designer-droge
spirits	['spɪrɪts]	Alkohol, Spirituosen, Branntwein
splash	[splæʃ]	bespritzen
split from	['splɪt ˌfrɒm]	sich trennen von
spoil a child	[ˌspɔɪl ə 'tʃaɪld]	ein Kind verwöhnen

sporty	['spɔːti]	sportlich
spots	[spɒts]	Pickel
sprained	['spreɪnd]	verstaucht
spread a rumour	[ˌspred ə 'ruːmə]	ein Gerücht verbreiten
squeeze	[skwiːz]	auspressen
stabilise	['steɪbəlaɪz]	(sich) stabilisieren
staff	[stɑːf]	Personal
staff meeting	['stɑːf ˌmiːtɪŋ]	Mitarbeiterbesprechung
staff room	['stɑːf ˌrʊm]	Personalraum
stalking	['stɔːkɪŋ]	Verfolgung
starchy products	[ˌstɑːtʃi 'prɒdʌkts]	stärkehaltige Produkte
start back	[ˌstɑːt 'bæk]	zurückschrecken
startling	['stɑːtlɪŋ]	auffällig
state's attorney	[ˌsteɪts ə'tɜːni]	Staatsanwalt
stay healthy	[ˌsteɪ 'helθi]	gesund bleiben
steal	[stiːl]	stehlen, entwenden
stem from	['stem ˌfrɒm]	stammen von
stepchildren	['steptʃɪldrən]	Stiefkinder
stepfather	['stepfɑːðə]	Stiefvater
stepmother	['stepmʌðə]	Stiefmutter
stereotypes	['steriəʊtaɪps]	Stereotypen, Cliché
stick together	[ˌstɪk tə'geðə]	zusammenhalten
stigma	['stɪgmə]	Brandmal, Stigma, Stigmatisierung
still water	[ˌstɪl 'wɔːtə]	stilles Mineralwasser
stodge (Slang)	[stɒdʒ]	Gebäck
stomach ache	['stʌmək ˌeɪk]	Bauchschmerzen
storage room	['stɔːrɪdʒ ˌrʊm]	Lagerraum
strain	[streɪn]	Stress, Belastung
strange face	[ˌstreɪndʒ 'feɪs]	fremdes Gesicht
strength	[streŋkθ]	Stärke
stretcher	['stretʃə]	Trage
strict	[strɪkt]	streng
stroke	[strəʊk]	Schlaganfall
stubborn	['stʌbən]	stur
stuff with	['stʌf ˌwɪð]	vollstopfen mit
subdivide	[ˌsʌbdɪ'vaɪd]	unterteilen
subdivide	[ˌsʌbdɪ'vaɪd]	unterteilen
subject matter	['sʌbdʒɪkt ˌmætə]	Betreffzeile
substance	['sʌbstəns]	Bestandteil, Substanz
subtitled	['sʌbˌtaɪtəld]	mit Untertitel, untertitelt
suffocate	['sʌfəkeɪt]	ersticken
suggest	[sə'dʒest]	vorschlagen
suicidal	[ˌsuːɪ'saɪdəl]	selbstmörderisch
suicidal thoughts	[ˌsuːɪ'saɪdəl ˌθɔːts]	Selbstmordgedanken
suicide	['suːɪsaɪd]	Selbstmord
sulky	['sʌlki]	schmollend, beleidigt
sunshade	['sʌnʃeɪd]	Sonnenschirm
supervise	['suːpəvaɪz]	beaufsichtigen
supply so. with	[sə'plaɪ ˌsʌmwʌn wɪð]	jmd. mit etwas versorgen
supply with	[sə'plaɪ ˌwɪð]	versorgen mit

support	[sə'pɔːt]	unterstützen, auch: stützen
support oneself with the hands	[sə'pɔːt wʌnˌself wɪð ðə 'hændz]	sich mit den Händen abstützen
surface	['sɜːfɪs]	hier: an die Oberfläche kommen
surgery	['sɜːdʒəri]	Operation, chirurgischer Eingriff
survey	['sɜːveɪ]	Studie, Umfrage, auch: Überblick
survival	[sə'vaɪvəl]	Überleben
survival rate	[sə'vaɪvəl ˌreɪt]	Überlebensrate
survive	[sə'vaɪv]	überleben
suspect	[sə'spekt]	hier: vermuten, auch: verdächtigen
suspend so.	[sə'spend ˌsʌmwʌn]	jmd. suspendieren, hier: von der Schule verweisen
swallow the wrong way	['swɒləʊ ðə ˌrɒŋ 'weɪ]	sich verschlucken
swap roles	[ˌswɒp 'rəʊlz]	Rollen tauschen
swearwords	['sweəwɜːdz]	Flüche
swell up	[ˌswel 'ʌp]	aufquellen
switch off	[ˌswɪtʃ 'ɒf]	hier: nicht mehr zuhören
swollen	['swəʊlən]	geschwollen
take a risk	[ˌteɪk ə 'rɪsk]	ein Risiko eingehen
take into account	['teɪk ɪnˌtu ə'kaʊnt]	in Erwägung ziehen
take into consideration	['teɪk ɪnˌtu kənˌsɪdə'reɪʃən]	in Erwägung ziehen
take precautions	[ˌteɪk prɪ'kɔːʃənz]	hier: verhüten
take responsibility	[ˌteɪk rɪˌspɒnsə'bɪləti]	Verantwortung übernehmen
take some blood	[ˌteɪk sʌm 'blʌd]	Blut entnehmen
take the mind off	[ˌteɪk ðə ˌmaɪnd 'ɒf]	hier: Kummer vergesssen lassen, ablenken von
tap on the shoulder	[ˌtæp ɒn ðə 'ʃəʊldə]	auf die Schulter klopfen
taunt	[tɔːnt]	verspotten
tax evasion	['tæks ɪˌveɪʒən]	Steuerhinterziehung
taxes	['tæksɪz]	Steuern
tear down/tore/torn	[ˌteə 'daʊn / tɔː / tɔːn]	herunterreißen
tell so. the facts of life	['tel ˌsʌmwʌn ðə 'fækts əf ˌlaɪf]	jmd. aufklären
temper tantrums	['tempə ˌtæntrəmz]	Wutanfall, Trotzreaktion
temperature	['temprətʃə]	Temperatur, hier: Fieber
tend to	['tend ˌtu]	neigen zu
term	[tɜːm]	hier: Schuljahr
terminally ill	[ˌtɜːmɪnəli 'ɪl]	unheilbar krank
terrace	['terəs]	Terasse
terrify	['terɪfaɪ]	verängstigen, einschüchtern
text so.	['tekst ˌsʌmwʌn]	jmd. eine Nachricht schicken
than	[ðæn]	als
theft	[θeft]	Diebstahl
therapeutic group	[ˌθerəpjuːtɪk 'gruːp]	hier: therapeutische Wohngemeinschaft
threat	[θret]	Drohung
threatening	['θretənɪŋ]	hier: Drohung, Angst einflößen
time out	[ˌtaɪm 'aʊt]	Auszeit
timer	['taɪmə]	Zeitmesser, Stoppuhr
tiredness	['taɪədnəs]	Müdigkeit
toddler	['tɒdlə]	Kleinkind (ca. 2-3 Jahre)

tolerant	['tɒlərənt]	tolerant, aufgeschlossen
tough	[tʌf]	hart
trainee	[ˌtreɪ'niː]	Auszubildende(r)
training	['treɪnɪŋ]	hier: Schulung, Fortbildung
tram	[træm]	Straßenbahn
transcript	['trænskrɪpt]	protokollieren
transfer so. to	[træns'fɜː ˌsʌmwʌn tu]	hier: jmd. überweisen an
transform	[træns'fɔːm]	umwandeln
transmitted disease	[trænsˌmɪtɪd dɪ'ziːz]	Übertragungskrankheit, Infektionskrankheit
transparency	[træn'spærənsi]	Overheadfolie
trap	[træp]	Falle
treatment	['triːtmənt]	Behandlung
treatment room	['triːtmənt ˌrʊm]	Behandlungszimmer
trickery	['trɪkəri]	Betrug, Hereinlegen
trolley	['trɒli]	Einkaufswagen
trouble kids	['trʌbl ˌkɪdz]	Problemkinder
troubleshooter	['trʌblʃuːtə]	„Problemfinder", Supervisor/-in
truancy	['truːənsi]	Schulschwänzen
trust	trʌst	Vertrauen
twist	twɪst	verdrehen
unbalanced diet	[ˌʌn'bælənst ˌdaɪɪt]	unausgewogene Ernährung
unbearable	[ʌn'beərəbl]	unerträglich
under supervision	[ˌʌndə sə'spɪʃən]	unter Aufsicht
undergo	[ʌndə'gəʊ]	hier: sich (einer Behandlung/Operation) unterziehen
underlying reasons	[ˌʌndə'laɪɪŋ ˌriːzənz]	tiefer liegende Probleme, versteckte Probleme
understanding	[ˌʌndə'stændɪŋ]	Verständnis
unemployed	[ˌʌnɪm'plɔɪd]	arbeitslos
unemployment	[ˌʌnɪm'plɔɪmənt]	Arbeitslosigkeit
unguarded	[ʌn'gɑːdɪd]	unbewacht
uninvolved	[ˌʌnɪn'vɒlvd]	gleichgültig
universal human right	[ˌjuːnɪ'vɜːsəl ˌhjuːmən 'raɪt]	allgemeines Menschenrecht
university entrance qualification	[ˌjuːnɪ'vɜːsəti ˌentrəns ˌkwɒlɪfɪ'keɪʃən]	Zulassung zur Universität/Fachschule, vgl. mit (Fach)Abitur
university graduate	[ˌjuːnɪ'vɜːsəti 'grædʒuət]	Universitätsabsolvent/-in
unpleasant	[ˌʌn'plezənt]	unerfreulich, unangenehm
unpredictable	[ˌʌnprɪ'dɪktəbl]	nicht vorhersehbar, unberechenbar
unscrupulous	[ʌn'skruːpjələs]	skrupellos, gewissenlos
unwanted pregnancy	[ʌnˌwɒntɪd 'pregnənsi]	ungewollte Schwangerschaft
urge so. to do sth.	['ɜːdʒ ˌsʌmwʌn tu 'duː ˌsʌmθɪŋ]	jmd. zwingen/dazu drängen etwas zu tun
urge so.	['ɜːdʒ ˌsʌmwʌn]	jmd. ermahnen
vaginal fluid	[və'dʒaɪnəl ˌfluːɪd]	Vaginalflüssigkeit
vandalise	['vændəlaɪz]	mutwillig beschädigen, verwüsten
vandalising	['vændəlaɪzɪŋ]	Vandalismus, Zerstörungswut
vandalism	['vændəlɪzm]	Vandalismus, mutwillige Beschädigung
vast	[vɑːst]	gewaltig, riesig
veer off	[ˌvɪər 'ɒf]	abdrehen, hier: einem Gespräch eine Wendung geben

vehemently	['viːəməntli]	vehement, heftig
vending machine	[ˌvendɪŋ məˈʃiːn]	Automat
vent	[vent]	hier: seinen Gefühlen freien Lauf lassen
vicious circle	[ˌvɪʃəs 'sɜːkl]	Teufelskreis
victimless	['vɪktɪmləs]	opferlos, ohne Opfer
view	[vjuː]	sehen
viewer	['vjuːə]	hier: Fernsehzuschauer
vigour	['vɪgə]	hier: Schwung, Elan
violence	['vaɪələns]	Gewalt
violent	['vaɪələnt]	gewalttätig
virginity	[və'dʒɪnəti]	Jungfräulichkeit
vision	['vɪʒən]	Sehvermögen
visiting days	['vɪzɪtɪŋ ˌdeɪz]	Besuchstage
visuals	['vɪʒuəlz]	visuelle Vorlagen
vital	['vaɪtəl]	hier: wichtig, entscheidend
voluntary	['vɒləntəri]	freiwillig
voluntary social year	['vɒləntəri ˌsəʊʃəl 'jɪə]	freiwilliges soziales Jahr
volunteer	[ˌvɒlən'tɪə]	Freiwillige/-r, Voluntär/-in
vomit	['vɒmɪt]	erbrechen
vulnerable	['vʌlnərəbl]	verletzlich
waste time	[ˌweɪst 'taɪm]	Zeit verschenken/ verschwenden
wall bars	['wɔːl ˌbɑːz]	Sprossenwand
wallet	['wɒlɪt]	Brieftasche
wander through	['wɒndə ˌθruː]	wandern durch
ward	[wɔːd]	Krankenhausstation
warning signs	['wɔːnɪŋ ˌsaɪnz]	Warnsignale
watch	[wɒtʃ]	beobachten, beaufsichtigen
weak	[wiːk]	schwach
weakness	['wiːknəs]	Schwäche
wealthy	['welθi]	wohlhabend
weapons possession	['wepənz pəˌzeʃən]	Waffenbesitz
week's quota	[ˌwiːks 'kwəʊtə]	wöchentliche Ration
weird	[wɪəd]	verdreht, komisch
well-balanced	[ˌwel'bælənst]	ausgewogene Ernährung
wheelchair	['wiːltʃeə]	Rollstuhl
whining	['waɪnɪŋ]	wimmernd, jaulend
white coat	[ˌwaɪt 'kəʊt]	hier: Schwesterntracht, auch Arztkittel
whole-grain	['həʊlgreɪn]	Vollkorn
whooping cough	['huːpɪŋkɒf]	Keuchhusten
wide variety	[ˌwaɪd və'raɪəti]	breite Vielfalt
wide-spread	['waɪdspred]	weit verbreitet
wilfully	['wɪlfəli]	absichtlich, mit voller Absicht
will	[wɪl]	letzter Wille
wink at	['wɪŋk ˌæt]	jmd. zuzwinkern
withdrawal	[wɪð'drɔːəl]	Rückzug, Sich-zurückziehen
withdrawal symptoms	[wɪð'drɔːəl ˌsɪmptəmz]	Entzugserscheinungen, Symptome des Entzugs
witness	['wɪtnəs]	Zeuge, hier: Trauzeuge
witness	['wɪtnəs]	Zeuge

work conditions	['wɜːk kən,dɪʃənz]	Arbeitsbedingungen
work experience	['wɜːk ɪk,spɪəriəns]	Berufserfahrung
working-class area	['wɜːkɪŋ ,klɑːs 'eəriə]	Arbeiterviertel
workout	['wɜːkaʊt]	hier: körperliche Belastung/Training
worn out	[wɔːn 'aʊt]	ausgemergelt
worry so.	['wʌri ,sʌmwʌn]	jmd. beunruhigen
wound	[wuːnd]	Wunde
wrapper	['ræpə]	Verpackung
wring hands	[,rɪŋ 'hændz]	Hände ringen
wrinkles	['rɪŋkəlz]	(Gesichts)Falten
wrist	[rɪst]	Handgelenk
x-ray	['eksreɪ]	Röntgenuntersuchung
yearning for	['jɜːnɪŋ ,fɔː]	Verlangen nach
yell	[jel]	schreien, rufen
yell at so.	['jel æt ,sʌmwʌn]	jmd. anschreien
Youth Welfare Department	[,juːθ 'welfeə dɪ,pɑːtmənt]	Jugendamt
zero tolerance	['zɪərəʊ ,tɒlərəns]	keine Toleranz (hier: für Straftaten)

Bildquellenverzeichnis

Aaron P. Stone, Rochester (England): 191.2
AIDS Healthcare Foundation: 99.1
CartoonStock, Bath (United Kingdom): 74.1, 84.1, 86 .1, 173.1, 174.1, 175.1
Childhelp® 1959–2012, US - Scottsdale, Arizona: 116.2, 116.3
Cornelia Kurtz, Boppard/Bildungsverlag EINS GmbH, Köln: 40.1, 79.1, 98.1, 98.2, 98.3, 115.1, 122.2, 127.1, 168.2, 174.2, 216.1
dpa picture-alliance GmbH, Frankfurt: 8.2, 126.1, 162.1, 214.1
Food Standards Agency, © Crown, UK: 126.2
Fotolia Deutschland GmbH, Berlin: 7.1 (mkrberlin), 8.1 (Bobby Earle), 8.3 (goodluz), 10.1 (Liv Friis-larsen), 15.1 (Alexander Raths), 21.1 (Gina Sanders), 25.1 (Kaarsten), 30.1, 31.1 (wwwebmeister), 32.1 (mangostock), 32.2 contrastwerkstatt), 32.3. (contraskwerkstatt), 32.4 (Sergej Khackimullin), 33.1 (opicobello), 36.1 (s_l), 39.2 (WONG SZE FEI), 41.1 (gornist), 43.1 (Minerva Studio), 46.1 (Ambrophoto), 46.2 (lisalucia), 51.1 (Andres Rodriguez), 101.2 (Andres Rodriguez), 56.1 (Robert Kneschke), 56.2 (Aaron Amat), 56.3 (somenski), 56.4 (Yuri Arcurs), 71.1 (klickerminth), 76.1 (ag visuell), 78.1 (Tomasz Trojanowski), 78.2 (Klaus-Peter Adler), 80.1 (Eléonore H), 80.2 (Matthias Lehmann), 85.1 (Jason Stitt), 87.2 (dedMazay), 87.3 (Hannes Eichinger), 89.1 (Artyom Yefimov), 92.1 (Klaus Rein), 100.1 (Tatyana Gladskih), 101.1 (Dasha Petrenko), 101.2 (Andres Rodriguez), 106.1 (Grischa Georgiew), 109.1 (S.Kobold), 112.1 (guukaa), 112.2 (Heiner Witthake), 116.1 (Firma V), 117.1 (klickerminth), 233.1 (Firma V), 120.1 (SHDR), 124.1 (D. Ott), 125.1 (Cult12), 128.1 (Ronny), 129.1 (juri semjonov), 133.1 (Hugo Félix), 133.2 (Jaimie Duplass), 135.1 (Graca Victoria), 136.1 (muehlberg), 138.1 (Sylvia Zimmermann), 140.1 (Alina Isakovich), 141.1 (Kzenon), 142.1 (Xenia-Luise), 143.1 (Eric Simard), 147.2 (Picture-Factory),148.1 (Teamarbeit), 155.1 (contrastwerkstatt), 155.2 (wwwebmeister), 159.1 (jd-photodesign), 160.1 (gina191), 164.1 (shootingankauf), 166.1 (Jeanette Dietl), 169.1, 170.1, 193.4 (pressmaster), 172.1 (Markus Bormann), 177.1 (iamsania), 178.1 (Piotr Marcinski), 182.1 (lukasvideo), 183.1 (Ademoeller), 184.1 (Sylvie Bouchard), 187.1 (beermedia), 187.2 (michaeljung), 188.1 (olly), 192.2 (Thaut Images), 193.2 (Bernd Kröger), 193.3 (Yuri Arcurs), 193.4 (pressmaster), 196.1 (ivanfff), 198.2 (ZIHE), 204.2 (Martin Schmid), 206.1 (Hemeroskopion), 207.1 (Mitarart), 209.1 (Nlshop), 210.1 (Otto Durst), 212.1 (Stefan Balk), 212.2 (Doris Heinrichs), 218.1 (Phoenixpix), 219.1 (contrastwerkstatt), 221.1 (Sandra Brunsch), 223.1 (Nicole Effinger), 224.3 (fotofrank), 225.1 (Peter Atkins), 226.1 (Monkey Business), 231.1 (Ingo Bartussek), 233.1 (Firma V), 234.1 (Barbara Winzer)
INKCINCT Cartoons, Australia: 96.1
Jennifer Hogan: 165.1
MEV Verlag GmbH, Augsburg: 8.4, 12.1, 13.1, 14.1, 14.2, 14.3, 14.4, 17.1, 39.1, 47.1, 55.1, 60.1, 61.1, 64.1, 65.1, 69.1, 122.1, 125.2, 129.2, 146.1, 147.1, 152.1, 158.1, 168.1, 180.1, 192.1, 93.1, 193.5, 194.1, 199.1, 200.1, 203.1, 204.1, 224.1, 224.2
Ruth Fiand, Aachen: 12.1, 12.2, 62.1, 63.1, 77.1, 94.1, 123.1, 123.2, 139.1, 149.1, 149.2, 149.3, 154.1
Stéffie Becker, Unkel/Bildungsverlag EINS GmbH, Köln: 16.1, 19.1, 19.2, 19.3, 20.1, 20.2, 37.1, 42.1, 43.2, 44.1, 48.1, 50.1, 59.1, 70.1, 81.1, 90.1, 100.2, 102.1, 105.1, 114.1, 134.1, 150.1, 161.1, 171.1, 186.1, 198.1, 201.1, 217.1, 217.2, 217.3, 217.4, 222.1, 236.1, 236.2, 236.3
The State of Queensland (Disability Services Queensland) - Queensland Government (www.qld.gov.au): 165.2
The Sun, London: 177.1, 191.1